MARJORIE GARBER

Shakespeare and Modern Culture

Marjorie Garber is William R. Kenan Jr. Professor of English
and American Literature and Language, and Chair of the
Department of Visual and Environmental Studies, at Harvard
University. She is the author of numerous books, including
Shakespeare After All, which was named one of the five best
nonfiction books of 2004 by *Newsweek* and received the 2005
Christian Gauss Book Award from the Phi Beta Kappa Soci-
ety. Garber lives in Cambridge, Massachusetts.

W9-ASF-987

Shakespeare
and
Modern Culture

Shakespeare
and
Modern Culture

MARJORIE GARBER

Anchor Books
A Division of Random House, Inc.
New York

FIRST ANCHOR BOOKS EDITION, DECEMBER 2009

Due to limitations of space, permissions to reprint previously published material
can be found following the index.

The Library of Congress has cataloged the Pantheon edition as follows:
Garber, Marjorie B.
Shakespeare and modern culture / Marjorie Garber.
p. cm.
Includes bibliographical references and index.
1. Shakespeare, William, 1564–1616—Criticism and interpretation. I. Title.
PR2989.G35 2008
822.3'3—dc22
2008026802

Anchor ISBN: 978-0-307-39096-7

Author photograph © Beverly Hall
Book design by M. Kristen Bearse

www.anchorbooks.com

Printed in the United States of America
10 9 8 7 6 5 4 3 2

To Erroll McDonald

and

Beth Vesel

CONTENTS

A NOTE ON THE TEXT

Unless otherwise noted, all references to Shakespeare's plays are from the *Norton Shakespeare Second Edition,* eds. Stephen Greenblatt et al. (New York: W. W. Norton & Company, 2008).

ILLUSTRATIONS

INTRODUCTION

THE PREMISE OF THIS BOOK is simple and direct: Shakespeare makes modern culture and modern culture makes Shakespeare. I could perhaps put the second "Shakespeare" in quotation marks, so as to indicate that what I have in mind is our *idea* of Shakespeare and of what is Shakespearean. But in fact it will be my claim that Shakespeare and "Shakespeare" are perceptually and conceptually the same from the viewpoint of any modern observer.

Characters like Romeo, Hamlet, or Lady Macbeth have become cultural types, instantly recognizable when their names are invoked. As will become clear, the modern versions of these figures often differ significantly from their Shakespearean "originals": a "Romeo" is a persistent romancer and philanderer rather than a lover faithful unto death, a "Hamlet" is an indecisive overthinker, and a "Lady Macbeth," in the public press, is an ambitious female politician who will stop at nothing to gain her own ends. But the very changes marked by these appropriations tell a revealing story about modern culture and modern life.

The idea that Shakespeare is modern is, of course, hardly a modern idea. Indeed, it is one of the fascinating effects of Shakespeare's plays that they have almost always seemed to coincide with the times in which they are read, published, produced, and discussed. But the idea that Shakespeare writes us—as if we were Tom Stoppard's Rosencrantz and Guildenstern, constantly encountering our own prescribed identities, proclivities, beliefs, and behaviors—is, if taken seriously, both exciting and disconcerting.

I will suggest in what follows that Shakespeare has scripted many of the ideas that we think of as "naturally" our own and even as "naturally" true: ideas about human character, about individuality and selfhood, about government, about men and women, youth and age, about the qualities that make a strong leader. Such ideas are not necessarily first encountered today in the realm of literature—or even of drama and theater. Psychology, sociology, political theory, business, medicine, and law have all welcomed and recognized Shakespeare as the founder, authorizer, and forerunner of important categories and practices in their fields. Case studies based on Shakespearean characters and events form an important part of education and theory in leadership institutes and business schools as well as in the history of psychoanalysis. In this sense Shakespeare has made modern culture, and modern culture returns the favor.

"I don't mind if something's Shakespearean, just as long as it's not Shakespeare."

The word "Shakespearean" today has taken on its own set of connotations, often quite distinct from any reference to Shakespeare or his plays. A cartoon by Bruce Eric Kaplan in *The New Yorker* shows a man and a woman walking down a city street, perhaps headed for a theater or a movie house. The caption reads, "I don't mind if something's Shakespearean, just as long as it's not Shakespeare."[1] "Shakespearean" is now an all-purpose adjective, meaning great, tragic, or resonant: it's applied to events, people, and emotions, whether or not they have any real relevance to Shakespeare.

Journalists routinely describe the disgrace of a public leader as a "downfall of Shakespearean proportions"[2]—as for example in the case of Canadian financier Conrad Black, whose plight was also called a "fall from grace of Shakespearean proportions,"[3] and who was described as the victim of a "betrayal of almost Shakespearean proportion."[4] In a book on the U.S. military involvement in Iraq and Afghanistan, a former CIA officer describes the results as "self-imposed tragedies of unplanned-for length and Shakespearean proportions."[5] Here the word "tragedies" makes the link between military misadventures and Shakespearean drama. The effect of a series of Danish cartoons that gave offense to Muslims was "Shakespearean in proportions";[6] the final episodes of *The Sopranos* were "a bloodbath of Shakespearean proportions";[7] and the steroid scandal in professional baseball was a plot that had "thickened to Shakespearean proportions."[8]

Vivid personalities like Lyndon Johnson, Richard Nixon, and William Randolph Hearst have likewise been described as figures of "Shakespearean proportions" or "Shakespearean dimensions."[9] Nor is it only national or international news that now makes the Shakespeare grade: a headline in the *Daily Telegraph* of London declared that "throwing a children's party can be a drama of Shakespearean proportions." And an article in the tabloid *New York Post* began, "A Shakespearean tragedy played out on a Long Island street where a boozed-up young woman unknowingly dragged her boyfriend under her car for more than a block as he tried to stop her from driving drunk."[10] "Shakespearean" in these contexts means something like "ironic" or "astonishing" or "uncannily well plotted." Over time the adjectival form of the playwright's name has become an intensifier, indicating a degree of magnitude, a scale of effect.

Why should this be the case? And what does it say about the interrelationship between Shakespeare and modern culture?

"SHAKESPEARE ONE GETS ACQUAINTED WITH without knowing how," says one earnest young man in a Jane Austen novel to another. "It is a part of an Englishman's constitution," his companion is quick to concur. "No doubt one is familiar with Shakespeare in a degree," he says, "from one's earliest years. His celebrated passages are quoted by every body; they are in half the books we open and we all talk Shakespeare, use his similes, and describe with his descriptions."[11] This was modern culture, circa 1814. In the view of these disarmingly ordinary, not very bookish observers, Shakespeare was the author of their common language, the poet and playwright who inspired and shaped their thought.

In 1828 Sir Walter Scott, already a celebrated novelist, "visited the tomb of the mighty wizard," as he wrote. He had a plaster cast made of the Shakespeare portrait bust in Holy Trinity Church, and he designed "a proper shrine for the Bard of Avon" in the library of his home at Abbotsford, making sure that the bust was "fitted with an altar worthy of himself." Scott noticed that the two of them—Scott and Shakespeare—shared the same initials, W.S. He had their head sizes measured and compared by a German phrenologist. A bust of Scott was designed to resemble that of the other Bard, and after Scott's

Gerard Johnson, William Shakespeare's Funerary
Monument, *Holy Trinity Church, Stratford-
upon-Avon*

death the bust of *his* head replaced that of Shakespeare in the library. Admiration here became identification—or perhaps a kind of rivalry.[12]

Shakespeare's modernity would also be proclaimed in nineteenth-century
America. In 1850 Ralph Waldo Emerson announced that, after centuries in
which Shakespeare had been inadequately understood, the time was finally
right for him: "It was not possible to write the history of Shakespeare till
now," Emerson wrote. The word "now" in his argument becomes the marker
of that shifting category of the modern, and it is repeated for emphasis a few
lines later. "Now, literature, philosophy, and thought, are Shakespearized.
His mind is the horizon beyond which, at present, we do not see. Our ears
are educated to music by his rhythm."[13] Thus Emerson could say of Shakespeare, simply and resoundingly, "he wrote the text of modern life."[14] We live
today in a new "now," a century and a half removed from Emerson's, but this
sentiment—"he wrote the text of modern life"—seems as accurate as it did
then.

Nor—as we have already noted—is this view the special province of literary authors. The frequency with which practitioners and theorists of many of
the "new" modern sciences and social sciences—anthropology, psychology,
sociology—have turned to Shakespeare for inspiration is striking, but not

surprising. Ernest Jones, Freud's friend and biographer, the first English-language practitioner of psychoanalysis, declared straightforwardly (in an essay he began in 1910, revised in 1923, and expanded in the 1940s) that "Shakespeare was the first modern." Why? Because he understood so well the issues of psychology. "The essential difference between prehistoric and civilized man," Jones argued, was that "the difficulties with which the former had to contend came from without," while "those with which the latter have to contend really come from within,"

> This inner conflict modern psychologists know as neurosis, and it is only by study of neurosis that one can learn the fundamental motives and instincts that move men. Here, as in so many other respects, Shakespeare was the first modern.[15]

Thus for Jones, Shakespeare's use of the soliloquy, the onstage, interior questioning of a character's conflicted thoughts and motives, anticipated the new science of psychoanalysis and Freud's "talking cure."

THE "TEXT OF MODERN LIFE" these days is embedded in a network of text messaging, Internet connections, video clips, and file sharing. Shakespeare in our culture is already disseminated, scattered, appropriated, part of the cultural language, high and low. An advertisement for rugged outdoors types advertised a sale: "Now Is the Winter of Our Discount Tents." This turned out also to be the name of a rock compilation by the label Twisted Nerve. At the same time, in London, the White Cube Gallery presented an exhibition of work by British artist Neal Tait, titled "Now Is the Discount of Our Winter Tents." Manifestly, none of these tweaked or inverted phrases would offer much in the way of wit or appeal if the cultural consumer did not recognize, or half recognize, the phrase on which each is based: the opening soliloquy of *Richard III,* in which the envious and aspiring Gloucester observes, in a classic of double-meaning enjambment, that "Now is the winter of our discontent / Made glorious summer by this son of York" (1.1.1–2). So we might say that Shakespeare is already not only modern but postmodern: a simulacrum, a replicant, a montage, a bricolage. A collection of found objects, repurposed as art.

Our Shakespeare is often "sampled" and "texted" in forms from advertising to cartoon captions. Lady Macbeth's exclamation in the sleepwalking scene, "Out, damned spot!" (*Macbeth* 4.1.33), is so well-known that it has been used to describe stain removers, acne medicine, and cleaning technologies for semiconductors. An ad for Hard Candy cosmetics extends the literary allusion, offering not only the "Out Damn Spot" concealer pencil to cover up blemishes, but also a coordinated line of makeup called "Macbare" and "Macbuff."[16] I call this a "literary allusion," but it is a quite different kind from those of an earlier period. Although the writers of copy here assume a recognition of *Macbeth* as the source, there is no extended expectation of familiarity with the text. The wit inheres in the *dis*location from context ("Lay on, Macbuff"?).

Popular culture examples of this kind are virtually ubiquitous. Hamlet's phrase "The undiscover'd country from whose bourn / No traveller returns" (*Hamlet* 3.1.79–80) has been used as the subtitle of *Star Trek VI*, the title of an art exhibition on representational painting at the Hammer Museum in Los Angeles, and the brand name of a company offering bicycle tours in California.[17] The bionic skeleton used for decades by the U.S. Food and Drug Administration to demonstrate artificial body parts was named Yorick, after "the exhumed skull in Shakespeare's *Hamlet*."[18] Sometimes the Shakespeare quotation has moved so far into the mainstream that there is little or no acknowledgment of any connection with the source. Economist Greg Mankiw chose the phrase "Strange Bedfellows" as the headline of a short piece on Al Gore and supply-side economists of the 1980s.[19] Although there may have been some tacit comparison between these figures and Shakespeare's Caliban and Trinculo, there's no evidence of it in the piece—and really no necessity. Shakespeare sampled, Shakespeare quoted without quotation marks, has become a lingua franca of modern cultural exchange.

The cultural "Q" value of something often goes up when its familiarity and utility go down. An antique shop that specializes in folk art will display objects like churns, crocks, quilts, and spinning wheels—once valued for their use and now many times more valuable, in sheer dollar terms, despite being useless.[20] And the further we get as a society from intimate knowledge of the language and characters of the plays, the more "love" of Shakespeare begins to be expressed as a cultural value. Shakespeare's plays are probably read and studied more, these days, *before* and *after* college—in high school and in reading groups, extension courses, lifelong learning and leadership institutes, and in the preparation of audiences attending play productions—than during the four years of traditional undergraduate college education. Preprofessional training starts earlier, college majors are more specialized than once they were, and there is less expectation of a broad general education or liberal arts foundation than was the case a generation or two ago. Shakespeare becomes the treat, as well as the all-purpose cultural upgrade, for which time is found later in life, after more basic, pragmatic skills and knowledge are acquired.

Thus it is not perhaps a surprise to discover that some of the most avid and interested students of Shakespeare today are businesspeople, CEOs and CFOs of major national and international companies. Shakespeare's plays are now being used, regularly and with success, to teach corporate executives lessons about business.[21] A few of the analogies the CEOs and their facilitators make may seem facile (the appearance of the ghost of old Hamlet is like the reminder that executives are accountable to their shareholders; CEOs, like the kings and queens in the plays, have to face the necessity of betraying—or firing—their friends). But the business of teaching Shakespeare-in-business has become popular and lucrative as a sideline for both government officials no longer in power and Shakespeare companies struggling to make a living.[22] The play that has most galvanized business leaders has been *Henry V,* whose protagonist, the leader of a "band of brothers," produced unit cohesion and triumphed against apparently insurmountable odds; I use some of the discussions among what might be called "business Shakespeareans" as examples in my chapter on that play.

In these encounters, "Shakespeare" often becomes a standardized plot, a stereotypical character, and, especially, a moral or ethical choice—not to mention the ubiquitous favorite, "a voice of authority," as if it were possible to locate "his" voice among the mix of Hamlet, Macbeth, Falstaff, Rosalind, Portia, Iago, the Ghost, and the Fool. (The CEOs are not often asked to see the play through the lens of a minor character, an old man, a young woman, an attendant lord, or a common soldier; they are kings and queens, generals, Machiavels, decision makers all.) What may sometimes drop out here, crucially, is the complexity of language and of plotting, the ultimate undecidability or overdetermination of phrases, words, and actions. Reading against the grain—trying to gather a multiplicity of sometimes conflicting meanings from any staged scene or passage—itself cuts against the grain of CEO management and decision-making. Perhaps the key phrase here ought to be, not "Falstaff, *c'est moi*"—as one executive was quoted as saying—but instead Iago's "I am not what I am."[23]

Politics, and politicians, often seem to be implicated, one way or another, in these cultural transactions. One September, during the presidency of George W. Bush, I was contacted by the *New York Times* columnist Maureen Dowd, who wanted to talk about Bush's summer reading list and the ways in which the Shakespeare plays he was then said to be reading might influence his political thought. I had written op-ed pieces for the *Times* on Shakespeare and culture on previous occasions, and Dowd thought I might have something to say about the present situation.

On President Bush's reading list—recommended, it was said, by his wife, Laura, who had been actively engaged in an NEA program called *Shakespeare in American Communities*—were a number of works of popular fiction, some books of American history (Nathaniel Philbrick's *Mayflower;* a study of the manhunt for Abraham Lincoln's killer; a book on naval battles that shaped American history), and biographies of Lincoln, Babe Ruth, and Roberto Clemente. Down at the bottom of the list, as provided by the White House Press Office, were two plays by Shakespeare: *Macbeth* and *Hamlet.*

That both plays were about usurpation, about the question of just election to high office, and about father-son or mentor-mentee tensions and conflicts, was not—necessarily—why these books had been chosen for the president's summer reading. Nor were they chosen (I imagine) because Hamlet was famous for having difficulty being a "Decider," or for Macbeth's battlefield comeback as commander in chief. I'd guess they were instead chosen because of their "greatness"—their cultural fame, their quotability, their ubiquity in American political and cultural discourse. In terms of their cultural power, these were American plays—plays that had shaped, and would continue to shape, the language of politicians, speech writers, motivational speakers, journalists—and us. *Macbeth,* I might note, was Abraham Lincoln's favorite play: a play about treason, "domestic malice," civil strife, moral courage, and resignation.

When I spoke with Maureen Dowd, I mentioned the fact that President Bush seemed not to have studied Shakespeare at Yale. Dowd asked how I knew this, and I told her that I had looked up his college transcript on the Web (it was available from both Republican and Democratic Web sites, with appropriate, or inappropriate, commentary). I started my teaching career at Yale, so I was able to decode the course names and numbers on the transcript to see that "Mr. George Walker Bush" had studied a great deal of history and taken some courses in philosophy, economics, and sociology, but only one English course, the basic entry-level introduction for nonmajors. No Shakespeare course, or indeed any other course in English lit.

What might the president have hoped to learn from these two famous plays—if he did find time to read them? Internet commentators and bloggers drew their own analogies between President Bush and both Macbeth and Lady Macbeth: Macbeth weary of endless struggle after the deed that would define his legacy—tomorrow and tomorrow and tomorrow; Lady Macbeth trying, without success, to wash blood from her hands. In this case George W. Bush was being *read through* Shakespeare, rather than reading him.

Other modern politicians have been more clearly conscious of the resonances of Shakespeare in their own politics and lives. One obvious example
here is Winston Churchill, but both John and Robert Kennedy also quoted
Shakespeare frequently in their public speeches to underscore the politics,
and the ironies, of modern life.[24] In contemporary American political debates
Shakespeare is often cited by lawmakers, though sometimes with scant attention to the context of the lines being quoted, and thus with occasional (and
unintended) comic results.[25]

When the plays are quoted, they are sometimes misquoted, whether by
accident or design. An inscription on the National Archives building in
Washington, D.C., the repository of important historical documents, cites
Shakespeare as a way of underscoring the value of the enterprise. But the
inscription, "What Is Past Is Prologue," is also a "correction"—expanding
Shakespeare's grammatical contraction in *The Tempest* ("what's past is prologue" [2.1.248]) into a more sedate and formal utterance, one perhaps
thought better suited for engraving on a public building.

Or, to compare small things with great, consider the tattoo on the shoulder
of a movie actress popular with young audiences—a tattoo described, in
many Web and tabloid citations, as a quotation from *King Lear.* An obliging
photo displays the quotation, in black letter print, which reads: "We will
all laugh at gilded butterflies." The implication is of a joyous celebration
of nature and serendipity. But this "Shakespearean" phrase is not (quite) in
Shakespeare. What King Lear says to his daughter Cordelia, in extremis, in
the fifth act of that dark play, is this:

> Come, let's away to prison.
> We two alone will sing like birds i' the cage.
>
> . . . .
> . . . So we'll live
> And pray, and sing, and tell old tales, and laugh
> At gilded butterflies
>
> *5.3.8–13*

There's no "all" in the passage. Lear's desperate appeal to his daughter is an
invitation to solitude in prison, now imagined as a kind of sanctuary against
the world. There are only two people in this scene, no collective audience.
The invitation is also, of course, an unrealizable fantasy—in the next scenes,
Cordelia will be hanged offstage, and the aged and distraught Lear will enter
carrying her body.

Nonetheless, the tattoo on the shoulder of Megan Fox testifies to a desire
to quote Shakespeare, and to take inspiration from him, or from his cited,

and slightly altered, phrases. Shakespeare in this case is, once again, a kind of inspirational sound bite, aphoristic, provocative, disseminated, and scattered far from its source. We should note, though, that both inscriptions—the one on the actress's shoulder and the one on the public building—are proudly "Shakespearean." Shakespeare here lends cultural credence, and cultural capital, whether the bearer of the message is an institutional monument or a performer of the moment.

BUT SHAKESPEARE'S EFFECT upon modernity, and modernity's effect upon Shakespeare, should not be confused or conflated with the idea of media or popular culture. Quite the opposite is the case, as we have already seen in the case of psychoanalyst Ernest Jones—and indeed with Jones's friend and mentor, Sigmund Freud. Some of the most engaged and passionate readers, quoters, and rewriters of Shakespeare have been philosophers and theorists, from Karl Marx to Friedrich Nietzsche, Ludwig Wittgenstein, and Jacques Derrida, as well as innovative novelists and playwrights from James Joyce and Samuel Beckett to Tom Stoppard, Barbara Garson (the author of the 1964 play *MacBird*), and Edward Bond, the author of a very dark play from 1971 called *Lear*. Individually and collectively in a wide range of genres, the body of work produced in dialogue with Shakespeare's plays, language, and characters has redefined and repositioned both the playwright and the modern world.

For philosophers and artists, thinking through Shakespeare has been a mode of intellectual engagement as well a kind of productive rivalry. To see how this works, it may be useful to have recourse to the category of thinkers whom the philosopher Michel Foucault described as "initiators of discursive practices"—a distinct kind of author that emerged to prominence in nineteenth-century Europe. These were figures like Freud, Marx, Georges Cuvier, and Ferdinand de Saussure, figures who "not only made possible a certain number of analogies that could be adopted by future texts," but also "cleared a space for the introduction of elements other than their own, which, nevertheless, remain within the field of discourse they initiated."[26] These writers, in essence, invented a way of thinking, about mankind, about language, about consciousness, about the world. Such writers, Foucault explained in his essay on authorship, "should not be confused with 'great' literary authors, or the authors of canonical religious texts, and the founders of sciences":

> The distinctive contribution of these authors is that they produced not only their own work, but the possibility and the rules of formulation of other

texts. . . . Freud is not simply the author of *The Interpretation of Dreams* or of *Wit and Its Relation to the Unconscious,* and Marx is not simply the author of the *Communist Manifesto* or *Capital:* they both established the endless possibility of discourse.[27]

Shakespeare too, I would suggest, has been just such an "initiator of discursive practices," at the same time that no one would disallow his right to be called a "great literary author." It is precisely this uncommon and perhaps uncanny double role, as both "great literary author" and "initiator of discursive practices," that marks Shakespeare's peculiar and remarkable modernity.

The chapters that follow will present extended evidence of this phenomenon with respect to one or another of the plays. But in order to clarify the point, an essential one for my general argument, I want here to mention in brief some symptomatic examples.

Shakespeare's plays were so well-known to Karl Marx that he alluded to them regularly in his writings, often with the assumption that his readers were as familiar with the plays as he was. Marx's early writings, from the period 1835 to 1843, include references to the following Shakespearean characters: Doll Tearsheet, Falstaff, Gloucester, Gratiano, Lear, Pistol, Portia, Mistress Quickly, Richard III, and Shylock. He quotes *Hamlet* all the time, but his most frequent and pointed references are to *Timon of Athens,* whose noble hero is appalled by the obsession with gold and money he finds in the society around him.

At the same time, Marx also often cites what we might consider unexpected Shakespearean moments and passages. Thus, for example, in a famous moment in *Capital* where he is talking about the "fetishism of commodities" and the question of use value versus exchange value, he free-associates, not, as one might expect, to *The Merchant of Venice,* but rather to the bumbling watchman of *Much Ado About Nothing:* "Who fails here to call to mind our good friend, Dogberry," Marx asks, "who informs his neighbor Seacoal that, 'To be a well-favoured man is the gift of fortune, but reading and writing comes by Nature.'"[28]

I would guess that most people today might fail to call Dogberry to mind in this connection—or perhaps any other. But to Marx the association was crystal clear. In another casual allusion that assumes that all readers know their Shakespeare by heart, he combines the figure of Puck in *A Midsummer Night's Dream* (here called by his folk name, Robin Goodfellow) with a reference to the ghost tunneling underground in *Hamlet* ("Well said, old mole. Canst work i'th' earth so fast?" [1.5.164]): "In the signs that bewilder the middle class, the aristocracy and the poor prophets of regression, we do recognize our brave friend Robin Goodfellow, the old mole that can work in the earth

so fast, that worthy pioneer—the Revolution."[29] Notice "we do recognize"—
as with "who fails here to call to mind," Marx is assuming, and creating, a
public sphere in which everyone talks and knows Shakespeare—knows it well
enough to allude, glancingly but tellingly, to incidents and characters as
proofs of a theoretical argument.

For a third example, consider this, from Marx's "Debates on the Freedom
of the Press":

> what an illogical paradox to regard the censorship as a basis for improving
> our press!
>
> The greatest orator of the French revolution, whose *voix toujours tonnante*
> still echoes in our day; the lion whose roar one must have heard oneself in
> order to join with the people in calling out to him, "Well roared, lion!"—
> *Mirabeau*—developed his talent in prison. Are prisons on that account
> schools of eloquence?[30]

"Well roared, lion!" is the jokingly appreciative response of the onstage audience in *A Midsummer Night's Dream* to the performance of the actor playing
the lion in the "Pyramus and Thisbe" play. Marx does not, presumably,
intend a real comparison between Mirabeau and Snug the Joiner; rather, his
quotation is a gesture of inclusiveness to his own audience—or perhaps just
the irresistible impulse to speak in and through Shakespeare.

"AGAIN AND AGAIN IN SHAKESPEARE," observed the German critic and theorist Walter Benjamin,

> battles fill the last act, and kings, princes, attendants and followers "enter,
> fleeing." The moment in which they become visible to spectators brings
> them to a standstill. The flight of the *dramatis personae* is arrested by the
> stage. Their entry into the visual field of nonparticipating and truly impartial
> persons allows the harassed to draw breath, bathes them in new air. The
> appearance onstage of those who enter "fleeing" takes from this its hidden
> meaning. Our reading of this formula is imbued with expectation of a place,
> a light, a footlight glare, in which our flight through life may be likewise shel-
> tered in the presence of onlooking strangers.[31]

The stage direction "enter, fleeing" contains, as Benjamin implies, a certain
built-in contradiction: characters appear onstage only so that they may be
seen to disappear. The idea that the theater audience constitutes a group of
"nonparticipating and truly impartial persons" describes a convention, rather
than a belief; it would be Benjamin who gave the fullest early articulation to

the theory of the "epic theater" that we associate with Bertolt Brecht. Benjamin wrote this passage in the 1920s, in a collection of extended aphorisms, dreams, and prose epigrams called "One-Way Street."[32]

But there is also, needless to say, a powerful historical irony operating here. Benjamin died in 1940, after trying to cross the border from France to Spain with a group of other refugees and being denied permission to enter the country. His ultimate goal was the United States. His death on the night of September 26, 1940, has been called a suicide; the others in his party were permitted to cross on the following day. As Hannah Arendt describes this tragic coincidence of events: "One day earlier Benjamin would have got through without any trouble; one day later the people in Marseilles would have known that for the time being it was impossible to pass through Spain. Only on that particular day was the catastrophe possible."[33] Thus in *his* "last act" Walter Benjamin himself entered, "fleeing," and was not rescued by the "nonparticipating and truly impartial persons" who made up the cultural field. His "flight through life" was, at the end, unsheltered by onlooking strangers.

To read Benjamin this way is to see Shakespeare as uncanny prognosticator—or emplotter—of the twentieth century. Indeed that is how Benjamin himself read Shakespeare. Consider these comments from his admiring essay on the Austrian satirist, essayist, and journalist (and quondam actor) Karl Kraus:

> "Shakespeare had foreknowledge of everything"—yes. But above all of Kraus. Shakespeare portrays inhuman figures—and Timon as the most inhuman of them—and says: Nature would produce such a creature if she wished to create something befitting the world as your kind have fashioned it, something worthy of it. Such a creature is Timon; such is Kraus. Neither has, or wants, anything in common with men. . . . A fool, a Caliban, a Timon—no more thoughtful, no more dignified or better—but, nevertheless, his own Shakespeare. All the figures thronging about him should be seen as originating in Shakespeare. Always he is the model.[34]

And again, discussing Kraus's assertion, "In me a capacity for psychology is united with the greater capacity to ignore the psychological" (itself a brilliant description of Shakespeare's dramatic technique), Benjamin draws a comparison between the twentieth-century satirist and his Renaissance precursor: "In Shakespeare's baroque tirades—when the cannibal is unmasked as the better man, the hero as an actor, when Timon plays the rich man, Hamlet the madman—it is as if his lips dripped blood. So Kraus, following Shakespeare's example, wrote himself parts that let him taste blood."[35]

This is not just another invocation of Shakespeare as a monumental figure of the past; it is a strong assertion of his anticipatory modernity. It might perhaps be suggested that Kraus (or Benjamin, for that matter) is a throwback to the early modern period, or to the baroque, rather than heralding Shakespeare as a protomodern. But Benjamin will always see these things in double time. Thus in a discussion of the way the advent of the new medium of film would produce not only a mass art form of immense social significance, but also a "liquidation of the traditional value of the cultural heritage" he cited the French director Abel Gance, who had written "enthusiastically" in 1927: "Shakespeare, Rembrandt, Beethoven, will make films." Benjamin's mordant comment was that Gance, without intending to, had "issued an invitation to a far-reaching liquidation."[36] "The angel of history," in Benjamin's famous description, "is propelled by the storm of progress into the future, while his face is turned toward the past."[37]

Shakespeare as journalist-aphorist-satirist. Shakespeare as filmmaker. These are only some of the avatars in which Shakespeare has reappeared upon the modern scene.

WRITERS AS DIFFERENT AS Nietzsche, Brecht, and Wittgenstein, each in his own way, claimed that Shakespeare's work led to an upheaval in the understanding of human character, feeling, and expression. Each of these thinkers rejected the mimetic, imitative idea about Shakespearean characters and Shakespearean actions, in favor of a view of disruption, of rupture. Nietzsche quotes approvingly the aphorism of the Austrian playwright Franz Grillparzer: "Shakespeare has ruined all of us moderns."[38]

Brecht asserted that Shakespeare's "great plays . . . are no longer effective" and need to be performed in the mode of his epic theater, to "destroy" the "old aesthetics" rather than to satisfy it.[39] That was in 1927. Two decades later, in 1949, Brecht would tell an interviewer that Shakespeare's works were among those most responsive to his theory of epic theater—a kind of theater that offers opposing sides of an argument, that always makes the audience aware that it is watching a play, and that resists the engendering of illusion.[40]

In the same year, the philosopher Ludwig Wittgenstein wrote his own "remarks" about Shakespeare, and Shakespeare's greatness, in his notebook:

> Shakespeare and dreams. A dream is all wrong, absurd, composite, and yet at the same time it is completely right: put together in *this* strange way it makes an impression. Why? I don't know. And if Shakespeare is great, as he is said to be, then it must be possible to say of him: it's all wrong, things *aren't like*

that—and yet at the same time it's quite right according to a law of its own. It is *not* as though Shakespeare portrayed human types well and were in that respect *true to life*. He is *not* true to life.[41]

The year was 1949. A cold war year. The year the first VW Beetle arrived in the United States. The first year of the Emmy awards. The year the NATO treaty was signed. The year the Soviet Union tested its first atomic bomb. That year the Shakespeare Festival in Stratford opened with *Macbeth,* and went on to productions of *Much Ado About Nothing* (with John Gielgud), *Othello,* and *Henry VIII.* Meantime, on Broadway in New York City, there was an opening of another show, this one of the musical *Kiss Me, Kate,* based on Shakespeare's *Taming of the Shrew,* with music and lyrics by Cole Porter. The play won the first Tony Award for Best Musical in 1949, and it suggested another use for Shakespeare: not Brechtian alienation or defamiliarization, but—as the witty choruses of "Brush Up Your Shakespeare" amply show— plain old sexual seduction:[42]

> Brush up your Shakespeare.
> Start quoting him now.
> Brush up your Shakespeare
> And the women you will wow.
> Just declaim a few lines from "Othella"
> And they'll think you're a helluva fella.
> If your blonde won't respond when you flatter 'er,
> Tell her what Tony told Cleopaterer.
> If she fights when her clothes you are mussing,
> What are clothes? "Much Ado About Nussing."
> Brush up your Shakespeare
> And they'll all kowtow.

Porter's lyrics were so risqué that they were censored by the movie industry when the film version came out in 1953. Family values. But here, clearly, was an ode to quoting Shakespeare—who says literature is useless?

IN RECENT YEARS scholars and theorists of modernity have often taken Shakespeare as a prescient example of ideas they themselves propose, in areas as diverse as science, social science, and the law. Anthropologist Victor Turner found Gonzalo's ideal commonwealth in *The Tempest* a useful example of communitas, a concept he also linked to the philosopher Martin Buber.[43] In his discussion of second-order observation and "the paradox of observing systems"—who observes the observer? how can an observer be both implicated and impartial?—the social systems theorist Niklas Luhmann cited as an instructive early example "Shakespeare's theater with its elaborate use of paradoxes and frames within frames."[44] And sociobiologist E. O. Wilson invoked Shakespeare's Iago in his account of "Group Selection and Altruism": "Selection will discriminate against the individual if cheating has later adverse effects on his life and reproduction that outweigh the momentary advantage gained. Iago stated the essence in *Othello:* 'Good name in man and woman, dear my lord, is the immediate jewel of their souls.' "[45] As we will see below in the chapter on *Othello,* this bromide about "good name," often taken out of context, has had a long and curious history of citation, as if it represented either Iago's views or Shakespeare's, rather than a disingenuous strategic maneuver by Iago. The ethical cliché may be appealing, but its use within the play is ironic. To make his point about the biological roots of human behavior, Wilson, a scientist well versed in classic literature, chose to ignore Iago's hypocrisy (as well as his "cheating" and its "later adverse effects on his life"). It was the expressed "Shakespearean" sentiment, not its sincerity or dramatic context, that Wilson remembered and found useful in adumbrating his own theory.

A memorable demonstration of the mutability of Shakespearean meaning across cultures was offered by an American anthropologist, Laura Bohannan, whose 1966 article "Shakespeare in the Bush," published in the general interest magazine of the American Museum of Natural History, has become a favorite of Shakespeare instructors.[46] Invited by members of the Tiv tribe in West Africa to tell "a story of her own country," she told them the plot of *Hamlet.* Bohannan's droll account purports to show her own attempt to "prove *Hamlet* universally intelligible," only to find that her hearers commended Claudius's marriage to Gertrude (marrying the brother's widow, the wife of the deceased chief, was a good act; had Gertrude delayed in remarrying, the crops would suffer). Hamlet's failure to woo and win Ophelia was put down to insufficient gift giving, his upbraiding of his mother for her conduct was deemed unseemly (a son should never criticize his mother), the Ghost was seen as a demonic figure, and various other elements of the story were likewise interpreted by the Tiv according to their own beliefs and customs. The last word in the article is given to an honored old man among the Tiv, who kindly invites her to tell more stories of her people, so that "we, who are your elders," can "instruct you in their true meaning."

The real butt of the joke, however, is neither the dignified Tiv elder nor the amused and amusing Bohannan herself (whose article in *Natural History* is written in the deadpan voice of the anthropologist as naïve observer), but

rather the Oxford acquaintance with whom Bohannan begins her narrative—
an acquaintance who has greeted her interest in Shakespeare with kindly, but
proprietary, condescension. "You Americans," he said to her as she was leaving Oxford for her stay with the Tiv, "often have difficulty with Shakespeare.
He was, after all, a very English poet, and one can easily misinterpret the universal by misunderstanding the particular." The putative lesson here, however
airily delivered—"one can easily misinterpret the universal by misunderstanding the particular"—is given a stringent double reading in Bohannan's apparently artless confessional tale, for *all* of the readers (the Oxford scholar, the
American anthropologist, the Tiv) are both "right" and "wrong." This story
could serve as an allegory of the process of anthropological investigation—or
indeed as an allegory of the reading of "Shakespeare," who emerges from the
narrative as at once very English, very American, (perhaps) very Tiv, and (in
any case) very modern.

THE ANTHROPOLOGIST CLAUDE LÉVI-STRAUSS wrote powerfully about the
ways in which myths were able to take on the power of objectified thought.
His goal was to show, he wrote, "not how men think in myths, but how myths
operate in men's minds without their being aware of the fact."[47] We might
substitute "Shakespeare" for Lévi-Strauss's "myth": exploring "not how men
think in Shakespeare, but how Shakespeare operates in men's minds without
their being aware of the fact." This, too, is a commutative equation, a trajectory that goes both ways; we think in Shakespeare, as Shakespeare thinks
in us.

Each of the plays interacts with our culture as if it were what psychoanalysis calls a *sujet supposé savoir,* the "subject supposed to know"—as if the play
(not the historical Shakespeare, but the imminent, all-pervasive, numinous
play) knew and knows something about us—something we can turn to it to
discover.[48] The play itself is the source of uncanny knowledge. It knows, but
it does not know it knows. Through our encounters and conversations with
the Shakespearean text, meanings are disclosed, debated, and assessed. The
play comes to stand for, to intercede on behalf of, to bear the weight of, our
most profound hopes, fears, identifications, and desires. Shakespeare has
become the "other scene" (the unconscious) of modern life.

THE SEQUENCE IN WHICH Shakespeare's plays are discussed in this book was
imagined, initially, to follow a rough chronology of the intersection between

each play and a significant moment, or set of moments, in modern culture. As the book expanded, however, and as I began to see the enormously wide range of contacts between the plays and various manifestations of modernity, it became increasingly clear to me that such a controlling structure was both a fiction and a functional impossibility. Historical and cultural events are reliably unruly, and do not fit neatly into a single focused moment. A case could be made for *every* year, and *every* interaction, as a turning point for the plays in question, since their effect—and their relationship with emerging themes, politics, and human events—has been both continuous and ongoing. As the reader will see, the moment of the "modern" has necessitated, from time to time, a glimpse of Romantic Shakespeare criticism, or of Victorian costuming and casting, as well as of the classic literary works and contemporary political events of more recent years. Furthermore, as one play led to the next, and as particular historical, coincidental, or contiguous links between them emerged, I began to see these reflections, as I hope the reader will as well, as both adjacent to one another and freestanding. This is not the story of a development, or of a progress or a progression, but rather, as I have been at some pains to insist throughout, the story of a set of mutual crossings and recrossings across genres, times, and modes.

One of my objectives has been to pair each play with a different modern genre, insofar as that is possible: a novel, a poem, a play, a detective story, a ballet, a dialogue, a rehearsal, a Broadway musical, a cartoon, a set of case studies for business executives. In many cases, perhaps most, there is more than one such genre, more than one cultural interlocutor, but the range itself has been both intriguing and instructive.

Throughout this book I will be suggesting a set of keywords, one for each of the Shakespeare plays under discussion—words that have seemed to me to be evoked by the criticism, performance, debate, and dissemination of that play in modern culture and that have been pivotal in the analysis of texts and contexts, behaviors and beliefs in the period from 1900 to the present—what might be called "the long twentieth century." This list of keywords provides an armature or spine for the book. Taken together, they exemplify my argument about Shakespeare's centrality to modern thinking and modern habits of thought. The list, I contend, names the central concepts and topics of literary and cultural investigation for the past hundred-plus years. In this sense, in setting the table for the ways in which we discuss, classify, and value substantive ideas, Shakespeare has shaped not only the reception and reconception of his own (and other) artworks, but also the very possibility of social analysis and cultural conversation in the present day.

I offer these keywords as part of each chapter's title, but it may be useful to look at them here in the form of a collective list of terms:

The Tempest	Man
Romeo and Juliet	Youth
Coriolanus	Estrangement
Macbeth	Interpretation
Richard III	Fact
The Merchant of Venice	Intention
Othello	Difference
Henry V	Exemplarity
Hamlet	Character
King Lear	Sublimity

Man, youth, estrangement, interpretation, fact, intention, difference, exemplarity, character, and sublimity. These are terms that have come to mark and ordain the questions we ask about ourselves and about our engagement with the mind and the world.

It is perhaps important to say that I did not begin with a preestablished list of terms, but rather with a desire, as much pedagogical as heuristic (and as much heuristic as pedagogical), to see if I could locate, isolate, and then analyze such a key term for each play.

I had chosen my group of plays because each seemed to have had a particular effect, or set of effects, in and for modernity. The question then became, Did the critical terms that emerged from these plays themselves add up to a story about modernity, and, indeed, about modern literary criticism and theory? As the reader will discover, that is my claim.

Each of the keywords I derive from the plays and what is said about them, whether in criticism, adaptation, rewriting, or staging, introduces, in a similar way, a central concept, or issue, for modern critical thinking. This was, as I say, the wager I made with myself at the beginning of the project. What I discovered, or uncovered, was not only how these plays changed the way modern culture (or modern cultures) dealt with issues from difference to sublimity to the idea of a "fact" or a "truth," but also how the plays themselves changed as modernity and postmodernity have overtaken them.

For example, I was interested to notice the ways in which the very notion of "character" and of certain inherently "human" qualities as they emerged in the early twentieth century seemed to be based upon readings of Hamlet (the play and the dramatic character). It's not surprising that Sigmund Freud's theories of character, personality, and neurosis should appear at the same time as does the emergence of "character criticism" in Shakespeare studies, and notably in the influential—and controversial—work of A. C. Bradley, the Oxford professor of poetry who was the younger brother of the philosopher F. H. Bradley. Both focused on Hamlet as a distinct personality type, indeed a "modern" type. It was Freud who remarked, trenchantly, that Hamlet's interior debates were an example, indeed perhaps the best example, of "the secular advance of repression in the emotional life of mankind."[49]

It is probably difficult for most people today to think about a mode of Shakespeare criticism that does not involve the question of character, and characters. But this category of analysis was hotly contested when it emerged, and it has been coolly dismissed by many critics and schools of criticism since. The primacy of "character" and the reign of *Hamlet* as the most canonical, the most famous, the "best" of Shakespeare's plays, began with Samuel Taylor Coleridge and William Hazlitt, and reached its peak of fame, arguably, with Bradley. "The centre of the tragedy," he maintained, speaking not only of *Hamlet* but by extension of all Shakespearean tragedy, "may be said with equal truth to lie in action issuing from character, or in character issuing in action."[50] Our contemporary use of "character" to denote moral strength or weakness—as in the so-called character issue for politicians and their suitability for office—and related questions of character building (or character assassination) are developments of this conviction that individuals in the world, like dramatic and literary characters, have what both Freud (from the vantage point of psychoanalysis) and Margaret Mead (from the vantage point of anthropology) called "character structures"—a system of traits that define and describe human motivation and action.

The keywords proposed in this book are *arbitrary* in that I have selected them myself, at my own discretion and for my own pleasure. But while they may be arbitrary, they are not *random*. A different set of keywords could certainly be offered, and generated, by other readers—and indeed I hope they might and will be, since this seems to me an interpretative activity of significant value. But what I have had in mind in proposing this list of terms, individually and in relationship to one another, is a kind of map, or rebus, of modern thinking. If we were to make a sentence of the words collected here (I think there may be a parlor game that sets the player such a task) the sentence would tell us something about current circumstances, current hopes and dreams, and who, or what, we think we are today.

———

THE PHRASE "Shakespeare makes modern culture; modern culture makes Shakespeare" takes the form of a *chiasmus,* or crossing of words—a rhetorical structure that depends upon internal parallelism and reversal to underscore its logic. This is a common device in rhetoric and political discourse, as well as in poetry. Perhaps the most famous chiasmus in modern American history was John F. Kennedy's "Ask not what your country can do for you—ask what you can do for your country."[51] The balanced clauses are satisfying, and they add up to more than the sum of their parts. It was a structure Kennedy liked, and one that he—or his speechwriters—used to good effect. "Let us never negotiate out of fear. But let us never fear to negotiate," he declared in the same inaugural address. Again the phrases work together to create a persuasive connection.

Shakespeare's own use of this inverted parallelism is powerfully effective in play after play. "I wasted time, and now doth time waste me," laments Richard II (5.5.49). "God send the prince a better companion," says the Lord Chief Justice in *Henry IV, Part 2,* and Falstaff replies, "God send the companion a better prince" (1.2.181–3). "What's Hecuba to him, or he to Hecuba, / That he should weep for her?" Hamlet asks himself, reflecting upon the real tears in the eyes of an actor playing a part (2.2.536–7). "Suit the action to the word, the word to the action," he advises the players (3.2.16–17). "Fair is foul, and foul is fair," proclaim the weird sisters in *Macbeth* (1.1.10). The device is never perfunctory and never trivial. In each of these instances—and in many others we could cite—the doubling effect is a *doubling back* that also becomes a *double take.*

The crossing pattern, the structure of an X, functions in the plays both at the level of language and at the level of plot (tragic figures like Richard II and King Lear actually grow in stature as they lose their power in the world, while both Macbeth and Richard III follow the reverse pattern, losing effectiveness once they have become kings). But what I want to note here is that the structure of thinking exemplified by chiasmus works both structurally and symbolically: the productive confusion between art and life, inside and outside, container and contained was essential to both the stability and the destabilization of Shakespearean theater. This structure, like a mirror facing a mirror, is closely related, in formal terms, to the play-within-the-play—like the "Mousetrap" (or "The Murder of Gonzago") in *Hamlet,* which both presents what has happened in the past and predicts and precipitates what will happen in the future. At the end of *A Midsummer Night's Dream* Puck teases the audience with the thought that the play they have watched may be only a dream, and a similar confusion is wrought upon the drunken tinker Christopher Sly in the introduction to *The Taming of the Shrew.* The effect can be dizzying, a kind of infinite regress: the mise en abyme, the enfilade, Freud's "navel of the dream." Chiasmus, the language of crossing, suspends for a moment the grounded logic of priority and reference: what we thought was solid ground (for example, the fact that Shakespeare's plays were written long ago, whereas "modern culture" is new and now) can be imaginatively put in question, even reversed. What we know of Shakespeare is inevitably colored and shaped by the times in which we live. Crucial to this structure, though, is its balance, which tips both ways. Hence the dizziness: how can something that is made by something else in fact make that something? The logic is itself Shakespearean and is found all over the sonnets, as well as in this perfect line from *Pericles:* "Thou that begett'st him that did thee beget" (21.182).

The same fascination with inversions and reversals—which is the inside and which is the outside? which the frame and which the framed?—was a consistent topic for modern, and "modernist," artists and writers.

René Magritte, The Human Condition

Perhaps my favorite images in this connection are a series of linked works by René Magritte, each entitled *The Human Condition.* A painting perched on an easel in front of a window merges indistinguishably with the "real" scene outside. The painting depicted on the easel is no more fictive than the scene outside the window—and the scene outside the window no more real than the painting on the easel. (Both are part of Magritte's *Human Condition*.)

M. C. Escher, Drawing Hands

Like the famous lithograph by M. C. Escher, *Drawing Hands,* in which two hands are in the process of drawing one another into existence, modern culture writes the plays of Shakespeare in works that range from fiction to film to plays to the daily news—while, at the same time, Shakespeare writes the modern culture in which we think we live.

*Shakespeare
and
Modern Culture*

ONE

THE TEMPEST

The Conundrum of Man

A T THE LUTHER LUCKETT CORRECTIONAL COMPLEX in Kentucky, inmates have the opportunity to join a Shakespeare production troupe (all male) that will rehearse and perform one of Shakespeare's plays, directed by a gifted Shakespearean actor, Curt Tofteland, who has been going to the prison since 1995. Some plays that have been produced by this group (or a subset of them; some are repeat performers, some are new) include *Othello, Titus Andronicus,* and *Hamlet*—all chosen in part because they engage the themes of crime, guilt, and repentance. A production of *The Tempest,* the culmination of that series, was the inspiration for a documentary, *Shakespeare Behind Bars,* in 2004. The film, which describes and shows scenes from this production, was singled out for mention at the Sundance Film Festival.[1]

The director, Hank Rogerson, presents rehearsal scenes and interviews with the actors. His technique is striking and effective: first you see them perform; then, gradually, you learn something about their crimes, and why they are in prison—many of them for life. These personal stories are given to us bit by bit, in small pieces of information, so that the actors we have grown to like and even to admire are only slowly revealed to have had other, in some cases startlingly violent, lives. What makes these stories so gripping is in part the relevance of the personal to the performative: each inmate discovers in his dramatic character some deep pertinence to his personal life, and even sometimes to his crime.

What is striking, too, is how different this version of the play is from those one might see in a modern theater or read about in contemporary Shakespeare criticism. Take the issue of race. Although several of the inmates are black, none of them is cast as Caliban. The Caliban of this production is a large white man with blond hair, who performs masterfully, shouting out curses, developing a distinctive crawl along the floor. Race and gender are not major factors in this performance, at least in any stereotypical way. Instead, the play is manifestly, to its actors, about redemption. At the very end of the play, the final couplet of Prospero's epilogue, spoken to the audience, is,

As you from crimes would pardoned be,
Let your indulgence set me free.

Epilogue 19–20

And these lines seem to have a special, direct, and contemporary pertinence to both the audience and the actors.

Some inmates hope that acting in the Shakespeare play—a recreation favored by the prison administration—will get them closer to parole. Others feel that the process is itself redemptive and cleansing, as well as engaging and exciting. Better than mopping floors. Trinculo—the actor seen in the opening moments speaking Prospero's speech—is a particularly affecting individual who acts as a recurring narrative presence throughout the documentary. At the end we see the performance, and find out what happened to the performers.

The film is effective both on its own, as an autonomous work of art, and also as a symptomatic and striking instance of the intersection between Shakespeare and modern culture. The play is not appropriated, trivialized, or merely thematized. It may or may not be "therapeutic." But the important thing, for the actors, the camera, and the viewers, is that it is *acted.* It is performed and experienced as a piece of theater. Shakespeare's "genius" is nowhere merely lionized. What we encounter, instead, is the contemporary relevance of Shakespeare as playwright—and the contemporary relevance of *The Tempest.*

THE TEMPEST ENGAGES THE QUESTION of modern culture in a number of different, direct, and overlapping ways. By "modern culture" here we might mean things as various, or as congruent, as colonialism, race relations, master-slave dynamics, psychoanalysis, cognition and the structure of the mind, "science" and "art" as (post)magical practices, feminism, geopolitics, environmentalism, governance, and the rationale for what we now call "general education." All presented in a marvelously compact package, a brilliantly conceived, tightly structured play that takes place in a short time, in a single space: an enchanted island located either in the New World, near Bermuda, or in the Old, somewhere between Naples and Tunis, or in the imagination.

In its dramatic form *The Tempest* is a comedy that recuperates what could have been a tragedy. It belongs as well to the genre of the revenge play, a popular mode in the period—but one that in its more usual form ends with death, and repetition: the ghost returns, a past wrong is recalled and righted. In this case the repetition comes at the beginning, as the very engine of transformation (storm, wreck, loss, plot, discovery). Events of twelve years ago are retold, recalled, and revisited, as the magical storm wrought by Prospero brings to the island the very same people who were the cause of his usurpation and exile. So it should come as no surprise to find that the internal mechanism of the play—repetition with a difference—becomes, as well, the mechanism of its history, or histories (in the plural) in modern culture.

There are several "histories" here, all interesting, all intertwined:

- the history of the play's performances
- the history of its adaptations
- political and cultural history (exploration and settlement; colonial and postcolonial)
- the history of literary criticism (romanticism, liberal humanism, new historicism, cultural materialism, psychoanalysis, postcoloniality)
- the history of "Shakespeare"—that is, fantasies about the author, in this case focusing on the persistent fantasy that the play is his "farewell to the stage"
- or the history of the sciences of "man"—theories of the self, the subject, the unconscious, and evolution

To further explain this last category: the play has been read and staged in recent years with a special attention to colonialism (both early modern and recent) and to race. But it also has powerful historical and conceptual resonances with the master narratives of the last century, the grand narratives generated by Darwin, Freud, and Marx, the narratives through which (and in reaction to which) "modernity" and "postmodernity" have come to position themselves. Jean-François Lyotard defines postmodernism as a skepticism or "incredulity" toward grand narratives—the refusal to believe that there are metastories about man and "progress" and, indeed, "liberation."[2] And this tension—between belief in a grand narrative and skepticism or distrust—could be said to animate the tensions both within Shakespeare's play and between the play and its various interpreters or appropriators. The play itself has been repeatedly "colonized," used as a staging area for arguments about the transcendence of poetry, about Shakespeare the Man, about cultural politics, and about mastery and subjugation.

GRAND NARRATIVES CREATE trajectories for thinking—and for categories of thought. Darwin mapped the "descent of man" and the evolution of species—and *The Tempest* can be seen (and was read, a hundred years ago) as a kind of ethnography or natural history of evolutionary life stages, with Cal-

Charles Buchel, Herbert Beerbohm Tree
as Caliban

iban related to beasts, fish, and animals, and Ariel to airy spirits. Many productions of the play at the turn of the last century featured a Caliban who
was, to cite the title of a book published in 1873, *Caliban: The Missing Link.*[3]
Caliban attempts to rape Miranda and people the isle with Calibans. (We
might say that the play in this period was evolutionary psychology, though
the term had not yet been invented.) But the nineteenth century and the early
twentieth century regarded Caliban as a figure of pathos, aspiring to a higher
condition ("I'll be wise hereafter, and seek for grace"). Percy MacKaye's 1916
"community masque," *Caliban by the Yellow Sands,* performed at New York's
Lewisohn Stadium, presented Prospero as guiding Caliban toward moral
improvement: "Caliban seeking to learn the art of Prospero . . . the slow education of mankind through the influences of cooperative art."[4] This was the
Darwin of his own time, the Darwin of the late nineteenth century and the
early years of the twentieth.

THE TWO THEORIES of human evolution, Darwin's and Freud's, are in a way
natural counterparts. One tells the long story of the species; the other the

short story of the individual. Both are "evolutionary"—they see a series of accidents, events, traumas, recuperations from trauma, beginnings over again: the history of "man."

My suggestion for a keyword for *The Tempest* and its effect upon modern culture would, in fact, be this problematic word "man."[5] "Man" as a general substantive for all mankind raised a number of problems for the late twentieth century. Did it include "woman"? Did its use flatten out important cultural differences and histories? What about its older use to mean "servant" (my man—"'Ban, 'ban, Cacaliban / has a new master.—Get a new man!" [2.2.175-6])? "Man" can mean a human being of either sex, a male person, the human race or species. The debates about the use of the term, among anthropologists, linguists, literary critics, historians, and professional writers and thinkers, have in a way defined some of the most trenchant conversations about culture (and that equally contested term, "civilization") for the last several decades. The wide range of meanings of "man" (mankind, man or spirit, man or beast, master and servant/slave, man and woman) and the tensions and injustices that arise in and around this set of definitions are themselves both prefigured, and encapsulated, in the dramatic action—and dramatis personae—of *The Tempest*.

That Shakespeare played with the meaning of this term is clear from a telling exchange in *Hamlet,* when Hamlet remarks to Rosencrantz and Guildenstern, "Man delights not me—nor woman neither, though by your smiling you seem to say so." This remark comes at the close of the very famous philosophical rumination about "What a piece of work is man," a passage that ends with "And yet to me what is this quintessence of dust" (2.2.293–98). The shift from the one meaning of "man," *mankind, humanity, mortal existence,* to the other meaning, *male person,* indeed *male desiring person,* is quick, shrewd, and definitive. The word "man" breaks apart into (at least) two meanings, one solemn, one erotic and comic.

In *The Tempest,* as we'll see, this process of parsing, or dividing up, the various meanings of "man" becomes the topic of constant investigation. And, as we will also see, this contributes to the sense of the play's current pertinence. In a way, all of the disciplines of knowledge that developed and were formalized from the end of the nineteenth century onward—anthropology, sociology, linguistics, psychology, all of what came to be known as "the sciences of man"—find their core narratives in *The Tempest*. The play is not only a parable of colonial appropriation and dispossession, but also, equally crucially, the story of art and science at a crossroads, of the aesthetic and the instrumental, the psychological, the biological, the creative imperatives and the death drive, all "bound up," to use Ferdinand's wondering phrase, "as in a dream" (1.2.490).

THE TEMPEST IN MODERN CULTURE has been the story of four characters, and of competing narratives, each bidding, at one time or another, to be the grand narrative of which this brilliant play is exemplar. The story of Prospero; the story of Miranda; the story of Ariel; and the story of Caliban. Each is intertwined with a certain view of history, and a certain view of man.

Other characters in the play have had their adherents and proponents. W. H. Auden thought Antonio was the strongest character in the play, because he is self-sufficient and content to be alone. Two female characters crucial to the narrative—the powerful witch Sycorax, Caliban's mother (whom Prospero supplanted), and Claribel, the daughter of the King of Naples (married to an African and sent to Tunis)—are absent from the play's dramatis personae, a fact that did not go unnoticed by feminist readers in the twentieth century. The poet H.D. identified herself with the "invisible, voice-less" Claribel, writing that "I only threw a shadow / On his page, / Yet I was his, / He spoke my name."[6]

Prospero's daughter, Miranda, the one woman we meet onstage, rebels against her father but, in doing so, falls in with his secret wish for her to marry Ferdinand. Her speech about the "brave new world / That hath such people in it"—describing, in glowing terms, the posse of usurpers and would-be murderers shipwrecked on the island—provided a title to the highly success-ful dystopian novel by Aldous Huxley.

But the cultural effect in particular of Ariel, Caliban, and Prospero, on realms of modernity from political manifestos to poetry, has been enormous. What seems to have happened is that artists, writers, psychologists, and the organizers of political movements have *recognized* Shakespeare's *Tempest* as a prescient allegory of their own situation. In part because the play is, or seems to be, a fantasy—and because it is, or seems to be, *both* a story about mental life and a story about politics and culture—it offers a different kind of alle-gory than that represented by a tragedy or a history play.

We might begin with Prospero, not because he has always been regarded as the central figure, but precisely because in recent years he has not.

Prospero is a magician, like the magician who was the title character in Marlowe's *Doctor Faustus* (1592). For Faustus's initial goal, too, was the achievement of knowledge. In his opening soliloquy Faustus, in his study, reviews the extant practices of intellectual life—disputation, medicine, law, and divinity—and decides that magic is the strongest of them:

> These metaphysics of magicians
> And necromantic books are heavenly,
> Lines, circles, signs, letters and characters—
> Ay, these are those that Faustus most desires.
> Oh, what a world of profit and delight,
> Of power, of honour, of omnipotence
> Is promised to the studious artisan!
> All things that move between the quiet poles
> Shall be at my command. Emperors and kings
> Are but obeyed in their several provinces,
> Nor can they raise the wind or rend the clouds;
> But his dominion that exceeds in this
> Stretcheth as far as doth the mind of man.
> A sound magician is a mighty god.[7]

In the early modern period magic was a recognizable profession—science and magic were just at this time beginning to be distinguished from each other. To be interested in mathematics, astronomy, navigation, geography, cartography—and also in alchemy, divination, and occult philosophy—was not a contradiction in terms. In fact, this combination of skills, talents, and interests is the very combination that marked the famous magician John Dee (1527–1608), on whom Shakespeare may, indeed, have partly modeled the character of Prospero.

John Dee was noted for his mathematical treatises, his library of books (the largest in the country and one of the best in Europe at the time), and his conversations with angels and spirits, whom he sought out as a way of increasing knowledge, often with the help of a crystal glass. John Dee was also a friend of Tycho Brahe and knew the work of Nicolaus Copernicus. Again, science and "magic," far from being at opposite poles, were often thought of as branches of the same kind of inquiry.[8]

And so they are again, in a way, today. "Genius" is often regarded as an aspect of scientific investigation and insight. Keys to the universe, whether through DNA, the splitting of the atom, relativity theory, or string theory, are envisaged as developing through science rather than through what we now call "the humanities"—literature, art, music, and philosophy. The split that developed in the seventeenth century, around the time of Francis Bacon and over the course of the succeeding century, between science and the humanities, and between science and "magic," is in some ways being repaired.

A renewed centrality for Darwin and Darwinian theories—now once more, a hundred years later, to be found all over the press, the publishing world, and academia, whether from the side of sociobiology or biography and history—may lead to a recentering of Prospero as both a naturalist and a magician, an artist and a scientist. Biotechnology, genetic engineering, cloning, mutations, and hybrids have brought Darwin back to the center of cultural attention. And in this framework, Prospero as scientist, and Caliban as hybrid exemplar, are also center stage.

If Darwin mapped the species, Freud mapped the internal workings of the psyche, the evolution of the individual's consciousness (and unconscious), through mental strategies like repression, displacement, condensation, and fantasy or wish fulfillment. And *The Tempest* can be—and has been—read as an allegory of the workings of the human mind, with the id (instinctual and desiring) represented by Caliban, kept in a cave when he is not needed for basic life functions: "we cannot miss him"—he carries wood and brings water. And the superego is represented by Ariel, who fulfills wishes and plans, and who also counsels the civilized qualities of mercy over revenge and retribution: "If you now beheld them," Ariel tells Prospero about the distracted and imprisoned courtiers, "your affections / Would become tender."

> PROSPERO   Dost thou think so, spirit?
> ARIEL   Mine would, sir, were I human.
>
> *5.1.19–20*

Prospero is struck, as we might be, that a human being is taught something about basic humanity by a spirit, and concludes that "The rarer action is / In virtue than in vengeance" (5.1.27–28).

One of the best popular culture explorations of the role of the unconscious (and of something explicitly called the id) in *The Tempest* is the film adaptation from 1956, *Forbidden Planet*, which introduced Robby the Robot as the Ariel figure. Dr. Edward Morbius, a philologist and the film's Prospero, discovers that the ultimate enemy to the planet Altair is his own unconscious— the monster that threatens the planet comes from his own id ("This thing of darkness I acknowledge mine" [5.1.278–9]). Meanwhile his daughter Altaira has fallen in love with the commander of the United Planets Cruiser. Morbius dies, Altaira prepares to return to Earth with the crew. (More recent pop culture spinoffs would include all the "desert island" television shows, from *Gilligan's Island* to *Lost*, as well as a film like *Cast Away* [2000], in which the Ariel character is a volleyball named "Wilson.")

But in the middle of the twentieth century Prospero was clearly associated in many minds with the humanities. In criticism he was regularly described as a "playwright"—the creator, onstage, of a play within a play. When the play was read as an art fable, he was the meta-artist, the artist who represented Shakespeare the Playwright.

In the 1950s and '60s, in fact, *The Tempest* was many an English professor's favorite play. It was, after all, a play about a man who preferred reading books to wielding political power. Here is how Prospero describes himself to his daughter Miranda (and to the audience) at the beginning of the play:

> —being so reputed
> In dignity, and for the liberal arts
> Without a parallel—those being all my study,
> The government I cast upon my brother,
> And to my state grew stranger, being transported
> And rapt in secret studies.
>
> *1.2.72–77*

> I, thus neglecting worldly ends, all dedicated
> To closeness and the bettering of my mind.
>
> *1.2.89–90*

Prospero, by this "neglect" of worldly things and focus on his scholarship, enabled his brother, Antonio, to "believe / He was indeed the Duke," and to make a deal with the King of Naples, Alonso, to remove Prospero and his daughter, Miranda, both from the dukedom and from Milan altogether, by placing them in a leaky boat and setting them out to sea.

But the good old councillor Gonzalo ("a noble Neapolitan") helped them, furnishing the boat with "rich garments, linens, stuffs and necessaries," all of which they have been using, and wearing, on the island from that time twelve years ago to the present. Also, most centrally,

> Knowing I loved my books, he furnished me
> From mine own library with volumes that
> I prize above my dukedom.
>
> *1.2.167–69*

Notice that he *still* prizes his books above his dukedom, his political place in the world. It's that preference, that choice, that led to his usurpation and exile, his loss of power in Europe.

In the mid-twentieth century this removal from the world, this choice of scholarship rather than political engagement (and what would have looked, presumably, like humanistic scholarship—"books"—rather than laboratory

science for human betterment [or for the arms race]), was, for some people, a
choice that seemed personal, self-involved, rather than selfless. "Ask not what
your country can do for you, but what you can do for your country." Was
scholarship and academic work—work, say, in literature, the classics, art, philosophy, even history—doing something, whether for "your country" or for
the world? The answer, for scholars from ancient times to the present, has
been yes. But the example of Prospero offered a model—indeed, perhaps even
a model for "having it all." For it is Prospero's attention to his books that
leads, ultimately, to the defeat of evil: the shaming and reformation of male-
factors, the conversion of sinners, a dynastic marriage that returns his family
to political power, and a triumphant return from exile. The ivory tower has
turned out to be a command post, even a panopticon.[9]

Nonetheless, this idealized figure encountered some serious critiques. In
the last part of the twentieth century Prospero began to be regularly read (or
appropriated) as a colonial exploiter of the indigenous population of what the
play text calls an "uninhabited" island—an island already inhabited by Caliban and his mother, Sycorax ("this island's mine, by Sycorax, my mother").
In Latin America, in Martinique, and elsewhere, versions of the play were
written that espoused the cause, and the character, of Caliban. And at the
same time there was some attention to the situation of Miranda; her father's
loving protectiveness could also be seen as a kind of condescension. " 'Tis new
to thee," his ironic (and indulgent) response to her exclamation "How beau-
teous mankind is! / O brave new world / That hast such people in't," is a
put-down as much as an affectionate aside (5.1.186–87).

The father's irony, in context, is perfectly appropriate; these beautiful
people have robbed him of his dukedom and sent him off in a leaky boat to
die. But taken out of context " 'tis new to thee" has had a career somewhat
comparable to the ironization of "brave new world."

The tension between parents and children, and especially between fathers
and daughters, so often encountered in Shakespeare's plays, is also present in
The Tempest. And if the play is read as an allegory of generational conflict, as
well as the story of a particular nuclear family (once again, as in all those other
Shakespearean incidences, with the mother absent and dead!), then the ironic
caution of the father (" 'tis new to thee") to the daughter embracing a brave
new world (and a husband, and a move to the city) may well stand, inadvertently and unheeded, as the mantra of the sixties. Critics, in other words,
began to rebel against Prospero. If one generation of professors thought of
themselves as Prosperos, the next generation would people the academy with
Calibans and with resistant and rebellious Mirandas. (And, of course, another

way to look at this is to say that once again the internal structure of the play is predictive and determinative: just as it began with the repetition of a rebellion, with the powerless and the powerful switching places, so its metatheatrical afterlife will be a return to that pattern of repetition.)

Magician, academic, scientist, playwright—Prospero, setting Ariel (the mind and imagination) free, acknowledging Caliban (the body, its needs and desires) to be part of him ("this thing of darkness I acknowledge mine"), would wind up, despite himself, in the Freudian position of the heavy father. And yet there remained, at the same time, this transferential desire, this wish to hear Shakespeare's voice in Prospero's, to believe—as Coleridge, Edward Dowden, and other Romantic critics long ago had believed—that through his dramatic figure of the father-playwright, Shakespeare was sending us a message, the message of his departure.

HOW CAN WE ACCOUNT FOR the persistent desire to hear the voice of Shakespeare in the voice of Prospero?

It is often observed that we live today in a "celebrity culture," a culture of public "confession," of "talking heads" and of "public intellectuals." The fantasy of putting Shakespeare on *Charlie Rose*—or on the analyst's couch—lies very close to the surface of our preoccupation with his elusive authority. And that authority, like the authority of all celebrities, is two-sided: we want Shakespeare's aura, and we also want his vulnerability.

This is one reason for the persistence of the idea that Shakespeare used one of his most authoritative dramatic characters to confess his own feeling about leaving the world of the theater, an event usually described, in defiance of history, as his "farewell to the stage."

The Tempest is the site of one of the most quoted of all of Shakespeare's gorgeous set pieces, a gorgeous set piece about a gorgeous set piece, the speech that begins "Our revels now are ended."

> Our revels now are ended. These our actors,
> As I foretold you, were all spirits, and
> Are melted into air, into thin air;
> And like the baseless fabric of this vision,
> The cloud-capped towers, the gorgeous palaces,
> The solemn temples, the great globe itself,
> Yea, all which it inherit, shall dissolve;
> And, like this insubstantial pageant faded,
> Leave not a rack behind. We are such stuff

As dreams are made on, and our little life
Is rounded with a sleep.

4.1.148–58

This is one of the passages in Shakespeare that I find real difficulty in reading aloud without a noticeable catch in my throat. It's written, we might say, to produce that effect. Written by a playwright still at the height of his powers. The pathos it induces is a stage effect, and—as a stage effect—it is very real.

But what this passage certainly is not is "Shakespeare's farewell to the stage." The imagined social pathos of his departure from London—which would not come for more than a year after *The Tempest,* and after he had written at least one more play, *Henry VIII, or All Is True,* and possibly parts of some others—is something some readers and commentators have wanted to elicit from these words, for a variety of reasons. So far from being "Shakespeare's farewell," it is not even, in the play, "Prospero's farewell," since it takes place in the fourth act of a five-act play.[10]

Prospero's not dying. He's furious. And worried. Caliban and the other low conspirators are still out there, plotting against his life, and "the minute of their plot / Is almost come" (4.1.141–2). And this play-within-a-play, the masque of Juno and Ceres, takes place in the fourth act. It isn't till the end of the fifth act, of course, that Prospero releases Ariel, marking the end of his magic ("Be free, and fare thee well") and speaks his Epilogue. In Patrick Stewart's performance of the part in the mid-1990s, Stewart, classically trained with the Royal Shakespeare Company but perhaps best-known for his role in *Star Trek: The Next Generation,* relinquished the microphone amplification that he had used throughout the rest of the play. His voice was suddenly, and only, that of a man, not a magician—or a demigod.

So why do we persist in calling the "revels now are ended speech" Shakespeare's farewell? (*Okay, it's not his literal farewell, but it's a kind of farewell, right?*) Freud had a name for this: disavowal. The refusal to believe something we really, really don't want to believe—or rather, in the case of Freud's patient, and in our case as readers of Shakespeare, the wish not to give up believing something we really, really want to believe. The desire, in this case, for Shakespeare to be talking to *us,* confessing his vulnerability to *us.* But like all overmastering desires, this one—the desire to know what is in Shakespeare's mind—cannot ever be wholly gratified, or satisfied.

NONETHELESS, IT ABIDES, in criticism, in the theater, and in film. In Peter Greenaway's 1991 film, *Prospero's Books,* the main character, played by the

Shakespearean actor John Gielgud, is called in the script at the end "Prospero/ Shakespeare," and is instructed to address the audience, "his last audience in his last play . . . as he takes leave of the island, the theater, and possibly his life."[11] Pathos can go no further, and Greenaway is not normally a sentimental man. I think this is hokum, as you can tell. But I'm mentioning Greenaway's script here not to deplore it but to point out something rather wonderful in it.

Prospero's Books takes as its structuring principle the "twenty-four books that Gonzalo hastily threw into Prospero's boat as he was pushed out into the sea to begin his exile."[12] The trope is a complete fantasy, of course. Greenaway invents the number twenty-four, invents the idea, creates an "unscene" that sets the stage (or rather, the screen) for the film.

1. The Book of Water
2. A Book of Mirrors
3. A Book of Mythologies
4. A Primer of the Small Stars
5. An Atlas Belonging to Orpheus
6. A Harsh Book of Geometry
7. The Book of Colours
8. The Vesalius Anatomy of Birth
9. An Alphabetical Inventory of the Dead
10. A Book of Travellers' Tales
11. The Book of the Earth
12. A Book of Architecture and Other Music
13. The Ninety-Two Conceits of the Minotaur
14. The Book of Languages
15. End-plants
16. A Book of Love
17. A Bestiary of Past, Present, and Future Animals
18. The Book of Utopias
19. The Book of Universal Cosmography
20. Lore of Ruins
21. The Autobiographies of Pasiphae and Semiramis
22. A Book of Motion
23. The Book of Games
24. Thirty-Six Plays

His detailed description of the books is smart, witty, imaginative, and worth reading—a paragraph apiece, including the "fact" that the *Book of Travellers' Tales* was much used by children; that Prospero used *The Book of the Earth* to seek for gold, not for financial gain but to cure his arthritis; and that *The Autobiographies of Pasiphae and Semiramis* is pornography, that steam rises from its pages whenever the book is opened and it is always warm—and that you have to handle it with gloves. You can see he must have had fun putting this list together—it reads like something out of Jorge Luis Borges. Here's what he has to say about that last book, the one called *Thirty-Six Plays:* "*Thirty-Six Plays.* This is a thick, printed volume of plays dated 1623. All thirty-six plays are there save one—the first. Nineteen pages are left blank for its inclusion. It is called *The Tempest.* The folio collection is modestly bound in dull green linen with cardboard covers and the author's initials are embossed in gold on the cover—W.S."[13]

By this powerful inventive fiction, one of the books that Prospero takes with him on his voyage is the First Folio of Shakespeare. The play has yet to be written, but the space for it stands waiting. (*The Tempest* is, in fact, the first play in the First Folio.) This is a version of the play-within-the-play (or the play-within-the-playbook)—a version that depends upon absence rather than presence, and thus upon performativity. It allows for "audience" input, as the process of the film will somehow produce the missing play. But from our point of view, I think the gap is as important as what fills it.

IN MANY ARTICULATIONS OF *The Tempest* in and for modern culture, Prospero is a defining presence, whether as father and mentor, benign scholar and artist, scientist, artful revenger, unrepentant colonial oppressor and exploiter, or stand-in for Shakespeare the man. In a Freudian allegory of the play as a model for the human mind, or for "humanity," he would be the conscious subject, whose unconscious could be split into the Ariel part and the Caliban part, whether we call those parts imagination or fantasy or superego (for Ariel) and lust or self-preservation or the id (for Caliban).

But for quite a long time in the modern history of this play, Prospero, although he is in some sense the "main character," was not the figure who most dominated the cultural imagination. Instead it was Ariel and Caliban, the "airy spirit" and what the list of roles calls the "savage and deformed slave," who captured the popular imagination—in art, in poetry, in criticism, and, increasingly, in politics and political theory. Here it will be useful to look at the long sweep from Romanticism to the present.

Two of the most popular Shakespeare plays in the nineteenth century were his two "fairy" plays, *The Tempest* and *A Midsummer Night's Dream.* Half a century or more before Freud, Romantic critics regarded these plays, with their invisible spirits and magical powers of transformation, as keys to Shakespeare's poetic imagination. Taken together with the "Queen Mab" speech in *Romeo and Juliet,* which is also about a tiny spirit who visits people at night and gives them dreams, the fairy plays seemed to say something powerful and consistent about the mind and about creativity.

Like so many other plays (*King Lear* and *Macbeth,* for example), *The Tempest* had been "improved" for modern—that is, eighteenth-century— taste, but was "restored" to the stage by the actor-manager William Charles Macready in 1838. Throughout this whole period, there was a raging debate between people who wanted to see Shakespeare's plays produced, and people, sometimes very major critics, who thought that any stage production ruined their imaginative potential. The Romantic critic Hazlitt, for example, felt strongly that "poetry and the stage do not agree well together"; that "fairies are not incredible, but fairies six feet high are so," and that "the boards of a theatre and the regions of fancy are not the same thing."[14]

But lest you think that all of these Victorian allusions are saccharine or benign, we might consider, for example, a painting called *The Stuff That Dreams Are Made Of,* by John Anster Fitzgerald, in which a dreaming woman is surrounded by narcotics, bottles, and spirits. It's clear that her dreams are produced by drugs and drug-induced hallucinations. The title, of course, is an adaptation of Prospero's famous line. Fitzgerald executed a series of "dream" paintings, like *The Artist's Dream,* in which the sleeper encounters frightening fairy creatures that resemble figures in works by Pieter Brueghel or Hieronymus Bosch.[15]

John Anster Fitzgerald, The Stuff That Dreams Are Made Of

———

WHEN THE SPIRITS OF *The Tempest* are depicted or performed, the artist, or the director, does make choices. The artist Henry Fuseli, who created many powerful images from Shakespeare, painted (between 1800 and 1810) an Ariel who was athletic and dancerlike, perched on a bat's back (as in the song Ariel sings in 5.1.88: "Where the bee sucks, there suck I"). You can see the six-footer problem here. In Macready's theater production, though, Ariel was played by a woman—this is Priscilla Horton, and the pose is very like that in the Fuseli. Subsequent Ariels throughout the century were female, gentle, and showed quite a bit of leg.

In fact, in productions of Shakespeare's other fairy play, *A Midsummer Night's Dream,* the parts of Puck and Oberon (the King of the Fairies) were usually in this period played by women, or by young girls. The Ariel in Charles Kean's 1857 production was the thirteen-year-old Kate Terry, whose "ethereal" presence struck audiences as preferable even to the "full-grown voluptuous-looking females" (I'm quoting from Kean's biography) who had played the part before.[16] Kean's Ariel looked like she could, indeed, be compressed within a pine tree. Remember, this is the same Victorian culture that produced *Alice in Wonderland* and *Peter Pan.* Hans Christian Andersen, author of fairy tales, was overcome with admiration for this figure, whom he described with a male pronoun ("All in white he stood . . .").[17] The character was imagined as male; the actor was female. (In the early modern period, of course, the reverse was true: the character—Miranda, Lady Macbeth, Portia—was female, but the actor was male.) Gender onstage is always an illusion. The case of Ariel makes that illusion palpable, since (as Milton's angels told a curious Adam and Eve) spirits have no sex. (But this does not mean that they always lack desire, as we will see in the epilogue to W. H. Auden's *The Sea and the Mirror,* where Ariel confesses his love for Caliban.)

THE GENDERING OF THESE SPIRITS is not without interest, since it creates onstage and conceptual structures: a "female" Ariel has a different relationship to a "male" Caliban than does a "male" Ariel (I put all these gender designations in quotation marks on purpose). And a "female" Ariel would have, perhaps, a different interpretive affinity to the character of Miranda (whose spectral equivalent she might, now, be imagined as being). In fact the female Ariels, since they were active, energetic, and able to fly about the stage and do wonders, quite overshadowed the Mirandas, who were reduced to resisting the command of fathers who secretly hoped they would resist.

Henry Fuseli, Ariel

Daniel Maclise, Priscilla Horton as Ariel

Miranda's one very strong speech, her attack on Caliban for his attack on her—

> Abhorrèd slave,
> Which any print of goodness wilt not take
> . . . .
> When thou didst not, savage,

> Know thine own meaning, . . .
> I endowed thy purposes
> With words that made them known.
> But thy vile race
> . . . had that in't which good natures
> Could not abide to be with; therefore wast thou
> Deservedly confined into this rock.
>
> *1.2.354–64*

—this very strong and aversive speech was for many years reassigned to Prospero, on the grounds that a sheltered maiden wouldn't—or shouldn't—think or say such things.

The nineteenth century introduced a female Ariel, in accordance with its own sense of what a sprite might be like. But most late-twentieth-century Ariels have been male. In a production directed by Mark Lamos at the Hartford Stage Company in 1985 I saw the part played by a male gymnast, who swung athletically in the air on ropes rather than the "fairy wires" that became popular for the Victorian Ariels (and Peter Pan). And as the introduction to the Arden edition of *The Tempest* points out, the actor Simon Russell Beale performed the part for the Royal Shakespeare Company in 1993–94 as a distinctly resentful figure, quite ready for his freedom.[18]

"ARIEL" AS A TITLE for a collection of poems—and for a poem—has been adopted by poets from T. S. Eliot to Sylvia Plath (although Plath's title is actually the name of her favorite horse). The character's name is related to the Hebrew word for "lion of God" (and is found in modern Israel as a man's name); Renaissance audiences might also have associated "Ariel" with "Uriel," the spirit with whom the magician John Dee was said to converse. The pathos of the character, with his insistent desire to be free (twelve years in the pine tree under Sycorax, twelve years' service for Prospero), is sometimes occluded or lost in these appropriations, which seem to focus on Ariel's other side, the embodiment of music ("Be not afeard. The isle is full of noises," says Caliban, who of course has never seen Ariel, "Sounds, and sweet airs, that give delight and hurt not" [3.2.130–31]).

The romantic poet Percy Bysshe Shelley, who thought that poets were the unacknowledged legislators of the world, considered *The Tempest* his favorite Shakespeare play, and identified with the character of Ariel. Using that name, he wrote a poem ("With a Guitar, to Jane") to the wife of a friend, calling himself "your guardian spirit Ariel" and calling her husband "thine own prince Ferdinand." The story has a sad ending, though, and one uncannily related to *The Tempest.* Shelley and "Ferdinand" (Edward Williams) drowned, shortly after the presentation of the poem and the guitar, when a sudden storm arose off the Italian coast. The boat they were sailing in sank: Shelley had named it *Ariel.*

YET WHILE "ARIEL" WAS being adopted by poets, it, or he, was also claimed as a principle of freedom and grace by politicians, especially those in Latin America. The Uruguayan philosopher and statesman José Enrique Rodó in 1900 published a book called *Ariel* that contrasted the elegance and power of Latin American culture with the "barbarism" of Caliban, the forces of northern invaders. In Rodó's book, which became an enduring best seller, an old teacher "who by allusion to the wise magician of Shakespeare's *Tempest* was often called Prospero," gathers his young disciples about him "one last time," and talks to them beside a statue of Ariel, beside which it had become his custom to sit.[19] "Shakespeare's ethereal Ariel symbolizes the noble, soaring aspect of the human spirit," writes Rodó. "He represents the superiority of reason and feeling over the base impulses of irrationality."[20] The plan was to be "evolution," a "continuous and felicitous acceleration of evolution," so that "the period of one generation" might be enough time to transform Latin American society.[21] The word "evolution" is repeated ("the later evolution of superior races").[22] Rodó goes on to claim that "Ariel will pass through human history, humming, as in Shakespeare's drama," until the reformation of society—the animation of "those who labor and those who struggle" is perfected, and he can be set free to return to "the center of his divine fire."[23]

Rodo's optimistic document makes good use of both the Prospero character in his relationship to Ariel and the play's double ending: Prospero's departure (from teaching? to death?) and Ariel's hoped-for freedom. This appropriation of *The Tempest* signaled a new era in the cultural history of the play. For the rest of the twentieth century it would be thought of—by some at least—as a "New World" play. The geographical location of the island seems (perhaps deliberately) problematic. It seems to be located somewhere between Europe (Naples) and Africa (Tunis), from which the Neapolitans have been voyaging, after Claribel's wedding to "an African" (the one emphatically black character mentioned in the play). But the references to the "still vexed Bermoothes" or "Bermudas" in act 1, scene 2 suggest that we are in that mysterious and uncanny space still known as the "Bermuda triangle."

But the identification of Latin American nationalism and culture with

Henry Fuseli, Shakespeare: *Tempest,* Act I, Scene II

"Ariel," so unproblematic and heralded in 1900, was by the middle of the twentieth century—fifty years later—superseded by an identification with Caliban. Since Caliban had been the abject, the despised and othered one, for so long, we may want to take a moment to see how this came about.

Even before Rodó's *Ariel,* Caliban had been cited as the monstrous equivalent of North (and Anglo-) American crudity. In 1898, Nicaraguan Rubén Darío wrote an essay called "The Triumph of Caliban" about U.S. imperialism and aggression in the Spanish-American War.[24] On a Manichean reading of Caliban and Ariel—which is, after all, Prospero's and Miranda's reading, what we might think of as the dominant-culture reading—Caliban was base, and Ariel noble; Caliban was low, and Ariel high; Caliban was "bad" and Ariel "good."

What had changed? Over the intervening half a century, the play had come to speak differently to some members of its global audience. Prospero, the "good colonizer" of traditional Anglo-American interpretations of *The Tempest,* became increasingly regarded—when he was regarded at all—as the "bad colonizer," the imperialist, imposing his own culture and mores on a victimized Caliban, the native inhabitant (and, as he claims, natural ruler) of the island. All the "civilizing" boasts made by Prospero and Miranda—we taught you (our) language, we taught you (our) cosmology, we taught you (our) manners, we taught you about (our) God—could be regarded as impositions rather than noble gifts. Native and African populations in Latin America were not so grateful for the gift of someone else's civilization, and in North America (as in France and elsewhere in Europe) a growing consciousness of the colonial present, as well as the colonial past, began to reverse the poles in Shakespeare's play.

One catalyst here was the publication of a book by a French intellectual and civil servant, Octave Mannoni, in 1950, and its translation into English six years later. In French the book was called *Psychologie de la colonisation*—in English it was retitled, simply and powerfully, *Prospero and Caliban*.[25]

Mannoni's theory of the "dependency complex" of the native and the unconscious inferiority complex of the colonizer had an enormous effect, pro and con, on discussions of colonial relations. It certainly elicited a ferocious rebuttal from Frantz Fanon. Clearly an appropriation of Shakespeare's fictional characters, Mannoni's reading of their relationship is not only an allegory of, but a psychoanalytic "explanation" for, the colonial relation.

Mannoni expresses the belief that "the dependence relationship requires at least two members"—that it is a dialectic.[26] And he seeks to find the "exact psychological nature of the relations which form between the European colonial and the dependent native"—a nature he, like Freud, finds "best" described in "the world of some of the great writers," who "projected them on to imaginary characters placed in situations which, though imaginary, are typically colonial. The material they drew directly from their own unconscious desires," he says, upping the ante by suggesting that the writers (and in this case Shakespeare) participate in the "complexes" they depict in their fictional characters.[27] His examples are two famous literary dyads: Prospero and Caliban, and Robinson Crusoe and Friday.

Prospero, says Mannoni, is "the least evolved of all these literary figures, according to the criteria of psychoanalysis," because, as a magician, he doesn't have to have a good grasp of ordinary interpersonal relations.[28] He is attracted to solitude, in part because "if the world is emptied of human beings as they really are, it can be filled with the creatures of our own imagination: Calypso, Ariel, Friday."[29] In other words, to use the language of modern pop psychology, Prospero prefers "imaginary friends" to real ones. Mannoni thinks Miranda is healthier, or better adjusted. When she sees Ferdinand and the other Neapolitans, and bursts out with her famous words of admiration (bringing her name to life), "O brave new world / That has such people in't," (5.1.86–7) Miranda is making an "adjustment" that her "neurotic father had so surely missed"—and that he confirms in his scornful dismissal, "'Tis new to thee."[30]

Colonial life, says Mannoni, is "the nearest approach possible to the archetype of the desert island," and people who choose such a life are avoiding adult reality.[31] "Man [notice the recurrence of this keyword, yet again] is both Ariel and Caliban, and we must recognize this if we are to grow up." "This same unconscious tendency" that led Shakespeare to write *The Tempest* "has impelled thousands of Europeans to seek out oceanic islands . . . or, alternatively, to go and entrench themselves in isolated outposts in hostile countries."[32]

As for the "dependency complex" of the colonial natives, "it would be hard," says Mannoni, "to find a better example of it in its pure state" than in the figure of Caliban, who is delighted to find a new master in Stephano and is eager to abase himself and show loyalty to this unworthy drunken butler. "The dependence of colonial natures is a matter of plain fact. The ensuing encounter between the European's unconscious and a reality all too prepared to receive its projects is in practice full of dangers."[33] Mannoni includes a substantial and detailed reading of *The Tempest,* which is not in itself an unconvincing reading. Where his account is deeply troublesome is in his mapping of this story, unproblematically, onto so-called natives and so-called colonials. "The typical colonial is compelled to live out Prospero's dream, for Prospero is in his unconscious as he was in Shakespeare's."[34] The "Prospero complex," as Mannoni calls it, is probably present, even if repressed, in any man who "chooses a colonial career."

This book, we might recall, was written in 1948, published in France in 1950, and translated into English in 1956. It appeared before various interested readerships at the height of colonial concern and the beginning of decolonization. Mannoni himself had been an official in Madagascar, one of France's largest colonies. His dual identity, as psychoanalyst and as government administrator, is not unusual in the context of French (or other European) intellectuals.

In 1952, Frantz Fanon, born in Martinique, who had fought with the Free French in World War II and remained in France to study psychiatry, published *Black Skin White Masks,* his extraordinary account, part manifesto and part analysis, of his experience as a black intellectual in a France permeated with racism, conscious and unconscious. Fanon, too, analyzed the relationship of the colonizer and the colonized. Among his strong influences was Hegel (the Hegel presented in Alexandre Kojeve's famous Paris lectures). And among his targets, in the chapter, "The So-Called Dependency Complex of Colonized Peoples," not surprisingly, was Mannoni's *Prospero and Caliban: Psychology of Colonization.*

Fanon is superbly dismissive of Mannoni's thesis, which he summarizes in this way: "It becomes obvious that the white man acts in obedience to an authority complex, a leadership complex, while the Malagasy obeys a dependency complex. Everyone is satisfied." Mannoni, he thinks, completely disregards issues of race and race prejudice, the imperative on the black man to "turn white or disappear." Here is what Fanon says about *The Tempest:* "Prospero, as we know, is the main character of Shakespeare's comedy, *The Tempest*. Opposite him we have his daughter, Miranda, and Caliban. Toward Caliban, Prospero assumes an attitude that is well known to Americans in the southern United States. Are they not forever saying that [black men] are just waiting for the chance to jump on white women?"[35] The "complex," Fanon argues, is in the culture, not in the buried childhood psyches of the individuals. And as for the idea that "the dependency complex" is intrinsic to the native populace, "it appears to me that M. Mannoni lacks the slightest basis on which to ground any conclusion applicable to the situation, the problems, or the potentialities of the Malagasy in the present time."[36]

This is a French-on-French dispute, a dispute between two French cultural theorists with psychoanalytic training. Fanon became, in the following year, the head of the psychiatry department in a hospital in Algeria; in 1956, appalled by stories of torture told him by his patients, he resigned his government post and began working for Algerian independence. He found the colonial mission at odds, completely, with his profession of psychiatric practice.

What is especially fascinating and germane here is how central the story of Prospero and Caliban—and indeed, in its details, the story also of Miranda, Gonzalo, Ferdinand, and others—was to the cultural reading, the reading of culture, in this case.

Fanon was a Martinican; so was the playwright Aimé Césaire, who in 1969 wrote his own version of *The Tempest,* a play called *Une Tempête,* in which Caliban is a field hand and Ariel a mulatto house servant. Here is a brief passage (in translation) of Caliban's words to Prospero:

> You must understand, Prospero,
> for years I bowed my head,
> for years I stomached it,
> stomached all of it:
> your insults, your ingratitude,
> and worst of all, more degrading than all the rest,
> your condescension.
> But now it's over!

Over, do you hear!
Of course, for the moment you're still
the stronger.
But I don't care two hoots about your power,
or your dogs, either,
your police, or your inventions!
. . . .

Prospero, you're a great illusionist:
you know all about lies.
And you lied to me so much,
lied about the world, lied about yourself,
that you ended up by imposing on me
an image of myself:
underdeveloped, in your words,
incompetent,
that's how you forced me to see myself,
and I hate that image!
. . . .

 I know that one day
my bare fist, my bare fist alone,
will be enough to crush your world!
The old world is falling apart!
. . . .

you can get the hell out
You can go back to Europe.
But there's no hope of that!
I'm sure you won't leave![37]

At the end of Césaire's version of *The Tempest* Prospero indeed decides to remain on the island with Caliban and sends Antonio and Gonzalo back to Naples with Ferdinand and Miranda. Years go by; Prospero ages and grows cold. "Ah, well, my old Caliban," he says. "We're the only two left on this island, just you and me. You and me! You-me! Me-you!"[38]

But when he calls out, Caliban is gone, and from offstage the audience hears the cry of "LIBERTY!"[39]

THE LATE 1960S WERE in the midst of a period of decolonization (the end of official European—or U.S.—rule) in countries from northern and southern

Africa to the Caribbean, the Indian peninsula, and the south seas. In the Caribbean and in Latin America, in that same year, 1969, *The Tempest* and its main characters were cited as prescient forerunners. And again (in Spanish-speaking former colonies) it was Caliban, not Ariel, who had become the hero. The Cuban Roberto Fernández Retamar, a poet, essayist, and literary critic who became the cultural spokesman for Fidel Castro, wrote a much-cited and much-republished essay called "Caliban: Notes Toward a Discussion of Culture in America." As Retamar wrote:

> Our symbol is not Ariel, as Rodó thought, but Caliban. This is something that we, the *mestizo* inhabitants of these same isles where Caliban lived, see with particular clarity: Prospero invaded the islands, killed our ancestors, enslaved Caliban, and taught him his language to make himself understood. What else can Caliban do but use that same language—today he has no other—to curse him, to wish that the "red plague" would fall on him? I know no other metaphor more expressive of our cultural situation, of our reality. . . . [W]hat is our history, what is our culture, if not the history and culture of Caliban?[40]

We might notice here that Caliban's racial or ethnic identity is really a role, not an identity—that is to say, it varies from context to context, depending upon the national, colonial, or relational situation. Scholars concerned with Shakespeare's sources and influences have suggested every early modern category of "otherness" to Englishmen, from Native American to Irish—all of them wild men or "natives" that explorers of the time would have encountered in their travels. Voyages of exploration and discovery had brought Native Americans, alive and sometimes dead, from the New World to the king's court. Notice the moment in *The Tempest* when the commercially minded Trinculo discusses with himself the possibility of exhibiting Caliban in England for profit: "There would this monster make a man. Any strange beast there makes a man . . . When they will not give a doit to relieve a lame beggar, they will lay out ten to see a dead Indian" (2.2.28–31).

Modern productions in the United States and Britain often cast Caliban as nonwhite. But, as we saw with *Shakespeare Behind Bars,* a white, blond Caliban can indeed be very effective. It depends upon the reasons (fictional, cultural, experiential, performed, and performative) for his abjection.

In fact, as the Prospero and Caliban dynamic (whether unpacked by Mannoni, Fanon, or Fernández Retamar) might suggest, "Prospero" and "Caliban" are not only characters, but also *positions in a structure:* Dominator/dominated. Exploiter/exploited. Master/slave. Parent/child. Teacher/student.

Insider/outsider. Mind/body. Each creates the role of the other, as well as his own. And as the master/slave discourse, whether in Hegel or elsewhere, has compellingly suggested to modern culture, the apparently abjected partner is often in charge of the scene.

We have been tracing the characters of *The Tempest* as they have been recast as social roles, but it would be equally true to claim that this play and its characters and language have had a powerful effect upon the history of poetry. The isle is full of noises, and Ariel as invisible singer—as well as fearsome Harpy and vengeful sprite—haunts the stage, and the play.

> Full fathom five thy father lies.
>   Of his bones are coral made;
> Those are pearls that were his eyes;
>   Nothing of him that doth fade
> But doth suffer a sea-change
> Into something rich and strange.
>
> *1.2.400–5*

The song sung by Ariel to Ferdinand haunts T. S. Eliot's *The Waste Land,* where "Death by Water" is a constant theme.[41]

But often it is Caliban who seems to have most caught the poetic imagination, whether in Robert Browning's dramatic monologue, "Caliban Upon Setebos," or in W. H. Auden's bravura performance in Chapter III of his long poem *The Sea and the Mirror,* a brilliant chapter, in the prose style of the late novels of Henry James, called "Caliban to the Audience."

What is the appeal of Caliban to poets? He is a fan of music, for one thing, as his great speech demonstrates:

> Be not afeard. The isle is full of noises,
> Sounds, and sweet airs, that give delight and hurt not.
> Sometimes a thousand twangling instruments
> Will hum about mine ears, and sometimes voices
> That if I then had waked after long sleep
> Will make me sleep again; and then in dreaming
> The clouds methought would open and show riches
> Ready to drop upon me, that when I waked
> I cried to dream again.
>
> *3.2.130–38*

That the speech is spoken to the tone-deaf Stephano and Trinculo suggests that it is really addressed to the audience, or to himself.

Robert Browning's "Caliban Upon Setebos, or Natural Theology in the Island" was first published in 1864, a few years after the publication of Darwin's *On the Origin of Species* (1859). "Natural theology" is opposed to "revealed theology" or "revealed religion"—it's the attempt to find and test the existence of God (or a god, in this case) without any supernatural manifestations. Setebos is the god of Caliban's mother, Sycorax, whom Prospero preempted on the island. The proof of his existence is in his similarity to Caliban (notice the refrains at the end of the verse paragraphs, "So He"):

Would not I smash it with my foot? So He.

'Shall some day knock it down again: so He.

'Doth as he likes, or wherefore Lord? So He.[42]

Caliban imagines that Setebos himself is subject to a higher being he describes only as "the Quiet"—an unapproachable, impersonal force, very unlike the highly personalized, cruel, and unpredictable Setebos, always spelled with a capital *H* for the pronoun. Caliban speaks of himself in the third person throughout the poem. (Brackets inserted by the poet at the beginning and end represent his unspoken inner thoughts.) Like all of Browning's dramatic monologues (such as "My Last Duchess") the speaker here is revealing more about himself than he knows or intends. "The best way to escape His ire / Is, not to seem too happy."[43] The poem ends with a storm—we could call it a tempest—("there, there, there, there, there / His thunder follows!"). Having dared to imagine Setebos either caught and conquered by the Quiet, or merely dozing off and dying, he decides he is being punished: "Fool to gibe at Him! / Lo! 'Lieth flat and loveth Setebos!"[44]

This is one picture of Caliban produced by Victorian England. But here is a very different one:

The nineteenth century dislike of Realism is the rage of Caliban seeing his own face in a glass.

The nineteenth century dislike of Romanticism is the rage of Caliban not seeing his own face in a glass.

These are maxims that Oscar Wilde added in a preface to his then-scandalous novel, *The Picture of Dorian Gray,* published in 1891.[45] The book was an enormous success—widely read, and also widely denounced as immoral. In reply to his critics, Wilde added, for a preface, a defiant set of maxims about art and life, including "There is no such thing as a moral or an immoral book. Books are well written, or badly written. That is all," and "No artist has ethical sympathies. An ethical sympathy in an artist is an unpardonable mannerism of style," and "All art is quite useless."[46] The "Caliban" aphorisms are among the most frequently quoted. "Caliban" is the boorish, antiaesthetic reader, or critic, the one who dislikes and disapproves rather than responding. "Rage" rather than exquisite sensibility is his only emotion. And of course *The Picture of Dorian Gray* is, exactly, a novel about a monstrous double, hidden from sight: a portrait, locked away, that tells the truth about the degeneration of the beautiful hero.

James Joyce has one of his characters quote (or misquote) this maxim at the beginning of his novel *Ulysses.* In the opening pages of the first chapter, Buck Mulligan finds Stephen Dedalus shaving in front of a cracked mirror and takes it away from him: "The rage of Caliban at not seeing his face in a mirror," he says, and adds, "If Wilde were only alive to see you."[47] Stephen mutters that the cracked looking glass is a symbol of Irish art. But Wilde's aphorism had clearly by this time (1922) become a recognizable, and quotable, classic. This is a Caliban more like the "Barbarian" satirically described by Matthew Arnold in *Culture and Anarchy* than like the Darwinian figure of Browning's poem. For Arnold's "Barbarians" were the aristocracy—willful, athletic, individualistic, fond of field sports, possessing culture only in an exterior sense, lacking in sensibility and spirit.

The rage of Caliban at seeing—or not seeing—his face in a mirror: in W. H. Auden's long poem *The Sea and the Mirror: A Commentary on Shakespeare's* The Tempest, the mirror is associated with Ariel, and with Art—the Sea with Caliban and Life.[48] Auden as a poet went through at least three phases—Freudian, Marxist, and Christian—and elements of each of these are present in his poem. Prospero is the ego, Caliban the id. The poem is divided into sections: Preface (The Stage Manager to the Critics); Chapter I (Prospero to Ariel); Chapter II (The Supporting Cast); Chapter III (Caliban to the Audience); Postscript (Ariel to Caliban. Echo by the Prompter).

The real tour de force, as all critics have agreed, is the long prose section of Chapter III, Caliban to the Audience, in which he begins, in impeccably Jamesian tones, by announcing that he is the inevitable substitute for the playwright:

If, now, having dismissed your hired impersonators with verdicts ranging from the laudatory orchid to the disgusted and disgusting egg, you ask, and, of course, notwithstanding the conscious fact of his irrevocable absence, you instinctively *do* ask for our so good, so great, so dead author to stand before the final lowered curtain and take his shyly responsible bow for this, his latest, ripest production, it is I—my reluctance is, I can assure you, co-equal with your dismay—who will always loom thus wretchedly into your confusing picture, for in default of the all-wise, all-explaining master you would speak *to,* who else at least can, who else indeed must respond to your bewildered cry, but its very echo, the begged question you would speak to him *about.*[49]

Caliban then proceeds to ventriloquize, to talk in the voice of the audience, offering a complaint to the playwright that in his too-famous phrase about holding the mirror up to nature he allowed for a reversal of value between the real and the imagined, with the dangerous result that art is made to seem as if it should be the model or "cause" of life, rather being than the "accidental effect" of living. It is this inversion, this reversal of the traditional poles of "art" and "life," that is the imagined audience's concern, and Auden's point:

Is it not possible that, not content with inveigling Caliban into Ariel's kingdom, you have also let loose Ariel in Caliban's? . . . Where is *He* now? For if the intrusion of the real has disconcerted and incommoded the poetic, that is a mere bagatelle compared with the damage that the poetic would inflict if it ever succeeded in intruding upon the real. We want no Ariel here.[50]

Responding to the audience in his own voice, Caliban addresses the audience "on behalf of Ariel and myself" and points out that he and Ariel work together, as the picture of what is and what might be:

you have now all come together in the larger colder emptier room on this side of the mirror which *does* force your eyes to recognize and reckon with the two of us, your ears to detect the irreconcilable difference between my re-iterated affirmation of what your furnished circumstances categorically are, and *His* successive propositions as to everything else which they conditionally might be.[51]

"Introducing 'real life' into the imagined," to quote Auden's phrase about the Caliban chapter, was, I think, the move of modernity.[52] In the modern period Caliban has been, by turns, a "missing link," a natural theologian, a revolutionary, an enslaved or scorned or exoticized "native," a foe of aestheticism; Auden makes him an actor. Furthermore, he puts him in the place previously occupied by Prospero, at the end of the play, in the epilogue, engaging with the audience—but in this case from a position of strength. And from the other side of the curtain, or the mirror. In putting his Caliban in charge, it was, as he wrote to a friend, "exactly as if one of the audience had walked onto the stage and insisted on taking part in the action."[53]

Caliban became the Prospero of the twentieth century. It remains to be seen who will hold the staff and book, and wear the magic robe of art, in the twenty-first.

TWO

ROMEO AND JULIET

The Untimeliness of Youth

I N T H E F I L M *Shakespeare in Love* the young playwright William Shakespeare suffers from the malady that the twentieth century would call "writer's block."[1] His current project, *Romeo and Ethel the Pirate's Daughter,* is stuck and going nowhere. When he falls in love with a noblewoman crossdressed as a boy, who auditions for the part of Romeo, Will courts her in scenes that closely echo moments from *Romeo and Juliet*—including the famous "balcony scene"—and bits of dialogue from this forbidden courtship will later make their way into the script of his new play, now rewritten and retitled. The inspiration of his secret muse has, in this cultural fantasy, made Will into a better playwright. Thus in her bedroom he speaks the lines that will become Juliet's speech in the orchard (or "balcony") scene: "My bounty is as boundless as the sea, / My love as deep" (2.1.175–76); later he brings her a copy of a "new scene" that is the famous nightingale-and-lark aubade from act 3, scene 5.

To make the connection between modern film and Shakespeare's play even more overt, the authors of the clever screenplay, Marc Norman and Tom Stoppard, have given the lady a nurse-companion, closely indebted to Juliet's Nurse in tone, in spirit, and, occasionally, in language. In the denouement, these "star-crossed lovers," although they are not destined to live (together) happily ever after—since he is married and she is engaged to the fictitious Earl of Wessex—play the parts of Juliet and Romeo onstage, in a production that delights the theater audience, including the queen, and sets Shakespeare on the path to success and literary immortality. (For this performance, it might be noted, the lady has forsaken her male attire and plays Juliet, leaving Romeo to the amorous Will.)

The film—which won the Academy Award for Best Picture in 1998—does not pretend to historical accuracy. The only one of its deliberate and often delicious falsifications I feel impelled to "correct" here is the idea that Shakespeare's successful and memorable plays begin with *Romeo and Juliet* (c. 1597), thus relegating to the reputational dust heap such works as *Love's Labour's*

Lost, The Comedy of Errors, Titus Andronicus, Richard III, and the three parts of *Henry VI.* It is not the case that Shakespeare was an average playwright who suddenly became a great one. And it is certainly not the case that some life-changing external event, even falling in love, switched the gears on his writing and permitted him to become himself.

But there is a reason, or a modern cultural logic, why *Romeo and Juliet* is the fulcrum of this fictional story about the "real" Shakespeare. Shakespeare's play has become the normative love story of our time, a cliché so firmly established that the screenwriters can assume the audience will be amused by the idea of *Romeo and Ethel the Pirate's Daughter,* instantly recognizing it as "wrong"—and that virtually any love scene, when played from a balcony with the female beloved above and the male lover below, is automatically assimilated to a version of *Romeo.* (One example I noted some time ago took place between two St. Bernard dogs in the film *Beethoven's 2nd*).[2] *Romeo and Ethel* may have the ring of bathos to modern ears, but the couple so famous to us now went by a variety of names in the period immediately prior to Shakespeare's play, from Romeo and Giulietta (or Julietta) to Halquadrich and Burglipha to the title characters of Shakespeare's immediate source, *The Tragicall Historye of Romeus and Juliet,* a long poem by Arthur Brooke.[3] In the French version, by Adrien Sevin, the lovers Halquadrich and Burglipha belong, respectively, to families called Phorhiach and Humdrum. The classical version, from Ovid, was the story of Pyramus and Thisbe, brilliantly sent up by Shakespeare in the love comedy he wrote at the same time as *Romeo, A Midsumer Night's Dream.*

Even "Romeus" will strike modern ears as an error, though. The name "Romeo" has long since passed into the English language, although, peculiarly, with a meaning pretty much opposite to that of Shakespeare's fatally faithful wooer. A "Romeo" today, with or without a capital R, is a ladies' man, a seducer, a "habitual pursuer of women"[4]—not a young man so transformed by the singularity of his love that he prefers death with her to life without her. Anne Bernays's novel *Professor Romeo* (1988) is about a tenured professor of psychology at Harvard who is charged with the sexual harassment of his female students. The novel's title, it can be imagined, was thought to be self-explanatory; readers were not to expect an idealized story of pure, self-sacrificing passion.

How Romeo became a Lothario is in itself an interesting question.[5] I suspect it may have to do with putting a kind of ironic distance between the speaker and the idea of an all-consuming young love—or, alternatively, with a recognition of the inevitable narcissism that insists on the immediacy and primacy of the love object; Shakespeare's Romeo, we might pause to remember, first thought himself totally and hopelessly in love with Rosaline, a character who never appears in the play. When the lovestruck Romeo, fresh from his nighttime visit to Juliet's garden, turns up early at Friar Laurence's cell, the Friar, rather like a modern psychotherapist, questions his charge:

> What a change is here!
> Is Rosaline, that thou didst love so dear,
> So soon forsaken? Young men's love then lies
> Not truly in their hearts, but in their eyes.
> . . . .
> Lo, here upon thy cheek the stain doth sit
> Of an old tear that is not washed off yet.
> If e'er thou wast thyself, and these woes thine,
> Thou and these woes were all for Rosaline.
> And art thou changed? Pronounce this sentence then:
> Women may fall when there's no strength in men.
>
> *2.2.65–80*

But perhaps of more central interest, in the interactions between Shakespeare and modern culture, is the question of how "Romeo and Juliet" became the unquestioned modern cultural shorthand for romantic love.

As our brief survey of Shakespeare's sources will have suggested, this story of two feuding "households" (Prologue 1) was hardly a household word in the early modern period. Shakespeare does seem to have drawn on at least two English-language versions,[6] and there is some evidence—based on reprintings of Brooke—that "the story of Romeo and Juliet was popular in the reign of Elizabeth."[7] But certainly the lovers had not attained anything like mythic status. There is no mention of "a Romeo" or "Romeos" as a generic type in any other of Shakespeare's plays. By comparison, consider the situation of another figure celebrated in the literature of the period: Troilus, of that other pair of "star-crossed lovers," Troilus and Cressida. Mentions of Troilus—knowing, shorthand mentions, assuming the audience's familiarity with the reference—appear in *The Taming of the Shrew,* in *Much Ado About Nothing,* in *The Merchant of Venice,* and in *Twelfth Night,* as well as in "The Rape of Lucrece." Cressida is mentioned not only in *Merchant* and in *Twelfth Night* but also in *Henry V* and *All's Well That Ends Well.* Pandarus, the go-between, who plays the same structural role in the Troilus and Cressida story as do the Friar and the Nurse in *Romeo,* is mentioned by name in *The Merry Wives of Windsor* as well as in *Twelfth Night,* and *his* name had indeed by then become a household word, in lowercase, appearing as a noun and also as a verb in several plays. In short, there was a ready-made pair of lovers available, a pair already so legendary in Shakespeare's time that the playwright has them speculate in his play, with maximum dramatic irony, upon the archetypes that—as the audience would clearly recognize—they had already, by that time, become:

> TROILUS True swains in love shall in the world to come
>   Approve their truth by Troilus. When their rhymes,
>   Full of protest, of oath and big compare,
>   Want similes, truth tired with iteration—
>   "As true as steel, as plantage to the moon,
>   As sun to day, as turtle to her mate,
>   As iron to adamant, as earth to th' centre"—
>   Yet, after all comparisons of truth,
>   As truth's authentic author to be cited,
>   "As true as Troilus" shall crown up the verse
>   And sanctify the numbers.
> CRESSIDA Prophet may you be!
>   If I be false, or swerve a hair from truth,
>   When time is old and hath forgot itself,
>   When waterdrops have worn the stones of Troy
>   And blind oblivion swallowed cities up,
>   And mighty states characterless are grated
>   To dusty nothing, yet let memory
>   From false to false among false maids in love
>   Upbraid my falsehood. When they've said "as false
>   As air, as water, wind or sandy earth,
>   As fox to lamb, or wolf to heifer's calf,
>   Pard to the hind, or stepdame to her son,"
>   Yea, let them say, to stick the heart of falsehood,
>   "As false as Cressid."
> PANDARUS Go to, a bargain made. Seal it, seal it. I'll be the witness. Here I
>   hold your hand; here my cousin's. If ever you prove false one to
>   another, since I have taken such pain to bring you together, let all
>   pitiful goers-between be called to the world's end after my name:
>   call them all panders. Let all constant men be Troiluses, all false
>   women Cressids, and all brokers-between panders. Say "Amen."
>   3.2.160–90

It is certainly understandable that a later age—one that would, with however different a reason, be dubbed "Romantic"—might prefer "positive" archetypes of love to these ironic self-namings. But the fact remains that Troilus and

Cressida, famous—or infamous—from their appearances in major works by Boccaccio, Chaucer, Robert Henryson, and Shakespeare, were not only ready to hand, but already celebrated. How many modern-day teenagers, or modern-day adults, for that matter, can identify them, or tell their stories? Or what about that third pair of larger-than-life lovers linked by name in a Shakespearean love tragedy, Antony and Cleopatra?

All three plays have very similar structures: a "feud" (in *Romeo and Juliet,* between the Montagues and the Capulets; in *Troilus and Cressida,* between the Trojans and the Greeks—a.k.a. the Trojan War; in *Antony and Cleopatra,* between Rome and Egypt); go-betweens and enablers who broker love affairs (Nurse and Friar; Pandarus and Ulysses; Enobarbus and Octavius); a well-meant intervention that goes wrong; and a tragic end that reflects upon the transformative role of the lovers as it moves forward into a diminished political and social world. But where Romeo and Juliet are relative unknowns (prior to the celebrity of Shakespeare's play), the other pairs of lovers are virtually equivalent, in the early modern period, to the idea of love itself. Octavius Caesar's final speech in *Antony and Cleopatra* underscores the unparalleled status of the lovers: "No grave upon the earth shall clip in it / A pair so famous" (5.2.349–50). Like Romeo and Juliet, they are to be reunited in death—and in art.

The Joseph Mankiewicz film *Cleopatra* (1963) is notorious both for having almost bankrupted the studio, Twentieth Century Fox, and for bringing together the incendiary real-life lovers Elizabeth Taylor and Richard Burton, who met on the set and began their own legendary affair. But aside from this "sword and sandal" epic, which covers the entire life of Cleopatra, and not—like Shakespeare's play—only the years when she was the "serpent of old Nile," already "wrinkled deep in time," the story of these transcendent and world-famous lovers has not retained the mythic status in modern popular culture that it clearly had for Shakespeare's audience. The romances of older lovers, however passionate, are, it seems, now consigned to *On Golden Pond* rather than the barge that burned on the water at Cydnus.

So youth and optimism (or rather a kind of optimistic, uncompromised fatalism) would seem to be two things that *Romeo and Juliet* has to offer, in contradistinction to the stories of lovers far more famous in myth and legend. Does this really account for its modern ubiquity?

I want to approach the question of how two characters called Romeo and Juliet became the phenomenon (or, in postmodern commercial parlance, the brand) "Romeo-and-Juliet" first rather obliquely, following the signifier of "youth," and its supposed antonym, "maturity," as the term is applied to both persons and plays. This is a move that will take us back to the fantasy belief, depicted in *Shakespeare in Love,* that there was a turning point for Shakespeare when he changed from being a tyro (or, in the film's harsher comic vision, a hack) to being "Shakespeare." In Norman and Stoppard's film, which based the "love story" of the playwright on the plot of *Romeo and Juliet,* that play— and its supposedly "real" inspiration—is the turning point. For many traditional critics of Shakespeare, however, *Romeo and Juliet* has remained in a kind of neutral zone called "the early tragedies," sometimes bracketed with *Titus Andronicus,* and set off clearly, by chronology and by certain interpretative claims about quality and theme, from what are termed, by contrast, "the mature tragedies," beginning with *Hamlet.*

The phrase "mature tragedies" has become conventional as a literary-critical term of art. It appears in the titles of books of Shakespeare criticism,[8] it is used confidently by the *Encyclopedia Britannica,* and it seems to point to a period in the playwright's work—and life—that is understood to be especially productive and significant. A. C. Bradley, the influential critic whose published lectures on Shakespearean tragedy set the tone for early-twentieth-century discussions, confidently described "Shakespeare's tragic period" as the period 1601 to 1608, even though Shakespeare "wrote tragedy—pure like *Romeo and Juliet;* historical, like *Richard III*—in the early years of his career of authorship," when he was also writing early comedies. Bradley regarded *Hamlet, Othello, King Lear,* and *Macbeth* as plays that are central to understanding the major contribution of Shakespeare. By contrast, *Romeo and Juliet,* he insists, "is an early work, and in some respects, an immature one."[9] The play, that is to say, has been accused, sometimes explicitly, sometimes by implication, of the same immaturity that characterizes its protagonists.

The German Romantic critic A. W. Schlegel had suggested something of the same, in more highly wrought language: "If *Romeo and Juliet* shines with the colours of the dawn of morning, but a dawn whose purple clouds already announce the thunder of a sultry day, *Othello* is, on the other hand, a strongly shaded picture: we might call it a tragical Rembrandt."[10] In this classic example of "purple prose" the language is literally purple, but Schlegel's "dawn" image—and the implication of dangerous weather on the horizon— is drawn directly from Shakespeare's play, not only from the aubade of act 3, scene 5 (Juliet's "Wilt thou be gone? It is not yet near day") but also from her fear, in the orchard/balcony scene, that their love may be "too rash, too unadvised, too sudden, / Too like the lightning which doth cease to be / Ere one can say it lightens" (2.1.160–2). Haste, youth, and impetuousness—the very elements that make this play so appealing to a modern audience, and indeed, we might say, make it so "modern"—are tied to an ominous anticipation of futurity.

"Mature" as a term *within* Shakespeare's plays is sparingly, but tellingly, used: the "more mature dignities" of the grown-up Leontes and Polixenes in *The Winter's Tale* are cited as the reason these former "young play-fellows" have grown apart (1.1.25); the contrast between youth and maturity is again made at the beginning of *Antony and Cleopatra*—"As we rate boys who, being mature in knowledge, / Pawn their experience to their present pleasure, / And so rebel to judgement" (1.4.31–33)—and yet again at the beginning of *Cymbeline* (1.1.48). "Dignities," "experience," "judgement" are the qualities to be expected of the "mature." The word implies age, gravity, consideration—and perhaps a slightly excessive self-distancing from the instinctive energies, pleasures, and rebellions of youth. Manifestly there is a time for maturity to replace heedlessness—the rejection of Falstaff by a newly matured King Henry V at the end of *Henry IV, Part 2* seems like a case in point. But as audience responses to this rejection scene have demonstrated, there is a certain sympathy generated by playful irresponsibility. Falstaff's comic averral in Part 1, "They hate us youth" (2.2.78), spoken by a character who, by his own subsequent accounting, is nearing the age of sixty, raises the question of whether youth is an age, a stage, or an attitude. In the history plays, as war, death, and the responsibilities of political succession overtake the playing space of the tavern, Falstaff's claim of eternal "youth" is disallowed by the stern new king: "How ill white hairs becomes a fool and jester" (*Henry IV, Part 2* 5.5.46).

Given *Romeo and Juliet*'s almost automatic modern association with youth culture, and the by-now-proverbial identification of its title characters, it is of some interest to remind ourselves that for many years the star parts were those of Mercutio and the Nurse—as is often still the case on the stage today. Dryden famously reports the story, traditional by his time, that Shakespeare said that "he was obliged to kill Mercutio in the third act, lest he should have been killed by him."[11] Samuel Johnson, retorting, does not doubt that Shakespeare could have kept him alive if he wished, without danger of the play being eclipsed, but says nonetheless that "Mercutio's wit, gaiety and courage, will always procure him friends that wish him a longer life." As for the Nurse, to Dr. Johnson she is "one of the characters in which the author delighted: he has with great subtilety of distinction, drawn her at once loquacious and secret, obsequious and insolent, trusty and dishonest."[12] In his notes on the play, this great eighteenth-century editor has nothing at all to say about either Romeo or Juliet as characters except that Romeo shows "thin" wit at one point and "involuntary cheerfulness" at another, and that Juliet "plays most of her pranks under the appearance of religion; perhaps Shakespeare meant to punish her hypocrisy."[13]

The humorous characters, like the mercurial Mercutio and the earthy Nurse, were what appealed to earlier audiences. The young lovers, the focus of our modern gaze, were all very well, but it was Mercutio or the Nurse who threatened to run away with the show. Furthermore—and this was a problem that would persist—the actors who played Romeo and Juliet were often too old for the parts. Performed by Sir William Davenant's company in the Restoration period, the play earned a scathing critique from that inveterate theatergoer Samuel Pepys: "To the Opera," Pepys wrote in his *Diary*, "and there saw 'Romeo and Juliet,' the first time it was ever acted, but it is a play of itself the worst that ever I heard in my life, and the worst acted that ever I saw these people do, and I am resolved to go no more to see the first time of acting, for they were all of them out more or less."[14]

John Philip Kemble played Romeo in 1789 in a Drury Lane production, opposite the famous actress Sarah Siddons, then thirty-four. As her biographer noted, "time and study had stamped her countenance" by that time "too strongly for Juliet." Siddons would have played the part more convincingly fourteen years earlier, he thought, when she would more closely have resembled Juliet's "youthful loveliness."[15] Kemble is described by *his* biographer as equally unsuited to the part of Romeo: "Youthful love was never well expressed by Kemble," he wrote. "The thoughtful strength of his features was at variance with juvenile passion."[16] David Garrick, in his 1748 production, had been a thirty-one-year-old Romeo; Charles Kemble, John Philip Kemble's younger brother, was still playing the part in 1819, at age forty-four. His daughter Fanny, who became a celebrated actress in her own right, was nineteen when she first performed Juliet, cast against a Romeo who was, she later wrote, "old enough to have been my father." Her father himself was in the production, too, now playing Mercutio; he would then have been fifty-four years old.[17] Her mother came out of retirement, in this family production, to play the part of Lady Capulet.

THROUGHOUT THIS PERIOD, I might point out, the final scene was played as rewritten by David Garrick, with Juliet awakening before Romeo's death. Shakespeare's version of the last scene, in which each dies alone, was not restored until the middle of the nineteenth century.

One of the most successful Romeos of this period was a woman, Charlotte

Benjamin Wilson, David Garrick and George Anne Bellamy
in *Romeo and Juliet,* V, 3

Cushman, who played opposite her sister Susan as Juliet. Cushman's production ran for eighty-four performances, and drew rave notices. It was not a stunt, but a straightforward portrayal, admired by audiences. Romeo was perhaps her most celebrated role, although she also played Lear, Shylock, and Hamlet in the course of her career. A poster advertising Cushman's Hamlet in 1861 called her "a lady universally acknowledged as the greatest living tragic actress." Charlotte Cushman was a lesbian and had a number of famous lovers; rumors about her life and even her relationship with her sister were said to have helped fill the London theater seats for their *Romeo and Juliet.* One audience member reported that the portrayal of Romeo was so "ardently masculine" and the Juliet so "tenderly feminine" that "the least Miss Cushman could do, when the engagement was over, was marry her sister."[18]

Cushman's Romeo was not played as a woman—gay or straight—but as a man. She was the most successful and striking of the female Romeos, but not the only one; at least thirteen other women played the part on the American stage from 1827 to 1859.[19] (This was some fifty years before Sarah Bernhardt played Hamlet, to great acclaim, on stage and in a brief silent film.)

In Shakespeare's own time, of course, the part of Juliet would have been played by a boy actor. Transvestite theater was the rule, rather than the exception, on the early modern English public stage (as it was indeed in ancient Greece). What we may regard as "natural" or "real" gender performances

Charlotte Cushman as Romeo

*Charlotte and Susan Cushman as
Romeo and Juliet*

(male actors playing men, female actors playing women) are the adaptations from the Renaissance to the modern stage—beginning in England after the Restoration, when the theaters reopened—and when not a few conventional theatergoers protested against the less lifelike performances of women playing women, as compared to the more familiar, and (to them) more persuasive, boys. Conceivably some members of the audience, now and then, watched the performance binocularly, or metatheatrically, seeing both the performer and the role, as today an audience can see both the "real life" performer (say, Patrick Stewart or Dame Judi Dench) and the roles they play on stage or screen. This willing suspension of disbelief is part of what makes drama into theater—as also is the occasional breaking of the frame, through, perhaps, a quotation (by the performer in gesture or onstage attitude) of a signature previous role.

I mention these questions of gender and sexuality because *Romeo and Juliet,* as the "classic love story" of modernity, has now—inevitably—been staged and adapted for male-male and female-female lovers. One successful example with playgoers was Joe Calarco's 1998 adaptation, *Shakespeare's R&J,* set in an all-boy Catholic prep school where *Romeo and Juliet* is a proscribed text, and the boys act out the roles and inhabit them. "What could be more dangerous than the first forbidden kiss of literature," Calarco asked, rhetorically, and answered his own question: "The first forbidden kiss of two schoolboys." Significantly, for our purposes, he described his play as needing to "radiate with a very young, very male energy" in performance. Very young, very male. Contrast this with Garrick and Kemble. This insistence upon youth is, it might be said, a particular fetish of modernity, especially when it comes to *Romeo and Juliet.*

One caveat, or at least a small pause to reflect: it seems conceptually possible to think that *age* on the stage might be as fictive, or as binocular, as gender. There seems no reason why one couldn't see a "mature" actor as—at the same time—a persuasive teen Romeo or fourteen-year-old Juliet. But in fact this seems seldom to have been the case, and, importantly, it seems to be even less so in the twentieth and twenty-first centuries than in the time of Garrick or Mrs. Siddons. Despite the fact that truisms about youth and love are ubiquitous in the Renaissance and earlier (in the works of poets like Chaucer and Petrarch, as well as Shakespeare), the circumstances of the theater often led to the casting of older actors in the parts of the young lovers. The 1936 film of *Romeo and Juliet,* directed by George Cukor, starred Leslie Howard, then forty-two, as Romeo, and Norma Shearer, then thirty-four, as Juliet. Shearer was married to Irving Thalberg, the producer, who insisted that Howard play the part under the terms of his MGM studio contract—though Howard protested vehemently to the press about doing so. (There's some small irony, under the circumstances, in the fact that Thalberg's nickname was "the boy wonder.") The film's Mercutio, John Barrymore, was fifty-four. In the film they do not look old, certainly, but they do look like adults.

Every authority will remind us that this is a casting convention of the time. But that, again, is exactly the point I want to stress. On the one hand we have the play, so regularly classed by critics among the earlier, even "immature," plays. The Romantic critic Hazlitt indeed claimed—against all available evidence—that it was Shakespeare's *first* play. "*Romeo and Juliet,*" Hazlitt writes, "is the only tragedy which Shakespeare has written entirely on a love-story. It is supposed to have been his first play, and it deserves to stand in that proud rank. There is the buoyant spirit of youth in every line."[20] So the play is early, concerned with love, has "the buoyant spirit of youth" inscribed all over it, and may be, in Bradley's somewhat more measured or dour account, therefore "immature," if also "pure" (a word that you will recall he uses to characterize this play's mode of tragedy). On the other hand, *productions* of the play, especially well-known or benchmark productions prior to the middle of the twentieth century, have tended to cast older actors and actresses, whose few flashes of youthfulness are often singled out by commentators precisely because these are contrary to the general tone of the "mature" (or even overripe) performance.

It might be imagined that one way of "universalizing" the love story in the play would have been through its translation into ballet, since without the specificity of words, and with the presumptive requirement that the dancers be young, lithe, and visually beautiful, the particulars of the plot would almost directly yield to the embodied ideology of young love. But, as it turns out, the ballet versions of *Romeo and Juliet* were often star vehicles, and the performers, at least at the beginning, far from young, at least in dance-world terms.

Shakespeare's plays were identified relatively early as ripe for choreographic treatment. *Antoine et Cléopâtre* and *Les Amours d'Henri IV,* ballets based on his plays, were both produced for the Duke of Wurtenberg in the mid-eighteenth century.[21] But *Romeo and Juliet* would surpass these, and all others, from the beginning of the nineteenth century to the present day. The first version, *Romeo og Giulietta,* produced by Vincenzo Galeotti for the Royal Danish Ballet in Copenhagen in 1811, was the most popular ballet of the season. It was produced, we should note, at a time when there was no Danish translation of the play yet available. The choreographer, Galeotti, had worked in London at a time when the play was performed there, and might have seen a production, but it is far from clear what story the audience thought they were watching. No play by Shakespeare was performed in Copenhagen until 1813; perhaps unsurprisingly, that play was *Hamlet, Prince of Denmark.*[22]

In any case, *Romeo og Giulietta* was not the opening salvo in ballet as the harbinger of youth culture. The Romeo for this first production, Antoine Bournonville (the father of the choreographer of *La Sylphide,* Auguste Bournonville), was fifty-one, and the seventy-eight-year-old Galeotti himself performed as the Monk Lorenzo (the ballet's version of Friar Laurence). Finesse and grace, not the raw energy of youth, were the criteria.

Sergei Prokofiev's ballet, composed in 1935 and 1936 under a commission from the Kirov Ballet, immediately ran into political difficulties. Widespread government criticism of "degeneracy" in modern art—largely aimed at the composer Dmitri Shostakovich—touched Prokofiev as well, and while a version of his *Romeo and Juliet* (which he rewrote only under protest) was danced at the Kirov, with choreography by Leonid Lavrovsky and a great deal of theatrical pantomime and a happy ending—the lovers share a final dance and embrace a new world—a ballet to Prokofiev's music did not return to the major canon till the 1960s, when John Cranko choreographed it for the Stuttgart Ballet, which then came to the United States in 1969. Rudolf Nureyev and Margot Fonteyn performed the parts, memorably, in a Royal Ballet production by Sir Kenneth MacMillan. Fonteyn was thought to be nearing retirement when her career changed, radically, through the partnership with Nureyev. (She was born in 1919.)

In this instance, then, and perhaps also—who knows?—in the case of the elder Bournonville, it is not that the *Romeo and Juliet* story so directly mirrors or enacts modern youth, but rather that it seems somehow to confer youth upon these brilliantly successful performers, no matter what their actual ages. Margot Fonteyn begins her career again rather than retiring once she partners with Nureyev. Nureyev's first experience of dance, at age seven, has been described as "love at first sight,"[23] and he described Fonteyn as his soul mate. He came from one world, or "family," that of Russia and the Kirov Ballet; she came from another, as the prima ballerina of England's signature company. His defection in Paris ("I am a dead man," he is said to have said, when it seemed as if he would be sent back to Russia rather than on to a London tour) put him at risk ("And the place death, considering who thou art," as Juliet says to Romeo in the orchard, or balcony, scene—to which Romeo famously replies, "With love's light wings did I o'erperch these walls, / For stony limits cannot hold love out, / And what love dares do, that does love attempt" [2.1.106; 108–10]). Nureyev's all-consuming love is for dance: in the partnership with Fonteyn that love found also a local habitation and a name. The celebrity of *Romeo and Juliet* as a ballet is intertwined, in modern culture, with the celebrity of this unlikely and perfect couple.

Meantime the story of the Prokofiev ballet is still ongoing. The Joffrey Ballet mounted the first American production in the 1980s, and in July 2008 the choreographer Mark Morris directed the first real world premiere of the ballet as Prokofiev composed and planned it, with support from Prokofiev's family and from the Russian State Archive, restoring the original ending. A press release issued on behalf of the Mark Morris Dance Group and the Fisher Center for the Performing Arts at Bard College, where the premiere was performed, offers the following historical account: "Prokofiev conceived the ballet in 1935 in collaboration with innovative Soviet dramatist Sergei Radlov, who reimagined the familiar tragedy as a struggle for the right to love by young, strong, and progressive people battling against feudal traditions and feudal outlooks on marriage and family. Much of Prokofiev's score addresses the theme of love's transcendence over oppression."[24] The analogy is straightforward: Stalin's repressive regime, where in the arts "conservative neoclassicism supplanted accessible innovation," is like the repressive parents of the

Shakespeare play. Prokofiev—like Romeo?—is helpless to reverse the events in which he has been an unwitting and unwilling participant ("he pleaded to no avail to undo the changes that he had strongly resisted").[25] In the new production the composer will be reunited—long after his death—with the original ballet score and choreography designed expressly for it.

Prokofiev died in 1953, on the same day as Stalin. For three days throngs in Red Square prevented his body from being carried to the headquarters of the Soviet Composers Union for his funeral service. Taped music of the funeral march from *Romeo and Juliet* accompanied the body; all the living musicians in Moscow were required for Stalin's state funeral. (In an earlier moment of historical irony, Prokofiev had been awarded the Stalin Prize in 1951, three years after the Soviet Union had formally condemned him.) The great Russian dancer Galina Ulanova is said to have remarked, "Never was a story of more woe than this of Prokofiev and his Romeo."[26]

WE ARE NOW PERHAPS in a position to return to a question that puzzled us earlier: why did a relatively unknown love story like that of Romeo and Juliet come to eclipse, in general popularity and cultural citation, high and low, the venerable and famous love stories of Troilus and Cressida and of Antony and Cleopatra? The "answer," it seems, is the same as the question: it was in part *because* these were unknown, relatively "new" (and insistently "young") lovers that their story could be adapted to numerous romantic situations. The quip attributed to Ulanova suggests an archetypal relationship of longing and loss between a creator and a work of art. And the enduring partnership of Nureyev-Fonteyn seemed to demonstrate that the play, rather than being *about* youth, could *produce* it, even—or especially—in "mature" performers.

The availability of *Romeo and Juliet* as a transposable love story, not tied to ancient myth or history like *Troilus and Cressida* and *Antony and Cleopatra,* may actually have helped move it in the direction of a modern myth. It would *become* "generic," generating its own taglines, but the relative obscurity of its sources was in some ways an asset. Certainly that was the case for high school students liberated from studying *Julius Caesar* (as had been the norm in the United States through the 1950s) and introduced to Shakespeare instead through *Romeo,* now the standard first Shakespeare text in many public schools. Here, too, we might imagine, it is not only the erotics and pains of young love but also the generational conflict that hold strong appeal.

What we might call the readiness for appropriation of the feud ("My parents don't understand me") was very much in evidence in the discussions that led up to the play's most important intervention in modern, twentieth-century culture: the musical *West Side Story,* with book by Arthur Laurents, lyrics by Stephen Sondheim, and a compelling and memorable score by Leonard Bernstein, all based on a conception of the director and choreographer Jerome Robbins. (The fact that the original inspiration came from Robbins may say something about the legacy of Shakespeare's play as a vehicle for dance.)

At the top of Leonard Bernstein's copy of *Romeo and Juliet,* scrawled in the composer's hand, is the annotation "An out and out plea for social tolerance."[27] The original idea for the adaptation of Shakespeare's play, though, would have been called "East Side Story" rather than *West Side Story.* As the director and choreographer imagined the show and discussed it with Bernstein, the conflict was to be religious, rather than ethnic or racial: "When we started a project about *Romeo and Juliet* in the slums," Bernstein told an interviewer, "the East Side was what we had in mind—a story about kids fighting in the streets of the Lower East Side of New York. We took the story from Shakespeare to that setting. . . . This was 1949. Arthur [Laurents] wrote a couple of scenes, and we began to see at a certain point that the show was dated. There was a faint odor of *Abie's Irish Rose* [a long-running Broadway play of the 1920s about an Irish Catholic girl who marries a Jewish man over the objection of both of their families]. So we gave it up. Five years later the right time came."[28]

The "right time" was the mid-fifties, and the place of inspiration Los Angeles, where an article in the *Los Angeles Times,* found at poolside at the Beverly Hills Hotel, offered the necessary spark: a headline in the paper described "Gang Riots on Oliveira Street, about Mexicans and so-called Americans rioting against one another."[29] Bernstein recalled suggesting that they do the musical about "the Chicanos," and noting that there were Puerto Rican gangs in New York. Within a short time Robbins, Laurents, Bernstein, and a new young composer named Stephen Sondheim were on board to do *West Side Story.*

In the musical as it ultimately developed—a "musical tragedy," as someone observed, rather than a "musical comedy"[30]—the feud is between the Jets and the Sharks, two rival gangs, the first gang presumptively white, the second gang Latino. Tony (Polish-American Anton) and Maria (from Puerto Rico) are the Romeo and Juliet. Anita, Maria's friend from the bridal shop where they both work, is both the Nurse-confidante figure and an age-mate for Maria; her love for Maria's brother Bernardo, who replaces Tybalt as the victim of Tony/Romeo's ill-advised but well-intentioned intervention, gives

Anita a powerfully tragic as well as a wittily knowing voice. Chino, Maria's hapless suitor, is a version of Juliet's suitor Paris, but with, again, a greater implication in the outcome, since it is Chino who kills Tony, precipitating the double tragedy. Riff, the leader of the Jets, is based in part on Mercutio—since his accidental death triggers the gang war—but Riff is from the first a partisan, not (as is the case with Mercutio) a kinsman of the Prince, and therefore a medial figure. The Friar Laurence of *West Side Story* is Doc, the owner of the drugstore where Tony works. Except for Doc, the clueless social worker Glad Hand, and Officers Krupke and Schrank, who represent all the repressiveness of a broken adult system, the entire cast is "young" (the printed cast list groups them last, in a category called "The Adults," contrasted with "The Jets," "Their Girls," "The Sharks," and "Their Girls"). Bernstein noted that casting the show was especially difficult "because the characters had to be able not only to sing but to dance and be taken for teenagers. Ultimately, some of the cast were teenagers, some were 21, some were 30 but looked 16."[31] In his diary at the time of the original rehearsals, he wrote: "I can't believe it: forty kids are actually doing it up there on stage! Forty kids singing five-point counterpoint who never sang before—and sounding like heaven. I guess we were right not to cast 'singers': anything that sounded more professional would ultimately sound more experienced, and then the 'kid' quality would be gone. A perfect example of a disadvantage turned into a virtue."[32]

Only occasionally does Shakespeare's language surface directly in the text of *West Side Story*. Riff's and Tony's ritual greeting—"Womb to tomb!" "Sperm to worm!"—cleverly updates it, appropriating Friar Laurence's sententiousness (and the encapsulated plot of the play) by translating his words into a racier, sexier idiom. The Friar's lines are uttered to himself as he gathers herbs in his garden, oblivious to the ironic and predictive significance of his words: "The earth, that's nature's mother, is her tomb; / What is her burying grave, that is her womb" (2.2.9–10). Riff and Tony, who repeat this salute several times, use it as a kind of loyalty oath, expressing their lifelong (and deathlong) friendship. Family here is subsumed into gang affiliation: only when Bernardo is killed is blood relationship explicitly mentioned in the Sondheim lyric "A Boy Like That" ("A boy like that, / Who'd kill your brother . . . Stick to your own kind"). The Shakespearean plot, of course, is clearly recognizable—part of the point was to have the audience see the relevance of *then* to *now,* of great dramatic tragedy to musical theater (and of Shakespeare to Bernstein, Robbins, Laurents, and Sondheim). Tenement fire escapes offered an inspired urban equivalent to Juliet's balcony.

But it is in energy, movement, tonality, and even body type that *West Side Story* makes its claims for modernity and youth as a kind of timeless timeliness. Just as Friar Laurence's lines unwittingly predict the tragic plot of a story he does not yet begin to know, so also Shakespeare's *Romeo and Juliet* is seen as a prescient precursor of youth culture. A movement then gathering strength in the still "conformist" but already restless fifties, with the civil rights movement rising through the end of the Eisenhower years, would lead, before the next decade was out, to the Beatles, the Rolling Stones, the assassinations of three prominent American leaders, and the revolutions of '68. All this still lay in the future as Bernstein and Robbins designed their fresh take on the Broadway musical, on dance and theater, on youth, on what Bernstein (in the unmistakable language of the fifties) called "social tolerance"—and on Shakespeare.

Irene Sharaff, the costume designer, described the way she differentiated the two gangs from each other onstage. "In the fifties, the teen-age boys one saw on the streets of New York had arrived at a uniform of their own—not yet taken up by fashionable men and women—consisting of blue jeans or chinos, T-shirts, windbreakers, and sneakers. . . . The modern windbreaker with a hood, particularly when worn with tight-fitting jeans, has a silhouette and line resembling that of figures in Florentine Renaissance paintings."[33] The Jets wore blues and ocher yellows, the Sharks purple, deep pink, red, and black. The Jets' girls wore pastels; the Sharks' girls, in brighter colors, carried the shawls, or rebozos, that marked them as Latino, and that became a sign of mourning when, in the last scene, they shrouded the girls' heads. "The T-shirt," Sharaff noted, "in the fifties was worn solely as underwear." She dyed the shirts, faced the windbreakers with contrasting satin edging, and produced an indelible sign of period style. The period evoked then was "now." Modernity. The immediacy and fragility of today.

But one of the many things that both *West Side Story* and *Romeo and Juliet* continue to demonstrate is that now is never now for long. The years between the writing of Sondheim's lyrics for "Cool" in the mid-fifties and the emergence of the Beatles and the Rolling Stones in the early sixties marked a sea change in youth culture and sensibility. There was a way in which the fifties predicted the sixties, and a way in which the sixties took the fifties (them, us) by surprise. The most commonly cited cultural quotation from *West Side Story* today is almost undoubtedly Maria's song "I Feel Pretty," sung in the bridal shop, as she dresses for a reunion with Tony that will never come. "I Feel Pretty," it is perhaps needless to say, has since become a camp classic. "I Feel Pretty" spinoff products are sold at the "West Side Story" online store

(T-shirts in sizes small, large, and extra large; charm bracelets; wallets, cosmetics, and iPod cases, all in pink). Leonard Bernstein's response to Shakespeare's play—"an out and out plea for social tolerance"—sounds a little dated, and even a little sententious.

The next major adaptations of the play would be a) on film and b) concerned with youth, sexuality, media, and generational conflict. Shakespeare's language, and Shakespeare's characters and plots, are in Franco Zeffirelli's and Baz Luhrmann's films paradoxically fresher, sexier, and more contemporary than *West Side Story*'s dance at the settlement house gym or rumble under the highway. The dynamics of the feud, which took center stage in the conflict between the Jets and the Sharks, the Anglos and the Puerto Ricans, again receded, and was replaced by the love story of two young people and the failure of parents to understand their idealistic and rebellious children. Romeo's outburst to Friar Laurence "Thou canst not speak of that thou dost not feel" (3.3.64) was, effectively, the cry of a generation.

THE SUPPOSED UNIVERSALITY of generational conflict—or rather, its rediscovery as a main theme of sixties political movements—gave renewed impetus to the play's energies.

Bob Dylan's song "The Times They Are a-Changin'" was copyrighted in 1963. It became the anthem for a generation. Its lyrics speak, almost uncannily, to the *Romeo and Juliet* situation:

> Come mothers and fathers
> Throughout the land
> And don't criticize
> What you can't understand
> Your sons and your daughters
> Are beyond your command
> Your old road is
> Rapidly agin'.
> Please get out of the new one
> If you can't lend your hand
> For the times they are a-changin'.
>
> The line it is drawn
> The curse it is cast
> The slow one now
> Will later be fast
> As the present now

Will later be past
The order is rapidly fadin'.
And the first one now
Will later be last
For the times they are a-changin'.[34]

This logic of inversion (the slow will be fast, the present will be past, the sons and daughters will be in command) is, as we have already seen, the logic of *Romeo and Juliet*. And it is also—as should not now come as a surprise—the logic of the play's intersections with modern culture.

In the second half of the twentieth century, and into the twenty-first, the play has been a favorite, even surpassing *Hamlet* or *Lear*, with both young people and edgy modern and postmodern movie directors (Zeffirelli, 1968; Luhrmann, 1996). And in these films the play's internal instructions about the age of the protagonists have been taken as literally as possible. Zeffirelli's Romeo, Leonard Whiting, was seventeen when he played the part, and his Juliet, Olivia Hussey, was fifteen. Leonardo DiCaprio was twenty-two and Claire Danes seventeen when Luhrmann's film, with the stylishly updated title *Romeo + Juliet,* was released (which means they were a few months younger when it was filmed).

The Zeffirelli and the Luhrmann films spoke directly to their young audiences, as well as to the text and staging of Shakespeare's play. Zeffirelli had directed the play on the London stage, with John Stride and Judi Dench as Romeo and Juliet in 1960, shortly after the success of *West Side Story*. The film version, in 1968, cast even younger actors in the title parts, aiming to approximate the ages specified in Shakespeare's text. Psychological backstories were developed for other characters. Mercutio (John McEnery, in both play and film versions) was a striking figure, described as "manic and desperate" in the Queen Mab speech (1.4.53–95), and, "in sharp contrast to performance tradition," as *"not in control"* of his language and associations.[35] Lady Capulet, in Zeffirelli's concept, was a key figure in the plot, unhappily married to an older man, attracted to the young Tybalt, and sexually competitive with her daughter.[36] The film was thus, as one critic described it, a version of *The Graduate* set in Renaissance Verona (*The Graduate* came out in 1967, Zeffirelli's *Romeo and Juliet* the following year). Clearly recognized as a "youth movie," it quickly became the standard representation of the play in middle schools and high schools.[37]

The actress Ali MacGraw described Zeffirelli's 1968 film as a breakthrough. "The play is about the volatile pressures of youth. Zeffirelli deftly turned Shakespeare's prose [*sic*] into the poetry of love. This is the first version to show Romeo and Juliet naked on their wedding night."[38] MacGraw's remarks came in a program sponsored by Waldenbooks, "your best source for romance novels." She was chosen as a spokesperson, we can presume, because of her relationship to another archetypal love story of the period, the love story called simply *Love Story*, with a screenplay and novel written by Erich Segal. *Love Story*, with a famous tagline ("Love means never having to say you're sorry") and equally famous first sentence ("What can you say about a twenty-five-year-old girl who died?"), has been described by booksellers as "the *Romeo and Juliet* of the twentieth century."[39] And in fact, as it happens, Erich Segal himself once played the part of Romeo: in a Harvard Players production in the summer of 1957, when he was twenty and a college student, some years before he imagined and wrote his screenplay.[40]

Baz Luhrmann's film, made almost thirty years later, updated the mise-en-scène and the sensibility, wittily taking the word "family" (which does not in fact occur in Shakespeare's play) as the linchpin, and offering mug shots of two crime "families," the Montagues and the Capulets. This device served the double purpose of a historical transposition and a list of roles, since many of the characters could be introduced, visually, before they appeared in action in the plot. Luhrmann, the Australian director of *Strictly Ballroom* (and also of Benjamin Britten's *A Midsummer Night's Dream*), staged the opening prologue, written in the form of a sonnet, as a TV anchor's news report:

> Two households, both alike in dignity,
>   In fair Verona, where we lay our scene,
> From ancient grudge break to new mutiny,
>   Where civil blood makes civil hands unclean. . . .
> *Prologue 1–4*

Verona, in this case, was Verona Beach, in southern California; the feud was between crime lords over control of the territory, and Mercutio (Harold Perrineau) performed the "Queen Mab" speech in drag, while Queen Mab herself and her capacity to inspire dreams were turned into drugs and drug-related visions and hallucinations. The Prince became Captain Prince, the chief of police; both the Prince and Mercutio were played by black actors. So the film was, in a parlance long outdated by the time of its release, "relevant." It was also fast-paced, effective, and retained Shakespeare's language, though some scenes were cut and others altered. The last scene was given to Romeo and Juliet alone (no Paris, no Friar Laurence), and as in the earliest Davenant revisions, the lovers encounter (rather than ironically miss) each other before they die. ("Welcome to Verona Beach, a sexy, violent other-world, neither future nor past, ruled by two rival families, the Montagues and the Capulets," read the production notes, while the film's tagline is Juliet's, "My only love sprung from my only hate.")

So it is that *Romeo and Juliet*, that "immature," "fresh," "pure," and "early" work, both anticipates and responds to what sociologists and cultural analysts have come to call "youth culture," or "youth subculture." It may be too strong a claim to say that *Romeo and Juliet* has *produced* youth culture, but nonetheless the composite idea Romeo-and-Juliet does function, today, as a recognizable signifier: a signifier of young love, obstructed passion, "star-crossed lovers" (one cannot improve upon Shakespeare, that master modernist), parents who just-don't-understand, peer groups who exert what we now so easily call "peer pressure."

Theories of youth culture and subculture were emerging, in Britain and the United States, during the period of the 1950s and '60s—just as *West Side Story* and then the Zeffirelli *Romeo and Juliet* moved to make connections between Shakespeare's play and modern youth, as performers and as audiences. "The seemingly spontaneous eruption of spectacular youth styles," wrote Dick Hebdige, "encouraged some writers to talk of youth as the new class."[41] In the fifties some sociologists saw the juvenile gang as compensating for the social achievements—success in school and work, parental status—that would otherwise have conferred self-esteem. Others noted a similarity between the gang and the parent culture, seeing in the values of the youth subculture distorted, exaggerated, or parodic versions of the "respectable" parental world.[42] So youth cultures could be both versions of, and resistances to, the "adult" culture to which they were subordinate, and upon which, to a certain extent, they were dependent. In the sixties and seventies, needless to say, it became more difficult—or more contestatory—to say which was the dominant, and which was the sub. Hebdige, whose interest was sparked by what he called "spectacular subcultures" (teddy boys, mods and rockers, skinheads), placed an emphasis on class and ideology, but also on display: the theatrical self-representation that identified these groups, both to one another and as apart from the majority culture.

But theater is not a direct transcription of society, either in Shakespeare's time or in ours. We might recall that Leonard Bernstein and Arthur Laurents had their epiphany about making a version of *Romeo and Juliet* as a racial gang war as they sat by the pool at the Beverly Hills Hotel and happened to catch sight of a headline in a discarded newspaper. As Laurents later wrote, "In Shakespeare, the nature of the conflict between the two houses is never specified. We began with religion, but that was dropped in the roomy pool of the

Beverly Hills Hotel. Instead the problems of Los Angeles influenced us to shift our play from the Lower East Side of New York to the Upper West Side, and the conflict to that between a Puerto Rican gang and a polymorphous self-styled 'American' gang."[43] They, too, became obsessed with the idea of "style," in this case theatrical style. Although he conceded that "juvenile delinquency is not the most lyric subject in the world," what they aimed for, Laurents said, was a "lyrically and theatrically sharpened illusion of reality," emphasizing "character and emotion rather than place-name specifics and sociological statistics." Faced with the fact that the entire second half of *Romeo and Juliet* depends upon Juliet taking a magic potion, a device that they thought "would not be swallowed in a modern play," they determined to use Shakespeare merely as a "reference point" rather than a detailed blueprint. The idea that the potion might correspond to drug-taking—or that the plan might speak to an epidemic of teen suicide—would have to wait for another adaptation, another direction, or another generation.[44]

For Arthur Laurents, the updated version in his musical would embody "the character of today's youth." But as we have seen, the "character of today's youth" (drugs, teen suicide, dumb parents, peer pressure, and hasty, irrevocable decisions) seems in many ways to have found its model, and its mode, in Shakespeare's *Romeo and Juliet*. The pattern is circular, not linear. "Today" is a shifter, a word that means something different depending upon when it is written or spoken (Laurents's "today" was 1957, a half century ago). Nonetheless, the "today" quality of *Romeo and Juliet,* the play's—and the myth's—capacity to be both a predictor and a shifter, is one of the most remarkable manifestations of the phenomenon we have been calling Shakespeare and modern culture. To locate the particular modernity of *Romeo and Juliet,* its insistence on a "now" when you-just-don't-understand, we need, in fact, to look not only at versions and adaptations of the story, but, in this age of sampling, advertising, and simulacra, at its citations and quotations.

The Reflections, a doo-wop group from Detroit, recorded their hit single, "(Just Like) Romeo and Juliet," in 1964. The refrain was "Our love's gonna be written down in history / A-just like Romeo and Juliet," and the verses move from optimism ("Findin' a job tomorrow mornin'"; "Gonna show (gonna show) how much I love her"; "I'm gonna put Romeo's fame / Right smack-dab on a date") to the imagination of loss:

> If I don't (if I don't) find work tomorrow
> It's gonna be (gonna be) heartaches 'n' sorrow
> Our love's gonna be destroyed like a tragedy
> Just like Romeo and Juliet.[45]

We might notice that the parents, the feud, and all the other "blocking figures" have disappeared from this compact narrative: in this case the problem is finding work and "get(ting) myself straight," and the phrase "Romeo and Juliet" is a recognizable shorthand for the perfect dyad of young love. (Try singing "Just like Troilus and Cressida," or "Just like Paolo and Francesca," or "Just like Petrarch and Laura," to see how striking it is that this one work of early modern literature has made its way so successfully into the lexicon of modernity.) "(Just Like) Romeo and Juliet" enjoyed renewed bursts of popularity in the seventies and eighties, as other groups recorded and performed it. And in the 1980s another classic rock song called "Romeo and Juliet" was produced by the British band Dire Straits and became one of their best-known hits. The "lovestruck romeo" tells his story in the form of a "lovesong," and thus creates a lyric version of the play-within-a-play:

> You promised me everything you promised me thick and thin
> Now you just say oh romeo yeah you know I used to have a scene with him.
>
> Juliet when we made love you used to cry
> You said I love you like the stars above I'll love you till I die
> There's a place for us you know the movie song
> When you gonna realize it was just that the time was wrong?

The lyric offers a fascinating (counter)historical trajectory, as the past and the present become enfolded, the one within the other. The phrase from a "movie song" being quoted, "there's a place for us," is from "Somewhere," written by Stephen Sondheim for Tony and Maria in *West Side Story*. The "lovestruck romeo" of the Dire Straits rock song cites not the 1956 stage musical, but the movie made of that musical in 1961. So this "romeo" (lowercase) from the 1980s cites a song from the film made from a musical based upon Shakespeare's play about Romeo and Juliet. Add to this the modern vernacular sense of "a scene," meaning in this case a kind of relationship (with the implication that the relationship is slightly self-dramatized or self-dramatizing, or perhaps just a kind of social performance); "oh romeo yeah you know I used to have a scene with him." The lyric is actually pretty close to Shakespeare's play in some ways. "You said I love you like the stars above I'll love you till I die" is a tight summation of Juliet's "Gallop apace" speech in act 3, scene 2:

> and when I shall die
> Take him and cut him out in little stars,
> And he will make the face of heaven so fine

That all the world will be in love with night
And pay no worship to the garish sun.

3.2.21–25

This is the passage that Robert F. Kennedy quoted in his tribute to his brother, the slain president, at the 1964 Democratic National Convention. Kennedy cited the passage directly, and with attribution; he also chose a variant reading, one authorized by the fourth quarto of the play (in contrast to the first three quartos and the Folio), but preferred by some editors, in which the "I" of line 21 is replaced by "he": "When I think of President Kennedy, I think of what Shakespeare said in *Romeo and Juliet:* 'When he shall die / Take him and cut him out in little stars / And he shall make the face of heaven so fine / That all the world will be in love with night.' "[46] The voice through which Robert Kennedy speaks on this occasion, unselfconsciously, is Juliet's. He is not "identifying" with any character; instead he is quoting "Shakespeare," the play and the spirit of young love and loss within the play.

Cosmic or local, tragic or "tragic," *Romeo and Juliet* has been, throughout its history and especially in its interactions with modernity, the story of a perfect love disrupted by circumstance: feud, plague, politics, parental opposition, unseemly haste, and unforeseen delay. That the "time was wrong," in the words of the Dire Straits song, was a verdict that could attach to both the personal and the national tragedies. Over all of these quotations hovers that sense of "star-crossed lovers," mentioned by the Prologue in the opening lines of Shakespeare's play, that seems already to foreclose the valiant struggles of individuals against the future. Whether it is the "mature" actors onstage (and in early version onscreen) caught in tension with their youthful parts, or the transformation into wordless ballet that paradoxically restored "youth" to its performers, or the determined relevance of a stage musical that seemed already, by the time it concluded its run, almost out-of-date with the youth culture of its time, the play, like its protagonists, has been consistently too early *and* too late. By the middle of the twentieth century Romeo-and-Juliet had become a cultural macro, a widely and instantaneously recognizable term for passionate (and doomed) young love. It was not a surprise to see the suicide of singer Kurt Cobain of Nirvana and his relationship to his wife, Courtney Love, compared to the characters and plot of Shakespeare's play.[47]

AS ONE MIGHT EXPECT, given its themes and content, *Romeo and Juliet* has provided rich fodder for social researchers. A phenomenon called "the Romeo and Juliet effect" was detected, in the early 1970s, by a team of psychologists investigating the relationship between parental interference and romantic love. The researchers found that "parental interference in a love relationship intensifies the feeling of romantic love between members of the couple," and concluded that this situation, applying the "well-supported psychological principles" of "goal frustration and reactance" to the circumstances of romantic love, was "perhaps novel enough to justify a distinctive name—the Romeo and Juliet effect."[48] What's in a name? Enough, at least, so that sociologists two decades later, in a highly technical "three-wave longitudinal investigation," came to the conclusion that "no evidence was found for the Romeo and Juliet effect." The earlier study was described as "classic," but the goals of the studies, apparently, differed. The "Romeo and Juliet effect" authors, according to the later account, "found the positive effect of parental interference only for a measure of romantic love from which trust had been partialled. As such, it was more of a 'need' measure. We had a general measure of love, the Braker and Kelley (1979) love scale."[49] As this brief quotation will suggest, the study from 1992 was far more technical and less "literary" than the one dated twenty years earlier; in the first article the authors summarized Shakespeare's plot, retold the myth of Pyramus and Thisbe, and cited Denis de Rougement's *Love in the Western World* among the scholarly sources. The second article mentions "Romeo and Juliet" only as a term used by their predecessors; Shakespeare is not mentioned, although there is an epigraph from his *Romeo and Juliet,* printed as a block quotation, but mislineating the verse so it actually reads as prose.

> Juliet: "O Romeo, Romeo! Wherefore art thou
> Romeo? Deny thy father and refuse thy name;
> Or, if thou wilt not, be but sworn my love, And
> I'll no longer be a Capulet."
> —*from Shakespeare's Romeo and Juliet*[50]

The mode of transcription and attribution makes it clear that the authors' relationship to the play is attenuated at best, and the play is not otherwise footnoted or included in the sources. By this time, in other words, the key issue for these social scientists—reasonably enough, given their topic and professional training—was not *Romeo and Juliet* but "the Romeo and Juliet effect." Their conclusion was that the support of parents, peers, and "social networks" help to stabilize romantic attachments. "Hazard analyses showed that the female partner's perceived network support increased the stability of the relationships." So much for Juliet's despairing rejection of her mother and the Nurse. But the authors here, of course, are seeking a "positive" outcome rather than a tragic one. In its adoption into the ordinary language of social science, Shakespeare's play has become not even a secondary but really a tertiary source.

That is also the case with the most current and perhaps most controversial adoption of the "Romeo and Juliet" brand, not by social scientists but by jurists and journalists, in the concept of the "Romeo and Juliet law." These laws, which have been adopted by several states (Kansas in 1999; Connecticut, Florida, Indiana, and Texas in 2007), are an attempt to mitigate harsh penalties meted out to teenage lovers who had consensual sex when one of them was still a minor. Well-publicized cases, including one in Georgia, drew attention to the situation of individuals, typically young men in their teens, who have received lengthy jail sentences as "sex offenders" because the parents of their underage partners pressed charges. As one commentator noted, because of Juliet's age, "even Romeo would be labeled a sex offender today."[51]

But as available as the play (or its title characters) has been to appropriation by social scientists, some of its most persistent avatars have been in the arts—not only in the "high culture" arts of dance and film, but also in the popular (and even "new media") arts. Here are two brief but effective visual and aural examples that "sample" the play in, and for, the early twenty-first century—two examples that bring together the play's cultural ubiquity (no one needs to be told the plot or who the protagonists are) with the key issues of haste, youth, and failed, private, or oblique communication. Modernity being what it is—and what it isn't—the play's famous declaration about "the two hours' traffic of our stage" (usually quite a bit more) as an index of brevity are here sharply and wittily compressed into two minutes, or less—the time of a cartoon, a text message, or an advertising spot.

In a Roz Chast cartoon from *The New Yorker*, published on February 4, 2002, and entitled "The I.M.s of Romeo and Juliet," the teenage Romeo and Juliet, both at their computers (she has a laptop, he has a Mac; it's 2002, before the most recent portable technology), are sending instant messages to each other: "romeo u there," asks Juliet, and he answers, "yo wassup." She replies "nothin, u?" He asks if she's going to a party, but she's "grounded." "Y" is the one-letter query—no question mark needed. And then it's on to the family feud. "btw, both my rents hate u," she writes. His parents, it seems, "hate u," too. This cozy exchange is interrupted by the impending arrival of the heavy father: "my dads coming gtg," she types. Here is where Chast's cartoon intersects with the famous "balcony scene":

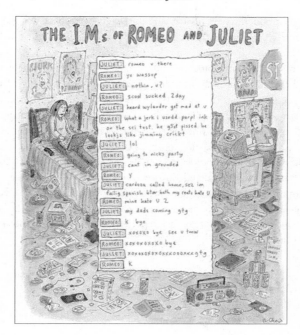

Romeo: k bye
Juliet: xoxoxo bye see u tmw
Romeo: xoxoxoxoxo bye
Juliet: xoxoxoxoxoxxxooooxxx gtg
Romeo: k

Compare this dialogue to the Shakespeare text as we thought we once knew it:

> Good night, good night. Parting is such sweet sorrow
> That I shall say good night till it be morrow.
>
> *2.1.229–30*

Chast's cartoon perfectly captures, in the mode of the consciously bathetic, the distinctive quality of this famous scene: the repetitions, the delays, the digressions, the excuses, the pleasurable pain of parting: *gtg k bye*. The cartoon is not only a snapshot double reading of Shakespeare and modern culture, but also, potentially, a commentary on dialogue, monologue, audience, gesture, speech codes, and language. For a play that has become so much of a modern/postmodern cliché that it is regularly cited by those who have never read it, this rescripting calls attention to the paradoxical discursive role of Shakespeare in modern life.

Very much the same could be said of a television advertisement that was produced the following year and that likewise took off from a technology of modern speech and performance. In October 2003 Nextel Communications ran a *Romeo and Juliet* spot in conjunction with an advertising campaign promoting "push-to-talk" cell phones. The humorous premise of the campaign was that people would use the "push-to-talk" feature even in situations in which they were next to, rather than separated from, each other. The *Romeo and Juliet* commercial depicted various characters, in Renaissance costume, performing the entire plot of the play in thirty seconds. The words spoken were brief and telegraphic, a modern-age version of the classical (and Shakespearean) device of stichomythia. Each participant clasped a phone and spoke his or her lines into it:

> *Juliet:*   Romeo!
> *Romeo:*   Juliet!
> *Juliet:*   I love you!
> *Romeo:*   Ditto.
> *Tybalt:*   Die.
> *Capulet:*   Marry him.
> *Juliet:*   Never. [*drinks potion*].
> *Romeo:*   No!
> *Paris:*   You! [*attacks Romeo; Romeo slays Paris; Romeo drinks poison.*]
> *Juliet [awakening]:*   Better now. [*Sees Romeo fall.*]
>   No! [*Stabs herself.*]
> *Friar Laurence:*   Kids.
> [*INTERTITLE:* Nextel. Done.][52]

I have arranged the lines here in some approximation of blank verse, since this tragedy-in-little is artfully designed to perform like a play. It takes two lines of iambic pentameter to get from love to death, with the Friar's final line, spoken from above, hovering over the action like a futile and resigned benediction. The intertitle, as it appears on the screen, puts the "done" tag on both the love-death plot and *Romeo and Juliet*: nano-Shakespeare.

Where the *New Yorker* cartoon—a print medium—produced a *script* (with an ease that the struggling writer Will of *Shakespeare in Love* might have envied)—the television ad was, in essence, a very short *movie*. Like the rock or pop love song, these are among the art forms of our time.

Play, ballet, film, musical, rock song, cartoon, advertisement: *Romeo and Juliet,* a play that anticipated, documented, and to a certain extent scripted the concept of "youth culture," has consistently found new genres, pertinent and impertinent, in which to stage the fraught dialogue between maturity and immaturity, experience and instinct, "we" and "you," "now" and "then." *All* of these terms are "shifters," the term given by linguist Otto Jespersen to words whose referent can be understood only from the context. Ask the baby boomers and the flower children and the Gen-Xers, once forever young. "Youth culture" as a concept is both time-bound (originating in the sociology of the fifties) and in flux: you never step into the same generation twice.

Shakespeare's plays are constantly aware of the "argument of Time," from Falstaff's "They hate us youth" (*Henry IV, Part 2*) uttered by that eternal optimist at the age of sixty, to Feste's "Youth's a stuff will not endure" (*Twelfth Night*), to Edgar's "We that are young / Shall never see so much, nor live so long" (*King Lear*). But Romeo and Juliet live short, not long. It is the brevity and compression of their story, the impressionistic sense that their *lives,* and not only the play that bears their names, constitute a "two hours' traffic" that has made this tragedy about untimely love so poignant, so "modern," and so timely. As for modernity's influence upon the play—that, we might say, is the *real* "Romeo and Juliet effect."

THREE

CORIOLANUS

The Estrangement of Self

"I F SHE SAYS YOUR BEHAVIOR IS HEINOUS / Kick her right in the Coriolanus / Brush up your Shakespeare / And they'll all kowtow."[1] In 1948 the gleeful mobsters in the musical *Kiss Me, Kate* caroled this courting advice to each other, having discovered that quoting Shakespeare could be an aphrodisiac, or at least a good line, when your goal is to "wow" women. With music and lyrics by Cole Porter, and book by Samuel and Bella Spewack, *Kiss Me, Kate,* based on Shakespeare's *The Taming of the Shrew,* was a hit on Broadway. The show ran for 1,077 performances in New York, and a London production, opening in 1951, held the stage for 400 performances in the West End. "Coriolanus" in Porter's sly lyric was a joke word, rhyming with "heinous" and gesturing toward the human posterior, the literal butt of the joke. It was what a later critical practice might call an empty signifier: present in the verse because it was a funny word, a kind of dirty or at least anatomical-sounding word, the title of a Shakespeare play that neither the gangsters, nor perhaps many in the audience, would be expected to know.[2]

Meantime, in a Germany where Shakespeare's *Coriolanus* had been banned by the American authorities after the defeat of Hitler, Bertolt Brecht was at work on an adaptation of the play for the Berliner Ensemble. Brecht tinkered with his script from 1951 to 1953, ultimately leaving it unfinished at his death in 1956. A production based on his adaptation was mounted by the Berliner Ensemble in 1963.

Coriolanus is not only a powerful tragedy but also a constant ideological temptation for directors; perhaps no other play of Shakespeare's has been so readily appropriated across the political spectrum. Coleridge long ago commented on "the wonderfully philosophic impartiality of Shakespeare's politics."[3] Laurence Olivier memorably played the part in two quite different productions, and in the early 1970s the British playwright John Osborne—who had gained fame in the 1950s as the author of *Look Back in Anger*—adapted the play for the modern theater, depicting the hero as an angry young man. This updated version (*A Place Calling Itself Rome*), with a black female tribune, a modern-day mob, and a helicopter for denouement, could not find a producer, and was never staged. It was in the Germany of the first half of the twentieth century, though, that *Coriolanus* struck a particular chord, coinciding—as it happened—with some extraordinary developments in theater, as well as in politics.

Many in prewar Germany had greatly admired Shakespeare's play. What one critic has called a "Coriolanus-Renaissance" resulted in at least thirty-four performances between 1911 and 1920—probably more than in Great Britain during the same time period—and German schoolbooks in the 1930s cited *Coriolanus* as a model of heroism. It was a favorite in Germany during the time of National Socialism, in part because it seemed to extol the status of the singular charismatic leader. The larger-than-life figure of Martius (later in the play called "Coriolanus") was described as offering an admirable example, "as Adolf Hitler in our days wishes to lead our beloved German fatherland."[4] Not surprisingly, then, after the war the play was *first* banned by occupation forces in the West, and then rewritten to make the plebeians more "heroic" and the martial hero more dispensable, as Brecht, and after his death, his wife, the noted actress Helene Weigel, reshaped Shakespeare for the Berliner Ensemble and for Communist East Berlin.

Two refractions of that revisionary moment, two rewritings of the Brechtian scene-of-writing, are worth considering in the context of Shakespeare and modern culture: the first is Brecht's own critical dialogue, "Study of the First Scene of Shakespeare's *Coriolanus*," staging a conversation among actors to discuss ways to interpret the first scene in light of Brecht's epic theater, Marxist dialectics, and Mao's essay *On Contradiction;* the second is Günter Grass's play *The Plebeians Rehearse the Uprising,* which imagines a rehearsal of *Coriolanus,* directed by a very Brechtlike figure called the Boss, as it is intersected by political events taking place just outside the theater.

It may be useful to recall something of Brecht's remarkable effect upon twentieth-century drama, staging, and acting, since all of these, as we will see, found an uncanny responsiveness in the Shakespearean text he was translating and adapting in his final years.

Brecht's ideas about theater developed and changed over his career, from the 1920s when he was a reviewer in Augsberg to his prominence as a director in Berlin. His involvement in political and social movements, his engagement with sociological theory and with Marxism, inflected the work he produced and, in particular, his ideas about the individual, the collective, and the relationship of the actor to the audience and of both the social and political world. During these years Hitler and National Socialism came to power; the day after the burning of the Reichstag in February 1933, Brecht left Germany for Denmark, Sweden, Finland, and then the United States, where he remained until 1947, and where some of his best-known plays were written.

Terms like "epic theater" and "gestic theater" (or the theater of *gestus*) are central to any analysis of Brecht, as is the celebrated element of *Verfremdung*, variously translated as "alienation," "estrangement," or "distancing," the signature quality of Brechtian drama.[5] Here is Walter Benjamin's explanation, from an essay first published in 1939, "What Is Epic Theater?" that framed some of the terms *for* Brecht. Benjamin writes, "Brecht differentiates his epic theater from the dramatic theater in the narrower sense, whose theory was formulated by Aristotle."

> Brecht's drama eliminated the Aristotelian catharsis, the purging of the emotions through empathy with the stirring fate of the hero . . . hardly any appeal is made to the empathy of the spectators. Instead, the art of the epic theater consists in producing astonishment rather than empathy. To put it succinctly, instead of identifying with the characters, the audience should be educated to be astonished at the circumstances under which they function.
>
> The task of the epic theater, according to Brecht, is not so much the development of actions as the representation of conditions . . . the truly important thing is to discover the conditions of life. (One might say just as well: to alienate [*verfremden*] them.) This discovery (alienation) of conditions takes place through the interruption of happenings.[6]

Brecht himself described the "alienation effect" in an account of a "new technique of acting," drafted in 1940. He cites in particular the resistance to empathy, "taking the incidents portrayed and alienating them from the spectator," and the purgation of the stage and auditorium from "everything 'magical.' " In using words like "alienation" and "empathy," Brecht thus incorporates Benjamin's account into his own. Thus, for example, he recommends showing the lighting apparatus rather than concealing it, so as to "destroy" the spectator's "illusion of being present at a spontaneous, transitory, authentic, unrehearsed event."[7] Among the techniques he singles out for the actor are direct address to the audience, speaking stage directions out loud, using the third person rather than the first person, and the refusal to be "completely transformed" into a character, instead speaking the lines as if quoting them. "He is not Lear, Harpagon, Schweik; he shows them."[8]

It is not an accident that one of Shakespeare's tragic figures comes first to Brecht's mind as he sets out to explain how estrangement or distancing might function for the actor in the theater. Admiration and ambivalence mark his engagement with Shakespeare—and Shakespearean drama—throughout his life and his work. In this same essay, for example, he has recourse to not one but two examples from Shakespeare to explain how a stage action could perform "alienation": "If *King Lear* [sic] (in Act I, scene i) tears up a map when he divides his kingdom between his daughters, then the act of division is alienated. Not only does it draw our attention to his kingdom, but by treating the kingdom so plainly as his own private property he throws some light on the basis of the feudal idea of the family. In *Julius Caesar* the tyrant's murder by Brutus is alienated if during one of his monologues accusing Caesar of tyrannical motives he himself maltreats a slave waiting on him."[9]

One more element of the *Verfremdungseffekt* is also worth noting, as we turn to this particular relationship between Shakespeare and modern culture, and that is what Brecht himself calls the "crucial technical device" of "historicization." Again, for him, this is a mode of psychic distancing rather than identification across time:

> The actor must play the incidents as historical ones. Historical incidents are unique, transitory incidents associated with particular periods. The conduct of the persons involved in them is not fixed and "universally human"; it includes elements that have been or may be overtaken by the course of history, and is subject to criticism from the immediate following period's point of view. The conduct of those born before us is alienated [*Entfremdet*] from us by an incessant evolution.
>
> It is up to the actor to treat present-day events and modes of behavior with the same detachment as the historian adopts with regard to those of the past. He must alienate these characters and incidents from us.[10]

When, therefore, Brecht himself undertakes a revision of a Shakespeare play for the stage, his selection of a play based upon ancient Roman history offers the opportunity for a multiple or many-layered distancing: of the modern German playwright from his early modern English "source," of Shakespeare from Livy and Plutarch (both of whose accounts of Caius Martius Coriolanus, Brecht will have read and will discuss), and of the actors from the "characters and incidents" of the play.

What might be called the collaboration between Brecht and Shakespeare, in Brecht's planned adaptation of *Coriolanus* for the Berliner Ensemble, offers an overdetermined instance of how Shakespeare makes modern culture and modern culture makes Shakespeare, because, as we will shortly see, Shakespeare's *Coriolanus* itself represents a striking instance of the performance of the estrangement (or alienation) effect *within* the play. Thus—to leap ahead for a moment toward a speculative theoretical claim—Shakespeare becomes the anticipatory coauthor of Brecht's ideas about alienation and acting.

Shakespeare revises Brecht just as Brecht revises Shakespeare. Furthermore, the revisions of Brecht's revision of Shakespeare are themselves—like Brecht's own unfinished version and its published preamble, the dialogue "Study of the First Scene of Shakespeare's *Coriolanus*"—formally marked as paratexts, supplementary to the "historical" object, Shakespeare's play.

The term *Verfremdungseffekt* is, as many scholars have noted, derived from an idea formulated by the Russian Formalist critics, a group of influential linguistic and literary theorists who flourished in Moscow in the early decades of the twentieth century. The movement ended at the close of the 1920s when Stalin came to power. Victor Shklovsky's phrase "making strange," or *ostranenie,* has been translated as "distancing" or "defamiliarization," as well as "estrangement." Brecht's coinage was invented after his return from a visit to Moscow, where he saw, and admired, a performance by a Chinese acting company in which, by design, "the audience was hindered from simply identifying itself with the characters in the play."[11] The Russian Formalists focused their work mainly on poetry, poetics, narrative, fable, and the concept of literariness, seeking to identify elements that were specific to literature, rather than part of a more general study of history, culture, or psychology. This attention to the literary is one of the aspects of Formalism that led Stalin et al. to condemn it as "elitist." So when Brecht borrows the concept of estrangement and recognizes it as an element of theater—whether in the classical Chinese tradition or in his own work—he resocializes the idea of distancing. What is defamiliarized, or made unfamiliar, is the attachment to the hero and the arc of his or her rise and fall, and also the idea of the "fourth wall," of theater as a self-contained unit walled off from the audience and from life.

When we come to look at Shakespeare's *Coriolanus,* we can see scene after scene in which the thematics of estrangement, distancing, defamiliarization, and alienation are performed, often (as will be immediately clear) in the context of an onstage performance-within-a-performance (standing for office in the marketplace; receiving embassies from Rome). Here are a few examples:

- Martius's astonishment at his mother Volumnia's instruction that he falsify himself in front of the common people in order to gain their votes for the consulate.

- His angry rejection of Rome ("I banish *you*") when popular favor turns against him.

- His rapprochement with the enemy general, Aufidius, formerly his foe.

- His expectation that the people of the vanquished city of Corioles will accept without ambivalence his honorific surname, "Coriolanus" (the man who defeated Corioles).

- His willed isolation from family and friends, and his ardent wish for self-invention ("as if a man were author of himself / And had no other kin").

- His refusal to admit entreaties on a personal level when the Roman general Cominius seeks his aid ("he was a kind of nothing, titleless").

- His capitulation to his mother's request, and to her stronger will, when, as the stage direction says, he "Holds her by the hand, silent," and his recognition that the outcome will be "most mortal" to him, even as it is a famous victory for Rome. "Mortal" in this phrase carries a doubled meaning of which the speaker may or may not be fully cognizant: fateful (and leading to death); human rather than determinedly inhuman.

- His ultimate stripping or unmasking by the crafty Aufidius, who removes, one by one, the names by which he has been known (Coriolanus, Martius), leaving him only with the insulting "boy," a word he repeats over and over in disbelief.

In Brecht's revision of Shakespeare's text Martius does not yield to his mother's entreaties in act 5, scene 4, because of filial love, pity for Rome, or pathos, but rather because Volumnia tells him the armaments industry of Rome is now superior to that of the Volscians:

VOLUMNIA   Enough of
         Your childish sentiment. I've something else
         To say. The Rome you will be marching on
         Is very different from the Rome you left.
         You are no longer indispensable
         Merely a deadly threat to all. Don't expect
         To see submissive smoke. If you see smoke
         It will be rising from the smithies forging
         Weapons to fight you who, to subject your
         Own people, have submitted to your enemy.

         . . . .

CORIOLANUS   O mother, mother! What have you done?[12]

His moving personal reflection on her actions as "most mortal" to him, the mark of Shakespearean pathos and humanism, are cut. The scene ends, abruptly, here.

Early in his career Brecht experimented with the term "dialectical drama," but replaced it with "non-Aristotelian," contrasting "the epic drama, with its materialistic standpoint and its lack of interest in any investment of its spectators' emotions," with the "dynamic, idealistically-oriented kind of drama, with its interest in the individual"—acknowledging that the latter was "more radical when it began life (under the Elizabethans) than it had become in later centuries."[13] Brecht scholar and translator John Willett notes that "the term 'dialectical' went into cold storage, to be taken out again in a somewhat different context at the end of Brecht's life."[14] "Epic" (as contrasted with Aristotelian tragedy) argued explicitly against empathy and pathos, and implicitly against the necessity of the unities of time and place.

Near the end of his life, though, Brecht returned to the idea of dialectical theater. First he wrote, in a draft appendix to his "Short Organum," that "an effort is now being made to move on from the epic theatre to the dialectical theatre," and then he organized, in 1956, a collection of theoretical writings called "Dialectics in the Theatre." He died that year, and the pieces did not appear until after his death. But the most central piece, the one Willett calls "the backbone of the whole affair, occupying two-thirds of the space," is the "*Coriolanus* dialogue."

That a dialogue should be dialectical is both structurally and intellectually reasonable. Two (or more) voices, two (or more) opinions, contradiction, argument, the possibility of resolution (whether contested or transcendent). Without contradiction, after all, how long does dialogue remain engaged, or engaging? "Dialogue" here presumably encompasses both Platonic and theatrical practice: contrapuntal ideas, contrapuntal "persons," whether visible or merely indicated by speech prefixes. Perhaps the Platonic dialogues employ the vocative ("Tell me, Glaucon . . .") so insistently because they are written and read rather than performed.

There are numerous ways to set a production in relation to a political moment, and not all of them are consonant with Brecht's idea of an epic theater. As one successful alternative, we might briefly consider the 1959 Stratford production of *Coriolanus* directed by Peter Hall and starring Laurence Olivier in the title role. (Hall was twenty-eight years old at the time, Olivier over fifty.) Olivier's Caius Martius in the early scenes, boasting of his victories to his mother, then exhibiting modesty about them to the Senate, was seen as the performance of a privileged English schoolboy behaving according to a familiar code: "Nobody," wrote Laurence Kitchin, "lacking knowledge of English public school *mores,* could have hit exactly this note of sulky pride, a result of the man of action's narcissism held back by the necessity to belittle success in the presence of social equals."[15] So Olivier as Coriolanus was at first a reticent young British public-school type, though gifted with a powerful tone of command—and disdain. By the close, however, in an athletic feat (and a visual tableau) that made the production and the performance legendary, he leaped headfirst from a twelve-foot platform without the support of wires, his ankles caught at the last minute by two (doubtless terrified) actor soldiers, and dangled upside down, the stage picture a deliberate echo of the dead body of Mussolini. After the Fascist dictator was captured and shot by Italian Communist partisans, Mussolini's body was taken to Milan and hung, upside down from a meat hook, as a lesson and a sign of ridicule.

Angus McBean, Coriolanus, 1959: The Death of Coriolanus, Act 5, Scene 6

The body of Benito Mussolini hanging in the Piazzale Loreto, Milan

This was in April 1945, almost fifteen years before the Hall production—but the memory of the image endured. Shakespeare's text indicates that "the Conspirators draw, and kill Martius," after the people have cried "Tear him to pieces! . . . He killed my son! My daughter! . . . He killed my father!" (5.6.121–23). But the Hall/Olivier image made Martius active rather than passive—and, at the same time, presented a visual quotation that associated him, for a brief but indelible moment, with Italian Fascism. (Mussolini, it might be noted, was killed—and then displayed—side by side with his mistress; Olivier/Martius, needless to say, is, as he declares proudly, and with no sign of his earlier reticence, "alone" [5.6.117].) As Cynthia Marshall nicely observed, "when Olivier played Coriolanus, a performer sometimes accused of overacting took on the character of a man who would be nothing but 'the thing I am.' "[16]

IN ACT 4 OF SHAKESPEARE'S PLAY, the self-exiled Coriolanus appears in Antium, the home of his former rival Aufidius. The stage direction tells us that he is in disguise: "*Enter* CORIOLANUS *in mean apparel, disguised and muffled*" (4.4), and almost immediately the word "strange" begins to be applied to him, in several, developing senses:

> THIRD SERVINGMAN [in Aufidius's house] What fellow's this?
> FIRST SERVINGMAN A strange one as ever I looked on.
>
> 4.5.19–20

> THIRD SERVINGMAN Prithee tell my master what a strange guest he has here.
>
> 4.5.33–34

The stranger refuses at first to give his name to his host, despite repeated demands, and, even after unmuffling, he seems not to be recognized:

> CORIOLANUS If, Tullus,
>   Not yet thou know'st me, and seeing me dost not
>   Think me for the man I am, necessity
>   Commands me name myself.
> AUFIDIUS What's thy name?
> CORIOLANUS A name unmusical to the Volscians' ears,
>   And harsh in sound to thine.
> AUFIDIUS Say, what's thy name?
> . . . .
> CORIOLANUS Prepare thy brow to frown. Know'st thou me yet?
> AUFIDIUS I know thee not. Thy name?
> CORIOLANUS My name is Caius Martius, who hath done
>   To thee particularly, and to all the Volsces,
>   Great hurt and mischief. Thereto witness may
>   My surname Coriolanus. The painful service,
>   The extreme dangers, and the drops of blood
>   Shed for my thankless country, are requited

But with that surname.

. . . .

Only that name remains.

4.5.53–73

By the end of the scene, the servingmen record a volte-face in their attitude toward the man they wanted to turn away:

FIRST SERVINGMAN Here's a strange alteration!
SECOND SERVINGMAN By my hand, I had thought to have strucken him
     with a cudgel: and yet my mind gave me his clothes made a false
     report of him.
FIRST SERVINGMAN What an arm he has! He turned me about with his
     finger and his thumb, as one would set up a top.
SECOND SERVINGMAN Nay, I knew by his face that there was something
     in him. He had, sir, a kind of face, methought—I cannot tell how
     to term it.
FIRST SERVINGMAN He had so, looking, as it were—would I were
     hanged but I thought there was more in him than I could think,
SECOND SERVINGMAN So did I, I'll be sworn. He is simply the rarest
     man i' th' world.

4.5.149–64

So Coriolanus arrives as a stranger, estranged from Rome and from his former self; his surname is another version of self-estrangement, both because, as he tells Aufidius here (and will be told by him in a confrontational "unmasking" moment at the end of the play), "Coriolanus" is a name divided against itself, naming the city that he vanquished and where he now seeks rehabilitation, and also because "only that name remains." The man he addresses as "Tullus," and who will call him, in turn, "Martius," learns that the Roman hero has been "whoop'd out of Rome" by "th' voice of slaves," and now comes to the land of his former Volscian enemies in search of revenge. The comical inability of the now starstruck servingmen to find words to describe the uniqueness of the man they once so easily spurned and rejected underscores the vacillation of fame, especially when the onlookers are themselves unnamed servants, plebians, and "slaves" distinguished only by number (First Servingman, Second Citizen, etc.).

Defamiliarized. Estranged. Alienated. Such terms are directly and literally applicable to the situation of Shakespeare's Coriolanus. But the performance of estrangement is not achieved through such "Brechtian" devices as the address to the audience. In fact, although most of Shakespeare's major tragedies depend upon the soliloquy as a hinge swinging outward toward the audience, whether to reveal the inner thoughts of a Hamlet or the Machiavellian plans of an Iago, *Coriolanus* is a play without major soliloquies, and indeed Coriolanus himself is a very unlikely candidate for confidential self-revelation. On the one hand, the typical theater audience might well strike him as composed of unequals, and, on the other hand, he seems a character whose language suggests that he is singularly out of touch with his own inner self, if one can posit such an interiority. Throughout Shakespeare's play Coriolanus seems startled or taken aback when confronted with other characters' impressions of him. Leaving aside, in the context of this investigation, whether various onstage observers are "right" or "wrong" about him, let us ask, instead, how to find the "him," or the "self," in Coriolanus.

The play continually returns to this problematic term, "self." By the time Coriolanus has left Rome, defying the "common cry of curs," which is the populace ("I banish you! . . . There is a world elsewhere"), he has resolved to resist the personal in favor of the aggressively—and defensively—depersonalized. As the Roman general Cominius explains, reporting on his own failed embassy:

> "Coriolanus"
> He would not answer to, forbade all names.
> He was a kind of nothing, titleless,
> Till he had forged himself a name o' th' fire
> Of burning Rome.
>
> *5.1.11–15*

And when, shortly thereafter, Coriolanus sees his mother, wife, and child approach to make the same plea on behalf of Rome, he tries to gird himself against it:

> But out, affection!
> All bond and privilege of nature break;
> . . . .
> . . . I'll never
> Be such a gosling to obey instinct, but stand
> As if a man were author of himself
> And knew no other kin.
>
> *5.3.24–37*

But no sooner does he make this famous—and wishful—statement about self-creation than he perceives the degree to which he is taking part in a performed fiction:

> Like a dull actor now
> I have forgot my part, and I am out
> Even to a full disgrace.
>
> *5.3.40–42*

This remark is an aside, a moment of confiding in himself—and in the audience. The Arden edition notes that it echoes Sonnet 23 ("As an unperfect actor on the stage / Who with his fear is put beside his part"), but it also recalls an earlier, and crucial, moment in the play, when Coriolanus's mother, Volumnia, urges him to mollify the people in the marketplace—whom he has brusquely insulted—and ask their support in the election for consul:

> Why did you wish me milder? Would you have me
> False to my nature? Rather say I play
> The man I am.
>
> *3.2.13–16*

For many characters in Shakespeare this onstage invention of the self is either not a problem—as in the case of Iago's self-satisfied "I am not what I am" (*Othello* 1.1.65)—or else, as with King Lear, it signals a crisis, a kind of pathetic break ("Doth any here know me? This is not Lear. . . . Who is it that can tell me who I am?" [*King Lear* 1.4.201–5]). Probably the closest, in phrasing, is the language of the disguised Viola in *Twelfth Night,* in costume as the "young gentleman" Cesario and addressing the Lady Olivia: "I am not that I play" (1.5.164).

Viola is in cross-dressed disguise; Iago declares himself a Machiavel; Lear articulates his dismay at Goneril's treatment of him now that he has abdicated the kingship. Yet at this point, early in his tragedy, Lear remains, as he thinks, in control of the scene. His questions here, however portentous in terms of dramatic irony, are meant to be rhetorical, not existential. His real break will come later, in the storm. But what about Coriolanus?

For him the dichotomy is a definitive shock. "You have put me now to such a part which never / I shall discharge to th' life" (3.2.105–6). Although Volumnia has tried to explain that deception in war is analogous to deception in politics (46–47), he is dubious, and her coaching offers a deliberate split between performance and truth:

> speak to th' people,
> Not by your own instruction, nor by th' matter
> Which your heart prompts you, but with such words
> That are but roted in your tongue, though but

Bastards and syllables of no allowance
To your bosom's truth.

3.2.53–58

Brecht's adaptation follows this scene closely, but minimizes the existential angst. From Coriolanus's refusal ("I will not do it") to his capitulation ("Pray be content / Mother, I am going to the market-place") in Shakespeare is a matter of ten lines (120; 130–31). In the Brecht, translated by Ralph Manheim, the attitude of concession is jauntier, less fraught: "Calm down. I'm going to the marketplace. Stop scolding." And where the Shakespeare has "Let them accuse me by invention: I / Will answer in mine honour" (143–44), Brecht/Manheim translates, "Inventive as may be their accusations / My repentance will be more so." The difference is slight, but indicative. Shakespeare's Coriolanus is torn between invention and honor, Brecht's—for the moment at least—more fully onboard for role-playing.

Here it may be useful to introduce a twentieth-century point of view about the linked concepts of self and performance, in Erving Goffman's idea of "the presentation of self in everyday life." Goffman's book of that title, a landmark in mid-century sociology, describes a "performance" as "all the activity of a given participant on a given occasion which serves to influence in any way any of the other participants."[17] The argument makes skillful and illuminating use of terms like "front," "back," "setting," and "sincere," applying the language of theatricality to encounters in social, business, and professional life. The title itself is an echo of Freud's *Psychopathology of Everyday Life* (1901) and, since Goffman wrote, there have been numerous other books and articles that take up not only the idea of "performance" but also the question of "everyday life," now a mainstay of cultural studies analysis.[18] But for my purposes the key word in Goffman's title is "self," a word that, as a noun or substantive meaning essential personality, only really comes into its own after Shakespeare. Definitions from the *Oxford English Dictionary* are sometimes overused in historical argument, but in this case they seem, collectively, suggestive.

Self, n.

> 3. That which in a person is really and intrinsically *he* (in contradistinction to what is adventitious); the ego (often identified with the soul or mind as opposed to the body); a permanent subject of successive and varying states of consciousness.
> [First historical use cited, 1674.]

> 4. a. What one is at a particular time or in a particular aspect of relation; one's nature, character, or (sometimes) physical constitution or

appearance, considered as different at different times. [First historical use cited, 1697.]

4. b. An assemblage of characteristics and dispositions which may be conceived as constituting one of various conflicting personalities within a human being.

[First historical use, 1595, from Spenser's *Amoretti*, 45:3: "And in my selfe, my inward selfe I meane."][19]

Critics regularly remind us that the source word for "person" is "persona," which means "mask," so that the idea of a person is, in a way, a back-formation from stage performance; the performed self, at least etymologically, produces the person, rather than the other way around. The example from Spenser's sonnet used by the *OED* underscores the fact that when "self" first begins its English career as an independent substantive (as contrasted with an adjective or pronoun), it is already divided ("in my selfe, my inward selfe I meane").

With this in mind, I want to take note of the relationship between performance and self in *Coriolanus,* and see why this play might have presented Bertolt Brecht with not one but two areas of particular interest: the political (plebians rise up against aristocrats) and the alienated "self."

Returning to Goffman for a moment, let us pause to reflect upon what might be called his moment of disavowal: when, having for over two hundred pages presented an engaging case for the applicability of theater terms to "everyday life," he offers, in the last two pages of his book, a "final comment" that in essence pulls the rug out from under, or (to use his terms) the scaffolding away from, his analogy. Like the moment when Puck tells the audience that what they have beheld is "No more yielding but a dream" (*A Midsummer Night's Dream,* Epilogue 6), Goffman's reader is now reminded that there are vital differences between art and life. The passage is lengthy but worth citing in full:

In developing the conceptual framework employed in this report, some language of the stage was used. I spoke of performers and audiences; of routines and parts; of performances come off or falling flat; of cues, stage settings and backstage; of dramaturgical needs, dramaturgical skills, and dramaturgical strategies. Now it should be admitted that this attempt to press a mere analogy so far was in part a rhetoric and a maneuver.

The claim that all the world's a stage is sufficiently commonplace for readers to be familiar with its limitations and tolerant of its presentation, knowing that at any time they will easily be able to demonstrate to themselves that it is not to be taken too seriously. An action staged in the theater is a relatively contrived illusion and an admitted one; unlike ordinary life, nothing real or actual can happen to the performed characters—although at another level of course something real and actual can happen to the reputation of performers *qua* professionals whose everyday job is to put on theatrical performances.

And so here the language and mask of the stage will be dropped. Scaffolds, after all, are to build other things with, and should be erected with an eye to taking them down. This report is not concerned with aspects of theater that creep into everyday life. It is concerned with the structure of social encounters—the structure of those entities in social life that come into being whenever persons enter one another's immediate physical presence. The key factor in this structure is the maintenance of a single definition of the situation, this definition having to be expressed, and this expression sustained in the face of a multitude of potential disruptions.

A character staged in a theater is not in some ways real, nor does it have the same kind of real consequences as does the thoroughly contrived character performed by a confidence man; but the *successful* staging of either of these types of false figures involves use of *real* techniques—the same techniques by which everyday persons sustain their real social situations. Those who conduct face to face interaction on a theater's stage must meet the key requirement of real situations: they must expressively sustain a definition of the situation: but this they do in circumstances that have facilitated their developing an apt technology for the interactional tasks that all of us share.[20]

Goffman's disavowal—I want to stick with that term for the moment—is itself analogous to two other, equally well-known, moments when major twentieth-century theorists draw upon theatrical imagery only to disclaim its pertinence for the stage. The first of these was Freud's declaration, in his essay on "The Uncanny" (1919), that events onstage (or in fiction) cannot be uncanny because the audience knows that they are part of a performance.[21] The second was J. L. Austin's remark in *How to Do Things with Words* that words used in onstage events could not be felicitous performatives for the same reason: because the circumstances make it clear to the audience that they are watching a fiction, a theatrical performance, not a *real* promise or marriage or pact.[22] Austin's lectures, later published in book form, were delivered in 1955. In their various ways, then, theorists like Austin, Goffman, and Brecht were all addressing questions of performance, felicity, and theatrical self-consciousness in a decade that was also marked by political concerns about treason, espionage, the cold war, and what Daniel Boorstin would shortly term the "pseudo-event" (an event staged entirely for its media or publicity effect, like a press conference or a photo opportunity).[23]

What has always struck me about Freud's and Austin's insistence on excepting imaginative literature from the categories of the uncanny or the felicitous performative is that they protest too much. If, as Freud says elsewhere, resistance marks the site of something important, these resistances are particularly suggestive. And when Goffman likewise ends his book on the performance of the self by saying that his use of "performance" was only a figure of speech, a scaffolding, I am tempted to ask why all of these subtle observers shy at the fence rather than jumping over it. For the radical interest of this problem—how to assess theatrical effects, noted in real life, when they appear in the theater—seems to me to lie in what it implies about the real power of theater.

If theater is a version of Freud's "other scene," his term for the unconscious, what is acted there is not *less* real, but rather *differently* real. Coriolanus encounters the demand to perform himself for an onstage audience, and discovers that the performance usurps and replaces the presumed authenticity of the self. In this emptying out of the concept—the estrangement, in effect, of the self from itself—we experience again the anticipatory modernity of Shakespeare.

CERTAIN NAÏVE OBSERVERS within Shakespeare's plays plainly do not make a distinction between theatrical performance and reality. (Consider for example Snug the Joiner's concern, in *A Midsummer Night's Dream,* lest the ladies in the audience be so frightened by his performance of a lion that the actors will be punished.) Others, like Polonius, who regard themselves as theatrical sophisticates, are nonetheless undone by their false sense of security about being safely in the audience.

The person/persona back-formation (the idea that the concept of a *person* is derived from the word for theatrical *mask*) reverses the common expectation about imitation: which, we may ask, is really imitating which? Thus for example the very first definition of "person" in the *Oxford English Dictionary* is "A role taken by a person." That this august reference work should commit what is normally a fundamental solecism in the world of definition—using a word to define itself—indicates something of the conundrum here. (The extended definition does not help to clarify the onstage/offstage problem, but rather instates it: "A role or character assumed in real life, or in a play, etc.; a part, function, or office; a persona; a semblance or guise. Hence: any of the characters in a play or story."[24]

The familiar cliché about life imitating art (based on an aphorism by Oscar Wilde) marks this uncanniness as a "modern" trait, or rather as a phenomenon of significance to modernism's—and postmodernism's—idea of itself: reflexive (in the case of modernism) and hyperreal. In the case of postmodernism, Jean Baudrillard's hyperreality has certain points in common with Boorstin's notion of the "pseudo." Indeed it is worth noting in this context that Baudrillard started his career as a teacher of German, and that his earliest publications included translations of Brecht (*The Refugee Dialogues*) and Peter Weiss (*Marat/Sade*).

Shakespeare's theatrical adeptness in having his characters address the offstage (as well as an onstage) audience provides one good model for this unsettling breaking of the frame. When Prince Hal says, "I know you all and will a while uphold / The unyoked humour of your idleness" (1.2.173–74) the offstage audience may feel falsely comforted in thinking that his deception is being practiced on his tavern friends, but the "you" here is certainly open enough, and the soliloquy form direct enough, so that he may be cautioning the audience as well as taking them into his confidence. The seductiveness of Mark Antony's "Friends, Romans, countrymen / Lend me your ears" is—as Kenneth Burke and others have argued[25]—a skillful piece of demagoguery, and one that influenced Brecht when he came to write *The Resistible Rise of Arturo Ui*.

In this play, written in 1941 but not produced until 1958 (and intended by Brecht for the American stage), the Chicago mob boss Arturo Ui, manifestly modeled on Adolf Hitler, takes lessons in performance from an actor who has him recite Mark Antony's speech. As soon as he concludes, and the lights fade out on him, a sign appears: "Herr Hitler coached by provincial actor. Lessons from Herr Basil in elocution and deportment."[26] The fact that this same speech, considered a straightforward model of virtue and patriotism and retitled "Antony Over Caesar's Body,"[27] was for many years a classic memorization piece in American elocutionary readers adds to the ironic effect of both Brecht's knowing appropriation and any modern restaging of *Julius Caesar*. Once again the addressees may hear a double message, at once seductive and patronizing, uplifting and manipulative.

IN THEIR READINGS OF *CORIOLANUS*, several critics have noted that Shakespeare's powerful play about failed eloquence and eloquent failure turns on a number of performatives, in Austin's terms—from the protagonist's illnatured attempt to win the "voices" or votes of the plebians for his election as consul to the promise to present himself to the people through the famous stage direction *Holds her by the hand, silent*. For me—as for Stanley Fish, in an important early essay on speech-act theory and literary analysis[28]—the most suggestive performative, and the one that acts as a fulcrum in many productions, is Coriolanus's defiant cry "I banish you!" spoken to the tribunes, the plebeians, and the city of Rome itself in act 3, scene 3 of Shakespeare's play.

Accompanied by the old counselor Menenius and the general Cominius, Coriolanus, following his mother's acting instructions in the previous scene ("Go to them with this bonnet in thy hand. . . . Thy knee bussing the stones" [3.2.73–75]), submits himself to the tribunes' verbal attack as they charge him with seeking tyrannical power and thus being a "traitor" to the people. The word "traitor" acts as a flash point here—as it will do, again, in the play's final scene—and despite Menenius's repeated promptings ("Is this the promise that you made your mother?" [3.3.90]) the scene culminates in a breakdown of communication and, inevitably, in mutual accusation. Sicinius, one of the tribunes, makes the initial declaration:

> in the name o' th' people,
> And in the power of us the tribunes, we
> E'en from this instant banish him our city,
> In peril of precipitation
> From off the rock Tarpeian, never more
> To enter our Rome gates. I' th' people's name,
> I say it shall be so.
>
> ALL THE CITIZENS It shall be so,
> It shall be so. Let him away.
> He's banished,
> And it shall be so.
>
> *3.3.103–11*

Brutus, the other tribune, picks up this refrain ("There's no more to be said but he is banished, / As enemy to the people and his country. / It shall be so!" and the people again shout, "It shall be so, it shall be so" [121–23]). It's at this point that Coriolanus delivers his speech of defiance and rejection, one of the high points of any performance:

> You common cry of curs, whose breath I hate
> As reek o' th' rotten fens, whose loves I prize
> As the dead carcasses of unburied men
> That do corrupt my air: I banish you.
> And here remain with your uncertainty.
> Let every feeble rumour shake your hearts;

> Your enemies, with nodding of their plumes,
> Fan you into despair! Have the power still
> To banish your defenders, till at length
> Your ignorance—which finds not till it feels—
> Making but reservation of yourselves,
> Still your own foes, deliver you
> As most abated captives to some nation
> That won you without blows! Despising
> For you the city, thus I turn my back.
> There is a world elsewhere!
>
> *3.3.124–39*

The tribunes and the plebians continue to celebrate as he departs, shouting "Our enemy is banished, he is gone!" And in the next scene we see Coriolanus calmly taking his farewell of his mother, wife, and what the stage direction calls "the young nobility of Rome."

"I banish you!" Who is banished in this utterance? Who is addressed? The onstage plebians and tribunes, the "common cry of curs" with reeking breath and cowardly habits? Or is this speech, like Hal's and Antony's, also conceivably aimed beyond the stage, at the audience in the theater?

What if—like Brecht—we take seriously the interrogation of the audience, and its castigation? What if "I banish you!" is aimed at *you*? A theater audience, or an audience reading the play text, may prefer, perhaps, to "identify" (as the modern phrase goes) with "the young nobility of Rome" rather than with the common people. But this is precisely what Brecht's theater resists.

Brecht did not complete his *Coriolanus* adaptation in his lifetime, but he did produce something else: a dialogue, "Study of the First Scene of Shakespeare's *Coriolanus*," dated 1953. This dialogue, written in the form of a "Brechtian" play, has achieved the status of a text in its own right, and became the source text for Günter Grass's *The Plebeians Rehearse the Uprising: A German Tragedy.*

ON JUNE 17, 1953, while Brecht was rehearsing a play with the Berliner Ensemble in East Berlin, the workers of East Germany revolted against repressive measures being imposed by the state, including the unilateral decision by the government to impose a general increase in work norms (that is, the units of work to be produced in a given time). Beginning on June 16 as a spontaneous march of construction workers on the Ministry and First Secretary Walter Ulbricht, it escalated on the following day to include political as well as economic demands. Food shortages, loss of electrical power, and other deprivations had led to widespread emigration. Berlin, like the rest of East Germany, suffered. The protesters, by this time some 100,000 in number in East Berlin alone—with others gathering in other cities to march— challenged the government, and were met, ultimately, with armed resistance. Soviet tanks, initially brought in as a show of force, fired on the demonstrators, and there were a number of deaths. The date, June 17, was subsequently commemorated as a national holiday in West Germany, until German reunification in 1990. Intellectuals and scholars took little, if any, part in these events, although Brecht afterward wrote a poem about them, ironically called "The Solution":

> After the uprising of the 17th June
> The Secretary of the Writers Union
> Had leaflets distributed in the Stalinallee
> Stating that the people
> Had forfeited the confidence of the government
> And could win it back only
> By redoubled efforts. Would it not be easier
> In that case for the government
> To dissolve the people
> And elect another?

The German novelist and playwright Günter Grass crafted his first full-length play as a reflection upon these events—and upon the politics and performance of theater—deftly drawing upon Brecht's dialogue on *Coriolanus,* Shakespeare's play, and Brecht's adaptation (*Coriolan*). The play that resulted, *The Plebeians Rehearse the Uprising,* announces its genre in the title.

This is a "rehearsal play," a genre that goes back at least as far as Kyd's *Spanish Tragedy* (ca. 1587), but has had a particular impact upon twentieth- and twenty-first-century theater, with its interest in metadrama, reflexivity, the mise en abyme and the theatrical enfilade—the Alice's-rabbit-hole effect. One celebrated example, immediately prior to *The Plebeians Rehearse,* was Peter Weiss's *Marat/Sade* (1963)—formally, *The Persecution and Assassination of Jean-Paul Marat as Performed by the Inmates of the Asylum of Charenton Under the Direction of the Marquis de Sade*—a play much in the spirit of Bertolt Brecht, with songs that comment on the political themes and issues of the play.

A slightly earlier example, which, like Grass's play, featured a revolt taking place in the city while performers play at governance in a "house of illusions," was Jean Genet's *The Balcony* (1956), set in a brothel, where the clients play-act at being judge, executioner, bishop, and general in their "scenes" with prostitutes, only to find themselves thrust into the public eye as simulacra of those public officials in an attempt to restore political order and authority. *Kiss Me, Kate* is another rehearsal play; in that case the play being performed, and interrupted, is Shakespeare's *Taming of the Shrew.* And it is perhaps need-less to say—though also important to remember—that *Coriolanus* itself is a version of the rehearsal play, with Volumnia and Menenius frantically coach-ing the recalcitrant and sulky Martius (a part for which the young Marlon Brando or James Dean, method actors both, might have been well cast).

Grass, himself a socialist and active in the German Social Democratic Party, had been critical of left-wing politics, preferring a slow (but sure) move toward democratic reform. He was already celebrated, on the basis of his nov-els *The Tin Drum* (1959) and *Cat and Mouse* (1961), as an important voice for the conscience of postwar Germany.

In 1964, on the four-hundredth anniversary of Shakespeare's birth, Günter Grass addressed the Berlin Academy of Arts and Letters on "The Prehistory and Posthistory of the Tragedy of *Coriolanus* from Livy and Plutarch via Shakespeare down to Brecht and Myself."[29] Much of his disquisition is taken up with a discussion of Shakespeare's play and Brecht's adaptation; his atti-tude toward the latter is critical, sometimes dismissive: Brecht, he says, is pro-grammatic, thesis-driven; he reduces Coriolanus from a "colossal fate-driven figure" to "a military specialist" so as to show how the world can do without him.[30] "The adapter is still more inconclusive, vacillating between partisan-ship and history, in his treatment of Menenius Agrippa."[31] "Brecht's intention of using Plutarch's pedagogy and Livy's constitutionalism as props for his own teaching comes out most clearly in the new version of Volumnia,"[32] who instead of sharing "the same heroic dimensions as her son" gets to tell him coldly, in Brecht's version, "You are no longer / Indispensable." "In the next scene of the adaptation, the upgrading of the tribunes who have used Volum-nia as a mouthpiece is shown even more blatantly."[33] And so on. Fidelity to source becomes a criterion for evaluation, despite the fact that no playwright used sources more freely, or changed them so frequently for dramatic effect, than did Shakespeare. Thus the final scene of Brecht's *Coriolan* comes in for particular dispraise: "Brecht here forsakes Shakespeare, Plutarch, and his spe-cial source, Livy. With no other foundation than himself and the intent underlying his adaptation, he makes the tribune Brutus censure the motion for a period of mourning with one final word: 'Rejected.' "[34] It seems only a slight overstatement, if at all, to read this sentence as Grass's own censure: "Rejected."

Ultimately Grass turns Brecht's verdict on Coriolanus, "You are no longer indispensable" (Brecht, *Coriolan* 5.4), back upon the Boss: "And you're not indispensable either," says the party official Kozanka to him as he exits the stage.[35] In its final moments *The Plebeians Rehearse the Uprising* stages the moment of bad faith as a scene of writing: the Boss writes a document that reflects Brecht's own ambiguous written statement, in a letter sent simultaneously to the governments of East and West Germany. The first two paragraphs of Brecht's letter had been critical of the East German government's handling of the uprising; the final paragraph expresses his solidarity with the Socialist Party.[36]

The Boss, whose new theater is being state-subsidized, nonetheless sends the original of his letter to the government, the copy "to friends in the West for safekeeping." He foresees a time when the date of the uprising, having become a national holiday, will be emptied out of meaning and of memory, and used only for beer drinking and picnicking. But Grass gives him, as his exit line, a version of the striking "banishment" lines of Shakespeare's Coriolanus: "Condemned to live forever with voices in my ears. You. You. . . . Bowed down with guilt, I accuse you!"[37]

Neatly blending Zola's famous *"J'accuse"* letter in the Dreyfus affair with Coriolanus's "I banish you!," this final phrase points up the difference between Zola, who was prosecuted and found guilty of libel, and fled France to avoid imprisonment, and Brecht, whose reputation in the East—and whose theater—remained unscathed by the events of June 17. And where Shakespeare's Coriolanus flings his final condemnation directly at the plebeians, the Boss speaks only to a tape recorder. What seems a bold estrangement effect in the epic theater is presented in *The Plebeians Rehearse* as something rather craven and futile.

OVER AND OVER AGAIN in Brecht's theoretical writings he inveighed against the "fourth wall," the illusion of closure that separated the audience from the play.[38] Breaking this powerful but imaginary barrier, a "wall" that one could not see but that nonetheless held the audience apart from the actors, became a signature of Brechtian theater. But historical events ironized this theatrical gesture by literalizing it, when in 1961 the Berlin Wall was constructed across the city, bisecting it and separating West from East. The material reality of the wall left Brecht's Berliner Ensemble in East Berlin, and many of his former audiences in the West.

Shakespeare's *Coriolanus* begins with the Roman hero's attack on the walls of the city of Corioli (1.4), and ends with his threat to attack the walls of

Rome (5.3). In Grass's play *The Plebeians Rehearse the Uprising*, set in 1953 but written more than a decade later, after the Berlin Wall was built, the striking construction workers seek the Boss's "gift of gab," his writer's eloquence, because their own trades are material, not literary.

> *Boss:* You build walls. I write. Straight walls—straight sentences. Who can build them without difficulty?

The workers see this as a ruse (*Plasterer:* "The government's building him a new theater." *Road Worker:* "That's why he won't do anything for us"). The Boss's dramaturge understands the position differently: "Great bastions are seldom taken at the first try."[39] But in fact, as will later become clear, the sentences the Boss finally writes are anything but "straight," and can be interpreted in a variety of contradictory ways. "Everybody will have his own interpretation," says Volumnia. "Cynical opportunist, home-grown idealist; all he really cared about was theater; he wrote and thought for the people."[40] Is the Boss the German enemy of Germany or its farsighted savior through his wall-busting theater? This question lingers at the end of Grass's play. But his rehearsal—the staging of a failed staging of the first scene of *Coriolanus*— would, as it turned out, prefigure another uncanny intersection between Shakespeare and modern culture.

WE HAVE NOTED THAT one of the characteristics of the play *Coriolanus* is its capacity to imitate the changing political alliances of its hero: at various times, and especially in recent years, the play has been read, and produced, as fascist and socialist, as a story of the title character's proud independence and of the empowerment of the nameless plebeians. The play itself returns insistently to the question of the performance of self. So it is perhaps a fitting twist to this history, the braiding together of Shakespeare, Brecht, and Grass, to add a word about the reversal in Günter Grass's own public reputation as a result of the publication of his memoir, *Peeling the Onion*. In it Grass disclosed that he had been a member of the Waffen-SS during World War II. Since he had always been an outspoken critic of the way Germany has dealt with its Nazi past, this belated revelation led some readers to accuse him of hypocrisy or deceit; others regarded the sensationalism as a gimmick to sell copies of his book.[41] In the immediate aftermath of these revelations calls went out for Grass to give back his Nobel Prize in Literature and his honorary citizenship in Gdansk (formerly Danzig), his native city.

The title of Grass's memoir alludes to a famous moment in Henrik Ibsen's *Peer Gynt,* a play about the quest for "self." Peer's search leads, ultimately, to a scene in which he peels an onion, layer by layer, in search of its heart, or ker-nel, or center, only to find that there is none. ("Nature is witty!" he exclaims in despair, tossing the pieces aside.[42]) Grass has said that his mother called him "Peer Gynt" because, like Ibsen's character, he was prone to telling tall stories.[43] What was the "self" of the man who was often called the conscience of postwar Germany?

Grass's rehearsal play seemed to accuse Brecht of complacency, at the least, and self-interest—carefully balancing his response to political events in order to keep his theater, and his art, ongoing. Now reviewers and editorialists accused Grass of dissimulation—and self-interest. "Does this revelation an-nul or impair Grass's work?" asked the *New York Times* editorial page, and promptly answered its own question: "To us, his novels have dramatized the problem of the conscience in history—and especially the battering it took in the 20th century—better than almost any other writer. Everything he has written will now be reread with an ironic eye, but the weight of the work will stand unchanged. With this revelation, Günter Grass has become, in a sense, his own final chapter."[44] So Brecht's ambivalence becomes a Brechtian play, and Grass's past a final chapter. Both are haunted by the story of Coriolanus. "Yet he shall have a noble memory" (5.6.154). As the last words of Shake-speare's play remind us, the last word is never the last word.

FOUR

MACBETH

The Necessity of Interpretation

THROUGHOUT ITS HISTORY, from the seventeenth century to the present, Shakespeare's *Macbeth* has intersected in striking and often disconcerting ways with both political events and stage history. Often, indeed, the two have been combined and conflated, so that it is not entirely certain where history ends and theater begins: as we will see, productions and interpretations of the play have created, as well as reflected, events in the public sphere.

Within the play, when the "weird sisters" appear to Macbeth and Banquo, there is a riddling moment—one of many—when Banquo tries to decipher their identity and their role. "You should be women," he says in surprise and consternation, "and yet your beards forbid me to interpret / That you are so" (1.2.43–45).

Interpretation and its risks and dangers are at the heart of the play, and provide the keyword for *Macbeth* in modern culture. From the witches' prophecies to the "equivocation" invoked by the drunken Porter, ambivalence and double meanings are everywhere on the scene. Equivocation in Shakespeare's time was associated in part with the Jesuit practice of "mental reservation"—saying one thing while holding in reserve another, more private thought or belief. In the seventeenth century, this sometimes led to accusations of treason, espionage, and double-dealing, and could result in a sentence of death.

The patron of Shakespeare's company at this period was King James I, who, as James VI of Scotland, had written a treatise on witchcraft and demonology. James had attended a number of trials of witches, and speculated about why there were more women witches than men. "The reason is easie," he wrote in his treatise, "for as that sexe is frailer than man is."[1] Intrigued by charms and conjurations, as well as by magic and the devil, James noted in particular the dangers of ambiguous messages and riddling language. In more recent years, concepts like ambiguity and undecidability have become central to the practice of literary interpretation, and here too

Macbeth has been an emblematic text. In the play, Macbeth calls the witches "imperfect speakers" because they will not answer all his questions. But in fact they are "imperfect" in another way as well, because their gnomic utterances, apparently so clear, will turn out to be riddles, imperfect in the sense of being unfinished: open, not closed, capable of—and ultimately demanding—further, even multiple, interpretations. This is as true of the play as it is of the witches' prophecies, and, once again, it accords strikingly with the role *Macbeth* has played in modern life.

If we begin in the nineteenth century, and then move to the modern day, what will be evident is the way the play of *Macbeth* crosses boundaries, spilling over from the stage to the street, from the past to an uncanny repetition in history and culture. As we will see, the appearance in the twentieth and twenty-first centuries of new media—including film, television, and 24/7 political journalism—has increased the rapidity and the ubiquity with which this particular Shakespearean play is invoked. The dangers of interpretation are, clearly, linked to its attractions, as was the case for Macbeth, for Banquo, and for Lady Macbeth.

ON MAY 10, 1849, at New York City's Astor Place Opera House there was a bloody riot. Some 22 people were killed, and more than 150 wounded or injured. The cause was a feud between the partisans of two very different actors playing the part of Macbeth—the American Edwin Forrest and the Englishman William Charles Macready.

Forrest's Macbeth was, by all accounts, appealing to the democratic sentiments of the populace. Forrest himself was an outspoken patriot. When his American production of *Macbeth* went to London in 1845, it was hissed at by the English audience. Forrest then actively entered the feud by attending a performance of Macready's *Macbeth* in Edinburgh, and hissing at his rival from a private box.[2] Macready's acting style differed, we are told, greatly from Forrest's—it was more "cerebral," more "aristocratic," appealing to and identifying with the wealthy and the genteel.[3] On May 7 in New York, the two actors had appeared in rival productions of *Macbeth*. Forrest was acclaimed; Macready was booed from the stage. But when the English actor was about to leave the United States he was persuaded, instead, to perform at the Astor Place Opera House. Apparently literary lights like Washington Irving and Herman Melville persuaded him that American audiences would behave.

They did not.

Eighteen hundred people took their seats inside the Opera House; some ten thousand, apparently, massed into the streets outside. The crowd began to storm the theater, the militia was called in, and shots were fired. The press reported this as a class riot, rich versus poor, high versus low.[4] It was a class riot fought over the ownership of Shakespeare. And the play, of course, was *Macbeth*.

Macbeth, as I noted, was also Abraham Lincoln's favorite play. "I think nothing equals *Macbeth*," he wrote to the actor James Henry Hackett.[5] Days before his assassination, in April 1865, he traveled on a steamer from Virginia to Washington, D.C., having just paid a visit to the headquarters of the army. For several hours, Lincoln read passages from *Macbeth* to those on board, including Senator Charles Sumner and a French nobleman, the Marquis de Chambrun. Both Sumner and Chambrun were struck by the fact that Lincoln lingered over Macbeth's lines about Duncan, which, they report, he read twice:[6]

> Duncan is in his grave.
> After life's fitful fever he sleeps well.
> Treason has done his worst. Nor steel, nor poison,
> Malice domestic, foreign levy, nothing
> Can touch him further.
>
> *3.2.24–28*

(Only a month earlier Lincoln had delivered his Second Inaugural Address, which contained the phrase "with malice toward none.")

Within a week of this scene of reading, Lincoln himself was dead, killed on April 15 by an assassin's bullet as he sat in Ford's Theatre with his wife, watching a comedy. His assassin, John Wilkes Booth, was a member of a famous Shakespearean acting company. He had played Mark Antony, one of the conspirators, in a production of *Julius Caesar* the year before, when his brothers played Brutus and Cassius. His brother Edwin became the most famous American Shakespearean actor of his generation.

MACBETH HAS ALWAYS BEEN regarded by actors as unlucky, and many accidents have befallen performers in the play, some of them fairly serious. Actors call it "the Scottish play," refusing to mention its name, especially onstage. Some years ago when I was giving some lectures at the Shakespeare Theatre in Ontario, Canada, an actor was taking a group around for a tour of the playhouse there, and he happened, inadvertently, to pronounce the name of the play while he was standing on the stage. He looked terrified for a moment,

John Wilkes, Edwin, and Junius Brutus Booth, Jr.,
in Julius Caesar

and immediately left the stage, performed one of the prescribed purifying rituals, and then returned.[7] Over the years, many alarming incidents have shadowed "the Scottish play" and its performers: in one production, for example, an actress playing the sleepwalking scene with her eyes closed—for verisimilitude—walked off the stage and fell into the orchestra pit. On more than one occasion, a real weapon was substituted for a stage prop, so that an actual murder took place on the stage.[8] Suffice it to say that the "curse" is strongly believed in by actors today, and that it specifically extends to not quoting the play within the theater (except, of course, when performing it) and to not mentioning the names of the main characters (they can be called "the Thane" and "the Queen," for example, or "Mr. and Mrs. M."). Not only is the play taboo, it also continually performs its taboo nature, since otherwise we would merely set it aside as too dangerous to stage. As with so many risky pleasures, the risk becomes part of the pleasure. When Macbeth is most assured of his inviolability, he is most vulnerable. And this is true for the actor and the audience of *Macbeth* as well.

One classic example of the "curse" at work involves the director Orson Welles. Welles actually staged two famous productions of *Macbeth*. The first, in 1936, became known as the "Voodoo Macbeth." It was performed at the

Lafayette Theater in Harlem, and set in Haiti. Welles's *Macbeth* production was part of the Depression's Federal Theater Project, had an all-black cast of more than one hundred, and was an enormous success. When at the end of the play Hecate says, "the charm's wound up," everybody cheered. Welles was barely twenty-one—and the performance made him famous.[9] In 1948, though, Orson Welles decided to make a film of *Macbeth*. His objective was to make the performance as "authentic" as possible—and so he insisted that his characters speak in a real Scots burr. The film was produced inexpensively and was shot in twenty-three days. The verbal sound track was prerecorded, Scots burr and all. The problem was, once the film had been made, audiences couldn't understand a word of it. So they reissued Welles's *Macbeth* in 1950, redubbing all the actors' lines in BBC accents.[10] A classic "curse" story. It was not until the film was restored, decades later, that the "original" Scots version was reinstated.

TO FIND A REASON or a motive behind behavior that may seem random or unmotivated is one of the interests of psychoanalysis, and it will come as no surprise that *Macbeth* attracted the interest of Sigmund Freud. Freud, whom we have seen to be a knowledgeable reader of Shakespeare, brought his attention to the play in the essay "Some Character-Types Met with in Psycho-Analytic Work" (1916). The title indicates the piece's seeming objective: to describe and categorize real patients in Freud's practice. But in a section on "Those Wrecked by Success" the Macbeths, and particularly Lady Macbeth, make an important appearance.

The general argument about "those wrecked by success" is that the very individuals who ought to feel satisfied that they have achieved their objectives nonetheless set up internal resistances, or self-judgments, which emerge when external obstacles to success are removed. Although he begins by discussing an unidentified patient who has consulted him, Freud, citing reasons of confidentiality, soon switches to the discussion of a fictional "patient," Lady Macbeth. "For the usual reasons," he writes, "I shall not discuss what we know or conjecture on the point in relation to cases of clinical observation, but in relation to figures which great writers have created from the wealth of their knowledge of the mind."[11]

Freud notes that the one hesitation Lady Macbeth seems to manifest is when she sees the sleeping Duncan: "Had he not resembled / My father as he slept, I had done it"—a useful piece of evidence for any analyst interested in his patient's past history and family life.[12] He records the fact that she keeps her composure the banqueting scene, and even lies on behalf of the dismayed Macbeth ("my husband is often thus")—Macbeth, of course, has seen the ghost of Banquo, which she has not. And Freud observes that a change comes over both Macbeth and Lady Macbeth after the murder makes Macbeth king. At this point, Macbeth becomes cold and resolute, where he had been fearful and self-divided; Lady Macbeth is suddenly overcome with doubts and fears, and, more signally, with an internal life, made clear (with brilliant dramatic inventiveness by the playwright) in the sleepwalking scene, where we see and hear her inner thoughts. But what is chiefly significant in this essay are two observations Freud makes toward the close of his treatment of Lady Macbeth: first, that we *cannot know* the motives that have changed Macbeth and Lady Macbeth, since they are fictional characters, figments of the author's imagination, created through the distillation of chronicle and legendary material ("What . . . these motives can have been . . . is in my view impossible to guess"); and second, that it is quite possible that Macbeth and Lady Macbeth are best regarded as split halves of a single character. Thus the themes that seem both to unite them and to distinguish them (inner guilt, bloody hands, remorse or remorselessness) are either/or aspects of a persona: "Together they exhaust the possibilities of reaction to the crime, like two disunited parts of a single psychical individuality, and it may be that they are both copied from a single prototype."[13]

So Freud begins by thinking that a fictional character will be a useful case study comparison for his real-life patients. He then conducts an analysis based upon "evidence" from the fictional patient's own testimony, then decides that such evidence, while internally consistent, is unreliable because the fictional construct is itself unstable and motivated by unknowable (undecidable) outside influences (textual transmission, authorial motives, allegorical and legendary resonances). Finally he decides that the character herself (Lady Macbeth) may well be just a symptom of a split within a larger consciousness of which she might be a constituent part: "In that case it would of course be pointless to regard her as an independent character and seek to discover the motives for her change, without considering the Macbeth who completes her."[14] It is striking that in this analysis Freud himself seems caught by ambivalence and undecidability. At the close of the essay, he will return to "clinical experience" and claim that there is complete agreement between literature and clinical work. But the question of whether the Macbeths are two characters or one remains unresolved, as does the role of literature, and literary interpretation, in the consulting room. Is a literary type a precursor or a reflection of perceived reality?

A few years later, in 1919, Freud returned to the relationship between psychoanalysis and literature in one of his most dazzling and influential pieces of writing, "The Uncanny." In this essay, which has had an enormous effect upon subsequent literary, philosophical, cultural, and film theory, he describes the "uncanny" as something frightening that leads us back to what is known and familiar. The sense of uncanniness (often related to automata, to doubles, to things that seem to have a "life of their own," and to witches, riddles, and prophecies that seem to know more than we do about ourselves) combines the undecidability of origins, motives, and effects with the sense that something is repressed, and returns. In other words, the "uncanny" is an effect of the unconscious, another story, or another scene, which we intuit but do not fully recognize or understand.

As I noted in discussing *Coriolanus,* Freud wants to exclude "the uncanny in *literature*" from his general sense of uncanniness, on the grounds that we accept the fictional conventions and are not therefore disconcerted or destabilized by them. But a play like *Macbeth* precisely challenges those conventions, since neither the central character (Macbeth, confronting the witches) nor his partner (Lady Macbeth, who is a normalized version of those witches) can escape the undecidability of knowing what is true or what is real. "So long as they remain within their setting of poetic reality," Freud writes, figures like ghosts or witches "lose any uncanniness they might possess."

> The souls in Dante's *Inferno,* or the supernatural apparitions in Shakespeare's *Hamlet, Macbeth,* or *Julius Caesar,* may be gloomy and terrible enough, but they are no more really uncanny than Homer's jovial world of gods. We adapt our judgment to the imaginary reality imposed on us by the writer, and regard souls, spirits and ghosts as though their existence had the same validity as our own has in material reality.[15]

In light of the celebrated *Macbeth* "curse" we might wonder if Freud is too certain here about the limits and boundaries of "material reality."

In any case it is not only the apparitions and the "weird sisters" who proclaim them who have sometimes seemed to transgress the space from page or stage ("the imaginary reality imposed upon us by the writer") to real life. Lady Macbeth, the object of Freud's professional as well as his literary scrutiny, has over the years become a powerful cultural type, the imposing, ambitious, and supposedly thwarted woman, a woman who threatened both manhood and womanhood by crossing into "male" space.

The particular kind of interpretation that baffled Banquo, confronted by bearded figures who "should be women," is a version of what is sometimes called "gender undecidability." The plot of *Macbeth* equates these bearded witches with Lady Macbeth, whether she is portrayed as an "unsexed" woman single-mindedly bent on political advantage (the famous "phallic woman" of psychoanalysis)[16] or as a hypersexual seductress.

Lady Macbeth has long occupied this cultural role of the (too-)powerful woman in visual images as well as verbal ones. In an eighteenth-century painting by Johann Zoffany, the Shakespearean actor and theater manager David Garrick, who was relatively short in stature, is shown onstage as Macbeth, dwarfed by his Lady Macbeth, the actress Hannah Pritchard. But this image is respectful and elegant in the extreme, especially when compared to a 1996 political cartoon by Pat Oliphant, in which the Lady Macbeth figure is then–First Lady Hillary Clinton. The theatrical context has entirely disappeared, but the idea of the witchy queen remains.

Comparisons between Hillary Clinton and Lady Macbeth proliferated throughout the period when she was First Lady and resurfaced with her campaign for the presidency—if indeed they ever went below the surface. (I once had a stack of Hillary/Lady Macbeth references an inch thick, which—in a spectacular act of historical shortsightedness—I discarded after the Bill Clin-

Johann Zoffany, David Garrick and Mrs. Pritchard in *Macbeth*

ton years in the White House.) A notorious article in the *American Spectator* described her, in 1992, as "The Lady Macbeth of Little Rock."[17] Although "The Lady Macbeth of Little Rock" article never actually mentions Lady Macbeth, except in the headline, the piece and the epithet were quoted all over the press and the Internet.

Before Hillary Clinton, it was British prime minister Margaret Thatcher who was Lady Macbeth in the public press. "Women, do you want to lead your country . . ." began an essay in *The New York Times*. "Study the progress of Margaret Thatcher. . . . Think of Lady Macbeth. Unsex yourself. Wear battle dress at every opportunity. Do not spare a thought about 'mothers' sons' when ordering men to war. But pity men for their weakness." And so on. You get the idea. "Feminists may dismiss you as an 'honorary man,' the royal family may mutter about your lack of compassion, but abroad you will be an honored guest."[18]

While the categorization of Hillary Clinton as Lady Macbeth did not let up, another candidate for this same position during the Bush years has been Secretary of State Condoleezza Rice. "Fill me from the crown to the toe top—full of direst cruelty" is the *Macbeth* epigraph of an article that made this point. "Secretary Rice has been labeled as the White House's Lady Macbeth–in–residence. Lady Macbeth surpassed her husband in ambition, guile, and ruthlessness. She beguiled and compelled him to assassinate his rivals for the throne of Scotland."[19] And once she became Speaker of the House, Nancy Pelosi got the same Lady M. treatment: in an article criticizing Pelosi for *stressing* the fact that she is a mother and grandmother ("On [the day] she took the gavel as the speaker of the House of Representatives, [she] was escorted to the podium by her six grandchildren, including a sleeping baby she carried in her arms"), a much-circulated article asserts that "Lady Macbeth had a child (act 1, scene 7), but she wouldn't be my first choice to run a country."[20] There seems no reason to drag in Lady Macbeth in a story about "us[ing] . . . womanhood and motherhood as a gimmick"—except that Lady Macbeth has become the modern-day macro for a powerful woman who scares men. The use of Lady Macbeth as caricature, however appropriate or inappropriate in a given political context, suggests something about the way *Macbeth* has lent itself to critique and social satire. Especially in a time of national political crisis—as we saw with Abraham Lincoln—the play seems often to be on, or behind, the scenes. This was especially the case in the decade of the 1960s, a volatile and exciting, but also terrifying, time.

A short list of the events of that era is worth recounting, since many echoes of them would appear, directly or in symbolic form, in a striking version of *Macbeth* that caught the cultural imagination in the latter part of the twentieth century: Barbara Garson's play *MacBird.*

The sixties were witness to a remarkable sequence of political and social developments that seemed to unfold in an unrelenting sequence. The Bay of Pigs invasion in 1961. The Cuban missile crisis in 1962. The assassination of John F. Kennedy on November 22, 1963. The assassination of Malcolm X on February 21, 1965. The assassination of Martin Luther King Jr. on April 4, 1968. The assassination of Robert F. Kennedy on June 6, 1968. The continuing civil rights movement in the American South. The beginning of the Vietnam War. The Free Speech Movement at Berkeley in 1964. The Watts riots in Los Angeles in 1965. The student uprisings in France in May 1968. The riots at the 1968 Democratic convention. Prague Spring, and the Soviet suppression of the uprising in Czechoslovakia. The Woodstock Festival and the Altamont Free Concert in 1969. The Kent State shootings in 1970. Second-wave feminism and the "sexual revolution." Sex, drugs, and rock and roll. Anything seemed possible.

That political assassinations of major U.S. public figures should have been so frequent may appear startling from the perspective of today. When I showed the Zapruder film of the Kennedy assassination to a lecture hall full of students there was absolute and horrified silence. The film is brief; I showed it a second time, and then once more. Many of the undergraduates present had, I was surprised to learn, never seen this film before, although their lives are often dominated by recorded moving images, from DVDs to YouTube. Older people in the audience, of whom there were several, responded—as I did—with memories of where they had been that day. But I was struck by the fact that this visual document, so familiar as to have become in my lifetime a monumental record of an unforgettable moment, was for some who watched it a new—and newly terrible—experience. The relevant point here is not just that time passes, or that 1963 has somehow become almost half a century ago. What I want to underscore, instead, is that for my students this event was "history"—like the history of medieval Scotland or of Jacobean England. Their encounter with it came, because of the way I presented it to them, as a secondary effect, a "source" for the play, *MacBird,* which we are about to consider. Until, of course, they saw the 26.6 seconds of Abraham Zapruder's home movie, intended to capture the joyous occasion of a presidential visit to the city where he lived.

The scene is Dealey Plaza in Dallas, Texas; the time is 12:30 p.m. Central Standard Time on November 22, 1963. President John F. Kennedy receives a fatal gunshot wound to the head while riding in a presidential motorcade. Then came the arrest of Lee Harvey Oswald, and, two days later, on November 24, Oswald's own death, when he was shot and killed by Jack Ruby on live television as the nation watched. From that time to this, conspiracy theories have abounded. Less than a week later, on November 29, the new president, Lyndon Johnson, appointed a commission to investigate the assassination of President Kennedy. Headed by Chief Justice Earl Warren, the commission found that Lee Harvey Oswald had acted alone.

In Barbara Garson's passionate and literate satire, Warren appears as "The Earl of Warren"—a witty inversion that uses his (very American) first name as a title, since Shakespeare's plays have earls in them. This coinage led to the other, comical titles in *MacBird:* the Egg of Head (for egghead Adlai Steven-

*Film still, from the Zapruder film of the assassination
of President John F. Kennedy*

son), and the Wayne of Morse (for Senator Wayne Morse, one of only two U.S. senators to vote against the 1964 Gulf of Tonkin Resolution that authorized further U.S. involvement in the Vietnam War).[21] Bobby Kennedy, who was attorney general in his brother's administration, is in this play the Lord of Laws.

Like all topical social satire, this play (like the satires of Pope and Swift in the eighteenth century, or of *Borat*, the *Colbert Report*, *The Simpsons*, or *Doonesbury* in the twenty-first century) requires us to know something about the people and events being satirized. We need a kind of social glossary to know, for example, that the "Miss Moya" to whom MacBird speaks on the telephone, saying "Okay, Miss Moya, send the newsmen in," is a send-up of Bill Moyers, the newsman who was a special assistant to President Lyndon Johnson from 1963 to 1967.[22] Moyers was a chief architect of the Great Society, Johnson's domestic social program for eliminating poverty and racial injustice. The Great Society is itself satirized, and parodied, in *MacBird* as the "Smooth Society," announced in MacBird's own "I have a dream" speech:

> My Smooth Society has room for all;
> For each, a house, a car, a family,
> A private psychoanalyst, a dog,
> And rows of gardens, neatly trimmed and hedged.[23]

As this will begin to suggest, *MacBird* is not only a satire but also a *parody* and a *burlesque,* basing itself on a "great" work of literature and registering that work's difference from modernity. Blank parody, parody that is not necessarily meant to be humorous, is one of the great twentieth-century art forms, following the pattern of what the anthropologist Claude Lévi-Strauss called "bricolage," a work of art created from whatever odds and ends happen to be available.

But *MacBird* itself *was* clearly intended to be humorous, in an urgent, political way. The author, Barbara Garson, was an activist at Berkeley in the sixties, working with Mario Savio and the Free Speech movement. The story goes that when Garson was addressing an antiwar rally in 1965 she accidentally misspoke, calling the wife of the then-president "Lady MacBird Johnson"[24] (rather than "Lady Bird" Johnson; Mrs. Johnson's given name was Claudia, but as a child she was described as being "as pretty as a ladybird," and the nickname stuck; all the members of the president's family had names that gave them the initials LBJ: the daughters were Lynda Bird and Luci Baines).

The slip of the tongue led to the idea of a play based on *Macbeth,* Shakespeare's play of assassination and insurrection. The time—August 1965—was just after the Watts riots and the attempt on the part of the Vietnam Day

Committee to stop a troop train in Berkeley—hence the play's first line, spoken by the three witches, a beatnik, a well-dressed black man, and an old leftist:

> When shall we three meet again?
>   In riot!
>   Strike!
>   Or stopping train!²⁵

Barbara Garson self-published the play, initially through the Independent Socialist Club in Berkeley, before an expanded edition was published by the Grassy Knoll Press (a wry reference to the place from which came the shots that killed John Kennedy). The play sold some 200,000 copies, and in 1977 it was produced on Broadway starring Stacy Keach, William Devane, Cleavon Little, and Rue McClanahan. More than a social or political phenomenon, *MacBird* is a remarkably literate and literary play. The better you know Shakespeare, the more you can appreciate its wit, and the way in which it incorporates many other plays in addition to *Macbeth* under the guise of a (deceptively) simple parody. Because of its historical timeliness and its some-times broad political humor, *MacBird* is more often cited than read. But it is well worth reading, and in what follows I will, by taking some time with its details, try to show how it works as a play, as an intervention in public cul-ture, and as a reading of Shakespeare.

MacBird opens with a prologue clearly based on Shakespeare's famous pro-logue to the first act of *Henry V.* But in this case things are comically reversed: invoking a "fireless Muse" rather than a "Muse of fire," the Prologue tells us that "our warlike leaders" should "*not* appear / Upon this stage in false resem-blances," and, instead of the audience being implored and invited to use its own imagination to piece out the events on the stage, we are told to do the opposite:

> O, don't employ your own imaginations
> To piece out imperfections in our plot. . . .
> Your very lack of thoughts must cloak our kings.²⁶

And so on to the play itself, set at the Democratic National Convention. This is, of course, before the assassination—the plot follows that of *Macbeth.* The Ken O'Dunc brothers (John, Robert, and Teddy) are conferring about their expected dynasty. Bobby is a schemer, Teddy infantile. Unfortunately they need MacBird (Lyndon Johnson) to bring in the southern and western votes, and so they decide with distaste and reluctance to offer him the vice presidential nomination. The three witches, on cue, encounter MacBird and his Crony, and hail them:

> All hail MacBird! All hail the Senate's leader.
> All hail MacBird, Vice President thou art.
> All hail MacBird, that shall be President![27]

The language closely follows the *Macbeth* plot, where Macbeth is about to become Thane of Cawdor, though he doesn't yet know it:

> FIRST WITCH All hail, Macbeth! Hail to thee, Thane of Glamis.
> SECOND WITCH All hail, Macbeth! Hail to thee, Thane of Cawdor.
> THIRD WITCH All hail, Macbeth! That shalt be king hereafter.
>
> *1.3.46–48*

Garson builds into her parody a number of famous set pieces drawn from other plays. John of Gaunt's celebrated "this England" speech from *Richard II* ("this earth of majesty, this seat of Mars . . .") is adapted to make John Ken O'Dunc predict the "New Frontier," while promising the presidential succession to "Bob . . . and Ted . . . and princes yet unborn."[28] Polonius's "Neither a borrower nor a lender be" speech becomes the advice of the oldest witch to a younger one:

> Be thou militant but by no means adventurist . . .
> Neither a burrower from within nor a leader be,
> But stone by stone construct a conscious cadre,
> And this above all—to thine own class be true
> And it must follow, as the very next depression,
> That thou canst not be false to revolution.[29]

MacBird, the Lyndon Johnson figure, speaks contemptuously of the too elegant, too handsome John Ken O'Dunc in a splendid version of Richard III's "Now is the winter of our discontent" speech, cataloging all the things that make such a "princeling" a lightweight:

> Grim-visaged politics has smoothed his face;
> Our manly wars give way to mincing words . . .
> He capers nimbly at a yachting party.[30]

And so on, only to be interrupted by the appearance of John himself, whom he greets heartily and invites to a Texas reception (we feel the foreboding of how that will turn out):

Well, how about that meeting on my ranch? . . .
My wife and I intend a bang-up show.
We'll hold a grand procession through the streets
So you can meet the people of my state.
You'll ride in rich regalia through the throng,
And feel the warmth and frenzy of their love.[31]

After the assassination, the Egg of Head (Lord Stevenson) echoes Ophelia far more closely than the old witch echoed Polonius:

Oh what a noble mind was here brought down!
The statesman's, soldier's, scholar's eye, tongue, sword,
The expectancy and rose of the fair state,
The glass of fashion and the mold of form,
Supreme in war and thus our hope for peace,
The believed of all believers—quite, quite dead.[32]

The assassination scene itself is set forth in what is called stichomythia— lines or half lines of verse spoken by alternating speakers, a technique often used by Shakespeare to show discovery and dismay. In *Macbeth* we hear exactly such a decrescendo when Macbeth reports to Lady Macbeth that he has "done the deed"—that is, killed King Duncan:

MACBETH   I have done the deed. Didst thou not hear a noise?
LADY MACBETH   I heard the owl scream, and the crickets cry.
    Did not you speak?
MACBETH   When?
LADY MACBETH   Now.
MACBETH   As I descended?
LADY MACBETH   Ay.
MACBETH   Hark!—Who lies i' th' second chamber?
                                        2.2.14–17

In *MacBird* this same blank horror attends the crowd's account of the Ken O'Dunc assassination, accompanied by a slideshow of the Texas Book Depository, the Grassy Knoll, the Railroad Overpass, and other now famous, iconic locations:

1ST VOICE   Oh, no!
2ND VOICE   Can't be!
3RD VOICE   They've shot the President!
5TH VOICE   Oh, piteous sight!
1ST VOICE   Oh, noble Ken O'Dunc!

2ND VOICE	Oh, woeful scene!
6TH VOICE	Oh, traitorous villainy!
2ND VOICE	They shot from there.
1ST VOICE	No, that way.
3RD VOICE	Did you see?
4TH VOICE	Let's get the facts. Let's go and watch TV.[33]

The bathos is deliberate—and the effect appalling.

The hand-washing moment from Lady Macbeth's sleepwalking scene—"out damn'd spot, out I say"—is deftly adapted to incorporate Lady Bird Johnson's famous commitment to the beautification of highways, as Lady MacBird enters, distraught, carrying a giant bouquet of flowers, followed by her two daughters with aerosol sprays:

LADY MACBIRD Here's the smell. Out, out damned odor, out!
    The smell of blood is still within my nostrils.
. . . .
DAUGHTER 1 She's been this way or worse for several days now.
DAUGHTER 2 We have to follow after her with air-wick,
    For every several steps she stops and sniffs
    And crying out, "There's blood upon this spot!,"
    She makes us spray to mask the phantom smell.[34]

The daughters go on to comment that "everywhere she goes she carries flowers," and Lady MacBird herself mutters distractedly, "flowers by the roadside . . . plant these flowers. . . . Yet all the petals of a summer's roses / Can never sweeten this accursèd land."

        Be calm, sweet bird. She's often like this . . . nerves . . .
        To ease your frenzied wits, we will decree
        That all our highways shall be lined with flowers.[35]

The sequence *odor/air-wick/flowers/highways* as it unfolds here is unexpected and clever. What begins as apparently a simple sight gag quickly turns itself into a mini-history of overcompensation.

The cauldron scene (adapted from act 4, scene 1 of Macbeth) is brilliant—all too raw and pertinent, with its painful chanting of what goes into the witches' "protest pot."[36] "Picket, sit-in, strike, and stir," chants the first witch (the college beatnik); "Bombed-out church and burning cross," chants the second witch (the African American); and "Sizzling skin of napalmed child," chants the third witch, reciting a horror from the Vietnam War.

And the final prophecies, the ones that MacBird, like Macbeth, thinks cannot possibly come true, involve a time "when burning wood doth come to Washington":

> No man with beating heart or human blood
> Shall ever harm MacBird or touch his throne.[37]

"Then Bobby, live!" exclaims MacBird in relief. "What fear have I from thee?"

But, as it turns out, these prophecies are—like those in *Macbeth*—uncanny riddles that tell the truth in the guise of an impossibility. The cherry trees in Washington are torched by rioters, so that burning wood does indeed come to Washington, and as for the man without a heart, Robert Ken O'Dunc reveals that the brothers—all but the hapless Teddy—were drained of blood by their ambitious father, "to free his sons from paralyzing scruples / And temper us for roles of world authority."

In fact, the Ken O'Duncs are heartless and bloodless. The prophecy comes true, MacBird dies of a heart attack ("thus cracks a noble heart"), and Bobby seizes the banners and the policies of the person he calls his "great predecessor," in order to hew out "the Smooth Society." The play ends with a typical Shakespearean couplet, the kind we find so often at the ends of tragedies:

> So, choked with grief, I pledge my solemn word
> To lift aloft the banner of MacBird.[38]

SOME IRONIES, HOWEVER, Barbara Garson could not have foreseen in 1966. She could not have imagined the assassination of Robert Kennedy in 1968, or, some forty years later, the uncanny return of the repressed in another Texas occupant of the White House and his own preference for his ranch and his disdain for eastern frippery. Not to mention the return of war and its victims. Double, double, toil and trouble.

If we learn anything from these repetitions, it is that the past refuses to stay in the past. In the spring of 2008 Hillary Clinton, that "Lady Macbeth of Little Rock," defended her decision to stay in the Democratic primary race through June by citing an unexpected event that changed the outcome in 1968: "We all remember Bobby Kennedy was assassinated in June in California."[39] Despite Clinton's immediate explanation and amplification—her intention, she said, was just to point out that campaigns are long and that circumstances may change without warning—the outcry was quick and loud.

One commentator described it as "Sick. Disgusting. And yet revealing. Hillary Clinton is staying in the race in the event some nut kills Barack Obama. . . . We have seen an X-ray of a very dark soul. One consumed by raw ambition to where the possible assassination of an opponent is something to ponder in a strategic way. Otherwise, why is murder on her mind?"[40] Whether Clinton's remark was the result of weariness, careless phrasing, or the disclosure of an unconscious half-wish (all motives put forward by pundits who pounced on her comment), the public outcry made clear that these assassinations were part of the *nation's* unconscious, and that repetition (JFK, Martin Luther King Jr., RFK) had brought them to the double status of a *plot*—at once a conspiracy and a narrative.

MACBIRD WAS, IN ITS OWN TIME, a cultural sensation. I've cited just a few of the many instances of passages and quotations from Shakespeare plays other than *Macbeth* within this capacious text (*Richard II, Richard III, Julius Caesar, Hamlet*). Each of these has its pertinence: *Julius Caesar* is also about an assassination, *Richard II* about the deposition of a king, *Hamlet* about a king's murder, *Richard III* about a jealous opportunist who manages to seize the crown. Each of them, that is to say, could have been the "host," or the framing device, for a Shakespearean parody about the Kennedy family, the Kennedy assassination, and the rise and fall of Lyndon Baines Johnson. But the choice of *Macbeth* is not really a choice, but rather an inevitability. It is, as we've seen, the Shakespearean play of uncanniness. Among the play's many painful—and powerful—elements is the insistence upon the return of the repressed. And what is repressed and returns in *MacBird* is not only the story, but also the underlying issues: inequity, poverty, rage, corruption, deceit, and war. What makes the witches' prophecies come true is the anger in the streets, and the cynicism of political education. The burning trees of Washington, and the political candidate trained to be without a heart.

If you want to see heartlessness, though, you might have a quick—very quick—look at a parody of this parody, a work called *Macbill,* written by Ronald Wilcox in 1998 about the Clintons.[41] Wilcox nowhere acknowledges that he is borrowing from Barbara Garson or *MacBird,* although his cast of characters includes:

Lady Macbill, Hillary of Rodham
Vincent of Foster, Earl of Defender
Starr, High Sheriff of Fax

Carville the Clown, Master of Spin
And
Sir George the Younger, Double-Ewe of Bush[42]

The three witches, the first one of whom is named—what else?—Monica,
ask:

When shall we three meet again?
In Subpoena, Summons, or Internet of Woe?
. . . .
When the Hurlyburly Inquiry's done.
When the Impeachment's lost and won.
. . . .
That will be at the quest of Starr.[43]

MACBIRD, WHICH TOOK SORROWFUL note of a national tragedy (and
quoted parts of Kennedy's inaugural address among the snippets of Shakespeare), seems almost benign when we compare it to the occasion that
produced Roman Polanski's 1971 film of *Macbeth.* For that occasion was a
set of senseless murders committed by Charles Manson and the women of
Manson's "family," including three—Susan Atkins, Patricia Krenwinkel, and
Linda Kasabian—who participated in the murder of Sharon Tate, Roman
Polanski's pregnant wife, at her house in the Bel Air section of Los Angeles.
Three other people were also killed. The next night the same group, plus Manson and a couple of others, also attacked and killed Leo and Rosemary LaBi-
anca, writing—and misspelling—the Manson Family credo, "Helter Skelter,"
in blood on the refrigerator door. Written on the porch of Sharon Tate's house,
in her blood, had been the word "Pig." The Manson "Family"—dominated by
the charismatic Charles, who regarded himself as a master and savior—were
high on drugs, including hallucinogens, and regarded these killings as the
beginning of a revolution.

When his wife was murdered Roman Polanski was in London, working on
a film, *The Day of the Dolphin.* He abandoned that project and flew to Los
Angeles, where he was photographed by *Life* magazine in the doorway of his
house, the path stained with blood. Polanski consulted psychics, hoping to
find clues to the murderers and their motives. He also determined upon a
new film project, a version of Shakespeare's *Macbeth,* with a screenplay written in collaboration with critic and writer Kenneth Tynan, the author of *Oh!
Calcutta!* Some of the financial backing for the film came from Hugh Hefner,

which produced a tendency—on the part of scholars as well as the general public—to call it "the *Playboy Macbeth*." But Polanski tried to distance himself from this sponsor, and his version of Shakespeare is no mansion romp.

The film is violent, powerful, and beautiful, with a number of scenes imagined as if the viewer were himself or herself on hallucinogens. The actors playing Macbeth and Lady Macbeth were much younger than is customary. Francesca Annis, at age twenty-six, was an atypical, sensual, and capricious Lady Macbeth; Polanski had her perform the sleepwalking scene in the nude. Jon Finch was a young Macbeth; neither conformed to stereotype, and Polanski was quoted as saying that "directors always present Lady Macbeth as a nagging bitch."

As a sidebar to this discussion, but one not without interest, I should point out that Lady Macbeth's career in modern culture here takes a forking path: in films and on the stage she has become more glamorous than in the recent past, while in the press, and as a cultural analogy—"the Lady Macbeth of Little Rock"—she has become an ambitious, often desexualized woman, envious and desirous of "male" power, a living caricature.

Two scenes from Polanski's film are especially worth our interest. The first is the scene of the slaughter of Macduff's family, the second, the play's—and film's—final scene.

The slaughter scene in *Macbeth* tells its own tale. Bloody, graphic, and nightmarish, it is the Tate-LaBianca murders uncannily retold. We experience it twice: once directly, once, equally painfully, through Macduff's slow coming to awareness of his incalculable loss:

> MACDUFF How does my wife?
> ROSS Why, well.
> MACDUFF And all my children?
> ROSS Well, too.
> MACDUFF The tyrant has not battered at their peace?
> ROSS No, they were well at peace when I did leave 'em.
>   *4.3.177–80*

It takes several more lines before Ross can be persuaded to tell his news:

> ROSS But I have words,
>   That would be howled out in the desert air
>   Where hearing should not latch them.
> MACDUFF . . . is it a fee-grief
>   Due to some single breast?

> ROSS No mind that's honest
>   But in it shares some woe, though the main part
>   Pertains to you alone.
>
>   *4.3.194–200*

The suspense is drawn out, as Ross begs pardon in advance—"Let not your ears despise my tongue forever."

And as Macduff guesses the news, the audience relives the horror that it experienced in watching the slaughter:

> ROSS Your castle is surprised, your wife and babes
>   Savagely slaughtered. To relate the manner
>   Were on the quarry of these murdered deer
>   To add the death of you.
>   . . . .
> MACDUFF My children too?
> ROSS   Wife, children, servants, all
>   That could be found.
> MACDUFF My wife killed too?
> ROSS   I have said.
>   . . . .
> MACDUFF He has no children. All my pretty ones?
>   . . . .
>   What, all my pretty chickens and their dam
>   At one fell swoop?
>
>   *4.3.205–20*

The second scene in Polanski's *Macbeth* that is worth special notice takes place at the end of the film, when he omits, completely, the final speech of Malcolm, the new king, and replaces it with a silent scene in which Donalbain, the second son, seeks out the witches' hovel. So instead of resolution and transformation, we have repetition.

Malcolm's speech had offered two kinds of change, official (state) and personal:

>   My thanes and kinsmen,
>   Henceforth be earls, the first that ever Scotland
>   In such an honour named. What's more to do,
>   Which would be planted newly with the time,
>   As calling home our exiled friends abroad,
>   That fled the snares of watchful tyranny,
>   Producing forth the cruel ministers

Of this dead butcher and his fiend-like queen—
Who, as 'tis thought, by self and violent hands
Took off her life—this and what needful else
That calls upon us, by the grace of grace
We will perform in measure, time, and place.
So thanks to all at once, and to each one,
Whom we invite to see us crowned at Scone.

5.11.28–41

Where the beginning of the play had centered on uncanny repetition (one traitorous Thane of Cawdor replaces another traitorous Thane of Cawdor; double, double, toil and trouble—the first line of the play is "when shall we three meet *again?*"), this resolution seems to turn a circle into a triumphant upward line (no more thanes, thus no more traitorous ones)—the mistakes Duncan made by being too soft, too unwatchful, finding the mind's construction in the face (taking things, and people, at face value) would not be repeated by his more cautious, less trusting son, who tests his men with false claims of sinfulness. The traditional Shakespearean ending points toward a notional sixth act offstage ("What's more to do, / Which would be planted newly with the time . . . We will perform in measure, time, and place") and so off to the coronation place at Scone.

But in Roman Polanski's version the circle is back—there is no escape from repetition. Donalbain returns to the witches, presumably to ask what the future holds in store for *him* after his brother Malcolm's ascendancy. Just as the mirrors within mirrors (the "perspective glass" with the show of eight kings) offered an endless enfilade, so here what is mirrored, reflected, is the past repeating itself. The film begins again, rather than ending. Act 6 will be act 1, as another jealous rival seeks supernatural help in gaining the throne. The timeliness of *Macbeth* as a play is always this untimeliness, untimely ripped from the headlines.

Macbeth in modern culture is in the position of Donalbain in the Polanski film—and of the witches at the beginning of the play, with their promise to "meet again." Over and over again, tomorrow and tomorrow, it shows that history and modernity are artifacts of uncontrollable recurrence. Whatever the tomorrows and yesterdays bring, the play is already there before us. What it prophesies is itself.

FIVE

RICHARD III

The Problem of Fact

WHICH IS MORE POWERFUL, fact or fiction?

If any era should be aware of the temptations to rewrite history, it is our own. Every day we meet up with new examples, from the relatively trivial to the profoundly serious. Saddam Hussein was said to be behind the World Trade Center bombings.

Saddam Hussein

Iraq was said to be harboring weapons of mass destruction. Former pro football player Pat Tillman was said to have been killed in combat; it was later revealed that he was killed by "friendly fire."[1] Jessica Lynch was said to have fought off her attackers with a gun during an Iraqi ambush; a made-for-TV program presented her as a hero. Lynch, who had nothing to do with this representation, and who was seriously wounded in the attack, said that she remained "confused as to why they chose to lie."[2] Mao Zedong, who for so long dominated Chinese politics, has now—to quote an article in *The New York Times*—been "airbrushed out of history."[3]

Mao Zedong

James Frey, the author of *A Million Little Pieces,* a best-selling "memoir" about his experiences with addiction and prison, turned out to have fabricated much of it. Oprah Winfrey, who had chosen the book for her book club, expressed her dismay. The Smoking Gun Web site called it "A Million Little Lies."[4] "I've never denied that I altered small details," said Frey.[5] "Spinning" news stories has become part of the practice of politics and public relations. John Kerry, a war hero in Vietnam, was "Swiftboated," his military service and patriotism criticized. "Spinmeisters" are hired by politicians as a matter of course to get out the messages they want and to suppress those that show them in an unfavorable light. Attack tactics, demonizing the opposition, "Borking," the "politics of personal destruction"—all of these are commonplaces of our recent political life.

When the Pulitzer Prize–winning journalist and author David Halberstam was killed in a traffic accident in 2007, many people in the press and in public life spoke out about his contributions to their fields. Columnist Bob Herbert took the occasion not only to praise Halberstam as an example and a model, but also to reflect upon questions of truth and falsehood. "If there was one thing above all else that David taught us," Herbert wrote, "it was to be skeptical of official accounts, to stay always on guard against the lies, fabrications, half-truths, misrepresentations, exaggerations and all other manifestations of falsehood that are fired at us like machine-gun bullets by government officials and others in high places, often with lethal results. 'You have to keep digging,' he would say, 'keep asking questions, because otherwise you'll be seduced or brainwashed into the idea that it's somehow a great privilege, and honor, to report the lies they've been feeding you.' "[6]

Which is more powerful, fact or fiction?

Shakespeare's play *The Tragedy of Richard III* is an eloquent testament to the power of fiction-making for two reasons, one dating to his time, the other to ours: first, because of the rewriting of history by historians in the early modern period; and second, because the history of this period many people know today is derived, in fact, from the plays of Shakespeare. The facts modern audiences know about Richard are the fictions invented by politicians and courtiers.

Shakespeare wrote and performed his plays in the time of Queen Elizabeth, the daughter of Henry VIII and the granddaughter of Henry VII, otherwise known as Henry Tudor, the Earl of Richmond. It was in the interest of the Tudors to delegitimize Richard's claim to the throne and to describe him as an unfit and unworthy king—since his claim was actually stronger than that of Henry VII. So historians attached to the Tudor court had a political job to do. The character of Richard III was rewritten by historians like Sir Thomas More into the literal embodiment of evil, his misshapen body (not attested to by other historical sources) used as a visual metaphor for his twisted mind.

Thomas More described Richard as "little of stature," "ill-featured of limb, crook-backed . . . hard-favored of visage" (and *therefore,* by some sleight of logic, deceptive and cruel).[7] None of this seems to be true. Portrait and other evidence suggest quite a different picture, including Richard's success as a general in the field, and his dedication to (rather than enmity toward) his family. The historical Richard was not a hunchback and did not have a withered arm. So far as we know, he was not born with a full set of teeth, nor (it seems relatively certain) was he carried for two years in his mother's womb before his birth. In this sense Richard III—Shakespeare's Richard III, one of the most remarkable dramatic characters ever produced—is a fiction.

But the political imagination that produced him was not, or not only, Shakespeare's. Thomas More, Polydore Vergil (an official historian for Henry VII), and a number of other interested parties contributed to this story. Their Richard is, by some counts at least, a monster: someone who would readily murder his nephews, the princes in the Tower.

Still, Shakespeare's Richard is different both from the one-dimensional monster of the Tudor historians, and the splendid general and loving family man of the modern Ricardian revisionists. And it is Shakespeare's Richard who seems to have won the day: a charismatic villain, sexy, super-articulate, flirtatious and seductive with the audience as well as with the Lady Anne. Should we care whether his story is "true" or not?

The debate about truth and fiction, truth and lying, truth and interpretation, is staged within the play—and indeed, within Richard's own soliloquies from the beginning of the play to the end. In this way Shakespeare can be seen to have *anticipated* the tension between fact and fiction that troubles modern-day commentators: it is that very tension that animates both Richard III and his play.

IN A DEVELOPMENT THAT was almost inevitable for this most famous and popular of plays, Shakespeare's *Richard III* was rewritten ("improved") for the stage by the eighteenth-century writer Colley Cibber, who made Richard into a one-dimensional, opportunistic, and ambitious villain, omitting, in the process, the characters of Clarence, Hastings, Margaret, and Edward IV. The Colley Cibber version was the only one staged in England from 1700 until the late nineteenth century, when Henry Irving restored some of Shakespeare's text in 1877.[8]

But from that time to this the literary character has triumphed over the rewriting of history with defenders and analysts of Richard, from Sigmund Freud to Helen Hayes, well into the present day.

Cibber's instinct for correcting Shakespeare was more recently exhibited in Al Pacino's film *Looking for Richard*.[9] The actors express their puzzlement about why the prophecy Clarence mentions should involve the letter *G,* since his name is Clarence. They don't realize that his first name is George, and that "Clarence" is his title. Therefore, to clarify the matter for the audience, they alter the Shakespeare text so that it refers to a prophecy about the letter *C* rather than *G*—thus neatly excising the playwright's deft dramatic irony, since *G* is an initial that fits Richard, Duke of Gloucester, as well as it does George, Duke of Clarence.

The appeal of Richard's character to the contemporary imagination has produced a number of timely comparisons with figures in political life in the past century. Thus, for example, W. H. Auden began his lecture on *Richard III* at the New School in 1946 by comparing Richard's opening soliloquy ("Now is the winter of our discontent") to a speech by Adolf Hitler.[10] During the presidency of Richard Nixon, analogies between one ill-fated Ricardian rule and the other were fairly commonplace. The journalist Molly Ivins recalled "a certain Richard III grandeur to Nixon's collapse because he was also a man of notable talents."[11] And during the aftermath of the 2000 election campaign, when he lost the nomination to George W. Bush, John McCain was compared to a "modern-day Richard III, consumed with bitterness and in pursuit of power at all costs."[12] The modernity of Richard's character is built into the structure of the play. Richard's actions and thoughts, dramatized through the theatrical device of the soliloquy—confiding in his audience, making them his accomplices—make him one of the most familiar and recognizable of Shakespeare's characters, a model not only for psychological complexity but also for the playwright as coiner of "plots."

"Plots have I laid, inductions dangerous," he says in his opening soliloquy. And a "plot" in this period was a *map,* a *plan,* a *scheme,* a *conspiracy,* and a *story line,* related at once to fact and to fiction. A *plot* in literary terms is the arrangement of events in a narrative to engage the attention of the reader—or viewer—and to arouse suspense or anxiety, utilizing elements of characterization, symbol, and conflict. It differs—as narrative theorists have argued— from *story,* in that the events in what is called *story* are chronological, but the details of a *plot* are told selectively, to produce a sense of causality as well as of suspense. The classic explanation of this comes from E. M. Forster's *Aspects of the Novel:* " 'The king died and the queen died' is a story. 'The king died and then the queen died of grief' is a plot."[13]

The earliest reference in the *Oxford English Dictionary* for the word "plot" in the other sense, as "a conspiracy to achieve an unlawful end," comes from the historian Polydore Vergil, who served King Henry VII, and who seems to have begun the narrative of the wicked Richard III (circa 1550).[14]

In this case, then, history and fiction, fictional history and historical fiction, seem to have emerged and developed together. That a "plot" should be both a conspiracy and a story line is not an accidental connection. It says something—something crucial, something fascinating—about the way in which Shakespeare's *Richard III*, again, both the character and the play, catches hold of the critical imagination.

Richard's startling modernity emerges out of his intimacy with us, apparently up close and personal. The audience is given a vivid sense of his interior struggles, his private thoughts, and his constant awareness of his own social performance. This effect is achieved not by some transcendent insight into the universality of human nature, but rather by a skillful and innovative use of a specific theatrical device, the soliloquy. We might compare this breakthrough to other "technological" advances in later eras, like the invention of photography and its effect upon painted portraits and landscapes, the advent of sound or color in film, or the "shot reverse shot" film technique in which one character is shown looking (usually offscreen) at another character, and then the other character is shown looking "back," so that the effect is to persuade the viewer that they are looking at each other.[15] Documentary interviews utilize a version of this same technique, sometimes shooting the interview first, then interposing an interviewer's question or comment after the fact, to create the impression of a continuous flow of conversation.

Shakespeare is not the only playwright of his time to use the soliloquy in this fashion, to impart a sense of "roundedness" and interiority to a character, but his use is surely among the most effective. Thus for example the famous opening line of *Richard III*, "Now is the winter of our discontent," set out a double frame of reference from the beginning. The line is enjambed—its sense carries over to the next line—and the second line "takes back" what seems to be the overt meaning of the first:

> Now is the winter of our discontent
> Made glorious summer by this son of York.
> *I.I.I–2*

The first line seems for a moment to be declarative and confessional: *now*— "at the present moment"—we, or I, are, or am, discontented. But the second line rewrites or recasts the meaning of *now* retrospectively, turning it into a word that means "in view of what has happened." Instead of "now I am discontented" we get "we [the Yorkist faction in England] used to be discontented but now we are pleased." But in fact, of course, the audience hears both, gets both: I ought to be contented, but in fact (I am telling you privately) I am not. The effect is one of interior disclosure. Nothing makes us believe we are actually in touch with the "reality" of a character like encountering both inner conflict and secret motives. A third meaning of *now* also lurks behind the speech, one from legal practice or debate: "introducing an important or noteworthy point in an argument."[16] Richard's soliloquy, as it unfolds, will take on the shape of a legal argument ("Now"; "But"; "And therefore" [1.1.1; 14; 28]), with the "logical" outcome his determination "to prove a villain" (30), "to hate the idle pleasure of these days" (31), and to set his two brothers, King Edward and the Duke of Clarence, "in deadly hate the one against the other" (35). Richard does this with confidence, because he is secure in his sense of comparative psychology: "And if King Edward be as true and just / As I am subtle false and treacherous" (1.1.36–37). The betrayal of the hapless George, Duke of Clarence, will take place on schedule. And indeed, on schedule, Clarence arrives onstage, "guarded" and under arrest: "Dive, thoughts, down to my soul," says Richard, "here Clarence comes" (41).

To whom is he speaking? To himself and to us, the audience, who have already become his confidants and coconspirators. It is a measure of the enormous effectiveness of this device that we do not experience it as artificial (why say these things out loud?), but rather as "natural." I do not mean any disrespect to Shakespeare when I say that in moments like this we can see the inception of—or, better, a forerunner of—both modern "war room" politics and tabloid television. The amount of risk, dare, and self-exposure produced by the soliloquy when it is aligned to a personality type (or theatrical convention) like Richard, at once self-advertising and self-protective, manipulative and narcissistic, makes for "good theater" both on and beyond the stage.

THE ELIZABETHAN STAGE HAD developed this persona as the type of the "Machiavel" (a schemer and politically ambitious man, patterned loosely after an Elizabethan understanding of Machiavelli's *The Prince*). Shakespeare puts the word into Richard's own mouth in a soliloquy in *Henry VI, Part 3,* the play that precedes *Richard III* in the "first tetralogy," his four early history plays about the Lancasters and the Yorks (*Henry VI, Parts 1, 2,* and *3,* and *Richard III*). With unerring theatrical instinct Laurence Olivier seized upon this speech as the first "revelation" of Richard's interior character, and grafted it onto his own production, the entry into both Richard's "plots" (*Richard III* 1.1.32) and Shakespeare's.

> Why, I can smile, and murder whiles I smile,
> And cry "Content!" to that which grieves my heart,
> And wet my cheeks with artificial tears,
> And frame my face to all occasions.
> . . . .
> I can add colours to the chameleon,
> Change shapes with Proteus for advantages,
> And set the murderous Machiavel to school.
> Can I do this, and cannot get a crown?
> Tut, were it farther off, I'll pluck it down.
> *3 Henry VI 3.2.182–95*

Not only is he a Machiavel, a stock Elizabethan villain, he is also a Vice, a figure derived from the old morality plays. At one point he says, to good comic—and deconstructive—effect, "Thus, like the formal Vice, Iniquity, / I moralize two meanings in one word" (3.1.82–83). His language is deceptive, witty, double-edged.

Again, much of this effect derives from the device of the soliloquy, which enables him to confide in us while fooling, and gulling, the dupes onstage. (Are we dupes too? Which position, which forced casting, does the audience prefer—to be dupes or coconspirators?)

Not all soliloquies have the same function. Hamlet's soliloquies, as they have been performed over the years, have given credence to the idea that he represents the apotheosis of human self-reflection, and thus of the qualities we like to think of as characterizing "humanity," among them the capacity for self-questioning and the instinct to philosophize or speculate. Richard of Gloucester's soliloquies—especially those spoken before he becomes King Richard, when he will try to consolidate his inner and outer voices in the service of political power—show us something different, although something that could with equal persuasiveness be described as something "human": manipulation, calculation, self-division as a strategy rather than a metaphysical condition. In both cases we need to bear in mind that the effect of "being human" or "being real" or being a "rounded" character is *produced*, rather than merely mirrored or imitated. Produced, that is to say, *as* a theatrical effect. We recognize the "reality" based upon a structure of perception and contrivance. To put it succinctly, Shakespeare manages us, as Richard manages the Lady Anne, and Buckingham and Hastings in the early moments of his play.

Throughout the play Shakespeare has the character of Richard deploy both self-exposure (even what a modern audience might conceive as self-pity) and the mocking, ironical aside to create this double effect of inside and outside: "Because I cannot flatter and look fair," he protests,

> Smile in men's faces, smooth, deceive, and cog,
> Duck with French nods and apish courtesy,
> I must be held a rancorous enemy.
> Cannot a plain man live and think no harm,
> But thus his simple truth must be abused
> With silken, sly, insinuating jacks?
>
> *1.3.47–53*

Whenever a Shakespeare character calls himself a plain man or a plain speaker the audience should be on the alert for dissimulation and contrivance. But Richard is perhaps the locus classicus of this move within the plays. "I am too childish-foolish for this world," he says, in the same scene (142). Thus in his own public performance, it is Richard, not the child king Henry VI or the princes in the Tower, who becomes the innocent child.

The "aside" as a device functions, like the soliloquy, as a tip-off to the audience that something else is going on, and often, as in this play, that words spoken are to be heard or taken ironically. Both Richard and his initial adversary, old Queen Margaret, deploy such asides liberally. Both are schemers, and survivors. I should note that although the terms "soliloquy" and "monologue" do not appear in the play texts, Shakespeare frequently has characters stand "aside," or urge others to join them "aside," for a private onstage conversation. In other words, the concept of a verbal *aside* develops out of, or concurrent with, an internal stage direction. What starts as a separation of characters from the main onstage action so they can "converse apart" becomes, as it were, psychologized into a conceptual, verbal, or tonal bracketing of an utterance so that the audience understands it to be an *aside* spoken to *them*. One example—taken from the same scene we have been discussing, act 1, scene 3—can serve for many. When Richard exclaims piously about the accusers of Clarence, "God pardon them that are the cause thereof," Lord Rivers commends his forebearance ("A virtuous and a Christian-like conclusion, / To pray for them that hath done scathe to us").

> RICHARD So do I ever—(*speaks to himself*) being well advised.
> For had I cursed now, I had cursed myself.
>
> *1.3.313–17*

In this early scene, even as Richard engages with his onstage adversaries, his wink to the audience is manifest: he himself is the one who has done harm "to us." As the play progresses, and especially at the point when Richard becomes King Richard and needs to play the protagonist rather than the antagonist, it will become increasingly difficult for him to control this kind of double dialogue.

For Richard is a better villain than he is a king. He is a betting man—"my dukedom for a beggarly denier"; "my kingdom for a horse"—and he is very successful at the beginning of the play. Take, for instance, the seduction of Anne, which takes place under the most difficult possible circumstances (he's killed her husband and is in the presence of her father-in-law's corpse). "Was ever woman in this humour wooed? / Was ever woman in this humour won?" (1.2.215–16) It's a high-wire act—Richard loves it, and so do we. But things begin to go wrong—his "plots" begin to fail and falter—almost from the minute he ascends the throne.

Contrast this with Queen Margaret's curse, the other—historical—"plot" of the play. Margaret, the widow of King Henry VI, was dead before the time in which Shakespeare sets his drama. Her presence in *Richard III* is Shakespeare's invention, another way in which he rewrites history. Margaret's curse—that all of Richard's henchmen would die—is remembered, over and over again. Rivers and Gray recall it en route to their deaths.

> GRAY   Now Margaret's curse is fall'n upon our heads
> . . . .
> RIVERS   Then cursed she Hastings; then cursed she Buckingham;
>   Then cursed she Richard. O remember, God,
>   To hear her prayer for them as now for us.
>
> *3.3.14–18*

In the internal world of the play, Margaret's curse *is* history, the story of what happened. And yet in modern productions the character of Queen Margaret is often cut, as Olivier cuts her from his film of the play, and, many years later, as Richard Loncraine would do in a well-received 1995 film version starring Ian McKellen. Revived from the dead by Shakespeare to act as a monitory chorus in his play, Margaret is often now "disappeared" by directors, as Richard continues to dominate the stage.

THE INTRIGUING PROBLEM that a consideration of *Richard III* thus presents for literary study, as for modern culture, is this vexed quesiton of truth or fact. What is "truth" in a literary text? What are "evidence" and "proof"? If something is historically inaccurate, how can it also be "true"? What this play suggests is that literary truth and literary facts are, or can be, as compelling as historical truth and historical facts, or even biographical truth and biographical facts. Literature creates and inhabits its own reality and reference points. Fictional characters, whether they are classical gods and goddesses, or characters from novels, films, television, or other modes of high and popular culture, often have as much influence upon how we behave as do models from "real life" and history.

In the special case of Shakespeare, of course, there is also something else at work, since so much of what modern-day Americans know as English history in fact comes from Shakespeare, rather than from a close reading of chronicle sources or contemporary historians. Here supposed fact and supposed fiction have exchanged places, and "Shakespeare says" becomes a cultural authority. Most centrally, we need also to keep acknowledging that history, too, is interpretation, and that historians—like playwrights, novelists, newspaper columnists, and college professors—are influenced, inevitably, by the times in which they live and the contexts in which they write.

Shakespeare's history plays—and indeed all of his plays, since they are all "historical" to the extent that they indicate a time and place—take place in triple time: in the time when they are set, historically; the time when they are written (intersecting with Shakespeare's own time, politics, and history); and the time when they are produced and performed, or read and interpreted.

So the question we want to be asking ourselves is not, is Shakespeare's *Richard III*—the play or the character—"true to history," but rather, why does it exercise such a powerful fascination upon us? Why has Shakespeare's account of historical events superseded other accounts, accounts that might be more true (whatever we think that means) to contemporary events, events contemporary to the time when they occurred?

When he read the play in the early part of the twentieth century, Sigmund Freud found Shakespeare's Richard to be psychologically "true"—a brilliant portrait of "ourselves." In the section "The Exceptions" in "Some Character Types Met with in Psycho-Analytic Work" (1916), he identified Richard as the kind of person who always regards himself as an "exception" to any rule.[17] Freud, who knew his Shakespeare well, singled out only a few characters for extensive analysis: the figures who fascinated him were Hamlet, King Lear, the Macbeths—and Richard III. What a topic for an analyst: a character whose fantasies are grandiose *and* fulfilled, and who is constantly assessing himself and lying to himself, both at once.

BUT PERHAPS THE MOST PASSIONATE admirers of Richard III in the early and mid-twentieth century were "amateurs"—in both senses: nonprofessionals, and lovers. In the summer of 1924 the Richard III Society was founded in Britain by a group of amateur historians convinced that history had not done justice to Richard. Similar groups of amateur sleuths had banded together in the nineteenth century to try to reverse another historical truism: the "fact" that the author of the plays was William Shakespeare of Stratford. That they were amateurs does not mean that they were unskilled or unknowledgeable.

The argument that Richard III has been unfairly maligned by history is strikingly parallel to the debates about who wrote Shakespeare's plays. Both the passionate defenders of Richard III and those who espouse the claims of the Earl of Oxford or of Francis Bacon as the true author of Shakespeare's plays regard themselves as crusaders of a sort, who can right the wrongs done by history.

Originally called the Fellowship of the White Boar, the British parent society renamed itself the Richard III Society in 1959 (and continues under that name still). The founding members of the American branch included a star-studded group of actors, writers, and artists, including Alfred Lunt, Lynn Fontaine, Dorothy Kilgallen, Salvador Dalí, John Gielgud, Helen Hayes, Tallulah Bankhead, and James Thurber. Ricardians today, worldwide, continue to maintain their hero's innocence, celebrating his accomplishments with an annual meeting, various publications, and several scholarships, including a $30,000 dissertation fellowship. Every year on Richard's birthday, October 2, they hold a commemorative event. The group is inclusive and democratic. But when it was begun, both in Britain and then in the United States, the defense of Richard was both heartfelt and chic or sophisticated. It was not only a cause célèbre, but also a celebrity cause.

The 1950s were the decade of Laurence Olivier's film version of *Richard III,* and of a new and sympathetic biography by Paul Murray Kendall. In the early 1950s, the time of McCarthyism, national and international conspiracy theories, and rampant accusations of disloyalty, the backstory of Richard III and his times might have had a particular appeal to revisionists. (Journalist Richard Rovere, writing in 1959 about McCarthy's last years, called them "seasons of discontent.")[18] Fact and fiction, in this era as in so many other recent decades, not only were hard to prise apart, but also depended upon where you stood.

BUT WITHOUT QUESTION the biggest literary boost to the defense-of-Richard movement came with the publication, in 1951, of a compelling mystery novel, *The Daughter of Time,* written by Josephine Tey (the pen name of the Scottish writer Elizabeth MacKintosh).

There have been innumerable detective novels about Shakespeare's plays, including, for example, two classics by the New Zealand–born writer Ngaio Marsh: *Light Thickens* (about *Macbeth*) and *Killer Dolphin* (about the discovery of a glove supposed to have belonged to Shakespeare's son Hamnet, who died at age eleven). Under the name of Michael Innes, the literary scholar J. I. M. Stewart wrote a terrific thriller called *Hamlet, Revenge*. Shakespeare's plays often provide titles (for example, Agatha Christie's *By the Pricking of My Thumbs*) as well as plots. None of these Shakespeare mysteries, though, had anything like the crossover effect of *The Daughter of Time,* a book that quickly became a classic and a key document for Richard hunters in the twentieth century.

That Josephine Tey herself was far from oblivious to the times in which she lived and wrote can readily be seen, not only in the kinds of plots that fascinated her, but also in, for example, what might seem to be a throwaway line in *The Daughter of Time,* when her main character, Alan Grant, reflects on the difference between the England of Richard's time and his own:

> For thirty years, over this green uncrowded land, the Wars of the Roses had been fought. But it had been more of a blood feud than a war. A Montague and Capulet affair; of no great concern to the average Englishman. No one pushed in at your door to demand whether you were York or Lancaster and to hale you off to a concentration camp if your answer proved to be the wrong one for the occasion.[19]

This mention of a "concentration camp" is effectively jarring; it brings in, for a moment, the horrors of the mid-twentieth century, in the midst of a daydreaming rumination about old, green England.

The Daughter of Time follows very much the pattern established in Tey's other, even more fictional mysteries:[20] a recurring conflict between figures who are highly admired, well liked, and trusted but turn out to be secret villains, liars, and even murderers, and figures who are easily vilified and wrongly accused. The phrase from which she takes her title, "Truth is the daughter of Time, not authority," comes from Francis Bacon's *Novum Organum* (1620).[21]

Here is the novel's situation: Detective Alan Grant is in the hospital, recovering from an injury suffered when he was chasing a criminal. He's bored, and an actress friend brings him a set of images of faces, from portraits, photographs, the newspapers, and so on. As a detective, Grant's business is reading faces, and he is struck by one, in particular, a face that seems to him serious, thoughtful, and showing signs of past illness or worry. To his astonishment, the face is not that of a judge or a statesman, but the face of Richard III. The rest of the novel is his investigation, with the help of a young American research assistant, of the story of Richard III. The investigation takes as its evidence books of various kinds, some lent him by the nurses, some found in the British Library by the research assistant.

Two quotations from the novel will illustrate something of its time; each is pertinent to the theme of truth and fiction. The first is a conversation between Detective Grant and a hospital nurse, prompted by Detective Grant's question about how the princes in the Tower died:

> "Who said they were smothered?"
> "My history book at school said it."
> "Yes, but whom was the history book quoting?"
> "Quoting? It wasn't quoting anything. It was just giving facts."[22]

And the second is from a letter written to him by his cousin, with whom he has been discussing what happens when you puncture the balloon of someone's certainty: "It's an odd thing but when you tell someone the true facts of a mythical tale they are indignant not with the teller but with you. They don't *want* to have their ideas upset."[23]

In addition to being a chronicle of the Richard story, Tey's book is in fact a series of reflections on history and on the reliability or unreliability of "fact," "truth," and apparent biographical detail, as filtered through a set of genres, times, writers, and readers. For Detective Grant has collected a large and heterogeneous bunch of sources, and they are all, in some ways, unreliable:

- A "Historical Reader," a book of famous anecdotes, many of them apocryphal. "It bore the same relation to history as Stories from the Bible bears to Holy Writ. . . . Raleigh spread his cloak for Elizabeth, Nelson took leave of Hardy in his cabin on the *Victory,* all in nice clear large print and one-sentence paragraphs. To each episode went one full-page illustration."[24]
- A school history, two thousand years of English history divided into reigns for easy reference. "It was no wonder that one pinned a personality to a reign, forgetful that that personality had known and lived under other kings. . . . It never crossed one's mind that someone who had seen Queen Elizabeth could also have seen George I. One had been conditioned to the reign idea from childhood."[25]
- A constitutional history of england, by the "real" historical author, J. R. Tanner (1860–1931).
- A modern authority on the period. In this case, a fictional author— Sir Cuthbert Oliphant, who comes in for quite a lot of gentle mockery. "Historians should be compelled to take a course in psychology before they write."[26]
- A historical biography: a real book (*The Rose of Raby: A Life of Cecily Nevile, Duchess of York,* Richard III's mother) attributed to a fictional

author, Evelyn Payne-Ellis, instead of the book's actual author, Guy Paget (1886–1952), the writer who was also the author of *The Rose of London* (a life of Jane Shore, Edward IV's mistress) and *The Rose of Rouen* (a life of Elizabeth Woodville, Edward IV's wife).

- A supposedly contemporary account, Sir Thomas More's *Life of Richard III.* Detective Grant and his research assistant, Brent Carradine, soon learn that More (1478–1535), the most authoritative source for Richard's villainy (and for Shakespeare), was five years old when Richard came to the throne and eight years old when he died. Everything in More's *Life of Richard,* therefore, is hearsay. Or worse. (Much of it turns out to be the ideas, if not the words, of John Morton, Richard's enemy and Henry VII's Archbishop of Canterbury.)
- A monkish chronicle that turns out to contain a political lie.

In addition to these variously unreliable sources, there are examples of, and references to, other forms of "history" and evidence-production:

- Historical myths with no factual basis: stories of martyrdoms, massacres, and other events that simply did not take place, but that have nonetheless been memorialized with statues, engravings, poems, and annual days of remembrance.
- A case history, in the form of Detective Grant's summation of the case of the murdered princes in the Tower (listing for both suspects—Richard III and Henry VII—things like "previous record," "motive," "right to the throne," relation to and knowledge of the deceased, etc.).[27]
- A historical drama: *Richard of Bordeaux,* the romantic tale about Richard II and his queen, Anne of Bohemia, that catapulted John Gielgud into stardom. This play, first produced in 1932 at the New Theatre, was a huge hit. The author's name, Gordon Daviot, is the pseudonym for a Scotswoman, Elizabeth MacKintosh—whose other pseudonym is Josephine Tey. So Tey, in her mystery novel about Richard III, informs the reader that her detective, Alan Grant, had seen *Richard of Bordeaux* at the New Theatre four times in his childhood, and, we are told, it was from seeing that play that he "knew all about" the history of England from the deposition of Richard II, to Henry V at Agincourt, and the sad tale of Henry VI.[28] Here's a good example of the *mise en abyme:* Tey's fictional detective has seen a play written by Tey under another name.

This veritable anatomy of literary forms also included, as is perhaps de rigeur, an expression of contempt for detective stories, voiced by an actress who is trying to persuade a writer to write a play for her instead (like Tey herself, this writer works in both forms): "After practically promising me that she would write it . . . now she decides that she must write one of her awful little detective stories." Detective Grant is sympathetic: "I don't suppose it will take her long to write her detective book." The actress airily agrees: "Oh, no. She does them in six weeks or so."[29]

Finally—although in this artfully nested series of books within books I hesitate to say that any layer is final—we have the disavowal of *this* book, the very book we're reading. Brent, the American research assistant, wants to write a book about the quest for the truth about Richard III. "I want to write it the way it happened," he says to Detective Grant. "You know, about my coming to see you, and our starting the Richard thing quite casually . . . and how we stuck to things that actually happened and not what someone reported afterwards about it . . . and that sort of thing."[30] Grant is agreeable; he himself, he says, would "never write a book" (not even his autobiography, a project he jokingly titles *My Twenty Years at the Yard*). But the young researcher, crestfallen, discovers that his findings are, alas, not new.

In fact, books on this topic had been written for centuries: "A man Buck wrote a vindication in the seventeenth century. And Horace Walpole in the eighteenth. And someone called Markham in the nineteenth."[31] The "someone called Markham," Clements Markham, was in fact the principal source for Josephine Tey's book.[32] Markham engaged in a public controversy on the question with the ranking historian of fifteenth-century England in his time, James Gairdner, whose own book on Richard is discussed within *The Daughter of Time*—though Markham, Tey's source, is not. So a book that was belatedly "discovered" by the fictional researcher within the novel is used to disallow the originality of the book that he would have intended to write, even as the novelist herself writes a book about the interruption and curtailment of this plan to write a book.

TWO LISTS, WHEN PLACED side by side, show that Tey knew exactly what she was doing:

Ella Darroll	Stephen Dedalus
Form III	Class of Elements
Newbridge High School	Clongowes Wood College
Newbridge	Sallins
Gloucestershire	County Kildare
England	Ireland
Europe	Europe
The World	The World
The Universe	The Universe

The first list is from the country nurse's schoolbook; the second is Stephen Dedalus's famous inscription, from the opening pages of James Joyce's *A Portrait of the Artist as a Young Man.*[33]

I have dwelt on the box-within-box-within-box (or book-within-book-within-book, or Russian doll–within Russian doll–within Russian doll) structure of what seems, on first—and pleasurable—reading to be a simple detective novel, in order to make a point not only about literature but also about the quest for "truth" and its relation to literary effect. As many scholars have pointed out, and as is manifest, I hope, from any reading or viewing of Shakespeare's play, the cultural power of Shakespeare's fictional Richard has been greater than any "historical" account of his reign and his deeds, whether favorable or unfavorable.

Play. Ballad. History book. Biographical romance. Chronicle. Myth. Case history. Detective story: all of these are modes of telling, or retelling, or reporting, or interpreting, issues of fact, or truth. To Tey's ample collection we could add some more modern ones (her book, remember, was published half a century ago, in 1951, and she died in 1952): television; film; documentary; "nonfiction novel"; embedded reporting; authorized biography; unauthorized biography; publicity release; press conference; blog.

I DON'T INTEND TO GIVE the impression that Tey's book is anything like the last word on the matter. Quite the contrary. There have been many, many books since, "fiction" and "nonfiction," "history" and "biography," "amateur" and "professional," written by historians, novelists, journalists, officials of the Richard III Society.

Some of these are deliberate fictions, some inadvertent ones, some serious historical accounts. All have been caught in the dialectic of pro and con. No one is indifferent, it seems, to Richard III. His story, his plot, is a double allegory: an allegory of supposed "evil" (the same spirit in which Shylock, Edmund, and Iago have been taken), and an allegory of the power of the lie. When public discourse is the "fiend that lies like truth," fiction is the ground on which we seek for (allegorical) fact. This is the power of Shakespeare.

SIX

THE MERCHANT OF VENICE

The Question of Intention

THE QUESTION "What was Shakespeare like?" often contains a not-so-secret wish that Shakespeare should be like us. Like the reader, like the actor, like the biographer, like the portrait painter, but also like the people of the nation, the interest group, the age. The word "Bardolatry," coined by George Bernard Shaw to characterize the Shakespeare worship he saw around him—and that had been in full galloping mode since the 1769 Shakespeare Jubilee—reflects the special situation of a poet-playwright whom some regard with an almost religious awe. And if worshippers tend to imagine their God in a personal form and appearance not unlike their own, so it has also been with Shakespeare. In appearance, in ideas, in beliefs, and in values and prejudices, Shakespeare, to paraphrase the old hymn, was a "man like me."

The history of Shakespeare portraits tells this tale: in generation after generation, the most admired images have been those that resembled and embodied the era and its values, whether for social standing, economic suc-

The Sanders portrait of William Shakespeare

Joseph Fiennes in Shakespeare in Love *(1998)*

Thomas Gainsborough, David Garrick with the
Bust of Shakespeare

cess, poetic glamour, or intellectual nobility. The actor and theater manager
David Garrick had a statue of Shakespeare carved for a temple in his garden,
and posed, himself, for the sculptor, so that the playwright's face bears Garrick's features.

As we have already seen, Sir Walter Scott, enthralled by the idea that his
initials matched those of the poet he admired and wished to emulate, had a
bust of Shakespeare installed in his library and took phrenological measure-
ments to compare Shakespeare's head size with his own. The intrigue of the
newly discovered Sanders portrait of Shakespeare, which came to light in
Canada a few years ago, was heightened both by the "cool" image of the
young sitter and his resemblance to the actor who played Shakespeare in the
film *Shakespeare in Love.*

There is, as the cliché goes, no accounting for taste: when some of the most
venerated images of Shakespeare have him looking like a merchant, a banker,
"an affluent and retired butcher,"[1] or, indeed, an accountant, we may wish
merely to say that seventeenth-century taste—or Romantic taste, or Victorian
taste—does not accord with our own. But one particular worry seems to

The Chandos portrait of William Shakespeare

have preoccupied many Victorian Shakespeare enthusiasts, both professional scholars and amateur "buffs," and this concern will lead us directly into our inquiry about *The Merchant of Venice* and modern culture.

Did the extant portraits of Shakespeare, and in particular the so-called Chandos portrait, make him look "too Jewish"?

George Steevens, an eighteenth-century editor of Shakespeare's plays, had already raised questions about the portrait's accuracy. "Our author exhibits the complexion of a Jew, or rather of a chimney-sweeper in the jaundice,"[2] Steevens wrote. This could not be Shakespeare. A mid-century Victorian, J. Hain Friswell, was similarly skeptical: "One cannot readily imagine our essentially English Shakespeare to have been a dark, heavy man, with a foreign expression, of a decidedly Jewish physiognomy, thin curly hair, a somewhat lubricious mouth, red-edged eyes, wanton lips, with a coarse expression, and his ears tricked out with ear-rings."[3] J. Parker Norris agreed: the Chandos portrait was "very Jewish," "foreign," "most disappointing."[4] The portrait painter Abraham Wivell, author of *An Inquiry into the History, Authenticity, and Characteristics of the Shakespeare Portraits,* greatly preferred the look of the Shakespeare bust in the Stratford monument (the same one that one eminent Shakespeare scholar had compared to a pork butcher), since it "has much less the look of a Jew than most of them."[5] The very "modern"-looking curly hair and fashionable earring, so appealing to mid-twentieth-century sensibilities, were to some of these observers—and "defenders"—of Shakespeare an unacceptable picture of their poet and hero.

"Too Jewish?" was the self-assured and gently self-mocking title of an art exhibition mounted at the Jewish Museum in New York City in 1997, curated by Norman L. Kleeblatt and featuring the works of artists like Deborah Kass, Cary Leibowitz, Elaine Reichek, and Art Spiegelman. But a hundred years earlier—at the time of the Dreyfus affair in France, and when Sigmund Freud encountered significant professional obstacles in his career because of his religious background—to be Jewish was sometimes to be "too Jewish." As we will see, the history of *The Merchant of Venice* from the time of its early performances through the transformative interpretations of late Victorian and early twentieth-century theater has encountered and staged these confrontations, as the figure of Shylock increasingly gained in importance, and moved, over time, from a comic butt to an archvillain to a noble figure of pathos and dignified loss.

We might say that the question for modern culture has now become: is *The Merchant of Venice* "Jewish enough?" Instead of the puzzle raised by the portraits—what did Shakespeare *look like?*—modern culture poses the question of the playwright's intention: what did Shakespeare *think like?* Was he "like me"—sharing the views (whether tolerantly liberal, tacitly or explicitly anti-Semitic, or defiantly proud) of the audience in the present day? And since both the present day and the cultural locations have continued to shift over time, the debate has continued, even, perhaps, intensified.

Why should it matter so much what the playwright's intention was in writing this play about a Jewish moneylender and his discomfiture in court at the hands of a strict law and a clever woman?

In a way, the question answers itself, and opens up to the wider twentieth-century debate about authorial intention. Despite the stringent arguments of William K. Wimsatt and Monroe Beardsley in their 1946 essay, "The Intentional Fallacy," that the author's intentions, whether we (think we) know them or not, do not govern the meaning of a literary work, there has remained a consistent critical interest in recapturing this elusive matter of intention and in tying the meaning of the work to what its author did or did not, or could or could not, have intended.

Just as some nineteenth-century connoisseurs of Shakespeare portraiture in England and America wanted their idol to look "essentially English," so some twentieth-century audiences (and directors and actors) have wanted their Shakespeare to share their own humane and ethical views. Their Shakespeare could not be an anti-Semite, so the play must contain a strong subtext that points toward his "real" opinions about universal human rights, dignity, and generosity. The famous response, attributed to Alexander Pope, upon seeing the actor Charles Macklin in the role of Shylock—"This was the Jew /

That Shakespeare drew"—could be said to voice the wishes of many later observers.[6] Macklin's revolutionary portrayal of Shylock as dignified rather than stereotypically villainous, a novelty in 1741, opened the door to modern, nuanced stage interpretations. On the other hand, as we will also see, individuals and regimes that sought justification for their own repressive or murderous policies toward Jews could look to *The Merchant of Venice* for "their" Shakespeare.

THE PECULIAR INFLUENCE of *The Merchant of Venice* on modern culture might be gauged by noting some of the current uses of what is perhaps the play's most proverbial and most misused phrase: the "pound of flesh." This phrase was used on the floor of the House of Representatives on February 7, 2007, when a representative protested the actions of the U.S. Attorney in trying to discipline two Border Patrol policemen who shot at suspects: "They wanted their pound of flesh. The maximum penalty, the maximum message to other border patrol agents: don't even think about firing your weapon at the border."[7]

The phrase also appeared as the headline of an article on February 2, 2007, in an Australian newspaper, about the national taste for healthy-looking models rather than overly thin ones: "Demanding Our Pounds of Flesh." Coming closer to the Shylockian original, an article on a proposed "friendly takeover" by one company of another that was rejected by the company president as an attempt "to extract an extra pound of flesh."[8] Going literal, a review of the film *Saw III* (2006) described the horror franchise as "giving a pound of flesh where it's due,"[9] and a front-page article in the *Washington Post* about the twenty-five-year prison sentence given WorldCom founder Bernard Ebbers asked, "How large a pound of flesh should society exact for serious white-collar crime?"[10]

But despite these free-floating phrases that seem deliberately to forget or flout their origins, the play worries us. Worries us individually and collectively. Worries us as readers, as performers, as teachers, as scholars, as students. Worries us as members of the modern world.

The now-current "ironic solution" to the play's problems—that the play's Christians are as bad as the play's Jews or worse, and that Shakespeare saw that and put it into his play—even if true doesn't really resolve the issue. The emotions and ideas it provokes are too powerful.

In a *New York Times* article theater critic Charles Isherwood reviewed twin productions, performed at the Theater for a New Audience in New York, of Christopher Marlowe's play *The Jew of Malta* and Shakespeare's *The Merchant of Venice*—with the same actor, F. Murray Abraham, playing the Jew in both. He is Barabas, the Jew of Malta, and he is also Shakespeare's Shylock. Marlowe's play preceded Shakespeare's, and its popularity with Elizabethan audiences is thought to be one reason why Shakespeare wrote *Merchant*. Isherwood begins his article by saying, "Welcome, ladies and gents, to the Theater for a New Audience's smackdown between two of the most notorious villains of the Elizabethan stage," and goes on to ask, not entirely rhetorically, "Who will prove the more noxious offender of 21st-century sensibilities?"[11]

Another article in the same newspaper, published just a few days previously, bore the headline "Essay Linking Liberal Jews and Anti-Semitism Sparks a Furor."[12] It discusses a recent publication of the American Jewish Committee in which the author criticizes a number of prominent intellectuals and artists for questioning whether the state of Israel should exist. The artists include the playwright Tony Kushner and the poet Adrienne Rich. Among the scholars criticized are Jacqueline Rose, a prominent British scholar who has published on Shakespeare and psychoanalysis; Tony Judt, a historian; and Daniel Boyarin, a scholar of the Talmud, who teaches at Berkeley. All of these scholars are Jewish.

The issues that have worried, concerned, and interested people—audiences, scholars, the general public—about *The Merchant of Venice* have been these: Is the play anti-Semitic? Was *Shakespeare* anti-Semitic? Did he knowingly ("intentionally") write a play that disparaged Jews (Shylock, but also Tubal, described by Shylock as "a wealthy Hebrew of my tribe" [1.3.52])? Or was he—as so many people have wanted to believe—a writer and thinker who transcended the prejudices of his own age, who was prescient, liberal before his time?

Some persistent questions about *The Merchant of Venice* include issues concerning Portia—is she a wise and exemplary figure or is she in fact herself flawed by prejudice, both against Jews and against Africans like her suitor, the Prince of Morocco? Others have to do with Antonio—how are we to understand his love for Bassanio, both in terms of the Elizabethan culture of ideal male friendship and in the wake of changing understandings about same-sex love both in Shakespeare's time and in our own? These issues are very much twentieth- and twenty-first-century concerns, and they have had some effect upon literary criticism as well as upon productions of the play. But the biggest question, sometimes explicit and always implicit, is Shakespeare's supposed attitudes toward Shylock and toward Jews and Judaism in general, and here, with this very tricky and often painful set of questions, is where we need to begin.

Here is a suggestive anecdote:

During the intermission of a production of the play at the American Repertory Theatre (ART), in which the part of Shylock was played by a young actor, Will LeBow, in a fedora hat and without the long patriarchal white beard—played for laughs, for discomfort, as had once been the staple of Shakespeare's stage—a number of audience members caught up with me to ask my response to his interpretation. Was it bad for Shakespeare, bad for Shylock, bad for the Jews? What had happened to the familiar "paternal" Shylock, and how could he have been replaced by this wisecracking guy who looked like he had come from the Lower East Side? A few weeks later I was part of a panel discussion on this question at the ART, during which several of the panelists—actors, directors, professors—told stories of their own sense of childhood slights and of feeling outside the mainstream, like Shylock. Is this really what the play is about in the modern era?

THE QUESTION OF Shakespeare's "intention" and Shakespeare's core beliefs in writing his play and designing the character of Shylock has been for many people in the twentieth and twenty-first centuries a besetting question. Many have *wanted* to find in this Elizabethan author a sensibility that transcended his time. Often the focus is on Shylock's great speech about humanity and revenge, from act 3, scene 1, the linchpin of many stage interpretations, as well as a speech frequently excerpted and quoted:

> I am a Jew. Hath not a Jew eyes? Hath not a Jew hands, organs, dimensions, senses, affections, passions; fed with the same food, hurt with the same weapons, subject to the same diseases, healed by the same means, warmed and cooled by the same winter and summer as a Christian is? If you prick us do we not bleed? If you tickle us do we not laugh? If you poison us do we not die? And if you wrong us shall we not revenge? If we are like you in the rest, we will resemble you in that.
>
> *3.1.49–57*

This speech gained new urgency, as one might expect, during the 1940s, and it has often been appropriated (or "repurposed") since: thus for example, after the reelection of Joseph Lieberman to the Senate as an Independent in Connecticut in 2006, a blogger writing to the conservative Republican Web site RedState.com cited Shylock's speech as if it had been spoken by Lieberman as a "gotcha" retort to the Democrats in his former party. The phrase "and if you wrong us, shall we not revenge?" was printed in bold.[13]

THE LEBOW/ART PRODUCTION played the "hath not a Jew eyes" speech for laughs—perhaps as a way of avoiding its powerful, aversive, and sentimental history. Is Shylock's moving speech a transhistorical plea for tolerance and understanding? Or is the fact that it ends in a cry for revenge a sign that Shakespeare saw his Jew as yet another vengeful villain?

The question returns us to the larger matter of intention and agency: Does the author, in this case the playwright, have the final say? How can we possibly know what he "intended"? And, in any case, does not the play develop and project meanings—meanings in the plural—that may well go against whatever an author had in mind? What Shakespeare "had in mind" is unknowable—which doesn't, of course, keep people from asking or wanting to know about it. But Shakespeare is famous for his capacity to speak through many characters, not just one. "Shakespeare," said the Romantic critic Hazlitt, "was the least of an egotist that it was possible to be. He was nothing in himself; but he was all that others were, or that they could become. He not only had in himself the germs of every faculty and feeling, but he could follow them by anticipation, intuitively, into all their conceivable ramifications, through every change of fortune, or conflict of passion, or turn of thought. . . . He had only to think of anything in order to become that thing, with all the circumstances belonging to it."[14] This capacity is related to what Keats called "negative capability," and it is one of the meanings of Coleridge's description of the playwright as "myriad-minded Shakespeare." Coleridge also wrote, in terms very close to Hazlitt's, that Shakespeare "darts himself forth, and passes into all the forms of human character and passion. . . . Shakespeare becomes all things, while ever remaining himself."[15]

Plays are not novels or lyric poems—there is no single speaker, but rather many first persons, many "I"s—all of them fictional, all of them "false." No matter how hard we look, we will not find "Shakespeare's opinion" in these plays—we will find instead his various opinions and other people's opinions.

Often his clowns know as much as his princes; even Launcelot Gobbo, whose social views we may consider deplorable, gives voice to a perceptively skeptical bromide: "it is a wise father that knows his own child" (2.2.66). Nonetheless, the question is posed and re-posed: What did Shakespeare know, and when did he know it? We are dealing here, at least in part, with what might be called both a cultural wish and a cultural fantasy: that Shakespeare was himself a modern before his time, and that he shared "our" views about questions of ethics, morality, and social justice.

ON THE ONE SIDE, then, the worry about a "too Jewish" Shakespeare; on the other side, the modern and postmodern wish that Shakespeare not be anti-Semitic, that he not have written an anti-Semitic play, that the problem posed by the attitudes voiced in this play—Portia's, Gratiano's, and Antonio's, as well as Shylock's—be somehow explainable, explained away through history or biography. But the play will not be controlled. It has a life of its own.

The story of this wish about Shakespeare—and its opposite, the fear that he is not "us," after all—can, however, be historicized, a little, which is to say that it can be situated by looking at the history of the character of Shylock.

"Anti-Semitism" in each of its iterations and manifestations is a prejudice against Jews and Judaism, culturally and ethnically as well as theologically. It may be useful—both in general and in looking at *The Merchant of Venice* over time—to distinguish among different historical moments of it. Inevitably times flow into each other, but we might point toward four such moments: the medieval and early modern heritage in which Shakespeare wrote; the nineteenth-century consciousness of capital at work; the "genteel" anti-Semitism of the early twentieth century; and the events of the Holocaust and the post-Holocaust period. Serious historians of these periods will see immediately what a broad-brush approach this is, and I ask their indulgence, since my preliminary objective is only to situate "Shakespeare" and "culture" in some relation to each other on this difficult and slippery topic. Although there are many more subtleties of prejudice to be teased out here, this will provide a framework for looking through various lenses at the play. What follows here, then, is a quick summary of themes, claims, slurs, and caricatures, leading up to some substantive issues for "modern culture."

In the medieval and Renaissance periods Jews were blamed for the death of Christ, for preferring the liberation of prisoner Barabbas to that of the imprisoned Jesus (one of the medieval Corpus Christi plays portrayed Jews "dancing around the cross" at the time of the crucifixion). Here, too, there developed the noxious "blood libel," the idea that Jews believed in ritual murder, and especially the ritual murder of children, sometimes as part of some unspecified cannibal practice. The Prioress's tale in Chaucer's *Canterbury Tales* is a significant example here: the genteel Prioress, with her "love conquers all" jewelry and her passionate affection for her little lapdogs, tells a chilling tale about the supposed murder of a Christian boy by a group of Jews as entertainment for her fellow pilgrims.

This medieval/Renaissance Jew was often portrayed as a monster and a caricature, as seen in one of the most famous speeches in Marlowe's *The Jew of Malta,* in which the Jew (*named* Barabas) boasts about his exploits:

> As for myself, I walk abroad a'nights,
> And kill sick people groaning under walls,
> Sometimes I go about and poison wells.
> *2.3.178–80*

T. S. Eliot accurately described the dramatic mode of Marlowe's play as not tragedy but farce[16]—Barabas speaks here in self-pleasuring modes of gloating hyperbole and winds up, at the end of the play, dunked into the cauldron of boiling oil he has prepared for his enemies.

Stage Jews in the period wore false hooked noses and red wigs and beards. (This is one reason why Portia's remarkable question, as she enters the courtroom in the *Merchant of Venice,* is so clearly an allegorical or political remark: "Which is the merchant here, and which the Jew?" Venetian merchants dressed like princes; Shylock is in his Jewish gabardine.) In medieval and Renaissance Venice, Jews were required to wear yellow badges and, when they began to cover those up, yellow hats.[17] Jews in the period were not permitted to own property; the trade of moneylending was one of the few open to them, and despite the noise about disapproving of usury, much of the European Renaissance world turned on credit and borrowing. As always, there is no need for a law unless there are violations of that law.[18]

Neither Chaucer nor Shakespeare would probably have known people who identified publicly as Jewish. The "Jews" in their writings are literary and cultural figures, not drawn from life. Jews were banned from England by the order of Edward I in 1290; if there were any English Jews—and doubtless there were—they worshipped in secret and pretended in public to be Christians. In 1490, Ferdinand and Isabella likewise expelled the Jews from Spain. Queen Elizabeth I had a Portuguese Jewish doctor, Rodrigo Lopez, who is sometimes thought of as a model for both Marlowe's Jew of Malta, Barabas, and Shakespeare's Shylock. Lopez became wealthy as a result of the favor of powerful Elizabethan sponsors, but was ultimately accused of conspiring to poison the queen and was hanged, drawn, and quartered. Lopez always claimed to have been a faithful convert to Protestantism. Right before he was hanged he supposedly declared that he loved the queen as well as he loved Jesus Christ—at which the crowd laughed, taking this as a confession.[19]

So the Jews in England in Shakespeare's time were either Marranos (Spanish and Portuguese Jews who had undergone supposed conversions, and practiced their religion in secret) or traveling musicians.

BUT WHAT ARE WE TO MAKE OF the open mockery to which Shylock is subjected, not only by Antonio, who is said to have "spet," or spat, upon his "Jewish gabardine," the long cloak traditionally worn by Jews, but also by Gratiano (who is the worst of them, and who nonetheless is "rewarded" by getting to marry Portia's friend and waiting-gentlewoman, the spunky Nerissa) and by Salerio and Solanio, Venetians who make "merry sport" of Shylock's deep distress at losing both his daughter, Jessica, and the money she takes away with her as a dowry for her Christian husband, Lorenzo. Salerio and Solanio mimic both Shylock's distress and his manner of speech in act 2, scene 8:

> SOLANIO   I never heard a passion so confused,
> So strange, outrageous, and so variable
> As the dog Jew did utter in the streets.
> "My daughter! O, my ducats! O, my daughter!
> Fled with a Christian! O, my Christian ducats!
> Justice! The law! My ducats and my daughter!
> A sealèd bag, two sealèd bags of ducats,
> Of double ducats, stol'n from me by my daughter!
> Stol'n by my daughter! Justice! Find the girl!
> She hath the stones upon her, and the ducats!"
> SALERIO   Why, all the boys in Venice follow him,
> Crying "His stones, his daughter, and his ducats."
>
> 2.8.12–24

Since "stones" is Elizabethan slang for testicles (compare our modern slang, "family jewels"), and it is clearly meant here in a double sense—this is one reason they laugh at him—the image is of a patriarch unmanned. Shylock's daughter now wears the stones (just, indeed, as Portia does, in commanding what was her father's household in Belmont). In losing his daughter, he loses not only his money but also his manhood. And, of course, this will become complicated and thematic in the trial scene, when the "pound of flesh" is forfeit, and the Jew Shylock approaches the Christian merchant Antonio with a knife.

And what about Shylock's forced conversion to Christianity at the end of the play? It is all very well to say that Renaissance Christians might believe that this is the only way he could find salvation—that it is *good* for him, even though he may not like it. But so much in the play pushes in the opposite direction for a modern audience. It is not only a violation of his religious freedom; it is also the final breaking point for him. In essence, Shylock dies twice for us onstage, even as he lives: when he loses his daughter, and when he is forced to convert.

Bear in mind that Shylock is not the "main character" in the play and that the play is categorized as a comedy, not a tragedy. It is called *The Merchant of Venice*, and the merchant of the title is Antonio. Jews could not own property and were not, therefore, merchants. Moneylending, the trade for which Shylock is reviled (and which Bassanio finds so useful), was one of the modes of livelihood open to them.

It is not clear which actor in Shakespeare's original company played the part of Shylock—it may well have been Richard Burbage. But by the middle of the eighteenth century, the character of Shylock had been established onstage by the actor Charles Macklin. His hat was red, not yellow, but it was clearly the sign of a Jew, an "other" in culture, to be noticed and avoided. Here is Macklin's own account of his initial portrayal of the part:

> I made my appearance in the green-room, dressed for the part, with my red hat on my head, my picqued beard, loose black gown, &c. . . . , I knew where I should have the pull, which was in the third act, and reserved myself accordingly. At this period, I threw out all my fire; and as the contrasted passions of joy for the Merchant's losses, and grief for the elopement of Jessica, open a fine field for an actor's powers, I had the good fortune to please beyond my warmest expectations—the whole house was in an uproar of applause.[20]

It was Macklin's interpretation that elicited Pope's affirmative praise: "This was the Jew / That Shakespeare drew." But Macklin's performance was hardly an exoneration of Shylock. A German visitor to England wrote, on seeing him in costume, "It cannot be denied that the sight of this Jew is more than sufficient to arouse once again in the mature man all the prejudices of his childhood against this race." The role apparently involved a distinctive mode of speaking: "The first words he utters, when he comes to the stage, are slowly and impressively spoken: 'Three thousand ducats.' The double 'th' and the two sibilants, especially the second after the 't,' which Macklin lisps as lickerishly as if he were savoring the ducats and all that they would buy . . . give the keynote of his whole character."[21] (Later caricatures of Jewish speech would include this "lisp" as an infallible indicator of identity, supposedly "too Jewish" once again; fin de siècle cartoons showed Jews who said "thith" for "this,"

Edmund Kean as Shylock

"thells" for "sells," and "sthoneth" for "stones."[22] And Solanio's mocking imitation, quoted above, of Shylock's "confused" language at the loss of his
money and his daughter suggests the possibility of such a lisp in the lines:
"She hath the stones upon her, and the ducats!")

SO IF WE WERE TO ASK the question about Shakespeare's "intention" and
Shakespeare's opinions and beliefs of Macklin—or perhaps of Pope—the
answer would have been to see Shylock as an ambivalent figure, neither the
one-dimensional monster of the past nor the humane, tragic victim of modern, post-Holocaust productions. But the play has always intersected, somewhat uneasily, with the politics of the times.

During the political debates surrounding the Jewish Naturalization Bill of
1753—universally referred to in the period as the Jew Bill, a bill designed to
make it possible for foreign Jews to become naturalized British subjects—
Shakespeare's play became part of the political rhetoric, as opponents revived
old claims about knife-wielding Jews and forced circumcision and quoted,
out of context, Shylock's remark about Antonio: "I hate him for he is a Christian." But most of the commentary centered on money, and on supposed
Jewish avarice: one of the key and most debated points of the Jewish Naturalization Bill was that it gave Jews the right to own English land. (Jews had been
readmitted to England under Oliver Cromwell in 1656.)[23]

By the early nineteenth century, the portrayal of Shylock had shifted a little. Edmund Kean played the part in a romantic spirit. Coleridge said of his performance style that "To see him act was like reading Shakespeare by flashes of lightning,"[24] and indeed Hazlitt thought him perhaps too "buoyant" for Shylock: "There was a lightness and vigour in his tread, a buoyancy and elasticity of spirit, a fire and animation, which would accord better with almost any other character than with the morose, sullen, inward, inveterate, inflexible malignity of Shylock."[25]

Nonetheless, Hazlitt marked a change in audience or reader response: Shylock, he wrote, is no longer "baited with the rabble's curse," but rather "he becomes a half-favorite with the philosophical part of the audience, who are disposed to think that Jewish revenge is at least as good as Christian injuries."[26] Shylock, said Hazlitt, was "*a good hater*"—this from a man who would a few years later write an essay called "On the Pleasures of Hating." Kean abandoned the traditional red wig, playing the part in a black wig instead. He was still clearly a villain, though a more romantic one.

By the mid-nineteenth century, the part of Shylock had become one of the great favorites for Shakespearean actors, together with Macbeth, King Lear, Richard III, Othello, and Hamlet. It was a star vehicle, a way of attracting attention—and customers—to the theater. Its moral values, or immoral values, were not really at issue. The play was the thing. Audiences went to the theater to be impressed, moved, excited, horrified.

But a certain shift was taking place as early capitalism gave way to the industrial era. Outside the theater (and ultimately inside it, too) anti-Semitism was not directed so much at the supposed biblical past, the myths and calumnies of the blood libel, as at the present sense that the Jews had money: the new myths had to do with international bankers and international conspiracies. John Gross quotes the poet and newspaper editor William Cullen Bryant: "It is true that moneychangers once spat on in the ghetto are now hugged in the palace. Rothschilds and Goulds, Belmonts and Benjamins are found in the antechambers of princes and presidents. But we fear that it is not so much that the prejudice against the Jews has ceased but that the love of money has increased—not that the Jews have become as Christians, but that the Christians have become as Jews."[27] The American railway magnate Jay Gould was in fact not Jewish, although his surname led not only Bryant but also Henry Ford and Henry Adams to conclude that he was a Jew. But on the other hand there is a certain charming irony in the fact that the Jewish financier August Belmont, who worked for the Rothschilds, became a figure in Democratic politics, and had the Belmont Stakes named after him, bears the same name—

his name from birth—as the distinctly un-Jewish Belmont that is the home of Portia in Shakespeare's play.

Edwin Booth, the son of the actor Junius Brutus Booth, and the brother of Abraham Lincoln's assassin, John Wilkes Booth, was a famous Shylock, and a single-minded one, driven by hatred and greed. "I have searched in vain for the slightest hint of anything resembling dignity or worthiness in the part," he wrote to a friend.[28]

There was also a real vogue for female Shylocks, both adult women and children. In the nineteenth century, this was not regarded as a scandal, and sometimes not even as a curiosity. Clara Fisher played the role successfully in both England and America, as did Charlotte Cushman and Catherine Macready. (Macready was the wife of a well-known Shakespearean actor; Cushman had been Portia in several productions of *Merchant,* and also played Romeo, Hamlet, and Iago.) Ellen Bateman, at the age of four, starred as Shylock opposite her sister Kate, a six-year-old Portia, and other female children were also cast, apparently successfully, as Shylock.[29] In 1929, however, when a woman played the part in a London production, the *London Times* critic wrote, "this Shylock occasionally left the Rialto; never the Contralto."[30]

Times were beginning to change by the last quarter of the nineteenth century and into the early years of the twentieth. The actor Henry Irving, the most celebrated Shylock of his era, was playing the part as a victim, as well as

Catherine Macready as Shylock

a villain. This was still not the humanist hero of the mid-twentieth century—far from it. But there was dignity in Irving's portrayal. The *Times* of London reported that he seemed to be performing "two distinct Shylocks," "the one erect, composed, dignified even in the complete overthrow of his long-cherished purpose, and almost by his bearing compelling our sympathies where they are most keenly raised against him; the other a screaming, incoherent old man, who seemed to have lost his wits together with his daughter and his ducats." The *Times* felt "strongly inclined to laugh" at the second Shylock, rather than to sympathize with him, "For," they wrote, "we must confess, we have never been able to share the sympathy that many commentators and critics have lavished on Shylock's ultimate discomfiture, or to understand in what way he was hardly treated by the Court of Venice." As for Shylock's motives, again the *Times* had little doubt: "It is an ancient grudge he bears; he hates them not so much because they call him Jew, but because he is a Jew."[31]

Famous people—like the prime minister of England, William Gladstone—came to see Irving play the part and thought it "his best." His exotic costume, as represented in a portrait of the period, might remind us, a little, of the criticisms offered of the Chandos portrait of Shakespeare: gold earrings, a dark tunic, a striped sash, a black cap with a yellow bar, majestic and vaguely "Oriental."

Henry Irving may not have been a Rothschild or a Belmont, but the shift to the modern period had, nonetheless, taken place. This slightly exoticized image may in fact mark a resistance to a more dangerous kind of realism—or it might suggest the "oriental Israelite Hebrew Jew" of which George du Maurier's Svengali, a native of German Poland, was a type.[32] Anti-Jewish pogroms in Russia were fueling the immigration of Russian Jews to England and America. In England, they settled in Whitechapel, a London area of pawnbrokers and shopkeepers. In New York, they populated the Lower East Side and began what would become a thriving Yiddish Shakespeare theater, often starring Jacob Adler, who also produced a play called *The Jewish King Lear.* *Mirele Efros, The Jewish Queen Lear,* was also a popular vehicle on the Yiddish stage.)[33] The contiguity of Shylock and Lear in the theater, both in New York City and in Germany, actually solved a small puzzle the answer to which I should have guessed long before: why Sigmund Freud might have thought to write an essay on "The Theme of the Three Caskets" that discusses both *Merchant* and *Lear.*

These were sometimes multilingual productions: when Adler's production of *Merchant,* which opened at the Bowery in 1901, was moved to Broadway two years later, Adler spoke Shylock's lines in Yiddish, while all the other

Jacob Adler as Shylock

actors spoke in English.[34] The play was a critical as well as a popular success. When it toured in Philadelphia, opening at the prestigious and high-culture Academy of Music, the *Philadelphia Inquirer* reported that many "veteran theatergoers and Shakespearean students" unhesitatingly declared "the Shylock of Jacob P. Adler" to be "the greatest ever seen on the American stage."[35] Adler's Yiddish apparently posed no obstacle for the audience. A review of the same production in Philadelphia's *Public Ledger* made clear that his language "did not grotesquely obtrude on Shakespeare's immortal English as many had feared, but seemed, as uttered by this actor, replete with gentle cadences and harmonies."[36] Later, when the German Jewish actor Richard Schildkraut, who had been a great success in the role in Germany before the rise of Hitler, moved to America and performed on the Yiddish stage, he played Shylock in German, while both the Antonio and the Portia in the cast spoke Yiddish.[37]

Jacob Adler saw Shakespeare's character as motivated by pride rather than revenge. In his own account he reverses what some might have regarded as the traditional image of Shylock in relation to the merchant Antonio:

Shylock, rich enough to forgo the interest on his three thousand ducats for the purely moral satisfaction of his revenge, such a Shylock, I say, would be richly dressed and proud of mien rather than the poor cringing figure time has made familiar. Antonio, on the other hand, is far from the chivalrous gentleman time has made familiar. . . . The two men are confronted in a supposed court of justice, a court packed with Antonio's friends, the judge openly committed to Antonio's cause, the prosecuting attorney a masquerading girl soon to be the bride of his bosom friend, and Shylock alone against them all without counsel, without advocate, with nothing on his side but the law.

The verdict, of course, goes against him. A quibble reverses the case, Antonio and the court divide the spoils between them and—*exit Shylock.* That's the end of him as far as Shakespeare's stage direction goes. But having bought so dearly the right to his contempt for his Christian enemies, would he not walk out of that courtroom head erect, the very apotheosis of defiant hatred and scorn? That is the way I see Shylock, and that is how I have played him.[38]

So the image of the Jew in modern culture was poised, or divided, at the turn of the twentieth century, between Whitechapel or the Lower East Side on the one hand, and the shadowy figures of international finance (and conspiracy, and world control) on the other: "Which is the merchant here, and which the Jew?" And when political troubles deepened in Germany, the figure of Shylock was, again, caught in the middle.

IN GERMANY, AS IN AMERICA, the play was popular, and its history in the twentieth century may, again, stand as an object lesson in the malleability of "intention," whether that of the author, the director, the actor, or the audience. Max Reinhardt, the celebrated director—who would ultimately emigrate to the United States—staged a 1905 production of *The Merchant of Venice* starring Richard Schildkraut, a production that was so successful that it played throughout Europe for the next thirty years. One theatergoer felt that "Schildkraut imbued the character with an unspeakable melancholy, which was elemental compared to the ennui of Antonio. Injustice was round him like a shroud. It is no mere chance," she added, "that this great actor created the most moving King Lear I have ever seen."[39] The verdict was widely shared. John Gross points out that Schildkraut's portrait was prominently displayed in Berlin's Deutsches Theater until the fateful year of 1933, when Joseph Goebbels ordered that it be taken down and publicly burned.[40] (Schildkraut's son, the American actor Joseph Schildkraut, played Hollywood roles as various as Judas Iscariot in Cecil B. DeMille's 1927 epic *The King of Kings,* and

Otto Frank, the father of Anne Frank, in the 1959 *Diary of Anne Frank,* thus ringing the changes on the question of Jewish agency and heroism on screen at some key moments in the twentieth century.)

While he was in Germany Reinhardt also directed Werner Krauss in the role of Shylock in a 1921 production. Krauss had starred in the title role of the film *The Cabinet of Dr. Caligari* and in a stage version of *Othello,* but initially, as Gross notes, Reinhardt had been skeptical about Krauss's portrayal of Shylock, suggesting that only a Jew could really understand the nuances of the part.[41] Krauss felt that this view was shortsighted and in response decided to put his own stamp on the part by acting with special aggressiveness onstage. The interpretation was effective, and Krauss played Shylock several times, for a number of directors, in the ensuing years.

But the political climate was changing rapidly. Werner Krauss was appointed an Actor of the State by Goebbels, and he appeared in the propaganda film *The Jew Süss* (1940), in which he played all the Jewish roles. In 1943 he performed in Vienna a very different Shylock from the one he had done in the twenties—another example of the "two Shylocks" theme, and also another piece of evidence to consider when assessing the effect of "intention." The Vienna production, described by Gross as "the most notorious *Merchant of Venice* of the Nazi years," directed by a longtime party member and staged at the express behest of the regional Nazi leader, presented the same Werner Krauss as a sinister and alien comic figure, with mannerisms designed to invoke the supposed "racial characteristics" of the "East European Jewish type."[42] Krauss's Shylock was praised in the Nazi press for its portrayal of Shylock as "pathological" and exhibiting "outer and inner uncleanliness."[43] Presumably, the audience was relieved to learn that, at least according to this production, Jessica was not in fact the Jew's daughter. In view of this fact, the light romantic comedy of her courtship by Lorenzo could be presented as the story of an "idyllic pair of lovers."[44] It was in the immediately following years that the full horror of the war, the concentration camps, and the consequences for European Jewry would become known to the world.

Postwar productions would have to take this into account, but they did so slowly and fitfully. The British director Jonathan Miller cast Laurence Olivier in the Shylock role for a production in 1970—which I saw—and which set the play in late Victorian England, with all the characters, including Shylock, identically dressed in top hats and frock coats. This was the assimilation Shylock, the Disraeli Shylock, the Rothschild Shylock, the Shylock as up-and-coming Englishman.

The part has been played in recent years by Patrick Stewart, by David

Suchet, by Antony Sher, by Al Pacino, and by Dustin Hoffman. Sher's Shylock was performed with "a heavy accent, a shuffling gait, a beard, long hair, and exotic clothes": the Royal Shakespeare Company described it as "a bold attempt to free the play from charges of anti-Semitism. In this production, Shylock is an ugly character who is only responding to the much worse behaviour of his tormentors." Will LeBow's wise guy/garment district Shylock at the ART was a deliberate return to both the "farce" theme of Shakespeare's own time and the "Whitechapel/Lower East Side" vision of Jews in modern culture.

BUT IT IS OFTEN OUTSIDE the theater that the most virulent use of the play, and of Shylock, is made. And not only in Nazi Germany and Austria. An example is available in the writings of an American who was not a sophisticated thinker, though he was an immensely powerful cultural presence— Henry Ford.

Ford was a car manufacturer, an innovator, and a classic American industrialist. But he also had some xenophobic ideas. He published in the 1920s a series of articles about Jews in the *Dearborn Independent,* a Michigan newspaper which, despite its name, was "published by the Ford Motor Company," and he was the author of several highly negative books on the topic, including one called *The International Jew: The World's Foremost Problem.*[45] A version of this book was published in German in 1921; it was edited and reissued, with a defiant preface by an admirer, in 1947, the year of Henry Ford's death. *The International Jew* includes chapters on "How the Jews Use Power," on "Jewish Supremacy in the Theatre and Cinema," on "The Battle for Press Control," and on how "Jewish Jazz Becomes Our National Music." Unsurprisingly, it also fixated on *The Merchant of Venice.*

Henry Ford was an enthusiast of the American schoolbook called *McGuffey's Reader,* the anthology that was the main textbook in American schools from 1836 through the 1920s. The readers went through six editions. As a child, Ford read and memorized them; as an adult, he could quote them from memory. He paid to have the entire series reprinted and distributed to schools across the United States.

One of the stories Ford had studied in the *Fifth Eclectic Reader* was called "Shylock, or the Pound of Flesh." "Why did Shylock choose the pound of flesh rather than the payment of his debt?" was one of the study questions, and another was, "How is Shylock punished? Is his punishment just? And why?" In 1914, the Detroit branch of the B'nai Brith Anti-Defamation League sought to have *The Merchant of Venice* removed from the public schools because it "maliciously and scurrilously traduce[d] the character of the Jew." Shylock, they wrote, "has become an unhappy symbol of Jewish vindictiveness, malice, and hatred." Henry Ford indicated that he took this as an affront to McGuffey, and his *Reader.*

In his chapter on "The Jews and Power" in *The International Jew,* Ford had noted a similar effort, on the part of "the Jews," that "force[d] *The Merchant of Venice* to be dropped from public schools in Texas, [and] Ohio" in 1906–7, and observed that "Rabbis force[d] [the] Hartford, Connecticut, school board to drop *The Merchant of Venice* from the reading list."[46]

This is not an uncomplicated issue, since it involves censorship. It might be argued that such efforts are especially shortsighted when what is censored is a play by Shakespeare—a play that can and has been read in many ways, not all of them, by any means, traducing the character of Shylock. But the incidents are indicative, if not of "modern culture," then of a kind of crisis of modernity-in-the-making.

In a chapter of *The International Jew* called "The World's Foremost Problem" (remember, this is written ten years before the Nazis come to power in Germany), Ford directly addresses the fantasy figure of his book's title:

> The International Jew rules not because he is rich, but because in a most marked degree he possesses the commercial and masterful genius of his race, and avails himself of a racial loyalty and solidarity the like of which exists in no other human group. He rules, at the top of affairs in every country worth while, by virtue of certain qualities which are inherent in the Jewish nature. Every Jew has these qualities even if not in the supreme sense, just as every Englishman has Shakespeare's tongue but not in Shakespeare's degree. And thus it is impracticable, if not impossible, to consider the International Jew without laying the foundations broadly upon Jewish character and psychology.[47]

Despite his personal attributes, his affection for his wife and for his daughter, Shylock on the Rialto is the uncanny prototype of Henry Ford's International Jew—commercial, masterful in business, imbued with "racial loyalty and solidarity"—and also (an irony Ford will not recognize) with Shakespeare's tongue. Not only does he outlive the play, he has been transmuted into a common verb—a very common, though uncomplimentary verb: to shylock. As Richard Hofstadter pointed out in *The Paranoid Style in American Politics* (1965), "The Shylock image pervades money crankery from the Greenbackers to Father Coughlin and Ezra Pound."[48]

"PARANOID" IS THE RIGHT WORD HERE. Persecution, grandeur, jealousy: these are the delusions, cultural as well as personal, that summon up the fear that is embodied in this character, as he makes his way through the ages, attached and detached from hatreds that evolve across the centuries. When the United States asked for the payment of war debts after World War I, it was taunted with the name "Uncle Shylock," a name that still recurs in print and Web references today.[49] Shylock is the ghost that will not be appeased. He marks a space of guilt, fear, transference, atavism. Along with "romeo," he is the only Shakespearean character to have become a noun on his own in the dictionary. Between these two lies the story of modern culture. Shylock's dictionary entry is so politically incorrect, and yet so pervasive. Although the word is not often heard today, Shylock himself is never wholly out of sight, or out of mind.

One of the greatest problems presented by *The Merchant of Venice* has always been that of genre: it declares itself as a comedy, even in some critics' estimate a "festive comedy"—it ends in three marriages, in the miraculous return of a fortune thought lost at sea, and in the exile of the destructive and blocking figure who seemed for a while to stand in the way of the happiness of the young lovers and the wealthy merchant.

And yet . . . and yet . . . right in the middle of the play there is Shylock. And he tends to steal the spotlight. Villainy is always attractive onstage; so is pathos; so, for that matter, is farce. Next to this deep interest in villainy, the other plot, the love plot and the casket choice, often seem minor to an audi-

"*Hey, just wanted to say loved 'Merchant.'*"

ence attuned to tragedy. Often in production, the Belmont scenes in act 5 are cut—they do not seem to fit the mood, and they are an anticlimax for a modern audience, rather than the fitting close to a happy comedy of marriage. Yet in Shakespearean comedy there is *always* a tragedy embedded, somewhere. In this one, the tragedy often wins out. Should it? This question of instability, of things turning into other things—comedy into tragedy, Christians into Jews and Jews into Christians, women into men and men into "women," Venice into Belmont and Belmont into Venice—is part of the affect of the play. It is one of the things that make this play so "modern," or even postmodern. Its instability is the only stable thing about it.

THE CHARACTER OF SHYLOCK EVOLVED over the years from a comic butt to a full-fledged villain, and then, gradually, to a victim of prejudice whose actions were explainable, if not excusable, because of the way he was treated by Venetian society.

By the second half of the twentieth century, after the unimaginable horrors of the Holocaust, Shylock had become a different kind of symbol. The social philosopher Theodor Adorno famously remarked that "to write a poem after Auschwitz is barbaric"—though he later qualified and explained his aphorism: "The statement that it is not possible to write poetry after Auschwitz does not hold absolutely, but it is certain that after Auschwitz, because Auschwitz was possible and remains possible for the foreseeable future, lighthearted art is no longer conceivable." In fact, Adorno saw "a withering away of the alternative between lightheartedness and seriousness, between the comic and the tragic, almost between life and death," as newly "evident in contemporary art." Thus, "the genres are becoming blurred," since "the tragic gesture seems comic and the comic dejected": "The art that moves ahead into the unknown, the only art now possible, is neither lighthearted nor serious; the third possibility, however, is cloaked in obscurity, as though embedded in a void the figures of which are traced by advanced works of art."[50] This was Adorno's reflection of his own century. But we could say that it is anticipated by Shakespeare, and by Shylock. The tragic gesture seems comic and the comic dejected. The "third possibility," "the only art now possible," is configured, "as though embedded in a void," by the complex dramaturgy of *The Merchant of Venice*.

Shylock after Auschwitz, as we saw, was changed, if only by the consciousness that made "Never again" a slogan for the times. For a while, he was a white-bearded patriarch, a damaged, secular Moses. The jokey young Shylock, played by Will LeBow, struck some audience members as a scandal.

Whether seen as a comic figure or a tragic one, a social-climbing Victorian (in Laurence Olivier's performance) or an aversive and vituperative presence, these Shylocks were mimetic as well as emblematic—that is, they were performed to represent a kind of person, whether a negative fantasy or a neighbor from down the block.

This was far from the only way *The Merchant of Venice* was taken up by its readers and performers, however. As the citations from Adorno will suggest, philosophers and cultural theorists have used and appropriated this play in ways very different from the mimetic or imitative: ways of reading that are allegorical, we could say, or allusive; ways that take the play as the starting point for another kind of discourse.

I NOTED IN THE INTRODUCTION that Karl Marx was so familiar with Shakespeare's plays that he quoted them frequently—and often rather unexpectedly—in his speeches and writings. *The Merchant of Venice,* with its reflections upon use value and exchange value, is, however, a play we might have expected him to cite. Through Marx's lens, Shylock becomes the allegorized voice of Capital.

In an excerpt from *Capital* about child labor, the humane workmen and factory workers protest against the exploitation of children, but since there is a loophole in the law they can do nothing about it:

> Workmen and factory inspectors protested on hygienic and moral grounds, but Capital answered:
>   "My deeds upon my head! I crave the law,
>   The penalty and forfeit of my bond."

> —The lynx eye of Capital discovered that the Act of 1844 did not allow 5 hours' work before mid-day without a pause of at least 30 minutes for refreshment, but prescribed nothing of the kind for work after mid-day. Therefore, it claimed and obtained the enjoyment not only of making children drudge without intermission from 2:00 to 8:30 p.m., but also of making them hunger during that time.
>   "Ay, his heart.
>   So says the bond."

Marx calls such cruelty—making children work long hours without food—"This Shylock-clinging to the letter of the law of 1844."[51] So Shylock has become a disembodied voice, a ghost, the ghostly cry of the literalizing law, the loophole that permits cruelty to children.

In another example, from a footnote to Marx and Engels's *Communist Manifesto*, a long discussion of the bourgeoisie and the rapidly changing means of production concludes with a phrase that the social theorist Marshall Berman used as the title of his classic 1982 book about modernity, *All That Is Solid Melts into Air: The Experience of Modernity*:

> All that is solid melts into air, all that is holy is profaned, and man is at last compelled to face with sober senses his real conditions of life, and his relations with his kind:
> "You take my life
>   When you do take the means whereby I live."
>
> *Shakespeare*[52]

Instead of "Capital," the disembodied voice of Shylock is now "Shakespeare"—quoted as a confirmation of the supposed voice of "man" under capitalism, caught up in what Berman calls "the dialectical motion of modernity," which "turns ironically against its prime movers, the bourgeoisie." Shylock *is* the bourgeoisie, for Marx, here forced to face "the real conditions" of his life and his relations with his fellow men.

In such intellectual moments as these, Marx—one of the primary theorists of modernity—ventriloquizes the voice of Shylock to embody an economic and cultural force in the world.

FOR MARX, HIMSELF BORN A JEW, Shylock is a figure for capital and for the literal law, and he is invoked frequently in Marx's writing. For Sigmund Freud he is a figure for the father—and his name is not even mentioned.

Freud's 1913 essay "The Theme of the Three Caskets" is a curious document, since it turns out not to be about *The Merchant of Venice* at all, but rather about *King Lear*. Freud begins by explaining the reason he is looking at these plays: "Two scenes from Shakespeare, one from a comedy and the other from a tragedy, have lately given me occasion for posing and solving a small problem."[53] This is very "Freud"—the easy tone, the "small problem," and Shakespeare's plays used as case studies. Freud writes two kinds of case studies, those based on real patients, though they are given pseudonyms, and those based on literary characters. From both, he derives principles about behavior, character, neurosis, and desire.

What does Freud have to say about *The Merchant of Venice*? Well, really, not much. He tells the story of the suitors' choice between the three caskets, and he digresses a little to say that he thinks Bassanio is blathering when he gives his big set piece speech about how the world is deceived with ornament: "what he has to say in glorification of lead as against gold and silver is little and has a forced ring. If in psycho-analytic practice we were confronted with such a speech, we should suspect that there were concealed motives behind the unsatisfying reasons produced."[54]

More important, for him, is that he finds concealed motives behind the unsatisfying (because overformulaic) casket choice: if one looks at it structurally rather than narratively, it is a man's choice among three caskets—and since (this is Freud) caskets, as symbolic containers, are emblematic of women, what we really have here is a *man's choice between three women*. In other words, behind Shakespeare's uneasy comedy lies Shakespeare's most profound tragedy: the choice is the choice of *King Lear,* a man choosing among three daughters.

Freud himself had three daughters, the youngest of whom was his intellectual heir, Anna Freud. By interpreting *The Merchant of Venice* as a concealed version of *King Lear,* he is able to set aside the problematic Jewish Shylock and replace him with a more appealing Shakespearean patriarch, the noble and universal Lear.[55]

Both Marx and Freud intersect with *The Merchant of Venice* in interesting and symptomatic ways—Marx by appropriating the play's language, and Freud by resisting and transposing its situation and characters. But for me perhaps the most interesting twentieth-century philosophical reading of Shakespeare's play is a 1944 essay by Jean-Paul Sartre, *Anti-Semite and Jew.*

Sartre's essay never mentions Shakespeare. He is writing from within the French tradition, rather than from an English, American, or German context where Shakespeare always lurks somewhere behind the scenes. It is entirely possible that he did not have Shakespeare, or *The Merchant of Venice,* in mind at all. What does it mean, then, to call *Anti-Semite and Jew* a reading of Shakespeare's play?

To see how we might read Sartre together with Shakespeare, it will be helpful first to return to the structure—the very balanced structure—of the play.

The Merchant of Venice is built on dyads and dialectics: pairs and opposites that mysteriously attract one another. For all of its peculiarities—this play combines a fairy tale structure (the choice of the three caskets) with a stock tale of a phantasmatic villain and an impossible wager whose payment would be death—this tale begins in symmetry and ends in symmetry.

The first two scenes give us Antonio and Portia, each melancholy, each for no reason he or she can name: "In sooth, I know not why I am so sad" is the opening line of the play. It is Antonio's line, and he suffers from a very "modern" condition of anomie: "It wearies me, you say it wearies you." Antonio's sadness is both over- and underdetermined. He does not know its cause: no cause is adequate, not worry about his ships at sea or their rich cargoes, not being in love. He scoffs at both—though it will turn out that he has reason to fear both.

The second scene presents Portia, equally sad, equally unwilling to fix her sadness on a single cause: "By my troth, Nerissa, my little body is aweary of this great world." She has a reason: what she considers to be her father's unjust will, which makes her marriage subject to the riddle of the casket choice— "so is the will of a living daughter curbed by the will of a dead father" (1.2.21). Love and fortune are issues for her, as for Antonio. Both could lose them; both could win.

But I want to focus on the structural symmetry here: Antonio and Portia. Because, of course, the play will bring them together as lovers of Bassanio. It is a collision-conflict waiting to happen. And for this reason, the end of the play is, in modern productions at least, a doubly "tragic" one, despite the fact that the play is billed as a comedy. The fourth act will give us the courtroom scene and the discomfiture of Shylock; the fifth act will give us Antonio as fifth wheel, the one Venetian left out of the love pairings (while the three sets of young lovers, each more selfish and self-regarding than the next, proceed to the happiness of marriage and of lovemaking, Antonio is the one left out, the one left over). Despite his lines of gratitude to Portia when she magically informs him that his lost ships have come home safe—"Sweet lady, you have given me life and living"—the Antonio of a contemporary production grinds his teeth: Portia has the real prize, Bassanio.

The play's other pairing, is, of course, equally obvious: Antonio and Shylock. "Which is the merchant here, and which the Jew?" The lines that Portia speaks in the courtroom, when she enters dressed as the Doctor of Laws, Balthasar, are exceedingly curious in naturalistic terms. Unless we imagine a production like Laurence Olivier's, where every man onstage wears a version of the same costume (in Olivier's case Victorian top hat and frock coat), she must easily be able to tell them apart. But this is "blind justice." Before the law, they are equal. Which is the merchant here, and which the Jew?

Both lend money; not only Shylock. Antonio lends money to Bassanio so he can wive it wealthily in Belmont: "In Belmont is a lady richly left." Indeed, Shylock names the very fact of their curious twinship, their curious union: it is a "merry bond" (1.3.169). The wager about the pound of flesh (that phrase that floats so oddly through modern language as if it were entirely and only a figure of speech) binds them, seals them, in what Shylock punningly calls "kindness," meaning both generosity and alike-ness. They are of the same kind, these two, he insists. Despite the fact that Antonio despises him and fails to recognize him. Fails, indeed, to recognize *himself* in Shylock.

Despite Shylock's famous entreaty, one also couched in the rhetoric of adequation, although it is seldom seen in that light ("Hath not a Jew eyes . . ."), [56] Antonio will not see this resemblance. And perhaps neither will the audience.

That is, until the courtroom scene—which is the merchant here, and which the Jew?—when the two are about to change places. And where the threat of Shylock with the knife and the scales—the pound of flesh to be taken from the heart, or from "what part of your body pleases me" (the play says it twice, locates it in two different places on the body)—this threat is, at the last minute, reversed, and instead of Shylock making Antonio a Jew ("This is kind I offer" [1.3.35]) Antonio makes Shylock a "Christian" (1.3.174). By forced conversion.

Critics as well as psychoanalysts—psychoanalysts as well as critics—have seen this threat as a symbolic threat of castration. Antonio by his own description is a "tainted wether of the flock" (4.1.113), and a wether is a castrated ram. Or they have seen it as a threat of circumcision, the two knife-events so often conflated in the hateful mythology of the anti-Jewish past.

Which is the merchant here, and which the Jew? Antonio's final lines to Portia, so ambivalently expressed in so many modern productions—productions where the love of Antonio for Bassanio is often played, these days, as sexual passion, not as platonic friendship—are these: "Sweet lady, you have given me life and living, / For here I read for certain that my ships / Are safely come to road" (5.1.285–87).

And Shylock's lines in the courtroom scene, when he is stripped of his wealth, are these: "You take my life / When you do take the means whereby I live" (4.1.371–72).

Which is the merchant here, and which the Jew? They construct each other; each is the other's Other, the other's fantasy and nightmare, both self and anti-self. This is true of the pairing of Antonio and Shylock and of the pairing of Portia and Antonio.

And this is the reading offered by Sartre's *Anti-Semite and Jew,* written in France in 1944. The anti-Semite creates the Jew. "The anti-Semite has chosen hate because hate is a faith," Sartre says. [57] "The anti-Semites . . . like to play with discourse. . . . They delight in acting in bad faith, since they seek not to persuade by sound argument but to intimidate and disconcert." [58] Might we here remember the courtroom scene, the triumphant Portia and the egregious, rejoicing Graziano ("A Daniel, still say I, a second Daniel! / I thank thee, Jew, for teaching me that word" [4.1.335–36])? Sartre says that "the phrase, 'I hate the Jews,' is one that is uttered in chorus: in pronouncing it, one attaches himself to a tradition and to a community—the tradition and community of the mediocre."[59] Here we can think only of the mocking voices of Graziano, Salerio, and Solanio as they race to outdo one another in mimicking Shylock's accent and his distress, as he laments the loss of his daughter and his ducats. And, most tellingly, Sartre describes the design of reciprocity—the very design that we have seen operate, centrally, in *The Merchant of Venice*. "The anti-Semite is in the unhappy position of having a vital need for the very enemy he wishes to destroy."[60]

In his preface to an edition of *Anti-Semite and Jew*, published in 1995, the political theorist Michael Walzer perceptively compares the book to a play:

> Sartre's book [says Walzer] should not be read as a piece of social science or even . . . as a philosophical speculation. His best work in the 1940s was in drama (*No Exit* was first performed in 1944; *The Respectful Prostitute* in 1946; *Dirty Hands* in 1948), and *Anti-Semite and Jew* is a Marxist/existentialist morality play, whose characters are produced by their dramatic interactions. The interactions are never actually enacted by people with proper names; the dialogue is never rendered in the first person. Everything remains abstract, impersonal, and yet the "situations" and the "choices" are highly dramatic. . . . The drama is grim, not tragic finally, but savagely critical of the world it describes. . . . This is the structure of the Sartrean drama: each character creates the others and chooses himself. . . . The drama arises from the interplay of social forces and individual decisions.[61]

As a theater critic, Walzer is ingenious and persuasive: he offers a reading of Sartre's reading and ties it to the question of modernity:

> The anti-Semite creates the Jew, but before that he creates himself within his situation. (But isn't this situation in part the creation of the Jew as the anti-Semite has created him? Sartre's argument is necessarily circular. The inauthentic Jew, who appears later on in the drama, is in fact an agent—though not the only or the most important agent—of the modernity to which anti-Semites react.)[62]

And again, most powerfully, "The anti-Semite 'chooses' the Jew only because he is available; any dispossessed, stigmatized minority, any 'unhistorical people' could as easily be chosen. The Jew in Europe is the exposed face of modern life."[63]

"The Jew in Europe is the exposed face of modern life." Those individuals who since World War II have been called "displaced persons"—refugees or prisoners removed from their native country—are also in this play bearers of Freudian "displacement," redirecting impulses onto a substitute target. It is this uncanny reciprocity—the finding of oneself in the hated (or beloved) Other one creates for oneself, and the pushing away of that unwelcome knowledge—that is the pattern produced within *The Merchant of Venice,* and reproduced in every social drama, often with destructive, even horrific results.

Michael Walzer's phrase "The Jew in Europe is the exposed face of modern life," as projected onto Sartre's text, offers what is, in my opinion, as good a reading of Shakespeare's play for our times as we are likely to find in a single sentence. Yet our central paradox remains the same: the modern life Walzer describes is informed by Shakespeare. Even if we bracket the question of intention as a cultural preoccupation, the couplet ascribed to Alexander Pope stands in equipoise with Sartre: this is the Jew that Shakespeare drew.

SEVEN

OTHELLO

The Persistence of Difference

W HAT'S BLACK AND WHITE AND READ ALL OVER?"
This is one of the oldest and corniest of riddles. And as we'll see, *Othello* is itself uncannily, and literally, illustrative of this riddle: a play about a (black) Moorish general and his (white) Venetian bride; a dark tragedy that turns on the loss of a white handkerchief embroidered with red strawberries; a play text printed in black and white, set up in type from papers that, if the editors of the First Folio are to be believed, scarce contained a blot.

"What's black and white and read all over?"

The riddle's joke, such as it is, turns on the homonym, or punning word-play, around the word "read" (R-E-D or R-E-A-D), and the answer to the conundrum is either "a newspaper" or "an embarrassed zebra," depending upon which spelling of "read/red" you choose. This "newspaper riddle" (as it is usually called) dates from the early part of the twentieth century and was frequently used by stage comedians in minstrel shows, vaudeville, and early radio. The joke's structure is one of deliberate and comic indirection, like other jokes popular in minstrelsy: Why did the chicken cross the road? To get to the other side. The listener finds that he or she has focused on the wrong element or on an element wrongly interpreted or misunderstood.

In the early 1960s variations on this familiar riddle—what's black and white and red all over?—were introduced by punning literal readings of the word *red* (R-E-D), making the joke a "catch," with a hidden element designed to trip you up. (We might call this catch the "Iago element" in the joke—"Honest, my lord? Think, my lord?"—since it makes the responder, the "mark," the targeted victim, rethink the very premises of the question.) The obvious answer, "newspaper," was triumphantly declared to be wrong, and the right answer was, variously, "an embarrassed (or blushing) zebra," "a sunburned penguin," "a skunk with diaper rash"—or other, even more desperate variations.[1]

A closer glance, or rather a closer listen, will make clear that it is not only wordplay, but also phrasing and what poets call the caesura, the place of the pause, that inflects the riddle text: the question "what's black and white / and read all over" is semantically as well as denotatively different from "what's black and white and red / all over." So the responder is asked to be a critic, as well as a wit—or a wit, as well as a critic. But no matter how shrewd the mark may be, he or she is doomed to fail.

Whichever version of the riddle you think you are hearing, your questioner will triumphantly reply with the *other* answer: if you guess, successfully, that the answer is "a newspaper," he or she will contradict you: "No, it's an embarrassed zebra"—or vice versa. The wit of this riddling exchange comes not, or not only, in the answer, or solution, to the riddle, but in the fact that the riddle has two solutions and that the "right" answer is always the *other* one, the one you didn't pick, or didn't guess, or didn't hear correctly. In other words, it is impossible to get the answer right. The right answer is always wrong.

If Sigmund Freud is correct in his assessment of how jokes work—and we will return to this question later—the effect is produced by a kind of dislocation: "we [are] obliged, *simultaneously or in rapid succession,* to apply to one and the same act of ideation two different ideational methods, between which the 'comparison' is then made and the comic difference emerges. . . . One of these two views, following the hints contained in the joke, passes along the path of thought through the unconscious; the other stays on the surface. . . . We should perhaps be justified in representing the pleasure from a joke that is heard as being derived from the difference between these two methods of viewing it."[2]

In what follows I will try to answer the riddle of my title both ways, by first proving that *Othello* is like a newspaper, and then that it is like a zebra. And, then, "taken together with the other proofs," I will try to see why this particular play by Shakespeare is so much like the riddle—why, that is to say, whatever "answer" we come up with about *Othello* turns out to be wrong.

What's black and white and read all over?
A newspaper.
How is *Othello* like a newspaper? Let us count the ways. The play and its characters are cited, insistently, consistently, persistently, and usually inaccurately, as the comparison text for events in the news. The press, the media, and the Web have appropriated *Othello* in black-and-white headlines, and, all too often, with black-and-white judgments that do not allow for shades of gray. What's black and white and misquoted all over? As we'll see in a moment, many of these citations and quotations are unintentionally comic.

Modern public speakers often get their "Shakespeare" from books of quotations, like *Bartlett's*, which identify the play (*Othello*) rather than the speaker (Iago, Roderigo, Cassio). So Shakespeare's sublime cleverness, in reusing phrases that had already become boring clichés in his own time by giving them to unreliable or untrustworthy speakers, is routinely and regularly undone by contemporary speakers and writers, who offer up these quotations "flat," as if they had the moral weight of Shakespeare behind them. They restore the banality that Shakespeare was at such pains to critique. Thus, for example, Iago is always quoted as believing in "good name in man and woman" when in fact he has no regard for public reputation at all, but only cites it as a way of gulling Othello and Cassio.

> Good name in man and woman, dear my lord,
> Is the immediate jewel of their souls.
> Who steals my purse, steals trash; 'tis something, nothing;
> 'Twas mine, 'tis his, and has been slave to thousands.
> But he that filches from me my good name
> Robs me of that which not enriches him
> And makes me poor indeed.
>
> *3.3.160–66*

And where Iago dismissively says that he'd be a fool to wear his heart on his sleeve for birds to peck at, generals, press secretaries, and congressional representatives all proudly testify to their sincerity by declaring, "I wear my heart on my sleeve."

Thus, for example, in a commencement address at the New School University in 2001, Theodore Sorensen, himself a former speechwriter, applied Iago's "who steals my purse steals trash" doctrine to America's reputation after the Abu Ghraib scandal, the Iraq War, and the low esteem with which this country was now held by allies, by the United Nations, and by the international community: "True, we have not lost either war we chose nor lost too much of our wealth. But we have lost something worse—our good name for truth and justice. To paraphrase Shakespeare: He who steals our nation's purse, steals trash. 'Twas ours, 'tis his, and has been slave to thousands. But he that filches our good name . . . makes us poor indeed."[3] The sentiments seem—to me, at least—irreproachable. But the "Shakespeare" component is a little shaky.

The business pages of the newspaper are likewise natural targets for today's Shakespearean references: the phenomenon of "identity theft," for example, has been a natural association for "who steals my purse steals trash," since in this case it is indeed a "good name" (and a credit rating) that can be stolen.

"Much has changed in the last 400 years," wrote a money columnist in *USA Today,* blissfully unaware of credit scandals in the Elizabethan era. "Those who filch our good names have come up with numerous ways to enrich themselves at our expense. They run up credit card bills, write bad checks and buy cars." Columnist James J. Kilpatrick, apparently eager to show that he knew Iago was a bad guy, prefaces his own article on credit bureaus by asserting that "the dastard gets off one great line"—and then quotes the passage ("who steals my purse steals trash") on his way to a consideration of the question of credit bureaus and bad credit reports.[4]

Othello has also in recent years come to the attention of what are perhaps today's most voracious consumers of Shakespeare, business professionals and motivational speakers. A wave of "Shakespeare on business," "the Bard in the boardroom" books has hit the stands in recent years, and some of these draw their "real life" experience directly from *Othello.* Sections on "Flatterers and Yes Men," "Office Politics," "Working Stiffs," and "Practicing Business Ethics" all cite key passages from the play, with Iago, unsurprisingly, at the center of most of them. Here, as a sample, is just one of these gems. (Bear in mind that this is offered as serious functional advice for business folk, not as fodder for the Jay Leno or Jon Stewart show.) From a section on "Dining Room Deals":

> Shakespeare knew that a major problem with wining and dining clients is the very fact that you have to eat and especially drink with them. . . . Even though Shakespeare did not invent the "happy hour" (he used this phrase at least a half a dozen times in as many plays, though not always in the context of drinking), he foresaw that the three-martini lunch of today, just like the drinking bouts of yore, could have unpleasant consequences. In *Othello* (Act II, scene iii) Cassio, a lieutenant in the army of Venice, says: "I have very poor and unhappy brains for drinking. I could well wish courtesy would invent some other custom of entertainment."[5]

And from a section on "Public Relations":

> Then there are always those unfortunate souls who feel, warranted or not, that they have no skill at presenting themselves, to the world. Such was Othello. In *Othello* (Act I, scene iii) he explains why public speaking is not his strong suit:
> Rude am I in my speech,
> And little bless'd with the soft phrase of peace; . . .
> And little of this great world can I speak
> More than pertains to feats of broils and battle,
> And therefore little shall I grace my case
> In speaking for myself.[6]

To Othello's eloquent self-analysis the author then adds this trenchant comment: "The problem is, if you don't speak for yourself, others will. And perhaps talk themselves into your job."[7]

Media attention to *Othello* has shifted quite a lot over the years, and in fascinating ways. In 1994 the country was awash in O. J. Simpson/Othello references—there seemed no Web site, no op-ed page, and no academic conference without them. The supposed analogies were simply too glaring: black hero, white wife, violent death. O.J.'s farewell ("suicide") letter, discovered before the famous televised Bronco ride through Los Angeles and his arrest, began with an assertion that if he and his wife Nicole "had a problem, it's because I loved her too much,"[8] prompting comparisons with Othello's final ("suicide") speech about loving not wisely but too well.[9] Every newspaper contained a version of this "American tragedy" and its Shakespearean counterpart. It was black and white and read all over.

But times have changed. Somehow, in the last few years, popular attention has shifted from Othello to Iago. We are now in an Iago moment. Indeed, we have been there for some time, in terms of popular culture. The Bill Clinton–Monica Lewinsky scandal (and how long ago that seems!) produced a multiplicity of Iago figures, from Bill to Hillary to Kenneth Starr to—most surprisingly and insistently, Linda Tripp. Tripp worked in the White House and was then transferred to the Pentagon Public Affairs Office; she became Monica Lewinsky's confidante, despite the difference in their ages. When she learned of Lewinsky's relationship with Clinton, she consulted a friend who was a literary agent, and began secretly taping her phone conversations. Ultimately she gave the tapes to the so-called independent prosecutor, Ken Starr, who was investigating the affair.

Almost immediately, in the public press, Linda Tripp began to be compared to Iago, in a startling number of instances.

- Columnist Mary McGrory described her as "an ex–White House employee with the malice of Iago."[10]
- Maureen Dowd of *The New York Times* called her the "Iago of Pentagon City" in a column that was widely reprinted.[11]
- Attorney Charles Ruff, representing Bill Clinton at the president's impeachment trial, supported Lewinsky's claim that no one had asked her to lie and cited her conversations with Linda Tripp, and Tripp's participation—"I have to say I was sort of reminded of Iago and Desdemona's handkerchief."[12]
- Andrew Morton, the author of *Monica's Story*, told Katie Couric that when he was writing his book, "I was trying to think of a literary figure

who was comparable to the malevolence and the evil that this woman has and I can think of Iago in *Othello,* but there's no female character who's betrayed another woman quite so comprehensively, quite so systematically, and quite so maliciously as this woman has."[13]

- Liz Langley remarked in the *Orlando Weekly,* "She's Monica's friend and then her Iago," calling Tripp "the most hated woman in America."[14]

Where did all this come from? The Tripp-as-Iago trope is quite a bit more far-fetched as a comparison than O.J. as Othello, but it received, as you see, a good deal of play in the media. Many other figures in the Clinton impeachment saga also got caught up in this web of analogies. *Othello* was on the country's mind. Karen DeCrow, a lawyer and former president of the National Organization for Women (NOW) varied the formula by focusing on Ken Starr and his evidence: "Iago had the handkerchief; Kenneth Starr has a blue dress," she wrote, in a column critiquing the invasion of Bill Clinton's sex life.[15] And Bruce Fein, the former associate deputy attorney general of the United States, held a news conference on Starr's investigation, in which he compared—or rather, contrasted—Bill Clinton with Desdemona. ("We have a president who seems to be imitating Raskolnikov in *Crime and Punishment* more than Desdemona in *Othello* in indicating what his own conscience speaks about these allegations."[16])

What cultural work is the analogy to *Othello* doing in the Clinton-Lewinsky narrative? Like the O.J. trial, the Clinton scandal now seems to belong to the mists of time, the long-ago 1990s, when newspapers, some of them, were indeed still printed in black and white, and read in hard copy rather than electronically. On the Web you can find references to Dick Cheney and to Karl Rove as the Iagos of the Bush administration, as well as to Ahmed Chalabi as "Iago in a silk suit," and to neoconservative Richard Perle as "America's Iago."[17] But post 9/11 we have a new Iago, and (surprise!) race is back in the picture, together with religion. And once again the story is interestingly displaced.

Othello is a "Moor," and much has been made of the question of his religious conversion from Islam to Christianity as part of his acculturation to Venetian society. Critic G. K. Hunter calls him "a great Christian gentleman," and asserts that "not only is Othello a Christian . . . he is the leader of Christendom in the last and highest sense in which Christendom existed as a viable entity."[18] (Yet as the Arden edition points out, "we cannot prove Othello to be a Christian convert," and there is no real reason to think of the Muslim religion, rather than paganism or a "worship of sun and moon and elemental forces of Nature," as the only alternative to Christianity.)[19] Is he one of *us,* or one of *them*?

The most recent development, in newspapers and on the Internet, is an explosion (if I may use so loaded a term) of references to *Iago*—not Othello—as a terrorist, and explicitly as an Islamic terrorist. Thus, for example, Ibrahim Amin, writing from the Free Muslims Coalition, made the strong claim, in an article called "Killing with One's Mind: Iago and the War on Terror," that the "mullahs and Imams . . . who constantly poison the minds of their pupils, constituents, or congregations . . . take the Iago approach," instilling in others, by insinuation and assertion, the will to kill. "They kill with their minds, moulding murderers who will kill for them." Amin's proposed remedy, for "dealing with the Iago form of villain," is to reconvert the mullahs and Imams, by the use of money and other means: "When we have such religious leaders in place, they can then play the role of Iago for our side. Each day they can manipulate their congregations, turning their thoughts against the terrorists and making them see such groups as enemies of Islam."[20]

But if Iago is now an Islamic terrorist, he is also, equally interestingly, a computer model for terrorism. Project IAGO is a model created as part of a war-gaming scenario at the U.S. Naval Postgraduate School in Monterey, California, "built on information about Ramsey Yousef, the Islamic Jihadist involved in the attack on the World Trade Center in 1993." The model is intended, in part, to simulate how Yousef, or someone like him, would respond to current events in the news. The basis of the program is something called "conceptual blending," a cognitive theory that tries to get at motivations below the level of consciousness, and regards the subject as an "adaptive agent." The next step, as the journal *Popular Science* noted cheerfully, was "a network of multidimensional cognitively complex villains that can act autonomously and in coordination (think terror cells)."[21]

"Shakespeare's Iago was the perfect starting point for what we wanted to explore," says John Hiles, the lead designer of the IAGO project. "How do you get inside the thought operations of another who is very, very different from you?" Hiles explained that although the word *IAGO,* in capital letters, is an acronym (for Integrated Asymmetric Goal Organization), "the acronym was an afterthought to make the project's rationale more accessible to people who haven't read the play." For Hiles, Shakespeare's play was the linchpin: "Iago's destruction of those around him and of himself wasn't driven by ideology or religion as far as I can tell. Shakespeare placed the destructiveness deeper than that. . . . I picked Iago as the name of my project because the research focuses on a terrible question that won't be easily answered."[22]

Iago has long been a type of the villain, a figure for "the allegory of evil."[23] What's new and startling here is that he has been moved across the color line to represent, now, the threatening foreigner rather than the resentful or resistant insider. No longer a working-class Englishman in Venetian drag, he is realigned with outsiderhood in just the way that the Venetians positioned Othello. And this reading of Iago as absolute and unmotivated evil also depoliticizes "the terrorists," removing any sense of their own motives or beliefs.

To sum up, then, the first answer to our riddle, "What's black and white and read all over?" is that *Othello,* the play and its characters, are used as a convenient, if often somewhat inaccurate, reference point for contemporary cultural and political events. The general outlines of the plot, and some of the play's most famous lines (again, often clichés that actually predate Shakespeare) are taken out of context in order to make the contemporary event, whether it is a war or a betrayal of confidence, both more serious ("Shakespearean," "tragic") and more recognizable. The commentator sounds profound and witty; the reader, listener, or audience feels gratified and flattered to "get" the reference, and Shakespeare is reconfirmed as the most trenchant and trusted observer of contemporary events since Walter Cronkite.

But if we review the topics that have brought *Othello* and the daily news together, we can see that one topic, although it is manifestly obvious, is often treated with great and nervous care, and that topic is race. Notice that none of the applications of *Othello* to questions of identity theft, credit, office behavior, or public speaking made any mention at all of race. To this set of readers and audiences, *Othello* was a play about interpersonal politics and professional, as well as personal, jealousy: Othello and Iago are, differentially but equally, versions of Everyman, or Everywoman.

When race *is* mentioned in the public press in connection with the play, however, the results are often incendiary. The O. J. Simpson trial polarized the public and led to symptomatic quoting—and misquoting—from the play. And attempts to link rape accusations against white members of the Duke lacrosse team by a black "exotic dancer" with Shakespearean references have been similarly loaded: citing Cassio's lament about the loss of his reputation (2.3.246–48), one commentator declared, "As Shakespeare wrote, they have lost the immortal part of themselves. And that is bestial."[24] It's hard to know where to begin in unpacking the complicated racial logics of this (mis)quotation from *Othello.*

When Brabantio hears of Desdemona's elopement with Othello, he blurts out his inner thoughts to Roderigo: "This accident is not unlike my dream, /

Belief of it oppresses me already" (1.1.143–44). In an interview with *The New Yorker,* the president of Duke, Richard Brodhead, remembered in particular the second line of Branbantio's speech, suggesting that this "belief" was a description of the "action of prejudice" or "preconceptions." But in the Duke lacrosse case the racial politics were reversed—the men accused of sexual aggression were white, the woman black. The line from *Othello* came to Brodhead's mind, the article insisted, "not for its obvious associations with interracial passions and violence, but for its lesson on prejudgment." Well, maybe so. But for a literary scholar turned administrator who then went on to address the "legacy of racism" in this country, the obvious associations with black/white relations must have lingered somewhere, too.[25]

What's black and white and red all over?
An embarrassed zebra.

"When you hear hoofbeats," says the diagnostician's adage, "think horses, not zebras." In other words, consider first the most common causes of disease, not the rarest or most exotic ones. But although Iago compares Othello to a "Barbary horse" (the equivalent of an Arabian stallion), I want to contend that the play is indeed a zebra—not so much because it is exotic, as because it presents certain perceptual, as well as conceptual, problems.

What is the "riddle" about zebras? "Is the zebra a white animal with black stripes, or a black animal with white stripes?" Evolutionary biologist Stephen Jay Gould called this "one of the persistent, unanswered questions about nature"—one of the kinds of questions that "refuse to go away because they . . . seem calculated, in their very formulation, to arouse argument rather than inspire resolution."[26] It doesn't take a zoologist come from the lab to see the analogy between this tantalizingly unanswered question and the besetting problems of *Othello* criticism, and of Othello—the play, the character, the actor, and the part. And those questions, too, "refuse to go away," for similar reasons.

For the record, although researchers in the 1950s came down on the "white with black stripes" side, the prevailing view these days is that the zebra is probably black with white stripes, since some zebras are born with genetic variations that make them all black with white stripes, or mostly dark with a striped pattern only on part of their coats. "Therefore, the 'default' color is black," writes a chief scholarly authority—an embryologist whose name, I am pleased to report, is Bard.[27] Stephen Jay Gould suggested that the topic "cannot be divorced from cultural contexts," and reported that, according to available research, "most African peoples regard zebras as black animals with white stripes."[28]

We might turn to Gestalt psychology and the history of art for a classic statement of this double view. Consider psychologist Joseph Jastrow's famous example of the rabbit-duck, an ambiguous figure that looks like either the head of a rabbit (facing right, with protruding ears) or the head of a duck (facing left, with a protruding bill). The image has been memorably discussed by E. H. Gombrich, as well as by Wittgenstein and others. Here is Gombrich's lucid account:

> We can see the picture as both a rabbit and a duck. It is easy to discover both readings. It is less easy to describe what happens when we switch from one interpretation to the other. . . . [T]here is no doubt that the shape transforms itself in some subtle way when the duck's beak becomes the rabbit's ears and brings an otherwise neglected spot into prominence as the rabbit's mouth. I say "neglected," but does it enter our experience at all when we switch back to reading "duck"? To answer this question, we are compelled to look for what is "really there," to see the shape apart from its interpretation, and this, we soon discover, is not really possible.[29]

Renaissance scholars may recognize this as a version of the art form known to Shakespeare as a "perspective," and to subsequent eras as an "anamorphism." And it is salutary, for literary scholars as well as for art historians, to be reminded that it is not really possible "to see the shape apart from its interpretation." But this famous rabbit-duck, derived from a German newspaper sketch and originally analyzed by an American psychologist at the turn of the last century, may have been superseded in our times by another, even more visually arresting animal.

The Op Art pioneer Victor Vasarely considered the zebra the perfect figure

Joseph Jastrow's rabbit-duck figure

for optical illusion. Beginning in the 1930s, Vasarely executed a series of zebra studies, made entirely of diagonal black and white stripes curved in such a way as to give the three-dimensional impression of a zebra. As "illusions," they are *undecidable*. Which is figure and which is ground? White on black? Or black on white?

What would be the difference between seeing *The Tragedy of Othello* as a black zebra with white stripes, and seeing *The Tragedy of Othello* as a white zebra with black stripes? The first kind of reading—*Othello* as a black zebra with white stripes—would view the play as about the *referent,* blackness, as the underlying "reality" toward which critical attention should turn. The second kind of reading—*Othello* as a white zebra with black stripes—would point instead toward the question of *representation,* of blackness as a theatrical (and political and cultural) *effect,* and thus as a template and touchstone for response on and off the stage. The history of the play, its performances and reception, has often blurred or confused these two. Another way of phrasing this would be to say that one kind of reading is *historical, cultural, and referential,* and the other kind of reading is *symbolic or allegorical.* The second kind of reading has, over time, focused on questions like "evil," where "black" and "white" are terms related to truth and falsehood, clarity and confusion, morality and amorality, and so on. While much useful scholarly excavation has tried to establish the root causes of an association between cultural color-coding and judgment (why is "black" devilish or sinful, and "white" angelic or

Victor Vasarely, Zebras, 1950

pure?), that is not my concern here. I want instead merely to indicate that some interpretations, and some stagings, of *Othello* have used the black/white theme as the surface structure of another kind of allegory, one that might concern itself with virtue and vice, say, or with triangulated jealousy. These readings cannot be dismissed as mere evasions of the "real" subject; at different times some topics (like sexuality or religion) have been as "loaded" as race, contributing to the "tragic loading" of this play.

Some influential readings—as I have already suggested—do not turn on the question of race at all. Critics like G. Wilson Knight and W. H. Auden focus on Othello as exemplary man and soldier-hero. T. S. Eliot, famously, speaks of Othello as "cheering himself up" in his final speech ("speak of me as I am . . . one that loved, not wisely, but too well").[30] The essay of Sigmund Freud's that I find most illuminating about *Othello* is called "Some Neurotic Mechanisms in Jealousy, Paranoia, and Homosexuality" (1922).[31] It describes the psychodynamics of the Othello/Iago/Desdemona triangle in unerring detail, although it never mentions their names. The single telltale clue, superbly "Freudian" in its displacement and diminishment, is a footnote to a song about infidelity sung by Desdemona in the fourth act of the play. Freud's point, in fact, is about universal erotic jealousy: "It is a matter of everyday experience," he writes, "that fidelity, especially that degree of it required in marriage, is only maintained in the face of continual temptations." Again, the play is viewed as universal: about all people—mainly Freud himself—not about racial difference.

The Caribbean-born black journalist and socialist thinker C. L. R. James, writing in the 1960s, contended that Othello's problem was not that he was black, but that he was a foreigner, an outsider in Venetian society: "I say with the fullest confidence, that you could strike out every single reference to his black skin and the play would be essentially the same. Othello's trouble is that he is an outsider."[32] Black zebra with white stripes, or white zebra with black stripes?

And yet through the years no topic has been more thoroughly explored or debated, either recently or over the play's history, than the question of Othello's own race or ethnicity. Is he "black" or "tawny"? An "African" or a "Moor"? Does he come from North Africa, or from farther south? Clues, such as they are, seem to abound in the play, and to be as confusing, or doubly directional, as the question of the zebra's stripes. As we've noted, Othello is described by Iago as a "Barbary horse," and "Barbary" was situated in north Africa, between Egypt and the Atlantic Ocean; Roderigo, clearly an unreliable authority, calls Othello a "thick-lips" (1.1.66). His mother received the embroidered handkerchief from an "Egyptian charmer"—does that mean they lived near Egypt? Othello himself says, "haply for I am black," but "black" could mean any number of things in the early modern period; the word was "applied, loosely to non-European races, little darker than many Europeans" (*OED* 1c).

In Shakespeare's source, a short story by the sixteenth-century Italian humanist Giovanni Battista Giraldi, also called Cinthio, Othello is a Moor, but this opens—and has opened for many scholars—the question of what Shakespeare thought a "Moor" was. The editor of the Arden edition reproduces a portrait of the Moorish ambassador to Queen Elizabeth, suggesting that "the ambassador's intense and aristocratic face seems to me right for Othello."[33] This "olive-skinned" portrait of 1600–1601 (the color-term is the Arden editor's) may strike us as somewhat at variance with Queen Elizabeth's order of the same date commanding the "transportation" out of England of unwelcome "Negroes and Blackamoors . . . which are crept into the realm . . . and are fostered here to the annoyance of her own people."[34] Was Othello imagined as an aristocrat or an unwelcome intruder, or both?

This quest for early modern authenticity—is Othello "supposed to be" a sub-Saharan black man or a North African "Moor"?—has had its counterpart in stage history. Early Othellos, played by white actors, seem to have been "black" rather than "tawny" until Edmund Kean introduced a "tawny" makeup in the early nineteenth century, an interpretation that quickly became fashionable with actors like Henry Irving and Edwin Forrest.

Meantime, much debate about the various meanings of "black," from sunburned to tawny to "negro," exercised the imaginations, and prejudices, of critics. Thomas Rymer's famous Restoration attack on the play, written in 1693, made mock of Othello's military rank and status, which he thought ludicrously improbable.

> [S]hall a poet . . . fancy that they will set a Negro to be their general, or trust a Moor to defend them against the Turk? With us a blackamoor might rise to be a trumpeter, but Shakespeare would not have less than a lieutenant-general. With us a Moor might marry some little drab or small-coal wench; Shakespeare would provide him the daughter and heir of some great lord or privy councilor, and all the town should reckon it a very suitable match.[35]

Rymer seems easy to ridicule—although T. S. Eliot remarked that he had never seen a persuasive refutation of Rymer's view of the play.[36] But it is disconcerting to find a distinguished poet and critic like Samuel Taylor Coleridge voicing a very similar opinion:

No doubt Desdemona saw Othello's visage in his mind; yet, as we are constituted, and most surely as an English audience was disposed in the beginning
of the seventeenth century, it would be something monstrous to conceive this
beautiful Venetian girl falling in love with a veritable negro. It would argue a
disproportionateness, a want of balance, in Desdemona, which Shakespeare
does not appear to have in the least contemplated.[37]

The difference here is that Rymer thinks Shakespeare a bad playwright for
imagining a love affair between Desdemona and Othello, whereas Coleridge
thinks Shakespeare can't really have meant it, since he was so good a playwright. "With us," "as we are constituted," "as an English audience was
disposed in the beginning of the seventeenth century": these appeals, as unwelcome as they seem today, are appeals to history, to reception theory, and to
cultural context. "We" and "us" are the most dangerous words in the English
language—or in any critical or political language.

And "we," when it comes to Shakespeare and Othello, are not, of course,
the audience Coleridge had in mind: we are not always "English." Americans
had their own cultural history, and their own prejudices, to contend with.
Abigail Adams, who had loved the plays of Shakespeare since she was a child,
went to the London theater and saw Sarah Siddons as Desdemona in the mid-
1780s. Mrs. Adams, who prided herself on her liberal views, was dismayed to
find herself recoiling from the image of a white Desdemona in the arms of a
black man—even when that black man was played by a renowned white
actor, John Kemble. The experience of seeing the play was different from that
of reading it. "Othello was represented blacker than any African," she wrote.
She could not say whether her instinctive dismay came from nature or nur-
ture (a "natural antipathy" or "the prejudices of education"), but she acknowledged, "my whole soul shuddered whenever I saw the sooty heretic Moor
touch the fair Desdemona."[38] Abigail's son John Quincy Adams felt if possible even more strongly on the question, echoing his mother's words (consciously or unconsciously) in an essay called "The Character of Desdemona,"
which was published in the *Atlantic Monthly* in 1836. Adams, by then an ex-
president, attributed all the disasters of the play to Desdemona's "unnatural
passion" for a "sooty-bosomed . . . thick-lipped wool-headed Moor."[39] The
tragedy, he thought, was due to her misbehavior, not to Iago's malevolence or
Othello's misconceptions. The American actor James Henry Hackett, who
corresponded with Quincy Adams, seconded this view, writing in 1863, "The
great moral lesson of the tragedy of *Othello* is that black and white blood cannot be intermingled in marriage without a gross violation upon the laws of

Thomas Dartmouth Rice as "Otello"

Nature; and that, in such violations, Nature will vindicate her laws."[40] I should note for the record that Hackett was born in New York, not in one of the southern states.

Meantime *Othello,* one of the most performed plays in America in the eighteenth and nineteenth centuries,[41] was also having a successful career in minstrelsy. The blackface entertainer T. D. Rice, who popularized the trickster figure Jim Crow, wrote and performed a burlesque opera called *Otello* in 1844. Although it is written in dialect-speech ("It am de cause, / It am de cause / Let me not tell you ob it, oh you lubly stars, / It am de cause," and so on), the "opera" follows the general plot of Shakespeare's play. There are, however, certain indicative changes. Othello and Desdemona already have a child, called "Young Othello," or "Young Lorenzo Othello"; only one side of his face was blacked up, indicating that he partially resembled each of his parents. Desdemona's handkerchief is replaced by a towel made of raccoon hide, and Desdemona herself comes back to life at the end of the play—much as Bottom does in the "Pyramus and Thisbe" play. Rice's *Otello,* which we would today call a subversive critique from below, played to packed—and segregated—houses.[42]

On the other hand, one postbellum American, a Maryland woman named Mary Preston, made it clear in her book, *Studies in Shakespeare,* that her identification with the protagonist required that he *not* be black. "In studying the play of *Othello,* I have always *imagined* its hero to be a *white* man." Shakespeare, she averred, was "too correct a delineator of human nature to have coloured Othello *black,* if he had personally acquainted himself with the idiosyncrasies of the African race." For Mary Preston the description of Othello as black was, in her view, "the *single* blemish on a faultless work. Othello was a *white* man!"[43] His color is a "blemish," a blot, on the whiteness of the page, and the stage. Here again we might note that it is Shakespeare's personality, as much as Othello's, that is being diagnosed. The Shakespeare whom Preston idealizes (or fantasizes) is not a Shakespeare who would make his soldier-hero a black man.

But as the English Shakespearean A. C. Bradley pointed out in 1904, the extreme views of (certain) Americans about the racial dynamics of the play were matched by the view of at least one highly regarded English writer: "The horror of most American critics (Mr. Furness is a bright exception) at the idea of a black Othello is very amusing, and their arguments are highly instructive. But they were anticipated, I regret to say, by Coleridge."[44] To Coleridge's claim that a Venetian girl falling in love with a negro "would argue a *disproportionateness,* a want of balance, in Desdemona, which Shakespeare does not appear to have in the least contemplated," Bradley's response is swift and uncompromising: "Could any argument be more self-destructive?" As he immediately notes, this is the very response that Brabantio expresses, and even Coleridge's word, "disproportionateness," echoes the voice of Iago: "Foul disproportion, thoughts unnatural." In other words, the play produces exactly the effect so disparaged by Coleridge as unlikely to have occurred to Shakespeare. "Thus," concludes Bradley with some justifiable satisfaction, "the argument of Coleridge and others points straight to the conclusion against which they argue."[45] Shakespeare aimed at melodrama, Bradley thinks, and he achieved it; a gentrified and genteel "Moorish" Othello would soften, or miss, the point. He is similarly contemptuous toward fainthearted critics and audiences who "consent to forgive [Desdemona] for loving a brown man, but find it monstrous that she should love a black one."[46] Bradley's emphasis here is theatrical, not social. He deplores Coleridge's racism, but his interest is in how the play works on the stage. The more horror expressed by the unenlightened and the bigoted, the better, from the point of view of good theater.

Yet Bradley has a relatively low opinion of his own cultural moment. Even though he is convinced that "Shakespeare's Othello was a black," he thinks it is probably risky to play him as one on the stage in 1904 (and here comes that dangerous word "we" again): "We do not like the real Shakespeare. We like to have his language pruned and his conceptions flattened into something that suits our mouths and minds."[47]

Despite this critical skepticism, it is important to note that a few black actors did perform *Othello* in "legitimate" productions of the play. In the nineteenth century Ira Aldridge, an American actor, played the title part, with Charles Kean as his Iago. (Aldridge never performed Othello in the United States, although he was celebrated throughout Britain, continental Europe, and in Russia, performing in St. Petersburg in 1863 to great acclaim.) The black actors Earle Hyman and Paul Robeson starred in productions in the early part of the twentieth century.

Robeson, famously, encountered negative press in Britain in 1930 when he played opposite white actress Peggy Ashcroft, and kissed her onstage. ("Ever

Ira Aldridge as Othello

so many people have asked me whether I mind being kissed in some of the scenes by a coloured man," Ashcroft told the *Daily Sketch,* "and it seems to me so silly. Of course I do not mind! It is just necessary to the play. For myself I look on it as a privilege to act with a great artist like Paul Robeson."[48]) But a little more than a decade later, when Robeson's American production of *Othello* opened for tryouts at the Brattle Theatre in Cambridge, Massachusetts, in 1942, the trade paper *Variety* declared that "no white man should ever dare presume" to play the role again.[49]

I will have more to say about Paul Robeson as Othello in a moment, but since Robeson's time many other black actors, from James Earl Jones to Laurence Fishburne, have successfully and effectively played the part, and the Puerto Rican–born Raul Julia was a memorable "tawny" Othello for Joseph Papp's New York Shakespeare Festival. White actors playing in black (or "tawny") makeup, from David Garrick to Orson Welles to the campy, eye-rolling, corked-up Laurence Olivier, had previously dominated the stage. Lately, however, this cross-casting has been regarded as—from a modern point of view—somehow "inauthentic" (as well as politically incorrect).

The actor Patrick Stewart, who spent many years with the Royal Shakespeare company, had always wanted to play Othello, but as he told an interviewer, "When the time came that I was old enough and experienced enough" to play the part, "it was the same time that it no longer became acceptable for a white actor to put on blackface and to pretend to be African." Later, in 1997, after his time in the *Star Trek: The Next Generation* television series was over, Stewart returned to *Othello,* to star in what he called a "photo negative" production. He and the actress playing Bianca were white; everyone else in the cast was black.

And yet of course Shakespeare's company contained no black actors, any more than it contained any women. Othello, Desdemona, Iago, Emilia, Cassio, and Bianca were all played by white males. The profound distinctions

Laurence Olivier and Maggie Smith in
Othello *(1965)*

among them with regard to color and gender are—like differences of age, rank, social class, and so on—artifacts of the playing space. All "race" in the plays is enacted, not essential, and it is enacted, not to reveal the supposed "truth" about Shakespeare's views, whatever they might have been, but rather to develop a dramatic situation that is entirely fictive. The authentic Othello, if by "authentic" we mean re-creating the stage conditions of Shakespeare's theater, would certainly be—or have been—a white man in "black" makeup.

When we cast a black actor in the protagonist's role, we are "modernizing" the play—just as we do when we cast a woman in the role of Desdemona. Did Shakespeare's audience then have a zebra/optical illusion experience when watching the play unfold, seeing both whiteness and blackness, but never both at once?

Black zebra with white stripes? Or white zebra with black stripes? What's black and white and read all over? Let me reframe the question so as to underscore the issue: should the play be thought of as a play centered on Othello, or a play centered on Iago? Again, the optical illusion may be at work. Which is figure, and which is ground?

It's not surprising to learn that there is a long tradition of pairs of actors alternating in the roles of Othello and Iago during the course of a theatrical run—as the great Shakespearean actors Henry Irving and Edwin Booth did in 1881. Jeremy Irons once told Maureen Dowd he was looking for another actor to alternate with him in a production of *Othello*.[50]

We may note that although Laurence Olivier, in a highly controversial performance, chose to play the part of Othello at the National Theatre and later in the 1965 film, when his imitator and admirer Kenneth Branagh came to do the play thirty years later, he was cast as Iago in the 1995 film directed by Oliver Parker, and Laurence Fishburne, an American black actor, was cast as Othello. In part this is an acknowledgment of the racial-political realities of 1995, the year of the O. J. Simpson trial.

But now, after centuries in which Othello was always portrayed by a white man in blackface (or brownface)—and then a few decades in which a black man playing the part was regarded as an advance in performative terms—some black actors in the twentieth and twenty-first centuries have queried both the politics and the theatrical inevitability of being cast in the role. These include the contemporary British actor Hugh Quarshie (born in Ghana, educated at Oxford) and the African-American expatriate Gordon Heath, who termed this obligatory rite of passage for black men in the theater "the Othello syndrome."[51] (The identical phrase, it is interesting to note, has been used by some psychiatrists to denote a state of fanatical jealousy.) At the same time, some scholars who have done much to bring the importance of race to bear on early modern studies have begun to question the degree to which *Othello* and other plays are "treated as texts which deal almost exclusively with race and racism."[52] There is always a corrective moment; perhaps the pendulum will swing back to the questions raised by Eliot and Auden.

THE DOUBLENESS OF FOCUS IS intrinsic to the very structure of the play. *Othello* in modern culture can certainly be said to have a "double consciousness" in the specialized sense used by W. E. B. DuBois: "this sense of always looking at one's self through the eyes of others, of measuring one's soul by the tape of a world that looks on in amused contempt and pity. One ever feels his two-ness—an American, a Negro; two souls, two thoughts, two unreconciled strivings; two warring ideas in one dark body."[53]

We should remember that the second answer to our riddle was not just "a zebra," but an "*embarrassed* zebra." And here, in terms of American culture, we return inevitably to race, sex, and politics.

Reviewing Gunnar Myrdal's *An American Dilemma* in 1944, Ralph Ellison wrote of the "sense of alienation and *embarrassment* that the book might arouse" because of its implied suggestion that it still took "a European scientist" to "affirm the American Negro's humanity."[54] Supreme Court Justice Ruth Bader Ginsburg, discussing in South Africa in February 2006 the international implications of the 1954 *Brown v. Board of Education* decision that desegregated American schools, cites a letter from then–Secretary of State Dean Acheson submitted in support of the Brown case: "The continuance of racial discrimination in the United States remains a source of constant *embarrassment* to this Government . . . it jeopardizes the effective maintenance of our moral leadership of the free and democratic nations of the world."[55]

The English-language homonym, read/red, here is joined by a French (near) anagram: *embrasser/embarrasser,* to embrace and to embarrass.[56] The Adamses, mother and son, recoiled in print from the spectacle of a "sooty heretic Moor" touching "the fair Desdemona." Two centuries later, Peggy Ashcroft was asked a related question: how did she feel about kissing a black actor, as the play required? And Paul Robeson reported that he felt like a field hand, backing away from her onstage (although both Ashcroft and the Desdemona of his American production, Uta Hagen, would ultimately be among his lovers).

But the *political* connotations of "red" also played a part in the saga of *Othello* in modern culture. The pre–civil rights era of the late 1940s to the mid-1950s, when the segregation of blacks and whites was still the law in many southern states, was also the time of the second "Red scare." Let me offer one indicative—and suggestive—example.

When Paul Robeson was summoned before the House Un-American Activities Committee in 1956, his supposed Communist past and his long history of friendship with Russia were very much on the minds of the members of the committee. The actor, who had toured triumphantly in *Othello*— and who was so closely identified with the role that his son and a friend founded the Othello Recording Company (1953–55) to release Robeson's music—had been seeking in vain to have his passport restored. Robeson was now testifying before skeptical and

Paul Robeson as Othello

accusing representatives, not even the "grave senators" who gave Othello a fair hearing in Venice. Robeson had refused to sign an affidavit stating that he was not a Communist, and he was badgered by several HUAC members ("Are you now a member of the Communist party?" they demanded several times). HUAC's counsel, Richard Arens, pressed Robeson about his supposed alias in a Communist cell, and the name he was accused of using is not without significance: "Have you ever been known under the name of 'John Thomas'?" attorney Arens asked.[57]

"Oh please," replied Robeson, "does somebody here want—are you suggesting—do you want me to be put up for perjury some place? 'John Thomas'! My name is Paul Robeson, and anything I have to say, or stand for, I have said in public all over the world, and that is why I am here today."[58] John Thomas. Readers of *Lady Chatterley's Lover* (originally published in 1928), or aficionados of British slang, will know that this is a slang term for the penis. The second (unexpurgated) version of *Lady Chatterley* was in fact published under the title *John Thomas and Lady Jane* (1972). One online dictionary of slang from the U.K. calls John Thomas "a well-established but ageing euphemism," an almost too-apt description for Othello. (We should not be so quick, though, to consign this term to verbal obsolescence; it surfaced in U.S. popular culture as recently as in the HBO show *Sex and the City*, where, in one episode, Trey asks Charlotte to "measure his John Thomas.")[59]

But by the time Robeson was testifying before HUAC another character called "Thomas" had also entered the cultural imaginary, in the character of Bigger Thomas, the protagonist of Richard Wright's *Native Son* (1940). As critics have noted, Bigger Thomas's murder of a white woman in that novel seems deliberately patterned on Shakespeare's *Othello*. And Bigger's name, critics agree, seems, equally deliberately, to evoke a derogatory racial term.[60] But the word "bigger," needless to say, also carries another connotation, equally tinged with racism, when combined with that other fetishized "Thomas"—John. The heroic, powerful, and sexy Paul Robeson—football player, baritone, actor, singer, public speaker—was for the House Un-American Activities Committee the embodiment of a "bigger" "John Thomas." Sexual threat and Stalinist spy. Their projections about this successful black man resemble those of Brabantio and the Venetian senators. Othello as John Thomas: the imagined and fantasized enemy of 1950s America.[61]

Instead of a hero and a cultural ambassador, Paul Robeson had become, in the eyes of his accusers, the "malignant" enemy, one who "traduced the state"—to quote Othello's words in the final act. Robeson's farewell performance of Othello's last speech at Carnegie Hall in May 1958, we might note, edited out the characterization of the enemy as a "circumcisèd dog," calling him instead a "damnèd heathen"—hence "John Thomas" is expurgated, and disappears. But it is worth noting that *Robeson's* final words turned the accusation back upon his inquisitors, and did so in ringing tones: "you gentlemen belong with the Alien and Sedition Acts, and you are the nonpatriots, and you are the un-Americans, and you ought to be ashamed of yourselves."[62]

"Shame" or embarrassment here returns, in the voice of the black actor reproving the dignitaries before whom he has been called to testify. What's black and white and red all over? The cultural politics of *Othello*.

I MENTIONED AT THE BEGINNING of this chapter that Sigmund Freud, in his inspired little book on jokes, claimed that the pleasure one gets from a joke is derived from the difference between two methods of viewing it: the conscious and unconscious, the literal and figurative, the manifest and latent, just has he had argued about dreams. The joke-work is like the dream-work; the joke is like a dream.[63] The play itself has the shape of a dream. It begins at night, with voices shouting in the dark, shouting about sex and desire. It ends with the "tragic loading" of a bed. In between there is always the insinuating voice of Iago, whispering to Othello the things he most dreads and fears: this accident is not unlike my dream.

But the play also has the shape of a joke. A tragic joke, a joke *on* Othello. One of the most famous of the jokes Freud cites is the one about the two Jews who meet in a railway carriage. "Where are you traveling?" asks the first one, and the second says, "To Cracow." "What a liar you are!" says the first, indignantly. "When you say you're going to Cracow, you want me to believe that you're going to Lemberg. But I know that you are really going to Cracow. So why are you lying to me?" Freud's reading of this is that it functions by use of absurdity, but also that the "more serious substance of the joke is the problem of what determines the truth. The joke . . . is pointing to a problem and is making use of the uncertainty of one of our commonest concepts . . . jokes of this kind . . . are attacking . . . the certainty of our knowledge itself."

A little reflection will remind us that a version of the same joke is actually told, or performed, toward the beginning of *Othello*. Instead of Jews in a railway carriage we have Turks on the seas, a Turkish fleet heading for Cyprus. No, says a sailor, the Turks are going to Rhodes. He has been told this on good report. But a senator corrects him: "This cannot be, / By no assay of reason—'tis a pageant / To keep us in false gaze" (1.3.18–20). Cyprus is more important to the Turks than Rhodes; and in fact, it turns out, that after a feint

Zebra in zebra crossing

in the direction of Rhodes, the ships have turned, "bearing with frank appearance / Their purposes toward Cyprus" (1.3.39–40). What a liar you are! You
tell us you are going to Cyprus, in order to make us think you are going to
Rhodes, but all the while you are intending to go to Cyprus. "'Tis a pageant /
To keep us in false gaze." This is the through line for the entire play, the short-
est version of its emphasis on false sight, on appearances and stagings, on lies
told with an ingratiating smile, and truths told with a leer or a sneer, so that
they sound like lies.

Freud calls this kind of joke a "skeptical" joke, and classes it with a larger
group of what he calls "tendentious" jokes, among which he includes exposing or obscene jokes, aggressive or hostile jokes, and cynical, critical, and
blasphemous jokes. A quick review of these terms—exposing or obscene;
aggressive or hostile; cynical and critical—will make it clear that this is a
description of Iago's technique throughout the play. Iago's, and also the playwright's. The translator's footnote in the *Standard Edition* of Freud's collected
works explains that "the German substantive '*Tendenz*' is throughout this
book translated 'purpose.' (Cf. 'a play with a purpose.') The German adjective
derived from it, however, (*tendenziös*) has become a naturalized word and
is accordingly translated here 'tendentious.' "[64] The word "tendentious" is
retained (without comment) in the new Penguin translation.[65] So here we

have, conceivably, a better answer to the puzzle of Iago's motive than Coleridge's famous phrase "the motive-hunting of a motiveless malignity."[66] Iago's motive, and Shakespeare's, too, is a *tendency,* or a *purpose,* at the level of the joke—or, to use Iago's word and Freud's, at the level of wit. Tendentious jokes, jokes "that have a purpose," are "jokes on which the difference in their hearers' reaction to them depends." Such jokes "run the risk of meeting with people who do not want to listen to them."[67] This is the structure of *Othello.*

The play is itself the most elusive and maddening of optical—and conceptual—illusions, figure and ground constantly exchanging places. If *Oedipus* is the myth and the play about a crossroads, we might invoke an everyday icon of modern life and say that *Othello* is the myth and the play about a crosswalk, or what in Britain is known as a "zebra crossing": a pedestrian crossing marked by broad black-and-white stripes on the road. Othello is a hero; Othello is a dupe. Iago is a devil, a scoundrel, a Machiavel; Iago is the type of the successful modern politician, from Richard Darman to Karl Rove. Iago is a terrorist; Iago is a strategy for combating terrorism, by getting into the minds of others. Othello is black, brown, Moorish, African; a white actor in blackface; a black actor; a cliché for black actors; a political challenge for white actors. Iago hates Othello; no, he loves him, but he doesn't know it, or can't admit it. The play is about race, about politics, about preferment, about jealousy, about desire, about evil, about innocence, about motiveless malignity. In the twentieth and twenty-first centuries it has also become a play about that most dangerous concept in the language, for we have made it a play about *us.*

EIGHT

HENRY V

The Quest for Exemplarity

April 23, usually described as "Shakespeare's birthday," was also recorded as the date of his death. Either this is an uncanny coincidence—and such things do happen—or we are again in the world of Shakespeare-larger-than-life, the Shakespeare who has already become a myth. Since Thomas Jefferson and John Adams both died on the same day, July 4, 1826, the fiftieth anniversary of the Declaration of Independence, perhaps we may rest happy here with the idea that coincidence rules. But in any case, it is another striking coincidence that April 23 is, and was in Shakespeare's time, also known as St. George's Day.

St. George is the patron saint of England, and from the fifteenth through the eighteenth centuries his feast day was celebrated on a par with Christmas. That Shakespeare's birthday (and death day) is also the feast day of the patron saint of England may again suggest either uncanny coincidence at work, and/or the operations of early Bardolatry.

St. George as patron of England also plays a part—at least a rhetorical part—in Shakespeare's play *Henry V*. At the close of his affecting and effective speech to rally the troops, "Once more unto the breach, dear friends, once more, / Or close the wall up with our English dead" (3.1.1–2), King Henry urges all those in the battle, the noblemen and the yeomen, to move forward:

> The game's afoot.
> Follow your spirit, and upon this charge
> Cry, "God for Harry! England and Saint George!"
>
> *3.1.32–34*

By the very next scene the rallying cry has already been made into a slogan, as Bardolph enters with his disreputable colleagues, crying, "On, on, on, on, on! To the breach, to the breach!" (3.2.1)—and trying to *escape* the battle. In a phenomenon familiar to anyone who follows modern political rhetoric in a time of 24/7 news cycles, words are here taken out of context, cited, recited,

Raffaello Sanzio, St. George Fighting the Dragon

and converted into a catchphrase for the speaker's own purposes. From "Nixon's the one" to "Where's the beef?" to "Yes, we can!" such phrases, consumer- and battle-tested, have been used to mobilize armies of voters in the era of the "selling" of presidents. But such slogans have always functioned in this floating fashion, coming to mean whatever the new context offers. King Henry's mention of "Saint George!" (designed in this ending couplet to rhyme with "charge") has the effect of raising the emotional war effort beyond the immediate moment ("Ask not what your country can do for you . . ."). At the same time, linking the three names (Harry, England, St. George) identifies and personifies them: for the moment of the battle the King *becomes* Saint George. Does the April 23 birthdate similarly identify and personify "Shakespeare" as "England"?

Henry V is the fourth play in a series, the so-called second tetralogy, or second group of four history plays, that Shakespeare wrote and brought to the stage. *Richard III,* the culminating play in the first group of four English history plays, is a play that brings "history" relatively close in time to Shake-

Laurence Olivier in The Chronicle History of King Henry the Fift with His Battell Fought at Agincourt in France *(1944)*

Kenneth Branagh in Henry V *(1989)*

speare's own day: Henry VII, who defeated Richard III, was Queen Elizabeth's grandfather. Shakespeare wrote the plays about a more recent time *earlier* in his career than the plays set in a more distant England: the years covered by the second tetralogy, from Richard II (who was king during the time of Chaucer) to Henry V (born in 1387, crowned in 1413, died in 1422), is squarely within the medieval period. The most salient "real world" fact about the Battle of Agincourt, for which the historical King Henry V is best remembered, is that it featured a relatively new kind of weaponry, the medieval (or "Welsh") longbow, sometimes described as "the machine gun of the Middle Ages." A skilled longbow archer could shoot around twenty aimed arrows a minute. Two modern films of Shakespeare's *Henry V*—the one with Laurence Olivier (1944, in the middle of World War II) and the one with Kenneth Branagh (1989, responding to the British engagement in the far less popularly supported Falklands War)—show the devastation this "humble" weapon was able to produce when arrayed against serried ranks of horsemen in armor and carrying pennants, spears, and other cumbersome regalia of war.

What does it mean for us to consider this one play on its own, without the context of the preceding three? I should note that in modern theater and cinema this is often done; the plays are almost always independently produced, staged, filmed, taught, and discussed. A classic film combining *Henry IV,* parts 1 and 2, and a staged "unscene" from *Henry V* (the death of Falstaff) was made by Orson Welles in 1965, and entitled—after a phrase from *Henry IV, Part 2*—*Chimes at Midnight* (Welles, of course, played Falstaff). Although *Henry V* may be read in part as a repetition and recuperation of the first play in the series, *Richard II,* and although there have been some marathon stagings of the four plays together—and, indeed, of the four plays of the first tetralogy together—these plays, as plays, are designed to be freestanding and to give you all the information about character, history, and plot that you need to understand and interpret what is going on. And unlike the other plays in the series, which are much admired, much performed, and much quoted, but usually in the context of "Shakespeare," this play, *Henry V,* has attained a double afterlife for modern culture: both in the annals of patriotic rhetoric and warfare, and in the peculiar and lucrative world of the business school, the realm of motivational speaking, and the leadership institute. As we will see, King Henry has been presented as an example of what might be called best practices for corporate executives in the twentieth and twenty-first centuries.

The play begins with an actor designated as the Chorus, who speaks at the beginning of each act, and also speaks an epilogue at the end of the play. The first prologue spoken by the Chorus, at the start of *Henry V,* has become one of the most famous speeches in Shakespeare, because it describes the theater, the (supposed) limitations of the actors, the stage, and the playwright, and the active, imaginative nature of the theater audience. As we have already seen, the Chorus's lines are so recognizable as Shakespeare that Barbara Garson was able to riff on them at the beginning of her political parody *MacBird*. This is a long passage, but it is worth quoting in its entirety, because the effect is cumulative, and the logic—both rhetorical and theatrical—something akin to magic. The movement from "O for" to "But" to "Suppose," "Piece out," and "Think" transfers the agency of the stage from the actor (and the playwright) to the audience.

> O for a muse of fire, that would ascend
> The brightest heaven of invention:
> A kingdom for a stage, princes to act,
> And monarchs to behold the swelling scene.
> Then should the warlike Harry, like himself,
> Assume the port of Mars, and at his heels,
> Leashed in like hounds, should famine, sword, and fire
> Crouch for employment. But pardon, gentles all,
> The flat unraisèd spirits that hath dared
> On this unworthy scaffold to bring forth
> So great an object. Can this cock-pit hold
> The vasty fields of France? Or may we cram
> Within this wooden O the very casques
> That did affright the air at Agincourt?
> O pardon: since a crookèd figure may
> Attest in little place a million,
> And let us, ciphers to this great account,
> On your imaginary forces work.
> Suppose within the girdle of these walls
> Are now confined two might monarchies,
> Whose high uprearèd and abutting fronts
> The perilous narrow ocean parts asunder.
> Piece out our imperfections with your thoughts:
> Into a thousand parts divide one man,
> And make imaginary puissance.
> Think, when we talk of horses, that you see them,
> Printing their proud hoofs i'th' receiving earth;
> For 'tis your thoughts that now must deck our kings,
> Carry them here and there, jumping o'er times,
> Turning th' accomplishments of many years
> Into an hourglass—for the which supply,
> Admit me Chorus to this history,
> Who Prologue-like your humble patience pray
> Gently to hear, kindly to judge, our play.
>
> *Prologue 1–34*

The Olivier film of 1944 famously began with an eagle's-eye view of the stage, gradually moving in closer, and providing a visual counterpart to the description of the "wooden O" that has become a proverbial description of Shakespeare's stage. Most theaters at this time were polyhedrons. This play may first have been performed at the Curtain, but its true home was the new public theater Shakespeare's company had built on the bankside of the Thames, the Globe, where most of his plays were then performed. (*The Tempest,* a play that we have seen to be full of magical devices, was performed at a smaller indoor theater, the Blackfriars, allowing for more in the way of artifice and lighting effects.) So the Chorus's prologue is a glimpse at the theater and backstage. This was mirrored at the end, when the grand sweep of filmic "realism" returned to the stage and to actors on it.

Kenneth Branagh, always competitive with his great (and admired) predecessor, Laurence Olivier, shot his version of the Chorus's Prologue not on a simulacrum of a stage but on a film set, with the Chorus, played by Derek Jacobi, in street wear (of a rather "theatrical" kind, overcoat and scarf), wandering through the empty studio. Again, the effect—already insisted upon in Shakespeare's language—was to give the audience a kind of double vision: a vision into the past (underscored in the Olivier film by a constant recourse to costumes and sets drawn from a medieval book of hours) and a vision of the supposed "present."

SO THE ISSUES ABOUT "what is real" and "what is now" are deliberately put in question. But look at the language of the speech, which is even more definitive and suggestive than the film images. The Chorus begins by wishing, or rather, pretending to wish for, a kind of hyper–stage realism—princes would act princes, monarchs would be watching, the stage would be a kingdom, the king (the warlike Harry) would appear as himself, and then take on the mythological costume of the god of war, Mars. But. But. Instead, the Chorus points out, we have actors ("flat unraisèd spirits"), a stage ("this unworthy scaffold"). No theater can hold real armies, or "the vasty fields of France."

This is a version of what in poetry is called an "inexpressibility topos" (for example, "No one could tell how many came to the feast . . ."). The teller is telling by *not* telling. And in the Prologue to *Henry V* the deficit is made a plus. Since we can't see these things, we need to use our imaginations.

> O pardon: since a crookèd figure may
> Attest in little place a million,

> And let us, ciphers to this great account,
> On your imaginary forces work.
>
> *Prologue 15–19*

A zero with an ordinal number in front of it may have great value. The players, as "ciphers" (zeroes) may be enhanced by the audience, which is given a crucial role:

> Piece out our imperfections with your thoughts:
> Into a thousand parts divide one man,
> And make imaginary puissance.
> Think, when we talk of horses, that you see them.
>
> *Prologue 23–26*

The "hourglass" image makes it clear that time is being compressed—"your thoughts . . . must deck our kings."

Every act of the play begins with this resituating of the action in the realm of the fictive and the imaginary. This is in part done in order to cover great stretches of time and history, explaining characters, their backgrounds, a shift of scene. But it is also both an old and a "modernist" device, destabilizing the realism of the front plane. The more "human" the characters seem—the frightened soldiers, the indomitable Welsh captain Fluellen, the thinking king—the more disconcerting it is to be pulled back into a narrative frame in which the fictionality and impermanence of what we are watching are emphasized.

> Thus with imagined wing our swift scene flies
> In motion of no less celerity
> Than that of thought.
>
> *3.0.1–3*

Begins the chorus to act 3,

> Suppose that you have seen
> The well-appointed king at Dover pier
>
> *3.0.3–4*

> Play with your fancies, and in them behold
> Upon the hempen tackle ship-boys climbing;
>
> *3.0.7–8*

> O do but think
> You stand upon the rivage
>
> *3.0.13–14*

> Grapple your minds to sternage of this navy.
>
> *3.0.18*

Similar language of supposing, imagining, and thinking dominates every one of these Chorus speeches. "Now entertain conjecture of a time," the Chorus begins act 4, and ends, "Yet sit and see, / Minding true things by what their mock'ries be." And this impermanence, this exchange of state between true things and mockeries, becomes thematic as well as formal at the end of the play, when, after the victory at Agincourt, the peace with the French, the dynastic courtship transformed into a love match with Kate (Catherine) of France, and the promise that "English may as French, French Englishmen, / Receive each other" (5.2.39–40), the entire play is unraveled by the sobering words of the epilogue. For no sooner has the king spoken his final words,

> Then shall I swear to Kate, and you to me,
> And may our oaths well kept and prosp'rous be
>
> *5.2.345–46*

than his place is taken onstage by the Chorus, who speaks a sonnet that undoes everything we (think we) have seen.

> Thus far with rough and all-unable pen
>   Our bending author hath pursued the story,
> In little room confining mighty men,
>   Mangling by starts the full course of their glory.
> Small time, but in that small most greatly lived
>   This star of England. Fortune made his sword,
> By which the world's best garden he achieved,
>   And of it left his son imperial lord.
> Henry the Sixth, in infant bands crowned king
>   Of France and England, did this king succeed,
> Whose state so many had the managing
>   That they lost France and made his England bleed,
> Which oft our stage hath shown—and, for their sake,
> In your fair minds let this acceptance take.
>
> *Epilogue 1–14*

This is postmodernity before modernism—a description of historical events as "always already," both imminent and belated—and it is highly characteristic of the English Renaissance. A fitting example from the early modern period is Hans Holbein's famous portrait *The Ambassadors* (1533). Men of substance, surrounded by images of permanence and power, are depicted as standing on a patterned floor that, viewed from an oblique angle, resolves itself into a human skull. Like the much later rabbit-duck anamorphism of Gestalt psychology, the painting contains both images, but only one can be

Hans Holbein, The Ambassadors *and detail of the foreground skull, undistorted when viewed from an angle*

seen at a time. This device allows for the presentation of two conflicting views at once, and for discrepant awareness and dramatic irony. All is vanity. Dust thou art. The viewer or audience sees what the protagonists do not.

So this play about victory and maturity is also about instability and impermanence, its formal nature deliberately at war with its heroic content. For a small and comic example of this, consider the way the English language continually deconstructs itself in the mouths of the French-speaking princess and her waiting woman in act 3, scene 4, turning apparently harmless phrases into dirty words. Words like "foot" and "cown" (for "gown") are (mis)understood by the Princess as "mots de son mauvais, corruptible, gros, et impudique" (evil-sounding words, easily misconstrued, vulgar, and immodest) (3.4.447–48). The four-letter English cognates for foot and cown would have been readily, and comically, heard by the audience in the theater, whether or not those audience members understood French. The larger thematic point is as striking as the topical comedy: language is treacherous, meanings shift, all speech is dangerous and not always under the control of the speaker. This insistent instability of meaning is in fact characteristic of the theme of language and languages throughout the play.

COMPARISON OF THE Olivier and Branagh films makes clear the wide range of "meanings" that can be attached to scenes, characters, settings, and speeches, depending upon the context and the historical moment.

As we have already noted, the "war" surround of the two films was very different. Olivier had delivered the Crispin Crispian speech as a World War II pep talk on the national radio, and it was clearly associated with Britain's sense of itself as a threatened smaller power in danger of being overwhelmed by the juggernaut of Nazi Germany. By the time Branagh remade the film, following, once again, in Olivier's path, the situation was quite different. Britain was the major power, and the aggressor. War was less heroic and muddier (in all senses). (In a later battle scene, the king walks through the devastation of mud, corpses, and disorder everywhere.)

Reviewing Olivier's film for *Time* magazine in 1946, James Agee observed that "the man who made this movie made it midway in England's most terrible war, within the shadows of Dunkirk." The soldiers with whom Henry talks on the eve of battle "might just as well be soldiers of World War II," Agee remarked, adding that "no film of that war has yet said what they say so honestly or so well."[1] Olivier took a speech originally assigned, by Shakespeare, to "a cynical soldier" ("But if the cause be not good . . ." [4.1.128ff.]) and put it "in the mouth of a slow-minded country boy" with a "peasant patience" and the accents of Devon in his voice. Olivier had been given leave by the Royal Navy in 1942 to make a romantic comedy called *Demi-Paradise* (also known as *Adventure for Two*) about a Russian inventor in England "in the interest of Anglo-Russian relations," and the navy then extended his leave so he could make *Henry V,* as Olivier quipped, "in the interest of Anglo-British relations."[2] (The title of *Demi-Paradise* is a reference to John of Gaunt's famous "this England" speech in Shakespeare's *Richard II.*)

Branagh's *Henry V,* too, was underwritten by a government subsidy. A distinguished professor of French, recalling that in his childhood Agincourt was viewed as a "perfidious" act perpetrated by the English against the "gallant French knights," wrote to *The New York Times* to speculate on why "the BBC and the British government" would give financial support to the film. "Could it be that Prime Minister Margaret Thatcher's crumbling popularity needs

Shakespeare to come to her rescue? With England in the wake of the Falklands crusade, and in a precarious position in the European community, anticipating the fateful union of Europe in 1992, is this a disguised effort to bolster British spirits?"[3] Others, predictably, disagreed that the film was good press for Britain. Branagh had restored several unflattering scenes cut by Olivier from his patriotic film, like the king's threat to the governor of Harfleur predicting rape and infanticide, the disgrace of three of Henry's former friends from the *Henry IV* plays, now exposed as guilty of conspiracy and treason, and the hanging of his friend Bardolph for robbing a church.

One critic thought that Branagh had made "a young male-rite-of-passage movie" in the tradition of U.S. Vietnam films, rather than "a critique of institutional power and class injustice," as the critic would have preferred, and thus was complicit in "whitewashing traditional autocracy and the logic of imperialism" while at the same time "giving us a Shakespeare that is genuinely popular, intelligent and enthralling, unforgettable if also unfaithful" to the details of the play.[4] Branagh himself said that "all the blood-and-guts was quite deliberate. In fact, if eyewitness accounts of the Battle of Agincourt are to be believed, we were rather modest in our representation of it. It was very unpleasant, undignified, inelegant butchery."[5] The battle scenes were, nonetheless, handled with a certain cinematographic sentimentality. Shakespeare's Henry had requested, after the battle, that the hymns *Non nobis* and *Te Deum* be sung in praise to God for the victory (4.8.117). Branagh envisages "the greatest tracking shot in the world," while "to the accompaniment of a single voice starting the *Non nobis* hymn, the exhausted monarch would march the entire length of the battlefield to clear the place of the dead."[6] Filmed in slow motion, in an homage to directors like Akira Kurosawa and Sam Peckinpah, the aftermath of the battle summoned images of *all* wars, *all* casualties and survivors. I saw it in the same week as another movie about heroic soldiers outnumbered and at a disadvantage, the American Civil War film *Glory* (1989), and was struck by the similarity between the two scenes of battlefield devastation and loss, from the swelling music to the heartsick leader.

IN ALMOST ANY VERSION OF THIS PLAY, however, whether onstage, on film, or excerpted as a stand-alone exhortation, it is the famous Crispin Crispian speech that remains the emotional high point of *Henry V.* This is the speech that has been appropriated, more than any other part of the play, for various players and plots in "modern culture" from politics to business, and it may be useful—as well as pleasurable—to revisit its language here. The speaker, of course, is King Henry, and his audience begins "small" (replying to his kinsman or "cousin" Warwick), and ends "big," addressing the audience, history, and the future.

By Jove, I am not covetous for gold,
Nor care I who doth feed upon my cost;
It ernes me not if men my garments wear;
Such outward things dwell not in my desires.
But if it be a sin to covet honour
I am the most offending soul alive.
. . . .
We would not die in that man's company
That fears his fellowship to die with us.
This day is called the Feast of Crispian.
He that outlives this day and comes safe home
Will stand a-tiptoe when this day is named
And rouse him at the name of Crispian.
He that shall see this day, and live t'old age
Will yearly on the vigil feast his neighbours
And say, "Tomorrow is Saint Crispian."
Then will he strip his sleeve and show his scars,
And say, "These wounds I had on Crispin's day."
Old men forget; yet all shall be forgot,
But he'll remember, with advantages,
What feats he did that day. Then shall our names,
Familiar in his mouth as household words—
Harry the King, Bedford and Exeter,
Warwick and Talbot, Salisbury and Gloucester—
Be in their flowing cups freshly remembered.
This story shall the good man teach his son;
And Crispin Crispian shall ne'er go by
From this day to the ending of the world,
But we in it shall be rememberèd,
We few, we happy few, we band of brothers.
For he today that sheds his blood with me
Shall be my brother; be he ne'er so vile,
This day shall gentle his condition.
And gentlemen in England now abed,
Shall think themselves accursed they were not here,
And hold their manhoods cheap whiles any speaks
That fought with us upon Saint Crispin's day.

4.3.24–67

Olivier, performing the speech for a 1944 audience, cut the lines "be he ne'r so vile, / This day shall gentle his condition." Branagh, in 1989, restored them. Why might this be? The egalitarian language of the fighting forces during the Second World War in an era when class consciousness was still vivid throughout Britain might have made even the glancing thought of a common soldier as coming from a "vile" or low social "condition" anathema to national spirit and national rhetoric. By Branagh's time, more than forty years later, these lines seemed merely "historical" and even quaint, not likely to be taken personally by any listener or social group. And Branagh himself, with his chunky body and his bouncy manner, seemed himself deliberately *ordinary* and classless, whereas the slim and elegant Olivier, distinguished though he might be in the film from the effete French, was clearly aristocratic and "noble" in his bearing. Branagh, in other words, was already "us" rather than "you" or "them," even *before* the battle that would, by Henry's redemptive rhetoric, transform the band of brothers, however "vile" their origins, into English gentlemen.

WHEN I WAS INVITED TO SPEAK to the Harvard College class of 1945—the war class—on the occasion of their sixtieth reunion, I began our discussion with the Crispin Crispian speech. The alumni, together with their spouses and partners, were a surprisingly large group, something between a hundred and two hundred people, graduates of coursework, battlefields, and three-quarters of a century of living, gathered on a Sunday morning to remember the past of the classroom, the past of the war and the ensuing histories. We noted on that occasion that the word "theater" itself marked the common ground of these endeavors. Since 1914, at least, when Winston Churchill used it to describe "the hand of war . . . in the Western Theatre," that word, denoting a place of action, has been in frequent use to describe a region of the world in which war is being fought.[7] What especially engaged these veterans was the idea that memories embellish the parts individuals played in the heroic conflict so long ago.

> Old men forget; yet all shall be forgot,
> But he'll remember, with advantages,
> What feats he did that day.
> . . . .
> This story shall the good man teach his son;
> And Crispin Crispian shall ne'er go by
> From this day to the ending of the world,
> But we in it shall be rememberèd.

Remembering "with advantages"—that is, with additions that make the story better—is, in fact, a good description of Shakespeare's *Henry V* as a play: a heroic reconstitution of a messy moment from centuries previous, reflecting positively upon both the older time and the present one, or, as we have seen in the case of all history plays, on *three* time periods at once: the one depicted in the fiction, the time of the play's original writing and performance, and the (shifting) present. So it was with the Greatest Generation— and so it has been with us.

A production by Michael Bogdanov in 1986 came after the Falklands experience, but it was Nicholas Hytner's 2003 version at the Royal National Theatre of Great Britain that took in the full panoply of the post-9/11 world. Tanks and television screens dominated the stage, and Henry's motives as commander in chief, leading his nation into war, were cast into serious doubt. "The play is a Rorschach test that can be made to fit a lot of political situations," said one American theater director. "You can turn it into a jingoistic production that serves in times when courage and patriotism are needed, or you can choose, as Hytner did, to use it to question military adventures. The depth and complexity of the play is such that it can work either way."[8]

But many modern appropriations of the play, in order to tell a political story, go directly from the text to its application, without the intervention of a stage or film performance. Numerous commentators saw the connection between Shakespeare's *Henry V* and the war in Iraq. Political journalist Arianna Huffington wrote that *Henry V* "contains far more truth about our present situation than anything coming out of the White House or the Penta-

President George W. Bush walks the deck of the U.S.S. Abraham Lincoln

gon."[9] George W. Bush's hard-drinking, hard-partying youth and his "conversion" seem directly to parallel the wild youth and reformation of Prince Hal; the tension with a strong paternal predecessor and namesake marks "George II" as a version of Henry V. The play's opening scene, in which the clergy are brought on board to support the war, rings a familiar warning bell. Indeed, the old king's advice to his son in *Henry IV* to "busy giddy minds / With foreign quarrels" (*2 Henry IV* 4.3.341–42) seemed as apt a description of the foreign policy of George W. Bush in Iraq and Afghanistan in the early years of the twenty-first century as it was—in the mind of the American historian Charles Beard—a description of "American interventionism and adventurism" in September 1939, when Beard published an article called "Giddy Minds and Foreign Quarrels" in the pages of *Harper's* magazine.[10]

King Henry the national hero, King Henry the living incarnation of England's Saint George, King Henry the adventurer, King Henry the opportunist, King Henry the cunning manipulator, King Henry the friend of corrupt politicians: none of these portrayals is inappropriate, and none disqualifies the others. In this context, there is no simple "truth," no one right answer. In looking at the arc of the character in the past half century it is of interest to see how the pendulum has swung, from the self-evidently "heroic" Henry of World War II who could summon an outnumbered wartime Britain to sacrifice and greatness, to the present-day suspicion of King Henry's motives and abilities when juxtaposed with American (mis)adventures in the Middle East. Depending upon your politics, it seems, you can find something to admire or something to deplore.

But as striking as has been this change in the fortunes of King Henry V, the one place he has remained almost unquestionably admirable is among those who regularly read—or appear in—*Fortune* magazine.

THE MANAGEMENT AND BUSINESS book industry—a booming business right now—garners much of its managerial "wisdom" from Shakespeare's works, as we can see from a list of recent titles, including: *Shakespeare in Charge: The Bard's Guide to Leading and Succeeding on the Business Stage* (1999); *Shakespeare on Management* (1999); *Inspirational Leadership: Henry V and the Muse of Fire—Timeless Insights from Shakespeare's Greatest Leader* (2001); and *Say It Like Shakespeare: How to Give a Speech Like Hamlet, Persuade Like Henry V, and Other Secrets from the World's Greatest Communicator* (2001). On the cover of this book the phrase "world's greatest communicator" is in capital letters, and the cover image shows a man in a modern business suit, but with an Elizabethan ruff, a high forehead, and a pageboy hairdo, earnestly addressing a table of male and female executives, one of whom is transcribing his words on a laptop.

For the authors of these books, and for those who run "leadership institutes" in Washington, D.C., and around the country, Shakespeare provides object lessons in real-life management and crises, and for them Henry V is the great exemplar of "leadership." Whole chapters are devoted to him, and whole sessions of the institutes focus on his example.

"Henry V is Shakespeare's great heroic leader," says Paul Corrigan in

Shakespeare on Management. "Above all the lessons for managers from Shakespeare's Henry concern his management of *people*. He listens to and talks with his troops in such a way as to motivate them to ever higher deeds of daring. This is a vital part of management."[11]

Corrigan cautions that one should not look to Shakespeare for simple heroics about leadership. His message is hard: "Even if you reach the top, even if you defeat your enemies against the odds, even if you get the girl as well, there are very dark moments. And they are at the core of senior management. Power is not clean."[12] A key case in point is the hanging of Bardolph (a scene that, as we've noted, was omitted from the highly patriotic Olivier film and restored in the more ambivalent Branagh version). For Corrigan, the choice is a good lesson for managers. King Henry, you will recall, says about Bardolph and his crime, stealing from a church, "We would have all such offenders so cut off" (3.6.98). Here is Corrigan's analysis:

> On Henry's orders a close friend is hanged, and for the purpose of the invasion necessarily so—the politics of an invading army compel it. . . . No modern managers are in the position to execute a friend. But many of us have had to make a decision in such a way as to forget some past personal relationship. . . . Shakespeare is teaching us a greater point on a wider field. . . . The execution of a friend makes a number of points with great clarity:
>
> - If I am prepared to hang him, since you know he is my friend, then the rest of you had better behave.
> - If I am prepared to hang him, since you know he is my friend, this an important principle.
> - If I am prepared to hang him, then the army is doing something much more important than what we all normally think of as important, that is, friendship.[13]

Likewise, commenting on the famous speech at Agincourt, Corrigan explains that it illustrates "a point that every major management guru stresses again and again: your staff will make or break your enterprise and your capability as a manager."[14] He inspires "pride of workmanship" in his troops, which "means more to the production worker than gymnasiums, tennis courts and recreation areas."[15] His speech "successfully motivates his troops."[16] "This is a clear example of human resource management at its highest."[17]

The long chapter on Henry V (the book contains others on less successful leaders, like Macbeth, Richard III, King Lear, and Coriolanus) is intercut with quotations from state-of-the-art books on business management, including those by Tom Peters and Peter Drucker, two of the architects of the field.

Shakespeare—and especially *Henry V*—supply the "proof texts" for the argument about making managers. In the introduction, Corrigan quotes the glorious "Once more unto the breach" speech from act 3, scene 1 (which, as we have already had occasion to notice, was immediately turned into a political slogan by the opportunistic and mercenary Pistol in the next scene of Shakespeare's play):

> Once more unto the breach, dear friends, once more,
> Or close the wall up with our English dead.
> . . . .
> On, on, you noblest English,
> Whose blood is fet from fathers of war-proof.
> . . . .
> For there is none of you so mean and base
> That hath not noble lustre in your eyes.
> I see you stand like greyhounds in the slips,
> Straining upon the start. The game's afoot.
> Follow your spirit, and upon this charge
> Cry, "God for Harry! England and Saint George!"
>
> *3.1.1–34*

And he follows it immediately with this observation: "Why is it that nearly all the managers I know would like to deliver a speech like this to their staff? They want to make this speech, not because they want to be in a war, but because they would love to be as certain as Henry is that their people will follow them."[18] I should note that Corrigan's book was published in 1999, before the Iraq War (and indeed before the terrorist attacks of 9/11). There are more than the usual set of ironically discrepant time periods here: Henry V's actual dates (medieval); Shakespeare's (early modern); management discourse of the late 1990s; and the (shifting) present day.

Former Reagan arms control director Kenneth Adelman and his wife, Carol, run a leadership training program wittily called Movers & Shakespeares. Here are some selections from their Web site:

> Drawing on their extensive experience in top positions in government, public corporations, and non-profit groups, Carol and Ken Adelman work closely with companies and universities to customize each program to address the key issues facing their particular organization at the time.

> The Adelmans select the most apt Shakespeare play to fit the program's purpose. For leadership and ethics, they draw on *Henry V,* for change manage-

Ken and Carol Adelman of Movers & Shakespeares

ment, *Taming of the Shrew,* for risk management and diversity, *Merchant of Venice,* and for crisis management, *Hamlet.*

No prior knowledge of Shakespeare is required. . . .

Participants divide into small discussion groups to relate the lessons of these Shakespearean scenes to their own company practices. The groups report back to the whole seminar on whether and how the company handled the situation better (or worse) than King Henry V, Portia or Claudius.[19]

Notice that the Shakespeare stuff is ancillary to the organizers' expertise and résumés: "their extensive experience in top positions in government, public corporations, and non-profit groups," to quote the Web site once again. Just as "no prior knowledge of Shakespeare is required" of participants (and quite reasonably so), likewise the directors of Movers & Shakespeares are, so to speak, Movers rather than Shakespeares. They have picked up their Shakespeare along the way. Carol Adelman is the president of Movers & Shakespeares, and her résumé tells us that she has "over 25 years of theatrical experience," but her doctorate is in public health, and she has worked in government as the "top official for the first President Bush on US foreign aid to Asia, the Middle East, and . . . Eastern Europe." Her husband, with "years of teaching Shakespeare" at Georgetown and George Washington universities (I am, again, quoting his résumé) has a doctorate in "Political Theory" and a master's in "Foreign Service Studies."[20]

In short, it is because of their credentials in government and business, not in English literature, that the Adelmans have clout in the world of the leadership institute. The real subject is leadership, and "Shakespeare" is the image or comparison being used to convey the point. Contented clients like Northrop Grumman Mission Systems, General Dynamics Armament and Technical Systems, Ocean Spray products, and the Wharton School of Business have written testimonials to Movers & Shakespeares, testifying to this program as a suitable authority to advise business executives. *Shakespeare in Charge,* the book Adelman coauthored with Norman Augustine, chairman and CEO of Lockheed Martin, was blurbed by Colin Powell and Warren Buffett.[21]

What does Ken Adelman have to say about Henry V? "Superb leadership, of the kind King Henry V displays, can compensate for shocking shortcomings elsewhere. . . . In Henry V we have a man at the apex of both the power and leadership scales. Watching Henry up-close-and-personal shows us a leader working brilliantly with his executive staff and lowly subordinates alike, a grand strategist who focuses on detail, a man whose private doubts and fears remain concealed as his public persona exudes confidence, a motivational speaker who peps up his team right before they take the field, and a warrior-commander who inspires them and drives them on to victory."[22]

The hanging of Bardolph is, for Adelman and Augustine, as it was for Corrigan, a crucial executive decision for King Henry, "the need to carefully evaluate his key staff and eliminate the bad seeds. Finding them, he gives them the *ultimate* pink slip."[23] About the Crispin Crispian speech, they say, "Successful corporate leaders inspire people to dig deep within themselves, which makes that critical difference between victory and defeat."[24] The longbows are said to come from "the Welsh forests—the Silicon Valley of that era."[25] Much of the rest of the book's opening chapter, "Act I: On Leadership," is devoted to the activities of "shrewd business leaders . . . like Henry," including Richard Branson of Virgin Atlantic; Todd Wagner, who pioneered putting sports events on the Internet; Jake Burton Carpenter, designer of the snowboard; and so on.[26] "While Henry doesn't have the luxury of a policy-planning staff and off-site strategizing meetings, he proves himself a great leader in identifying and then pursuing a clear vision."[27]

Just about every book on Shakespeare and business singles out Henry V as a model for modern leadership. In Jay Shafritz's *Shakespeare on Management* the "once more unto the breach" passage in *Henry V* is called "one of the greatest motivational speeches of all time," and Henry himself "a practitioner of the path-goal leadership style."[28] "A little touch of Harry in the night" is said to illustrate Tom Peters's theory of "management by wandering around," and the Crispin Crispian speech shows Shakespeare as a "managerial psychological par excellence."

What should we think about such an appropriation of Shakespeare? Certainly nothing is more symptomatic of "modern culture" than using Shakespearean characters and plots as the jumping-off points for discussions about business ethics and management decisions. Nor are these "readings" of the plays bad readings. They're perfectly sensible, as far as they go. They are presented, of course, as if they had been generated independently of any scholarship on the topic (there are no footnotes to literary scholars, Shakespeareans, or Shakespeare editors, although there are periodic footnotes to, or citations from, business texts). Corrigan devotes a substantial chapter to a reading of *Henry V* and to the story of King Henry as it was set out in the two previous plays, *Henry IV,* parts 1 and 2, where, as the madcap Prince Hal, he goes about consolidating his support with the underclasses by drinking with them, speaking their jargon, and associating with marginal characters in taverns and brothels. This is described as good preparation for leadership, as indeed it is. Adelman and Augustine are far less systematic in their treatment of the plays, using specific lines and incidents as springboards to discussions of modern-day tycoons and business decisions.

If we look at yet another one of these books, Thomas Leech's *Say It Like Shakespeare,* we find the role of each play and character even further fragmented, since the chapters are divided not by play but by business or management topic. Thus King Henry's nighttime walk among the troops on the eve of battle is cited in a chapter that urges "First, Do Your Homework," under a heading called "Know the Territory" that also includes "the sales guys" in *The Music Man* and the miscalculations of Custer and of Butch Cassidy and the Sundance Kid.[29] A chapter called "Gather Your Team: Once More Unto the Breach!" begins with the "we few, we happy few, we band of brothers" quotation to introduce the idea of working in "tiger teams, task forces, and IPTs (integrated project teams)" for optimal communication in business today.[30] The book ends with the Crispin Crispian speech, printed in full, followed by the suggestion that "if you read this aloud, you may feel an irresistible urge to head off for the recruiting office. This is regarded by many as one of the most powerful communications in the entire Shakespeare repertoire."[31] Again, this book's footnotes are all to business books, newspaper articles, books of famous insults, *People Skills,* and so forth.

There seems no reason not to welcome any modern discussion of Shakespeare, however attenuated from the actual plays and their language—as with films and books that take off from Shakespeare plays, like *A Thousand Acres* or *10 Things I Hate About You* (a "teen remake" of *The Taming of the Shrew,* in which my favorite character, the father, is called "Walter Stratford"). But this kind of work is not useful in illuminating, analyzing, or interpreting Shakespeare. It uses Shakespeare, but the use is not commutative. It does not go both ways. Taking problem sets from Shakespeare's plays and posing them as moral or ethical or decision-making problems flattens them out rather than teasing out their ambiguities and internal contradictions. The "Henry V" of these examples is a construct, a product of a management exercise or of a motivational speaking course.

Leadership is not a literary, intellectual, or analytical category. It is a word of instrumentality, avoiding ambiguity rather than seeking it. And it assumes that Henry, whoever he is, has a plan, a design, and an objective that can be imitated with profit—and *for* profit. (Thus none of these motivational exercises allow for the reversal of fortune that is announced by the epilogue, or for any of the myriad hints in the play that trouble may be just outside the boundaries of its controlling myth.) Yet the richness of the play depends, precisely, upon its eluding these determinative, end-stopped boundaries. The darker Branagh interpretation is always encoded within the more optimistic Olivier interpretation. The 2003 Nicholas Hytner production at the Royal National Theatre of Great Britain was described as "hugely controversial" because of its "deglamorization of Henry's war and its implied criticism of those who mount the ramparts under false pretenses."[32]

What is the literary keyword I would suggest for *Henry V*? It is certainly not "leadership." But it is a deceptively close, and deceptively distant concept— the concept of "exemplarity." Being fit to serve as a model or pattern.

Henry V's great speeches, both "once more unto the breach" and the Crispin Crispian speech ("we few, we happy few, we band of brothers") are taken by these motivational professionals as the exemplar of what a good leader should and can do, in the office as on the battlefield, in the warfare of multinationals as well as in the football locker room before the big game. But the literary-critical category of "exemplarity" is more complex and more double-sided.[33]

How can something be an example, if it is also an exception, and a unique event? Of what is it exemplar? Literary characters are often taken to be "examples" of something that is also "universal"—thus Henry is a king, a young man with a wild past, a general, an Englishman (or a Welshman), a historical figure, and so on. And some generalists will want to claim that such categories are examples of "human nature." Motivational books tend to present him as an exemplar of the good leader, the manager, the decisive business professional. But because he is embedded in a literary text, and is in fact constituted by that text, "Henry" is also a site of contestation and contradiction. Is he really in love with Kate, or is the marriage purely a political convenience? In the play he speaks plausibly on so many occasions, to so many publics and individuals—and in *Henry IV, Part 1,* the character of Prince Hal (who will become Henry V) says in soliloquy, to his offstage low companions (and to *us* in the audience), "I know you all, and will awhile uphold / The unyoked humour of your idleness" (1.2.173–74). That Hal was using his friends, and using us. Is this the same character? When Henry V is taken as an example, whether of the ideal military leader, or the concerned king, or the motivational speaker, what does his language really say? Making him an "example" of these categories is a back-formation, drawing his supposedly exemplary nature from our presuppositions about what the text, the play, means. The reasoning is circular; he becomes an example of that of which we posit, on the basis of our interpretation—or use—of his character, that there is a universal to be exemplified.

Ralph Waldo Emerson's *Representative Men* labels Shakespeare "the poet," Plato "the philosopher," and Napoleon "the man of the world."[34] This is a kind of exemplarity in biography, history, and citation—somewhat different from exemplarity when applied to a literary character or work. Critic Jonathan Culler writes:

> The power of literary representations depends upon their special combination of singularity and exemplarity: readers encounter concrete portrayals of Prince Hamlet or Jane Eyre or Huckleberry Finn and with them the presumption that these characters' problems are exemplary. But exemplary of what? . . . It is as critics and theorists that readers take up the question of exemplarity.[35]

In a similar spirit, the philosopher and theorist Jacques Derrida discusses the word "iterability," that which can be repeated, which is related to the concept of exemplarity, that which is taken as an example: "iterability makes possible idealization—and thus, a certain identity in repetition that is independent of the multiplicity of factual events—while at the same time limiting the idealization it makes possible: *broaching* and *breaching* it at once."[36]

Once more unto the breach. The breach in the wall is what allows for broaching the beginning of a conversation or discussion. It does not close; it opens. Henry V has been taken as an exemplar for the extraliterary world, the world of business, commerce, government, politics, and war. But he remains also a figure both broached and breached, presented and riven, divided within himself and within the play that bears his name. Infinitely repeatable, every time the same but different. Like acting, like theater—like Shakespeare.

Shakespeare's plays almost never end where you think they are going to end, and where they seem to "promise" to end. In *Much Ado About Nothing* the wedding is deferred till after the play is over; in *Macbeth* we do not yet see Malcolm "crowned at Scone." We tend to say that comedies "end in marriage," but often—as, for example, in *Twelfth Night*—the marriage is promised but not performed. *Henry V* is no exception: It ends not with the marriage of the English king and the French princess, although act 5, scene 2 seems to close on that promise ("Prepare we for our marriage," says the king, and concludes in the future tense and in the optative mood, expressing a wish: "Then shall I swear to Kate, and you to me, / And may our oaths well kept and prosp'rous be" [5.2.342; 345–46]).

But neither the royal couple nor the audience gets to enjoy this promised end. Instead the Chorus enters to tell us that this was all a moment, and that it is already over. In the space of a sonnet, a short fourteen lines (much shorter than any of the Chorus's prologues) we learn that Henry V lived a "small time," though "in that small most greatly lived," and that his young son, Henry VI, though he was left "imperial lord" of France and England, was badly advised: "Whose state so many had the managing / That they lost France and made his England bleed" (Epilogue 5–14). I suppose that we could regard this as a direct lesson in leadership: take control, don't put your business in the hands of too many managers, make sure the person in charge knows what he is doing. But if this is the "takeaway," then perhaps we no longer need the play, but only a set of prose maxims.

Henry V ends where it begins, with the Chorus describing—brilliantly and eloquently—the inadequacies of the playwright and the stage: "Thus far with rough and all-unable pen / Our bending author hath pursued the story, / In little room confining mighty men, / Mangling by starts the full course of their glory" (Epilogue 1–4). The sonnet epilogue here is in tension with the drama, with the dramatic action we have just seen and heard. Like a news bulletin, these unwelcome words interrupt the program. We "know" that, offstage somewhere in the imagined world of act 6 of this play the marriage took place, the lands were unified, the love story continued, the heir was born. But what we see and hear is something different, a story of death and of loss, not what we thought we were watching, a story of love and of victory. The king, the hero, the motivational speaker, disappears. What remains is the image of the "bending author" and the brevity of the moment, historically and theatrically speaking. The paradox of exemplarity, the impossibility of a singular paragon who is also an example or a model, requires us to remember the frame, to take the Chorus seriously as part of the play, and to recognize that what is most "Shakespearean" about this ending is the way in which it refuses to let us think we have clinched the deal.

NINE

HAMLET

The Matter of Character

ONE OF THE MOST CONTESTATORY PROBLEMS for literary study in the past century has been the question of character, which can be divided into at least two equally troublesome parts: Can a literary character be considered and analyzed as if he or she were a "real" person, with motivations and a history, "mimetic" (that is, imitative) of "reality"? What dramatic effects and cues are given in the text that produce this illusion of roundedness or interiority? Or, from the opposite end of the spectrum, is a character—especially a dramatic character, a character in a play—nothing more, or less, than a piece of writing, identical to his or her lines in the play, and having no existence (psychic, gestural, conceptual, historical) beyond the lines he or she speaks?[1]

That the word "character" originally meant writing, or handwriting, and did so in Shakespeare's time, further complicates the issue—and certain theatrical and dramatic effects, like, for example, the soliloquy, obviously give the *illusion* of interiority, inwardness, personal history, and feelings, even though those effects, too, are purely fictional and gestural.

Literary characters have, over time, in a variety of kinds of works and kinds of readings, been regarded as *rounded, flat, symbolic, allegorical, realistic, representative, historical,* etc. Consider, just for example, the fact that in *Hamlet* the character of Claudius is never named but always given the speech prefix "King." Does that make him more symbolic, one-dimensional, allegorical? And what kind of a character is a Ghost?

In a phenomenon we might call "the Hamlet effect," much criticism of the play holds the mirror up to nature and finds the critic reflected there. Readers, scholars, and actors have over the years consistently identified with the character of Hamlet, finding in his gifts and his foibles an image of themselves. The English Romantic critic Samuel Taylor Coleridge famously observed, "I have a smack of Hamlet myself, if I may say so."[2] Goethe wrote of Hamlet in 1756:

> A lovely, pure, noble, and most moral nature, without the strength of nerve which forms a hero, sinks beneath a burden which it cannot bear, and must

not cast away. All duties are holy for him; the present is too hard. Impossibilities have been required of him; not in themselves impossibilities, but such for him. He winds, and turns, and torments himself; he advances and recoils; is ever put in mind, ever puts himself in mind; at last does all but lose his purpose from his thoughts; yet still without recovering his peace of mind.[3]

Some twenty years later, Coleridge drew a direct connection between the idea of Shakespearean character and the inner life of Hamlet:

[O]ne of Shakespeare's modes of creating characters is, to conceive any intellectual or moral faculty in morbid excess, and then to place himself, Shakespeare, thus mutilated or diseased, under given circumstances. In Hamlet he seems to have wished to exemplify the moral necessity of a due balance between our attention to the objects of our senses, and our meditation on the workings of our minds,—an *equilibrium* between the real and the imaginary worlds. In Hamlet this balance is disturbed: . . . we see a great, an almost enormous, intellectual activity, and a proportionate aversion to real action . . . he vacillates from sensibility, and procrastinates from thought, and loses the power of action in the energy of resolve.[4]

Each critic describes a Hamlet who corresponds to something in himself. Goethe's Hamlet lacks "the strength of nerve which forms a hero," while Coleridge's Hamlet "procrastinates from thought, and loses the power of action in the energy of resolve." The time-honored question of Hamlet's delay is here linked to the question of character, in concepts like moral nature, weakness and greatness, an excess of sensibility, or a time "out of joint" for action.

Later in the century Edward Payson Vining wrote a book called *The Mystery of Hamlet* that set out to solve this problem of Hamlet's character. Published in 1881, this book might be considered a curiosity of its time—but it was also a *symptom* of its time, and it had some interesting effects, including the production of a fascinating film. Vining's Hamlet initially sounds a lot like Goethe's and Coleridge's: "a hero who, weak and vacillating, continually does those things which he ought not to do and leaves undone those things which he ought to have done, [but about whom] there is yet revealed a depth of human feeling." "[I]n the character of Hamlet we have a bundle of contradictions, as yet inexplicable and mysterious," says Vining. "The character of Hamlet reveals a depth of humanity which all earnest students infallibly recognize."[5]

But Vining thought he could unravel that mystery. His answer, painstakingly revealed through a series of chapters called "The Existence of a Mystery," "The History of the Story," "The Development of Hamlet's Character," and "The Type of Hamlet's Character," was that Hamlet was a woman. This is what made sense of Hamlet's "unnatural timidity" and his preference for "stratagem" over "strength."[6] Thus, Vining provides a chapter called "Hamlet's Nature Essentially Feminine" that contains the following subheadings: "Hamlet's Impulsiveness," "His Love for Mockery," "His Disgust with Revelry," "His Pretty Oaths," "His Fear of Breaking into Tears"—and so on.[7] A later chapter was called "Hamlet's Love for Horatio and Jealousy of Ophelia," and still other sections dealt with "His Bodily Characteristics" ("Small, Delicate, yet Plump," "His Daintiness"), "His Sensitiveness to the Weather and to Odors," "Hamlet Is Hysterical . . . ," "Hamlet Faints . . . ," "The Ghost Never Calls Hamlet 'Son,' " and other tantalizing clues.[8]

Vining supplies his character with a backstory: the throne of Denmark must pass through the male line. On the day when (offstage, and before Shakespeare's play begins) Old Hamlet fought and killed Old Fortinbras, the false rumor developed that Old Hamlet too had been killed; when a baby girl was born, Hamlet's mother decided to pass the child off as a son in order to protect the succession, and this decision, of course, could not be reversed when Old Hamlet returned to Elsinore. And Vining reminds his readers that Shakespeare wrote a number of plays that included women who cross-dressed as men, such as Portia (and Rosalind, and Viola), in order to play a part in world affairs.[9]

I SHOULD EMPHASIZE THAT Vining does not say that Shakespeare *intended* the character of Hamlet to be a woman. "It is not claimed that any such thought was in our immortal poet's mind when first he conceived and put the drama into shape," he says. "The evidence is strongly to the contrary":

> It is not even claimed that Shakespeare ever fully intended to represent Hamlet as indeed a woman. It *is* claimed that in the gradual evolution of the feminine element in Hamlet's character the time arrived when it occurred to the dramatist that so might a woman act and feel, if educated from infancy to play a prince's part.[10]

By this reasoning, Hamlet was sensitive, thoughtful, reflective, not quick to fight—all signs pointed in one direction. The secret of his character was revealed:

> The question may be asked, whether Shakespeare, having been compelled by the course and exigencies of the drama to gradually modify his original hero

into a man with more and more of the feminine element, may not at last have
had the thought dawn upon him that this womanly man might be in very
deed a woman, desperately striving to fill a place for which she was by nature
unfitted.[11]

Interest in this question persisted in the early years of the twentieth century,
and E. P. Vining's book and theory inspired a 1921 German silent film starring
the famous Danish actress Asta Nielsen, and directed by Sven Gade.

Asta Nielsen in Hamlet *(1921)*

The time was right for such a reflection. This was a moment in Europe,
England, and America when gender stereotypes, sexual "inversion," and psychology were developing as topics of scientific investigation and interest.
Havelock Ellis, a British doctor, social reformer, and "sexologist," published
books titled *Man and Woman* (1894) and *Sexual Inversion* (1897).[12] When the
great French actress Sarah Bernhardt played the title part, in 1889, she declared, "I cannot see Hamlet as a man. The things he says, his impulses, his
actions entirely indicate to me that he was a woman."[13] Notice if you will that
Bernhardt is (just) following the well-worn path of identifying herself with

James Lafayette, Sarah Bernhardt *(Hamlet)*

Hamlet, like Goethe and like Coleridge. She played the part successfully for many years, acting in a film version of the duel scene in *Hamlet* late in her life, when she had a wooden leg.

Moreover, there was, of course, yet another famous critic and observer of sexual norms and character who identified himself with Hamlet in this period and whose influence on Hamlet studies was immeasurably greater: Sigmund Freud. Freud's famous theory of the Oedipus complex was founded not so much on Sophocles' play *Oedipus the King* as on Shakespeare's *Hamlet.*

Freud developed this theory initially in a correspondence with his friend and fellow doctor Wilhelm Fliess, dated October 15, 1897 (the same time as Ellis and shortly after Vining). In this letter, Freud wrote:

> I have found, in my own case, too, [the phenomenon of] being in love with my mother and jealous of my father, and I now consider it a universal event in early childhood. . . . If this is so, we can understand the gripping power of *Oedipus Rex.* . . . Everyone in the audience was once a budding Oedipus in fantasy and each recoils in horror from the dream fulfillment here transplanted into reality. . . .
>
> Fleetingly, the thought passed through my head that the same thing might be at the bottom of *Hamlet* as well. I am not thinking of Shakespeare's conscious intention, but believe, rather, that a real event stimulated the poet in his representation, in that his unconscious understood the unconscious of his hero. How does Hamlet the hysteric justify his words, "Thus conscience does

make cowards of us all"? How does he explain his irresolution in avenging his father by the murder of his uncle—the same man who sends his courtiers [i.e., Rosencrantz and Guildenstern] to their death without a scruple and who is positively precipitate in murdering Laertes? How better than through the torment he suffers from the obscure memory that he himself had contemplated the same deed against his father out of passion for his mother?[14]

Notice that Freud, like Vining, says he is not claiming this to be Shakespeare's conscious intention. But where Vining suggested that the complications of the plot produced a female Hamlet ("this womanly man might be in very deed a woman"), Freud suggests that it is the unconscious of the playwright that understands the unconscious of his hero. If his hero has an unconscious, then he is "real" in some sense. Freud calls him an "hysteric," and this is a clinical diagnosis. And, of course, Freud, like Goethe, like Coleridge, like Sarah Bernhardt, like everybody, finds that—surprise!—Hamlet is just like him. "I have found, in my own case, too . . ."

A few weeks later Freud wrote again to Fliess, wanting to know what he thought about the new theory: "You said nothing about my interpretation of *Oedipus Rex* and *Hamlet.* Since I have not told it to anyone else, because I can well imagine in advance the bewildered rejection, I should like to have a short comment on it from you."[15] By 1900, the idea Freud proposed in his letter three years earlier had become a cornerstone of both his sexual theory and his theory of dreams. In *The Interpretation of Dreams,* Freud wrote:

> Another of the great creations of tragic poetry, Shakespeare's *Hamlet,* has its roots in the same soil as *Oedipus Rex.* But the changed treatment of the same material reveals the whole difference in the mental life of these two widely separated epochs of civilization: the secular advance of repression in the emotional life of mankind. In the *Oedipus* the child's wishful phantasy that underlies it is brought into the open and realized as it would be in a dream. In *Hamlet* it remains repressed; and—just as in the case of a neurosis—we only learn of its existence from its inhibiting consequences. Strangely enough, the overwhelming effect produced by the more modern tragedy has turned out to be compatible with the fact that people have remained completely in the dark as to the hero's character. The play is built up on Hamlet's hesitations over fulfilling the task of revenge that is assigned to him; but its text offers no reasons or motives for these hesitations and an immense variety of attempts at interpreting them have failed to produce a result.[16]

Freud mentions Goethe's belief that Hamlet's "power of direct action is paralysed by an excessive development of his intellect" (in effect Goethe as Hamlet), and notes that in fact Hamlet is able to act efficiently with respect to many other rivals and dangers, just not in the killing of the king: "What is it, then, that inhibits him in fulfilling the task set him by his father's ghost? The answer, once again, is that it is the peculiar nature of the task. Hamlet is able to do anything—except take vengeance on the man who did away with his father and took that father's place with his mother, the man who shows him the repressed wishes of his own childhood realized."[17]

It was not until 1910 that Freud himself began to refer to this as the "Oedipus complex."[18] Suppose that he had termed it the "Hamlet complex" instead—how might views of the play and its character have altered? That year, 1910, was the same that Virginia Woolf would proclaim the beginning of a new modern era—tying the notion of modernity to *character*. "On or about December, 1910," wrote Woolf, "human character changed."[19] In that same year Freud's disciple and friend, the Welsh psychoanalyst Ernest Jones, had begun expanding the Oedipus theory into what would become an entire small book called *Hamlet and Oedipus*.[20]

The Freud-Jones theory of Hamlet and the Oedipus complex was to have enormous effects upon productions as well as readings and interpretations of the play. Laurence Olivier's classic treatment, made into a film in 1948, cut the roles of Fortinbras and Rosencrantz and Guildenstern completely, and reduced the script by about half. The political plot thus disappeared, replaced by an emphasis on character formed by family circumstances. The production was framed between the opening voice-over murmur, "[T]his is the tragedy of

Film still of the marital bed in Hamlet *(1948)*

a man who could not make up his mind," and the final, or almost final, shot of the marital bed.

A small but indicative section of Jones's *Hamlet and Oedipus* speaks directly to this question of "what is a character." He is about to embark on a discussion of Hamlet and his problems—to use the title T. S. Eliot would give to a rather different essay in a few years' time—and he wants to justify his treatment of the character of Hamlet as if he were a living person, not a fictional construction. Jones puts the issue squarely to the reader: "I propose to pretend that Hamlet was a living person—one might parenthetically add that to most of us he is more so than many a player on the stage of life—and inquire what measure of man such a person must have been to feel and act in certain situations in the way Shakespeare tells us he did."[21]

As he well knew, this way danger lay. A few years earlier, in 1904, the literary critic A. C. Bradley had published his famous Shakespeare lectures on *Hamlet, Macbeth, Othello,* and *King Lear,* and although the book was greatly praised, it was also roundly criticized for treating Shakespeare's characters as real people. The hallmark of this kind of reading is a sort of ungrounded critical speculation. Here is a quick example from Bradley—speaking about Hamlet's own gifts for speculation: "Doubtless in happier days he was a close and constant observer of men and manners, noting his results in those tables. . . . Doubtless, too, he was always considering things, as Horatio thought, too curiously. There was a necessity in his soul driving him to penetrate below the surface and to question what others took for granted."[22] "[T]hroughout this kingdom of the mind . . . he moved (we must imagine) more than content," wrote Bradley.[23] And in a discussion of Hamlet's attitude toward his mother's remarriage, Bradley commented, "All his life, he had believed in her, we may be sure, as such a son would."[24] "Doubtless." "We must imagine." "We may be sure." Like the person who tells you "frankly" or "candidly" or "to be honest" that something or other is the case, these overemphases sow doubt. "Doubtless" is not proof—it is the avoidance of proof. "We must imagine" empties out the certainty of "must" (why *must* we?); "we may be sure" allows us exactly the uncertainty it seems to preclude. Bradley is a brilliant critic in many ways, but these speculations are not evidence, except of his own conviction.

The speculations of the psychoanalysts were different, although still speculative, because their aim was different. After all, Freud had written, "I have found, in my own case, too . . ." Ernest Jones would claim that Shakespeare was a psychoanalyst before the concept was invented: "Shakespeare's extraordinary powers of observation and penetration granted him a degree of insight that it has taken the world three subsequent centuries to reach."[25] Hamlet's "plight," Jones thought, "is given the name of psychoneurosis, and long ago the genius of Shakespeare depicted it for us with faultless insight."[26]

IN THE COURSE OF THE twentieth and twenty-first centuries, there have been at least three kinds of psychoanalytic readings associated with literature: a psychoanalysis of the author (Shakespeare's symptoms), a psychoanalysis of the character (Hamlet's symptoms), and a psychoanalysis of the text (the symptoms exhibited by *Hamlet* the *play*, like the splitting of characters into good father and bad father, or the linguistic symptoms like repetition, metaphor, or other figures of speech). In this last kind of reading the play is like a dream, an imaginative work made of signs and symbols, available for interpretation. It is really only this last kind of work that escapes from "character criticism" in the old speculative style, and moves toward an understanding of the text's multiplicities, the way it can be read and performed at different times in different ways, each persuasive. The business of the literary critic is not diagnosis but interpretation.

HERE IS A QUOTATION TO PONDER: "Few critics have admitted that *Hamlet* the play is the primary problem, and Hamlet the character only secondary."[27]

This is the opening sentence of T. S. Eliot's brilliant and cranky essay on

"He's, like, 'To be or not to be,' and I'm, like, 'Get a life.'"

Hamlet, published in 1919. Eliot goes on to critique both Goethe, "who made of Hamlet a Werther,"[28] and Coleridge, "who made of Hamlet a Coleridge." "Probably," he comments acerbically, "neither of these men in writing about Hamlet remembered that his first business was to study a work of art."[29] Eliot characterizes *Hamlet* as "the 'Mona Lisa' of literature,"[30] an echo (perhaps unconscious) of Ernest Jones's description of the mystery of Hamlet's delay as "the Sphinx of modern Literature."[31]

But for Eliot Shakespeare's play is not an assured success, but rather "an artistic failure."[32] Why? Because it lacks what he calls an "objective correlative," a set of objects, a situation or a chain of events "which shall be the formula of that *particular* emotion. . . . Hamlet (the man) is dominated by an emotion which is inexpressible, because it is in *excess* of the facts as they appear."[33] The "objective correlative" has become a kind of will-o'-the-wisp, with subsequent critics trying to chase it down and accusing Eliot of failing to create such things in his own poetry. But the very absence of the objective correlative is what makes the play interesting, and what makes the play work. This is not a play that functions by adequation. The *excess* is the Hamlet effect. And it is also the effect of modernity. The final two sentences of Eliot's essay make this point despite themselves. After claiming that "We must simply admit that here Shakespeare tackled a problem which proved too much for him," he ends his argument this way: "We should have, finally, to know something which is by hypothesis unknowable, for we assume it to be an experience which, in the manner indicated, exceeded the facts. We should have to understand things which Shakespeare did not understand himself."[34]

THE OMNIPRESENCE OF *Hamlet* in the masterpieces of modernism has itself become something of a cliché. Shakespeare's play is the touchstone, the proof-piece, the mark itself of canonicity.

Of course, not every modern writer felt this way. Some were frankly irritated by Hamlet, his literary celebrity, and his reputation. Inevitably, there was something of a backlash against the Romantic Hamlet. George Bernard Shaw gave it as his opinion that "all the sentimental Hamlets have been bores," and praised the "gallant, alert" portrayal of Johnston Forbes-Robertson;[35] D. H. Lawrence confessed that "I have always felt an aversion from Hamlet: a creeping unclean thing he seems, on stage . . . his nasty poking and sniffing at his mother, his setting traps for the king, his conceited perversion with Ophelia make him always intolerable. The character is repulsive in its conception, based on a self-dislike and a spirit of disintegration."[36]

Lawrence also produced a poem called "When I Read Shakespeare" that has some particularly pointed things to say about Hamlet as a character:

> When I read Shakespeare I am struck with wonder
> that such trivial people should muse and thunder
> in such lovely language.
>
> Lear, the old buffer, you wonder his daughters
> didn't treat him rougher,
> the old chough, the old chuffer!
>
> And Hamlet, how boring, how boring to live with,
> so mean and self-conscious, blowing and snoring
> his wonderful speeches, full of other folks' whoring!
>
> And Macbeth and his Lady, who should have been choring,
> such suburban ambition, so messily goring
> old Duncan with daggers!
>
> How boring, how small Shakespeare's people are!
> Yet the language so lovely! Like the dyes from gas-tar.[37]

"Gas-tar" is coal-tar, a chief fuel of the time. It smells bad, but it is the source of beautiful aniline dyes in blue, red, purple, yellow, and other shades. This image itself is arguably a good icon of modernity: progress and art linked together, stink and beauty—or, in Lawrence's rather jaundiced view, boring people and lovely language.

JAMES JOYCE'S SHAKESPEARE WAS anything but boring. His Hamlet was derived in part, as the library chapter from his 1922 novel *Ulysses* makes clear, from the French poet and essayist Stéphane Mallarmé—and Mallarmé's fin de siècle Hamlet was himself already a ghost: "struggling against the curse of having to appear," "the potential master who cannot become," "with the hesitation of unfinished deed" ("*sous le mal d'apparaître*"; "*le seigneur latent qui ne peut devenir*"; "*avec le suspens d'un acte inachevé*").[38]

For Mallarmé, Hamlet thus became the type of the poet: all the other characters in the play were aspects of himself, embodiments of his mind.

And for Joyce's protagonist, Stephen Dedalus, himself an aspiring writer, Hamlet is a compatible figure: he walks (*il se promène*), "reading the book of himself," as one of the librarians translates Mallarmé's phrase. "Reading the book of himself" would also be an apt description of both Stephen Dedalus's project, and Joyce's.[39] But where the inherited tradition (from Coleridge, Goethe, and others) closely identified Shakespeare with the character of Hamlet, or Hamlet with the character of Shakespeare, Stephen Dedalus has a different theory, a theory that links Shakespeare with the father, not the son.

THERE IS SOME SCHOLARLY EVIDENCE that Will Shakespeare the actor did play the part of the Ghost (the "perturbed spirit," "this thing") in his company's productions of *Hamlet*.[40] For Stephen and for Joyce, though, it is not just a matter of historical research, but rather a matter of theory and transference.

In Joyce's great modernist novel, published in the same year as T. S. Eliot's *The Waste Land*, a different kind of writing and a different kind of reading are taking place. The *writing* is usually called "stream of consciousness," or interior monologue, while the *reading* is a kind of allegory—what I might call a humanistic or cultural allegory—in which, for Joyce and also (though differently) for Stephen Dedalus, you are reading, simultaneously, several of the great narratives of the past. This is a technique allied to structuralism, a critical practice that emerged from semiotics and anthropology, positing a "deep structure" behind the surface of the text, a structure that tells a story. Such a structure may be briefly summarized here, in chart form:

Ulysses	Telemachus	Penelope
Bloom	Stephen	Molly
Shakespeare	Hamnet	Anne Hathaway
Ghost	Hamlet	Gertrude
God	Christ	Mary

The *story,* or the relationships among its major characters, seems to offer a pattern for other stories: from the Homeric story of Ulysses, his son Telemachus, and the faithful wife Penelope (whom Ulysses left at home), to Joyce's modernized version, in which the son, the Hamlet figure, is Stephen Dedalus, the aspiring Irish writer; the father, the Old Hamlet figure, is Leopold Bloom, the wandering Dublin Jew; and the wife, the Gertrude figure, not at all faithful but joyfully sexy, is the irrepressible Molly Bloom. Notice that by this time, 1922, *Hamlet* has itself become a kind of *myth*—the same kind of ur-story or ancestral story that Shakespeare's play was said, in its own time, to be echoing and refracting.

FROM THE BEGINNING OF "Scylla and Charybdis," chapter nine of *Ulysses,* set in the Dublin library, Shakespeare allusions abound:[41]

The Quaker librarian walks in a "sinkapace," a "coranto," and a galliard-dance step, comically invoked in *Twelfth Night* as the proper gait for a man of culture. In Shakespeare's play Sir Toby Belch says to the feckless Sir Andrew Aguecheek: "Wherefore are these things hid? . . . Why dost thou not go to church in a galliard, and come home in a coranto? My very walk should be a jig. I would not so much as make water but in a cinquepace" (1.3.105–9).

Later this librarian, Lyster, will be compared to the boy player who performs the women's parts in the traveling company that visits Elsinore in *Hamlet* ("tiptoeing up nearer heaven by the altitude of a chopine,"[42] the high-heeled shoe worn by women in the period). This is literary "insider" talk—Shakespeare quotation and clever juxtaposition as a shared secret among readers. Such embedded references demonstrate clearly that Joyce and his protagonist Stephen Dedalus both know the plays intimately.

Joyce evokes Goethe's view of Hamlet: the Quaker librarian considers Hamlet to be "the beautiful ineffectual dreamer who comes to grief against hard facts."[43] He incorporates Matthew Arnold's sonnet "Shakespeare" ("Others abide our question"), Coleridge's "myriad minded" Shakespeare, and Ben Jonson's praise of Shakespeare "this side idolatry." A famous anecdote told by John Manningham in his diary about Shakespeare's good-humored sexual rivalry with his chief actor, Richard Burbage, surfaces too: as Shakespeare boasted while in bed with the contested woman, "*William the Conqueror came before Richard the Third.*"[44] Robert Greene's put-down of Shakespeare in his own time—calling him the "only Shakescene in the country"—becomes, in Joyce's terms, "his glory of greatest shakescene in the country."[45]

Joyce also alludes to E. P. Vining's theory about Hamlet ("Vining held that the prince was a woman") and Oscar Wilde's theory about Shakespeare's sonnets ("The most brilliant of all is that story of Wilde's . . . where he proves that the sonnets were written by a Willie Hughes").[46] In effect, what is presented here, in montage/palimpsest form, is a compendium or anthology of received notions about the modernity or subjectivity or mystery of Shakespeare, and Shakespeare's Hamlet.

STEPHEN DEDALUS'S "THEORY" about Shakespeare and Hamlet is first mentioned in the opening pages of *Ulysses;* it is succinctly and ironically encapsu-

lated by Stephen's friend, the medical student Buck Mulligan: "He proves by
algebra that Hamlet's grandson is Shakespeare's grandfather and that he himself is the ghost of his own father."[47]

One of the themes of the novel is Stephen's search for a "father" who is not
his biological father, Simon Dedalus, but a spiritual or notional father—a figure who becomes equated in the course of the day (the fictional time of the
novel is a single day) with the Jewish small-businessman and advertiser Leopold Bloom. This quest maps onto the complicated reading of *Hamlet* that
Stephen offers to his friends in the library—a reading he himself may not
believe, but that he is pressed to present.

"What is a ghost? Stephen said with tingling energy. One who has faded
into impalpability through death, through absence, through change of manners."[48] In Stephen's imagination—one followed, I should say, by a number of
subsequent critics—Shakespeare was haunted by the death of his son Hamnet, who died in 1596, and identified himself with the role of the father—the
Ghost—rather than with Hamlet, the son. (The names of Hamlet and Hamnet were functionally the same in Shakespeare's time, like different spellings
of Alan or Stephen today.)

By following the Spiritual Exercises of St. Ignatius of Loyola (the vivid
visual imagining of a scene to be contemplated, the "composition of place"),
Stephen invokes the scene of the theater in Shakespeare's time, with Burbage
in the part of Hamlet: "It is the ghost, the king, a king and no king, and the
player is Shakespeare who has studied *Hamlet* all the years of his life which
were not vanity in order to play the part of the spectre."[49]

> To a son he speaks, the son of his soul, the prince, young Hamlet and to the
> son of his body, Hamnet Shakespeare. . . . Is it possible, I want to know, or
> probable that he did not draw or foresee the logical conclusion of those
> premises: you are the dispossessed son: I am the murdered father; your
> mother is the guilty queen, Ann Shakespeare, born Hathaway?[50]

Here Stephen is interrupted by AE (the pseudonym of George Russell, the
Irish painter, poet, economist and political thinker), who objects to "this pry-
ing into the family life of a great man."[51] It's the same point of view expressed
in Ralph Waldo Emerson's essay on Shakespeare in *Representative Men*[52]—
"Interesting only to the parish clerk," says AE. "I mean, we have the plays."[53]

But others in the library feel something like the opposite—they want
Hamlet to be the story, not of the father and husband, but of the son: "*Hamlet* is so personal, isn't it? Mr. Best pleaded. I mean, a kind of private paper,
don't you know, of his private life. I mean, I don't care a button, don't you
know, who is killed or who is guilty."[54] For Best, the biography/confession is

the *only* thing. For Stephen, though, the story is the story of the Ghost: "Two deeds are rank in the ghost's mind: a broken vow and the dullbrained yokel on whom her favour has declined, deceased husband's brother."[55] And behind the story is the story of Shakespeare at Stratford, who left his wife, in his will, his "second-best bed."

Here we might return to our chart of superimposed stories, history, and narrative as a palimpsest. The ghost who "fades into impalpability through death, through absence, through change of manners" is Shakespeare of London when he returns to Stratford and Stephen Dedalus when he returns to Dublin from Paris (and James Joyce who does the same). And it is also Leopold Bloom, a ghost in his own home, where his wife, Molly, is having an affair with Blazes Boylan.

The reader of Joyce's novel will know, though Stephen Dedalus does not, that Bloom, like Shakespeare, lost a son—in his case, Rudy, aged eleven days; in Shakespeare's case, Hamnet, aged eleven years. Will Shakespeare's father, John Shakespeare, died in 1601. "A father, Stephen said . . . is a necessary evil. He wrote the play in the months that followed his father's death."[56]

Can a father who has no son be a father? Can a son who has no father be a son? Shakespeare for Stephen is *both* Hamlet the Father and Hamlet the Son. "He is the ghost and the prince," says John Eglinton.[57] Stephen will go on to claim that Shakespeare's three brothers, Gilbert, Edmund, and Richard, are—like the wife/mother, Anne Hathaway—to be found all over the plays, though Gilbert never by name.

Stephen is fascinated by the authorship controversy, referring to the author of the plays and sonnets at one point as "Rutlandbaconsouthamptonshakespeare or another poet of the same name" (a joke about the famous view that the Homeric poems were written by Homer or a poet of the same name).[58] As with Homer, so with Shakespeare—the man is a mystery, and the authorship controversy itself is an emblem of the problem of paternity. It is, says Stephen, "founded . . . [u]pon incertitude, upon unlikelihood. . . . Paternity may be a legal fiction."[59] In this sense authorship is, precisely, a kind of paternity.[60]

Stephen sees Shakespeare in Shylock, too. "He drew Shylock out of his own long pocket. The son of a maltjobber and moneylender,"[61] Shakespeare sued a fellow player for money and wrote plays with an eye to profit—but clearly Stephen (unlike his friend Buck Mulligan) has some empathy for Shylock. There is talk of two prominent Jewish Shakespeare scholars: the Englishman Sir Sidney Lee, who changed his name from Solomon Lazarus Lee, and the Danish critic Georg Brandes, whose full name was Georg Morris Cohen Brandes.[62]

And meantime, in the background, is a dark, bowing figure who comes to the library to consult a local newspaper ad—it is Leopold Bloom, whom Mulligan labels "the wandering jew," and whose quietly interruptive presence marks the episode at its middle and end. The quest for the son and the quest for the father, which have been the theme of this whole bravura *Hamlet* debate, will continue for the rest of the novel.

The figure of Shakespeare, in a sense, frames—haunts—all of *Ulysses*. In the first chapter Buck Mulligan, the medical student, paraphrases Claudius and Gertrude to puncture Stephen's sadness about his mother's death. Elsewhere there are echoes of Ophelia's drowning, a passage that would also haunt T. S. Eliot's verse. And in a wonderful passage in the book's next-to-last chapter we learn that Leopold Bloom was in the habit of consulting "the works of William Shakespeare more than once for the solution of difficult problems in imaginary or real life," although, despite careful study and the consultation of a glossary, "he had derived imperfect conviction from the text, the answers not bearing on all points."[63] Bloom, a pragmatist and an optimist, not a poet or philosopher, goes to the plays for practical wisdom.

But the focus of *Ulysses,* and of the chapter in the library, is clearly on Hamlet—and on the question of the Ghost.

"WHAT IS A GHOST?" Stephen asked, rhetorically, and supplied his own answer. "One who has faded into impalpability through death, through absence, through change of manners." And again, he speaks of "player Shakespeare, a ghost by absence, and in the vesture [costume] of buried Denmark, a ghost by death, speaking his own words to his own son's name."[64]

Portraits and sketches of some of the stage's most famous Hamlets often registered this sense of the power of absence by showing the actor in the theatrical version of a reaction shot—the famous "start" when Hamlet first sees the Ghost—rather than depicting the Ghost itself. The negative becomes a positive: the invisibility of the ghost is what, paradoxically, makes its effect more real.

By the mid-nineteenth century and increasingly into the twentieth, though, technology had also introduced another kind of ghost, through the new technique of photography, with its language of photographic negatives and its capacity to reproduce the unseen. As Walter Benjamin observed, "In photography, process reproduction can bring out those aspects of the original that are unattainable to the naked eye yet accessible to the lens. . . . And photographic reproduction, with the aid of certain processes, such as enlargement

David Garrick as Hamlet

Edmund Kean as Hamlet

Eugene Thiebault, Henry Robin
and a Specter

or slow motion, can capture images which escape natural vision."[65] This kind of process, he added, "enables the original to meet the beholder halfway."[66]

Later twentieth-century writers have agreed. "Photography," wrote the novelist and essayist W. G. Sebald, "is in essence . . . nothing but a way of making ghostly apparitions materialize by means of a very dubious magical art."[67] Susan Sontag offered a tantalizing link to Shakespeare in an aside in her essay "On Photography" suggesting that Bardolators would treasure a photograph of the playwright as a kind of fetish or talisman, even if it were faded or barely legible: "Having a photograph of Shakespeare would be like having a nail from the True Cross."[68]

The visual "ghosts" that appear in reproductive media, from photography to film and television, are often regarded as errors to be adjusted or corrected. But in their appearance, they remind us of the material nature of illusion. In effect, they reverse the paradigm, as these "ghosts" become the mark of the real.

A DIFFERENT KIND of mark of the real as projected on and through the Ghost in *Hamlet* made its appearance in Jacques Derrida's *Spectres of Marx,* written after the fall of the Berlin Wall.[69] "A spectre is haunting Europe," Marx and Engels had declared, "the spectre of communism."[70] Derrida's reading begins with an epigraph from *Hamlet:* "the time is out of joint." What he will call "the dramaturgy of modern Europe"[71] is haunted by returning spectres, for "the logic of haunting" is that the end is always also the beginning: the revenant, the returning one, *"begins by coming back."*[72]

This is the pattern of revenge tragedy as well as the pattern of *Hamlet.* Many of the most popular tragedies in Shakespeare's time began with the return of a ghost. For what can a ghost do *except* return? The ghost's stage appearance is always a paradox, for its first entrance is also a repetition. "One cannot control its comings and goings because it *begins* by coming back." If this is true of history—and of literary history—it is also preeminently true of Shakespeare: in contemporary life he begins by coming back. For philosophy and literary theory in the later twentieth century, *Hamlet* was a revenant—the ghost that haunts both modernity and postmodernity.

What we see in the spectral appearance and reappearance of Hamlet in modern culture—whether in fiction, poetry, stage plays, films, or political theory—is both the longing for dramatic—and human—character and also a worry about its stability and persistence. The ghostly negative becomes a theme as well as a character without character. This, we might say, is the move of postmodernism. And it finds its dramatic embodiment, or disembodiment, in Tom Stoppard's 1996 play *Rosencrantz and Guildenstern Are Dead.*

STOPPARD'S PLAY and his clueless characters "read" (and misrecognize) Shakespeare's play—as Shakespeare's play also, wittily, "reads" Stoppard's. The intercutting and crosscutting of passages of Shakespeare with passages of Stoppard are one of the many things that make this play so powerful, and so funny.

Hamlet's great soliloquies have set the pattern for interior monologues, the pattern of thinking—from "O that this too too solid flesh would melt" (1.2.129) to "How all occasions do inform against me" (4.4.9.22). In chapter nine of Joyce's *Ulysses,* Stephen Dedalus's self-questioning and self-mocking interior monologue creates the effect of interiority and inwardness—the literary style of a man thinking out loud. But in Tom Stoppard's comic, searing, and postmodern play *Rosencrantz and Guildenstern Are Dead,* the two protagonists, who don't at all understand the Shakespeare play in which they are trapped, call this habit on the part of Hamlet "talking to himself," a habit that seems to them to be either suspicious or crazy. It is one of Stoppard's many witty moves in a play that makes those indistinguishable ciphers, Rosencrantz and Guildenstern, just as "real" and just as emblematic of their own time as Hamlet himself.

TWO KEY THEMES IN *Hamlet* play out on the stage through *Rosencrantz and Guildenstern Are Dead.* One is formal and structural: the device of the play-within-the-play; the other is existential: the confrontation with death, here imagined not only philosophically and poetically, but in terms of its theatrical impossibility.

Paradoxically, as we will see, stage death is always a simulacrum—despite the fact that Guildenstern tells the player that "you cannot *act* it," that "no one gets up after *death,*" the opposite turns out to be the case.[73] As Hamlet suggested long ago, we are all actors. Death onstage in modern culture is *life*—life without purpose, goal, or identity.

PLAYGOERS FAMILIAR WITH twentieth-century theater will recognize that metadrama—drama about drama—is one of its most familiar and effective devices. From Luigi Pirandello's *Six Characters in Search of an Author* to the plays of Jean Genet, Edward Albee, and David Henry Hwang, plays-within-the-play have followed Hamlet's advice to "catch the conscience" of onstage watchers by mirroring their experiences in a fictional guise. For a modern era when "appearance and reality" was a cultural and philosophical preoccupation, the play-within-the-play structure emphasized, as well, the fictionality of the real.

The play-within-the-play has strong roots in the early modern period. In Shakespeare's time the device was constantly exploited, by revenge tragedies and comedies alike. The revenger in Thomas Kyd's *Spanish Tragedy* contrives to kill his enemies during the plot of a play they are performing. Both *Love's Labour's Lost* and *A Midsummer Night's Dream* present the spectacle of onstage audiences watching plays that—although they do not realize it—tell versions of their own stories, to comic effect. In Beaumont and Fletcher's *The Knight of the Burning Pestle* a grocer and his wife go to see a stage play, complain that its characters are too uniformly high-born, and insist that an apprentice be given a starring role.

But it is in *Hamlet* that the metadramatic play finds perhaps its most extended and effective expression. The famous "Mousetrap," or "The Murder of Gonzago," in act 3, scene 2, is the central event, the play that authorizes all the others. In this scene Gertrude and Claudius are in the audience to watch a play about a Player King, a Player Queen, a nephew who poisons the king, and the wife's rapid second marriage, despite her protestations that she would never remarry ("The lady protests too much, methinks" [3.2.210], says Gertrude to Hamlet, in the audience). This play begins with a dumb show, a pantomimed version of the play that is about to take place. Later the play is broken, or interrupted, when "[t]he King rises" (3.2.243) in anger and departs.

And there are other plays as well: the First Player's passionate performance of a scene from a play about the fall of Troy ("What's Hecuba to him, or he to Hecuba, / That he should weep for her?" [2.2.536–37]); the scene in the Queen's closet, or bedroom, in which Polonius hides behind the arras, or curtain, and is stabbed through it by Hamlet, who thinks it is the king hiding there; and the dumb show reported by Ophelia, in which Hamlet appeared silently—like a ghost—in her closet. He has, indeed, already become a ghost.

> Lord Hamlet, with his doublet all unbraced,
> No hat upon his head, his stockings fouled,
> Ungartered, and down-gyvèd to his ankle,
> Pale as his shirt, his knees knocking each other,
> And with a look so piteous in purport
> As if he had been loosèd out of hell
> To speak of horrors, he comes before me.

. . . .

He took me by the wrist and held me hard,
Then goes he to the length of all his arm,
And with his other hand thus o'er his brow
He falls to such perusal of my face
As he would draw it. Long stayed he so.
At last, a little shaking of mine arm,
And thrice his head thus waving up and down,
He raised a sigh so piteous and profound
As it did seem to shatter all his bulk
And end his being. That done, he lets me go,
And, with his head over his shoulder turned,
He seemed to find his way without his eyes,
For out o' doors he went without their help,
And to the last bended their light on me.

2.1.78–101

Ophelia's narrative is an example of what I call a Shakespearean "unscene"—a scene that is not seen, but that is evoked so particularly and meticulously by a dramatic speaker that we seem to see it, and to see an actor or character within it. Shakespeare's plays are full of these "unscenes," too—it is one of his favorite, and most appealing, devices.[74]

It is this particular "unscene" from *Hamlet*—Ophelia startled by Hamlet as she is sewing in her closet—that Tom Stoppard uses to interrupt the action of the "modern" play, *Rosencrantz and Guildenstern Are Dead*, a play that seems to be about two Elizabethans and a disreputable bunch of players. Ophelia's appearance establishes the fact that the whole of *Rosencrantz and Guildenstern* is an unscene *seen*, the backstory only. And this mode of narration, from the backstory (the history or background story created for a fictional character), is, we can notice, another icon of modernity.

HOW DOES JAMES JOYCE'S TREATMENT OF *Hamlet* differ from Tom Stoppard's? It is far too simple to say that it is the difference between modernism and postmodernism (binaries are always a little misleading), but some of the ways in which those two movements have been distinguished can be useful. The critic Ihab Hassan, for example, suggests the following set of oppositions.

MODERNISM	POSTMODERNISM
form	antiform
purpose	play

design	chance
presence	absence
origin-cause	difference-trace
determinacy	indeterminacy[75]

In our case, then, the left-hand column would describe the methods and shape of the Joycean version of *Hamlet,* and the right-hand column Stoppard's version.

But we might recast these roles in an interesting way, if we imagined, instead of Joyce as the modernist and Stoppard as the postmodernist, which is what conventional literary chronology dictates, that *Shakespeare* is the modernist, and Stoppard—or Joyce—the postmodernist. Or, indeed, the other way around. For both the left-hand (modernist) list and the right-hand (postmodernist) list perfectly well describe the theatrical potential—and achievement—of Shakespeare's *Hamlet.*

Joyce assumed readerly familiarity with *Hamlet.* The play is assumed to be canonical, important. His narrator quips and jokes, sometimes to himself, with Shakespearean tags from dozens of plays. The Hamlet story is told and retold and assumes the status of a foundation myth, a founding story of human culture. Stoppard, who knows *Hamlet* equally well, allows it to become faintly ridiculous, without, of course, losing any of its power. It is still canonical, but it is also part of an anti-canon. There is a certain element of desperate farce. Many of the main characters, speaking their actual Shakespearean lines, intercut and crosscut and interrupt the very modern, Godot-like aimlessness of what is happening on the stage.

Samuel Beckett's *Waiting for Godot* is the play to which Stoppard is most indebted. (He has said that the two chief influences on this play were *Waiting for Godot* and T. S. Eliot's poem "The Love Song of J. Alfred Prufrock," which is also about an attendant lord.)[76] The scene with the three barrels, on board ship in act 3, is clearly written in homage to Beckett (Hamlet in a barrel, Rosencrantz and Guildenstern in another, and the entire troupe of players stuffed into, and emerging from, the third). Two characters, stuck on the stage, not knowing what's going on, waiting for something, having been summoned to do something, but why? And how? And when? Notice, though, that there is no ghost. The Ghost has become part of the machine. The whole action is a revenant, an endless repetition. Everything and everyone is already emptied out.

So the play begins with coin tossing. This is the modern, probabilistic version of the theme of fate in *Hamlet.* The destiny that shapes our ends, the providence in the fall of a sparrow, the other half of that "time is out of joint"

line—"O cursèd spite / That ever I was born to set it right!" (1.5.189–90).
But in this case it is not fate: just a lazy, aimless, and at the same time desperate game. Coin tossing, and every coin is heads. Something strange is
happening—even though, by the laws of probability, maybe this is not in fact
so strange.

The players arrive, and they are not noble but tawdry. They can perform
deaths, tragedies, heroes, villains—but mostly they get asked for sex and
voyeurism. It is the times. Blood, love, and rhetoric are their stock in trade.
But by the end of the play they will prove to be the real thing. Whatever that
is. *Real actors.* A contradiction in terms—and a postmodern parable. The very
embodiment of a simulacrum.

Like Beckett's characters, like Albee's, these everymen try to keep themselves occupied—in an empty world, and on an empty stage—by playing
games. They are two characters in search of an author. Though they dimly
sense that somewhere out there there *is* an author, or a playwright, or a play.

But their nemesis is Hamlet. He is better at these games than they are.
They rehearse, by playing the game of "questions." In another very funny
scene, a kind of version of the game show *Jeopardy!,* they have to talk to each
other in questions:

> *Ros:* Are you counting that?
> *Guil:* What?
> *Ros:* Are you counting that?
> *Guil:* Foul! No repetitions. . . .
> *Ros:* Whose go?
> *Guil:* Why?
> *Ros:* Why not?
> *Guil:* What for?
> *Ros:* Foul! No synonyms![77]

And so on.

Again, this is comic in itself—the play is a terrific stage vehicle—but it is
also a "reading" of Shakespeare's play, a play that is so very full of questions
("To be or not to be"; "What a piece of work is a man . . . And yet to me what
is this quintessence of dust?"; "Why would'st thou be a breeder of sinners?";
"What's Hecuba to him, or he to Hecuba?"; "What should such fellows as I
do crawling between earth and heaven?"; "Dost thou think Alexander looked
o' this fashion th' earth?"). Noting these questions and others, the critic Maynard Mack once observed finely that Hamlet's world was "preeminently in the
interrogative mood."[78]

Stoppard's characters have taken their cues, and their orders, from the floating phrases in Shakespeare's play: "[G]lean [what] afflicts him" (*Hamlet* 2.2.16–17). Their method will be question and answer.

But when in act 2 we meet them after their session with Hamlet—the session, remember, that has taken place offstage but that is act 2, scene 2 of Shakespeare's play, the first encounter between Hamlet and Rosencrantz and Guildenstern—we can see that the game of question and answer was itself a kind of interpretation:

> *Guil:* I think we can say we made some headway.
> *Ros:* You think so?
> *Guil:* I think we can say that.
> *Ros:* I think we can say he made us look ridiculous.
> *Guil:* We played it close to the chest of course.
> *Ros* (*derisively*): "Question and answer. Old ways are the best ways"! He was scoring off us all down the line.
> *Guil:* He caught us on the wrong foot once or twice, perhaps, but I thought we gained some ground.
> *Ros* (*simply*): He murdered us.
> *Guil:* He might have had the edge.
> *Ros* (*roused*): Twenty-seven–three, and you think he might have had the edge?! He *murdered* us.

The casual-seeming metaphor ("He *murdered* us") that will all too soon become literal is typical of Stoppard. Its repetition here is a prompt to the audience, an aural double take: "Remember this," it says. "Even if Rosencrantz doesn't understand what he is saying, *you* should: *you* know the play."

> *Guil:* What about our evasions?
> *Ros:* Oh, our evasions were lovely. "Were you sent for?" he says. "My lord, we were sent for . . ." I didn't know where to put myself.
> *Guil:* He had six rhetoricals—
> *Ros:* It was question and answer, all right. Twenty-seven questions he got out in ten minutes, and answered three. I was waiting for you to *delve.* "When is he going to start *delving*?" I asked myself.
> *Guil:* —And two repetitions.
> *Ros:* Hardly a leading question between us.[79]

Twenty-seven questions to three. If you go back and read the scene you can count them up. Here are the three questions Rosencrantz and Guildenstern manage to ask:

> "Prison, my lord?"
> "What should we say, my lord?"
> "To what end, my lord?"
> *Hamlet 2.2.238; 270; 275*

He murdered them.

There is a similarly wonderful incorporation of literary interpretation into dramatic action in the playacting scene where Guildenstern pretends to be Hamlet, and Rosencrantz asks him questions:

Ros: So—so your uncle is the king of Denmark?!
Guil: And my father before him.
Ros: His father before him?
Guil: No, my father before him.
Ros: But surely—
Guil: You might well ask.
Ros: Let me get it straight. Your father was king. You were his only son. Your father dies. You are of age. Your uncle becomes king.
Guil: Yes.
Ros: Unorthodox.
Guil: Undid me.
Ros: Undeniable. Where were you?
Guil: In Germany.
Ros: Usurpation, then.
Guil: He slipped in.
Ros: Which reminds me.
Guil: Well, it would.
Ros: I don't want to be personal.
Guil: It's common knowledge.
Ros: Your mother's marriage.
Guil: He slipped in.[80]

The play contains within it a version of every scene in which Rosencrantz and Guildenstern appear, and in each scene they have no idea what is going on. Why are they taking Hamlet to England? Why is he always talking to himself? (A down-market reference, again, to the famous soliloquies, which of course we never get to hear.) They fancy themselves psychoanalysts—and this allows Stoppard to make a joke about psychoanalytic interpretations of Hamlet:

> *Guil:* It really boils down to symptoms. Pregnant replies, mystic allusions, mistaken identities, arguing his father is his mother, that sort of thing; intimations of suicide, forgoing of exercise, loss of mirth, hints of claus-

trophobia not to say delusions of imprisonment; invocations of camels, chameleons, capons, whales, weasels, hawks, handsaws—riddles, quibbles and evasions; amnesia, paranoia, myopia; day-dreaming, hallucinations; stabbing his elders, abusing his parents, insulting his lover, and appearing hatless in public—knock-kneed, droop-stockinged and sighing like a love-sick schoolboy, which at his age is coming on a bit strong.

Ros: And talking to himself.

Guil: And talking to himself.[81]

Those pesky soliloquies again. But Hamlet when we meet him is a kind of trickster, a man of action. The substitute letter, which sends Rosencrantz and Guildenstern—rather than Hamlet—off to their deaths in England, is, I would suggest, done *better* in Stoppard's play than in Shakespeare's, because it has been set up by so very much in the way of repetition and substitution beforehand, including the reading aloud of the *first* version of the letter. Again, what may seem at first like aimless, or merely phatic, performative repetition turns out by the end of the play to have a powerful point. The main actors in Stoppard's play are the two minor characters of Shakespeare's *Hamlet,* whose names are so metrically similar as to be interchangeable ("Thanks, Rosencrantz and gentle Guildenstern," says Claudius, and Gertrude echoes him, "Thanks, Guildenstern and gentle Rosencrantz" [2.2.33–34]). In Stoppard's version they themselves can't even remember which is which (or at least Rosencrantz can't)—a joke that is funny the first time we hear and see it, very funny the next time, even funnier the next time—and ultimately *tragic* in the last moments of the play, when Guildenstern, the more self-possessed and self-knowledgeable of the two, is left alone onstage.

Rosencrantz disappears from view. Guildenstern, busy rehearsing one more time the story of how they got into this business in the first place, does not notice at first. He speaks:

> *Guil:* Our names shouted in a certain dawn . . . a message . . . a summons . . . There must have been a moment, at the beginning, where we could have said—no. But somehow we missed it. (*He looks round and sees he is alone.*)
> Rosen—?
> Guil—?[82]

It is at this point that he gathers himself and walks offstage, observing, as he goes: "Well, we'll know better next time. Now you see me, now you—(*and disappears*)."[83] Immediately the lights come up full onstage and we are in the middle of the great last scene of *Hamlet,* which contains both the title phrase ("Rosencrantz and Guildenstern are dead") and Horatio's promise to tell the audience—after the play ends—the story of the play:

> give order that these bodies
> High on a stage be placèd to the view;
> And let me speak to th' yet unknowing world
> How these things came about. So shall you hear
> Of carnal, bloody, and unnatural acts,
> Of accidental judgements, casual slaughters,
> Of deaths put on by cunning and forced cause,
> And, in this upshot, purposes mistook
> Fall'n on th' inventors' heads. All this can I
> truly deliver.
>
> *5.2.321–29*

But before Horatio can do so *"the play fades out, overtaken by dark and music."* Anticlimax.

TOM STOPPARD'S PLAY both interprets and upends *Hamlet.* It is *Hamlet* inside out, so to speak, seen from the green room or the wrong end of a telescope.

Reading *Hamlet* inside out does not, so much, make it a different play as show us the existential, postmodern repetitions that are embedded in the play we thought we knew. Defamiliarization—forcing the audience to see familiar things in a strange way—is, it turns out, an element not only of Stoppard's *Rosencrantz and Guildenstern,* but also of Shakespeare's *Hamlet.*

The title of Stoppard's play, of course, is *Rosencrantz and Guildenstern Are Dead.* And while this phrase is a quotation from the very end of Shakespeare's *Hamlet,* the title is also a simple description. In a sense they are already dead, existing in a no-person's-land onstage, what Stoppard's stage direction describes as *"a place without any visible character,"*[84] engaged, seemingly endlessly, in a coin-flipping contest that has no point, and will never end. *"Guil is well alive to the oddity"*[85] of the run of heads in the coin toss, writes the playwright in his stage direction. But these characters are waiting—waiting to die again.

There is no ghost, there is no skull, there is no gravedigger (though there is, as we have seen, a wish to "delve"). The fascination of the early modern period with death as a familiar companion—Martin Luther wore a skull ring, and vanitas paintings featured skulls as part of an assemblage of earthly vanities—is transmuted, in Stoppard's rewriting, into the conundrum of stage death, of dying onstage. "Do you ever think of yourself as actually *dead,* lying in a box with a lid on it?" asks Rosencrantz. "I mean one thinks of it like being *alive* in a box, one keeps forgetting to take into account the fact that one is *dead.*"[86] This is a not inelegant paraphrase of some of Hamlet's lines, but the contemplation of death on the part of these characters is somehow bathetic rather than ennobling. The true artists of death in the play are the players, who know it is a fiction.

WHEN ROSENCRANTZ AND GUILDENSTERN walk out on the players' performance, they are mortified, because acting needs to be done before an audience: "We're *actors*—we're the opposite of people!"[87] And what actors do best is die.

> *Guil* (. . . *rattled* . . .): You!—What do *you* know about *death*?
> *Player:* It's what the actors do best. They have to exploit whatever talent is given to them, and their talent is dying. They can die heroically, comically, ironically, slowly, suddenly, disgustingly, charmingly, or from a great height. . . .
> *Ros:* Is that all they can do—die?
> *Player:* No, no—they kill beautifully. In fact some of them kill even better than they die. The rest die better than they kill. They're a team. . . .

Guil: . . . You die so many times; how can you expect them to believe in your
   death?
Player: On the contrary, it's the only kind they do believe.[88]

To drive home the point, he tells an anecdote about an actor who was actually
condemned to die, and who was utterly unconvincing in the part.

The two kinds of death, "stage death" and "real death," will come together
in the closing moments of the play, when Rosencrantz and Guildenstern open
up the substitute letter and find that it requests the English king to put them
to death. Shakespeare's language is moving, and so is Stoppard's. "Who are we
that so much should converge on our little deaths?"[89] This is Guildenstern,
resisting knowledge.

Player: In our experience, most things end in death.

But Guildenstern is frightened and angry, and he picks up the Player's dagger: "I'm talking about death—and you've never experienced *that*. And you
cannot *act* it. . . . [N]o one gets up after *death*—there is no applause—there is
only silence and some second-hand clothes, and that's—*death*—"[90] And at
this he stabs the Player, who falls, clutches himself, weeps, and dies. And gets
back to his feet, as the Tragedians, his company, applaud.

"You see, it *is* the kind they do believe in," he tells the baffled Guildenstern, "it's what is expected."[91] The dagger was a trick weapon—and now all
the players turn on one another and "kill: each other," in, as it turns out,
exactly the manner of the duel scene in *Hamlet*: "*Alfred, still in his Queen's costume, dies by poison; the Player, with rapier, kills the 'King' and duels with a
fourth Tragedian, inflicting and receiving a wound.*"[92]

AGAIN, THE AUDIENCE SEES the play inside out—"I am dead, Horatio."
This phrase was, said Roland Barthes, a "scandal of language." Something
that was impossible to say. But Hamlet says it.[93]

> I am dead, Horatio. Wretched Queen, adieu!
> You that look pale and tremble at this chance,
> That are but mutes or audience to this act,
> Had I but time—as this fell sergeant Death
> Is strict in his arrest—O, I could tell you—
> But let it be. Horatio, I am dead,
> Thou liv'st. Report me and my cause aright
> To the unsatisfied.
>
> 5.2.275–82

"Report me and my cause aright / To the unsatisfied." That's us. You and me. Unsatisfied, despite what Horatio says that he can truly deliver. Unsatisfied, as Rosencrantz was unsatisfied:

> *Ros:* Couldn't we just stay put? I mean no one is going to come on and drag us off [No fell sergeant . . .]. . . . They'll just have to wait. We're still young . . . fit . . . we've got years . . .
>
> . . . .
>
> We've done nothing wrong! We didn't harm anyone. Did we?
>
> *Guil:* I can't remember. . . .
>
> *Ros:* All right, then, I don't care. I've had enough. To tell you the truth, I'm relieved.[94]

And Guildenstern, as we've already seen, disappears in the middle of a sentence: "Now you see me, now you—"[95]

But if both "stage death" and "real death" are staged, what is the difference? In Stoppard's play the final "tableau of court and corpses" is arranged in the same positions as those "*last held by the dead Tragedians,*"[96] that is, the troupe of tawdry actors who have died, so melodramatically and metadramatically, in the final "show." The decentering of the hero—the placement of the bit players, Rosencrantz and Guildenstern, in the place where we are accustomed to find Hamlet—goes along with the reversal of "stage death" and "real death," or rather, with the theatrical conundrum of how to tell them apart.

In his advice to the players Hamlet says that the purpose of playing is to hold "the mirror up to nature" (3.2.20). But the metadrama of modernity does, in a way, the opposite. It holds nature up to a mirror, and it believes the mirror. Never more than when it juxtaposes stage death and real death on the stage—and stage death wins.

TEN

KING LEAR

The Dream of Sublimity

A S FAR BACK AT LEAST AS the late eighteenth century, *Hamlet* had been considered as perhaps the "greatest" of Shakespeare's plays, and certainly as his most popular tragedy. Coleridge said so in England. Goethe said so in Germany. But in the middle of the twentieth century, a shift occurred in the public consciousness of two of Shakespeare's plays, *Hamlet* and *King Lear*. This shift was clearly and cogently noted in a 1993 book by R. A. Foakes called *Hamlet versus Lear*.[1]

Foakes argued that the primacy of *Hamlet* changed at mid-century in part because of a change in how audiences understood *King Lear*. When *Lear* was read as a play about redemption, and particularly Christian redemption, it had a host of fervent admirers, but it nonetheless stood apart from the experience of many. In the late 1950s and '60s, Foakes contended, the "meaning" of *Lear* for audiences and readers began to change in response to cataclysmic world events like the exploding of the hydrogen bomb, political turmoil in Eastern Europe and Cuba, the assassination of President John F. Kennedy, and the start of the Vietnam War. The play then "became Shakespeare's bleakest and most despairing vision of suffering, all hints of consolation undermined or denied."[2]

In support of this thesis Foakes presented three lists: a list of critics who called *Hamlet* Shakespeare's "best" or "greatest" play, or at least his greatest tragedy; a list of other critics (some as early as the nineteenth century or the first years of the twentieth) who made similar claims for *King Lear;* and a list of major events of the period 1954–65, beginning with the explosion of the H-bomb on Bikini Atoll and the consequent spread of nuclear fallout to Japanese fishing boats and to islanders in the region, and ending with the first bombing of North Vietnam and the Watts riots in Los Angeles.[3] His claims are not causal but relational; the world, or at least the world of Shakespeare readers, directors, teachers, and students, was ready for a new *Lear,* or receptive to the *Lear* that they now found or made.

Had he continued his list beyond 1965, Foakes might have listed two more tragic American assassinations, those of Robert Kennedy and Martin Luther King Jr.; as well as the growth of the counterculture and the 1967 "Summer of Love"; the intensification of both the Vietnam War and resistance to it; and the "events of '68" in France, Prague, and around the world. "Never trust anyone over thirty" was a saying that emerged out of the Free Speech movement at the University of California, Berkeley, in the mid-sixties,[4] but its resonances continued through the next several years, in politics, generational conflict, music, and popular culture.

How can we calibrate and document the reasons why *King Lear* rose on the Shakespearean stock market in the middle of the twentieth century? In doing so we will see that the trend was not "universal" (to use yet another one of the words of high praise characteristically applied to both *Hamlet* and *Lear,* as well as to Shakespeare himself). Praise for the relevance and moral power of *King Lear* was not usually, if ever, linked to any dispraise of *Hamlet.* It was rather, as Foakes claimed in the last sentence of his book, that in his view, and the view of several other critics at the time, *King Lear* "speaks more largely than the other tragedies to the anxieties and problems of the modern world."[5]

We should note, from the perspective of the first decade of the twenty-first century, that there has been a certain, perhaps inevitable, fluctuation in the market, with high-school and college students, particularly, returning to a closer identification with *Hamlet* than with *Lear.* Fueled by the spate of new action-oriented *Hamlet* films starring Mel Gibson and Kenneth Branagh—not to mention the "slacker Hamlet" played by Ethan Hawke in director Michael Almereyda's version, filmed in 2000—younger viewers find it easier to identify with Hamlet than to find a place for themselves within *King Lear.* When I met with a group of secondary school teachers to discuss the presentation of Shakespeare in the classroom, several of them mentioned that *Lear* was a hard play to teach. Although the instructors responded to the play's bleakness and sublimity, the students tended to find it somewhat estranging. If their mode of reading is not existential or allegorical, the plight of the old king may strike them as distant from their own concerns, and none of the younger generation—Edmund or Edgar, Goneril, Regan, or even Cordelia—is so readily available as a transferential "hero."

THE ROLE OF *Hamlet* in the formation of modern culture seemed to have been predicated on one of several scripts, like personal identification, as in Coleridge's "I have a smack of Hamlet myself, if I may say so"; biographical detection, as in psychoanalyst Ernest Jones's claim that "the play is almost universally considered to be the chief masterpiece of one of the greatest minds the world has known. It probably expresses the core of Shakespeare's philosophy and outlook on life as no other work of his does"; or allegorical extrapolation, as in Emerson's famous declaration in his "American Scholar" address that "the time is infected with Hamlet's unhappiness,—'Sicklied o'er with the pale cast of thought.' "[6] When Emerson made this observation in 1837, it was already something of a truism—a commonplace phrase that would be recognized by his listeners. (Indeed he went on to say that things were in fact not "so bad," that the time was "a very good one," in which literature was responding to the "topics of the time," the complex political and social needs of the era.) But the sentiment continued to be expressed for the next hundred years and more.

For Georg Brandes, the Danish critic, author of an influential study of Shakespeare published in English translation in 1902, Hamlet was emblematic of "the typical modern character, with its intense feeling of the strife between the idea and the actual world."[7] Notice the recurrence of this word "modern," which seems almost reflexively to have come to indicate something of the affinity critical observers felt with Hamlet as a character. They recognized themselves, as well as their times, in him.

In Europe, especially, this overthinking, underacting Hamlet was considered a version of the irresolution of political intellectuals, whose ideas could not be translated into action—and it was but a short step to identifying the malaise of an entire nation in this way. Foakes notes that "Germany is Hamlet" was the beginning of a poem written in the mid-nineteenth century, and both Poland and Russia had moments of thinking of themselves, explicitly, as Hamlet.[8] In France, Mallarmé saw Hamlet as a kind of ghost, tormented with the necessity of having to appear. The French poet and dramatist Paul Claudel reflected on Mallarmé's observations: "With Hamlet there appeared a theme . . . which waited two centuries to find an atmosphere it could develop in: the attraction to Night, the penchant for unhappiness, the bitter communion between the shadows and this anguish of being mortal."[9]

"HAMLET" BECAME CULTURAL CODE for "a troubled, indecisive, or capricious person" (*OED*).[10] A character in Eugene O'Neill's play *A Moon for the Misbegotten* (written in the period 1941–43) confides that "suddenly, for no reason, all the fun went out of it, and I was more melancholy than ten Hamlets."[11] Not only was "a Hamlet" moody, though; he was also often ineffectual, rendered immobile by too much consideration. The shorthand notion of Hamlet as a delayer who misses his moment has continued in political discourse throughout the twentieth century and to the present day. Thus, for example, Ronald Reagan's Secretary of State, George P. Shultz, cautioned that "We cannot allow ourselves to become the Hamlet of nations, worrying endlessly over whether and how to respond."[12]

To a certain extent this version of the modern Hamlet has been recuperated by actors and critics who have made him into an action hero in a time of inaction. In this view, it was the time that was out of joint, not the hero. If Olivier's Hamlet was, famously, "a man who could not make up his mind," he was, nonetheless, a heroic figure, struggling against a corrupt world.

In any case, though, whether heroic or neurasthenic, athletic or languorous, thinking too much or just thinking, Hamlet became a byword, a figure for intense (even overintense) subjectivity—personality, individuality, consciousness.

But this has never been the case with *King Lear.* For all of its use of soliloquy, and Lear's impassioned and brilliant speeches in the storm scene in act 3, the play of *King Lear,* which has been interpreted in a wide range of ways over time, has come for us to signify something else that is modern: the emptiness, illogic, terror, and absurdity of the modern condition. The play has been read in the twentieth and twenty-first centuries as an existential allegory, as a social treatise, as a philosophical statement: an icon of modern life, not of modern man.

SOME EARLIER CRITICS HAD already elevated *Lear* above *Hamlet.* William Hazlitt, the Romantic critic, for example, expressed the opinion that *King Lear* "is the best of all Shakespeare's plays," basing his argument, interestingly, in part on a claim of sincerity: "it is the one in which he was most in earnest." For Hazlitt "the *Lear* of Shakespeare cannot be acted," since "the greatness of Lear is not in corporal dimension, but in intellectual," and if we read the play rather than watch an actor in the role, "we see not Lear, but we are Lear."[13] A. C. Bradley, in his Oxford lectures on Shakespearean tragedy, expressed the view that *Lear* was "Shakespeare's greatest achievement" (although he thought it "*not* his best play"):[14]

> *King Lear* has again and again been described as Shakespeare's greatest work, the best of his plays, the tragedy in which he exhibits most fully his multitudinous powers; and if we were doomed to lose all his dramas except one, probably the majority of those who know and appreciate him best would pronounce for keeping *King Lear.*

Yet this tragedy is certainly the least popular of the famous four. The "general reader" reads it less often than the others, and though he acknowledges its greatness, he will sometimes speak of it with a certain distaste.[15]

Hamlet, by contrast, is several times described by Bradley, admiringly, as "the most popular of Shakespeare's tragedies on our stage" and as the play that is highest in "general esteem."[16] But popularity was only one gauge. In trying to explain why and how *King Lear* could be Shakespeare's "greatest" without being his "best play," Bradley had telling recourse to the comparison with other arts. He says that *Lear* is "greater than" *Hamlet, Othello,* or *Macbeth,* and "the fullest revelation of Shakespeare's power" ("I find that I am not regarding it simply as a drama, but am grouping it in my mind with works like the *Prometheus Vinctus* and the *Divine Comedy,* and even with the greatest symphonies of Beethoven and the statues in the Medici Chapel.")[17]

As we will see, this intuition, linking *King Lear* to the profoundest achievements of Dante, Beethoven, and Michelangelo, speaks not only to the language of suffering, but also to the question of sublimity. In fact the story of *King Lear* in the twentieth and twenty-first centuries offers a striking example of the intersection between timeliness and timelessness that has been a hallmark of Shakespeare's persistent modernity since Ben Jonson eulogized him as "not of an age, but for all time." In the case of *King Lear,* this meant not so much an "identification" with the hero's dilemma, as with the way in which the hero's consciousness of catastrophe became a cultural mise-en-scène.

FROM THE 1960S ON, *King Lear* held pride of place among Shakespeare's "greatest" plays, at least in the view of many. In its first edition, in 1962, *The Norton Anthology of English Literature,* the basic canonical textbook for college English majors across the United States, printed only two plays by Shakespeare: *Henry IV, Part 1* and *King Lear* (not *Hamlet*).[18] In 1965 the Yale English scholar Maynard Mack published a short book called *King Lear in Our Time,* based upon lectures he had given at Berkeley in the previous year. At the same time there appeared for the first time in English translation another, equally influential book that also put *King Lear* at its center, the Polish writer Jan Kott's *Shakespeare Our Contemporary.*[19] Kott's interpretation became vastly important for the itinerary of *King Lear* in the theater and on film from the sixties on. In both of these books—books which could not, in other ways, be more different—the word "our," a classic shifter (*whose* time? *whose* contemporary?) signals both a problem and a marker for modernity.

But the story begins much further back.

When Dr. Samuel Johnson, the Shakespeare editor, dictionary maker, poet, and moralist, came to edit the scene of Cordelia's death for his edition of 1765, he added a personal note in his edition: "I was many years ago so shocked by Cordelia's death, that I know not whether I ever endured to read again the last scenes of the play till I undertook to revise them as an editor."[20]

Johnson's shock was, we might think, salutary and indicative of the play's power—but for critics, writers, and audiences in the years before this, the death of Cordelia was a major flaw, and one that could be, and was, corrected. Shakespeare was a great poet, no doubt, but he lived in a barbarous age, and his works could be "improved" according to modern taste—the modern taste of the Restoration, the last years of the seventeenth century. Shakespeare died in 1616; the First Folio of his plays was published, by friends, in 1623, "according to the true and perfect copies" of the plays he had left them; in 1681, only half a century later, Nahum Tate had rewritten the play, as Shakespeare would have written it had he only known how to do so. From 1681 until 1838, some 150 years, only Nahum Tate's *King Lear* was performed on the English stage. You could *read* Shakespeare's play, but you could not see it performed. Hazlitt and Keats read Shakespeare, but they saw Shakespeare as rewritten by Tate.

WHAT KINDS OF "IMPROVEMENTS" did Nahum Tate make? Well, centrally, he invented what he clearly felt lay close beneath the surface: a love affair between Cordelia and Edgar. Cordelia thus consciously "tempts" her father to leave her no dowry, so that Burgundy will refuse to marry her, and she will be free to pursue a relationship with Edgar. (Both the King of France and the Fool are eliminated completely from the plot, since the first seemed superfluous and the second, indecorous.)

Cordelia is indeed fairly crafty. She at first refuses Edgar, so as to test his love for her, driving him into the device of disguising himself so that he may prove his love and be of potential service to his lady. (This is also what Kent does in Shakespeare's play, disguising himself as a common man so as to serve the exiled and broken King.) In Tate's version, Cordelia is abducted by ruffians at the behest of Edmund, who plans to rape her. She is rescued by the disguised Edgar, who then can reveal his real identity, and the lovers exit, satisfactorily, together. At the end of the play Lear, who has been sleeping in his prison with his head in Cordelia's lap, rouses himself when soldiers come

"Don't remind him it's Father's Day."

to kill her, dispatches two of them, and holds on valiantly until Edgar and Albany come to rescue them. The play, in short, has become a melodrama—very effective theater, though not the play that Shakespeare wrote.[21]

Nonetheless, Tate's version was "Shakespeare" on the English stage for a century and a half, until the great actors and theater managers of the middle of the century restored Shakespeare's words and actions. William Macready was the first, in 1838, and from that time Shakespeare's play displaced Nahum Tate's. The Fool, banished as coarse and grotesque—the very elements that would make him a perfect figure for twentieth-century modernity—returned to the play, but initially, for Victorians, more like a sprite than a sage. (Maynard Mack reminds us that this was the time of Peter Pan.)

And what about Lear himself? For a long time on the nineteenth-century stage he was almost a kind of Polonius—a doddering lunatic, an "old man tottering about the stage with a walking stick," as Charles Lamb said.[22] The majestic actor Edmund Kean, wrote Hazlitt, "driveled and looked vacant."[23] The magnificent language of the play, the towering speeches, the enormous pathos of conception and experience, were often turned into something like bathos instead. It was only gradually that the change was perceived, a return to the region of the sublime.

The later nineteenth century, and the early twentieth century, insulated itself in a way from the raw emotions produced by the play by overproducing it—elaborate stage sets, caves, huts, storms mechanically evoked, where the noise of the stage machines overwhelms the actor and the voice, leaving nothing to imagination—and also by situating the play in deep time—at the time of Stonehenge, or early Britain, with a kind of resolute primitivism. That was then; this is now. The language of the play permits an early modern as well as an ancient British ambiance—"robes and furred gowns hide all," says Lear.

AS WITH DR. JOHNSON's strong response to the death of Cordelia, the level of feeling evoked by the play is very high and very strong, and can sometimes, unknowingly, tip over into its opposite. Just as the modern theater of the mid-twentieth century would find when it located itself in the terrain of the absurd, the grotesque is the obverse of the sublime, as bathos is the obverse of pathos.

Pathos, and the emotions it generates, has often been associated with productions—and readings—of this play. Over the years the politics of the play have often been translated into family dynamics as much as European struggles for power. The king as father of something like a modern nuclear (and dysfunctional) family tends often to displace the king as father of the kingdom; paternity has drawn as much attention as patriarchy: Lear is given his rage and his high-handedness, but the fairy tale elements often emerge and predominate. There is a certain desire, evident, for example, in Freud's essay "The Theme of the Three Caskets," to see the play as centered on Lear and Cordelia, the love test, and the king's abrupt and painful fall.[24]

In recent years the play has sometimes become a story about aging and old age, the pathos not of a bad decision but of an inevitable fate, as the daughters become caretakers, impatient with their failing father. But the family dynamic between Lear and Cordelia, which fascinated nineteenth-century painters, was as much a romance as a contest of wills.

The Cordelia of Freud's essay is a good daughter but a silent one, and her silence, for Freud, equals death. Lear takes the whole of the play to understand what she means when she says nothing: the king, the old man, the patriach, has to come to terms with dying. We might note, though, that there is another family story going on here. "Cordelia" was Freud's nickname for his future wife, Martha Bernays—and also the nickname that Freud's teacher and collaborator, Josef Breuer, gave to *his* wife, "because she is incapable of displaying affection to others, even including her own father," as Freud reported in a tender letter to Martha.[25] This phenomenon of a wife fondly addressed by the name of the patriarch's daughter, may tell us something not only about

Freud or Breuer, but also about the place of Cordelia, who loves and is silent, in the modern culture of their time.

A long-standing theatrical tradition, now disputed by some scholars, suggested that the parts of Cordelia and the Fool were once doubled: as she exits the stage he enters, and when he exits for the last time—"I'll go to bed at noon"—she returns to Lear's side (3.6.78). The king's despairing cry in the last act, "And my poor fool is hanged," would then be seen to bring the two figures together (5.3.304). But it is the grieving father, not the broken monarch, who dominates the stage picture and the play's afterlife in the imagination.[26]

ON THE EVE OF World War II, in 1938, W. B. Yeats published a poem called "Lapis Lazuli" about the transformative emotion of tragedy. In the central stanza, Hamlet and Lear are yoked together as, implicitly, the greatest or most canonical figures in Shakespeare's works:

> All perform their tragic play,
> There struts Hamlet, there is Lear,
> That's Ophelia, that Cordelia;
> Yet they, should the last scene be there,
> The great stage curtain about to drop,
> If worthy their prominent part in the play,
> Do not break up their lines to weep.
> They know that Hamlet and Lear are gay;
> Gaiety transfiguring all that dread.
> All men have aimed at, found and lost;
> Black out; Heaven blazing into the head:
> Tragedy wrought to its uttermost
> Though Hamlet rambles and Lear rages,
> And all the drop scenes drop at once
> Upon a hundred thousand stages,
> It cannot grow by an inch or an ounce.[27]

A drop scene is an alternative term for what is more usually called, in the theater, a drop or act-drop—that is, the painted curtain lowered on the stage between acts to shut off the audience from a view of the stage. But the term "drop scene" was also used, as early as the mid-nineteenth century, in explicitly political and cultural contexts, to mean the final scene of a drama in real life.[28] And "blackout," another technical term from theater, means "the darkening of a stage during a performance," or "a darkened stage." But by 1938 the term was also frequently used in Britain to describe the compulsory extinguishing or covering of lights at night to protect against air raids. (Pilots, both German and Allied, also sometimes suffered "blackouts" of consciousness because of sharp turns in the air or fast acceleration.)

So in Yeats's poem, all Europe is a stage. Everyone is a Shakespearean character, whether he or she knows it or not. "There struts Hamlet, there is Lear / That's Ophelia, that Cordelia." Both on and off the stage we are actors, and we hold to our parts. "If worthy their prominent part in the play / [They] do not break up their lines [i.e., come out of character] to weep." Art is cognate to life; it anticipates it and scripts it. And art in this vision is even ameliorative—"gaiety transfiguring all that dread." Art is what we are trying to save the world *for*. As well as what may, unwittingly, save it.

> Tragedy wrought to its uttermost
> Though Hamlet rambles and Lear rages,
> And all the drop scenes drop at once
> Upon a hundred thousand stages.

But this vision, so close upon apocalypse of a kind—the glimpse of an Ireland and a Britain caught between terrifying modernity and elusive transcendence—is still offered at the level of high art. "Tragedy" is an aesthetic category, and, indeed, a saving one.

WHAT HAPPENED TO *King Lear* in the 1960s and after, what propelled it past *Hamlet* into the top place in the pecking order of Shakespeare's plays was the way, precisely, that it combined the affective sublime (Lear and Cordelia) with the bathetic grotesque (the Fool, the blinding of Gloucester). In other words, the very thing that the seventeenth and eighteenth centuries objected to—a certain indecorum, a certain excessiveness, a certain nihilism—was what made the play so modern, and so devastating. A few lines stand as suggestive signposts:

- Kent's "Is this the promised end?" followed by Edgar's "Or image of that horror?"
- Edgar's "I would not take this from report; it is, / And my heart breaks at it."
- Lear's "Howl, howl, howl, howl!"
- And the final lines of the play: "[W]e that are young, / Shall never see so much, nor live so long."

Against the array of world-disrupting events that took place in the late fifties and sixties, *King Lear* came to look, perhaps, all too familiar. Even the tensions between father and outspoken daughter had their local resonances. Poor Tom and the Fool seemed very familiar characters. The bleakness of the Lear landscape was like the bleakness of an atomic winter—or the bareness of a stage.

Here is the voice of William Butler Yeats again, this time as essayist, commenting on what makes a play work. Yeats was a brilliant modern playwright, very involved in staging as well as in the text. His own plays are very spare, as are the plays of Samuel Beckett. But what he found so exciting and successful about Shakespeare was what he called "emotion of multitude":

> The Shakespearean Drama gets the emotion of multitude out of the subplot which copies the main plot, much as a shadow upon the wall copies one's body in the firelight. We think of *King Lear* less as the history of one man and his sorrows than as the history of a whole evil time. Lear's shadow is Gloster, who also has ungrateful children, and the mind goes on imagining other shadows, shadow beyond shadow till it has pictured the world.[29]

It is never the case that "influence" goes only one way. The terrifying developments on the world stage, from the atom bomb to the Korean and Vietnam wars, were certainly contributory causes to the new view of *King Lear,* but so, equally, were the New Theater and anti-theater then being developed and staged in Paris, New York, London, and other places around the world. The fifties and sixties were also a time of enormous creativity and growth in theater, from the so-called Theatre of the Absurd to the kind of conceptual art event, improvised performance, or situation known as a "happening." The term *happening* was coined by the artist Allan Kaprow, whose first exhibition in this mode—an "event" consisting of eighteen "happenings"—took place in 1959. The term enjoyed a lively currency for the next decade. As for "Theatre of the Absurd," a label that is sometimes contested, its invention has been credited to the theater critic Martin Esslin, who used it as the title of a 1962 book on playwrights like Eugene Ionesco, Samuel Beckett, Jean Genet, and Harold Pinter.

This was *King Lear* time—or one of its times. We have seen that Bradley and Hazlitt and in fact many others, like Keats, thought of *King Lear* as Shakespeare's crowning achievement one hundred and almost two hundred years ago. But to the cold war generation and the postwar art world, the play seemed like a prescient vision of the present moment. And, importantly, it was not so much because of the pathos of its title character (or his daugh-

Paul Scofield in King Lear *(1971)*

ter), but because of the worldview the play seemed to body forth—a bleak, bombed-out landscape of nihilism. In fact the characters that seemed most "modern" and familiar to this contemporary world were not the kings, dukes, or courtiers, but the Fool, Poor Tom (the disguised Edgar), and the mutilated Gloucester, stumbling across the stage, perched on what he thinks is the top of Dover Cliff without the use of his eyes, persuaded into a pratfall (falling from flat stage to flat stage), which is a comic gesture and not a tragic one. Chaplin's Little Tramp was the social and sartorial model here, a ragged figure who faced each new and unexpected and impossible task with aplomb, and without self-pity.

How did *King Lear* come to be both the icon of Shakespearean greatness for the mid- to late twentieth century and, at the same time, the most "modern," modernist, and indeed postmodern of Shakespearean plays?

There is, of course, never an answer to "how" something like this happens. But history, politics, and theater were becoming, perhaps had already become, versions of one another. And in this case, perhaps surprisingly, the spark that lit the fire was a book of literary criticism.

POLISH CRITIC JAN KOTT'S BOOK *Shakespeare Our Contemporary* (1964) had an enormous influence on the director Peter Brook.[30] Martin Esslin's introduction to the American edition of *Shakespeare Our Contemporary* ends by praising Brook's production of *Lear* as "by now generally acknowledged as one of the finest Shakespearean performances within living memory."[31] Paul Scofield's portrayal of the title character struck audiences with a new force. Here is Esslin's account:

> In that production a play which had been regarded as unactable for many generations came to life with tremendous impact, and as a highly contemporary statement of the human condition. And this because it was presented not as a fairy-tale of a particularly stubborn story-book king, but as an image of aging and death, the waning of powers, the slipping away of man's hold on his environment: a great ritual poem on evanescence and mortality, on man's loneliness in a storm-tossed universe.[32]

"Great ritual poem" and "man's loneliness" both seem terms bound to another era, although they had their powerful resonances then, and still carry some effect today. But that the play is a "highly contemporary statement of the human condition" seems itself a highly contemporary statement.

From the time of the 1960s *King Lear* was read, produced, and thought of as a bleak and despairing play. The idea of sublimity, long associated with the play of *King Lear,* was now connected to the idea of modernity. And that connection made the mid-twentieth century the age of Lear.

SAMUEL BECKETT's *Endgame* and *Act Without Words* were perfomed together at their premiere in London in 1957. It was Jan Kott who had the idea of comparing them to Shakespeare's play, in a chapter called "*King Lear* or *Endgame.*" In each the tragic and the grotesque coexist, and exchange places without warning.

Kott took somber note of the new theater then emerging in postwar Europe. "[B]uffoonery," he claims, "is not only a philosophy, it is also a kind of theatre. To us it is the most contemporary aspect of *King Lear*."[33] And again, "In Shakespeare clowns often ape the gestures of kings and heroes, but only in *King Lear* are great tragic scenes shown through clowning."[34]

> Both the tragic and the grotesque vision of the world [Kott writes] are composed as it were of the same elements. In a tragic and grotesque world, situations are imposed, compulsory, and inescapable. Freedom of choice and decision are part of this compulsory situation, in which both the tragic hero and the grotesque actor must always lose their struggle against the absolute. The downfall of the tragic hero is a confirmation and recognition of the

absolute; whereas the downfall of the grotesque actor means mockery of the absolute and its desecration.[35]

The absolute is transformed into a blind mechanism, a kind of automaton. Mockery is directed not only at the tormentor, but also at the victim who believed in the tormentor's justice, raising him to the level of the absolute. The victim has consecrated his tormentor by recognizing himself as victim. "In the final instance," Kott continues, "tragedy is an appraisal of human fate, a measure of the absolute. The grotesque is a criticism of the absolute in the name of frail human experience. That is why tragedy brings catharsis, while grotesque offers no consolation whatever."[36] But it is not always easy to distinguish the tragic from grotesque. Lear with his Fool, or mumming in front of an unresponsive and unamused Goneril and Regan, is always, it seems, precariously balanced between majesty and folly, grandeur and the "new pranks" of which Goneril accuses him. Yet it was the story of the blind Gloucester, as much or more than that of the mad Lear, that seemed perhaps most emblematic of the modern condition. But the most sublime and most grotesque play within the play is the scene on "Dover Cliff," where Gloucester, blinded onstage by the unspeakable cruelty of Cornwall, encounters (and does not recognize) his disguised and loyal son.

> GLOUCESTER   Dost thou know Dover?
> EDGAR   Ay, master.
> GLOUCESTER   There is a cliff, whose high and bending head
> Looks fearfully in the confinèd deep.
> Bring me but to the very brim of it,
> And I'll repair the misery thou dost bear
> With something rich about me. From that place
> I shall no leading need.
>
> *4.1.71–78*

He intends, of course, to commit suicide—to kill himself by leaping from Dover Cliff into the sea.

A few scenes later Edgar and Gloucester reappear onstage, *not,* of course, actually at Dover Cliff, but on a flat piece of open land. Edgar is pretending that they are climbing to the cliff top:

> GLOUCESTER   When shall we come to the top of that same hill?
> EDGAR   You do climb up it now. Look how we labor.
> GLOUCESTER   Methinks the ground is even.

EDGAR   Horrible steep.
   Hark, do you hear the sea?
GLOUCESTER   No, truly.
EDGAR   Why, then, your other senses grow imperfect
   By your eyes' anguish.
GLOUCESTER   So may it be indeed.
   Methinks thy voice is altered and thou speakest
   In better phrase and matter than thou didst.
EDGAR   Y'are much deceived; in nothing am I changed
   But in my garments.
GLOUCESTER   Methinks y'are better spoken.
EDGAR   Come on, sir; here's the place. Stand still. How fearful
   And dizzy 'tis, to cast one's eyes so low!
   The crows and choughs that wing the midway air
   Show scarce so gross as beetles. Halfway down
   Hangs one that gathers sampire, dreadful trade!
   Methinks he seems no bigger than his head.
   The fishermen, that walk upon the beach,
   Appear like mice; and yond tall anchoring bark,
   Diminished to her cock; her cock, a buoy
   Almost too small for sight. The murmuring surge,
   That on the unnumbered idle pebble chafes
   Cannot be heard so high. I'll look no more,
   Lest my brain turn, and the deficient sight
   Topple down headlong.

4.6.1–24

This is a consummate Shakespearean "unscene"—entirely conjured up by language, even though it seems terrifyingly real.

"Set me where you stand," says Gloucester, and the disguised Edgar says:

   Give me your hand. You are now within a foot
   Of th' extreme verge. For all beneath the moon
   Would I not leap upright.

4.6.25–27

And aside to the audience, he says:

   Why I do trifle thus with his despair
   Is done to cure it.

4.6.33–34

When Gloucester does "leap upright," of course, he jumps, or falls, from flat ground to flat ground. In the Peter Brook production Gloucester faints, and thus "awakens" thinking he is at the bottom of the cliff. He is met "there," and "discovered," by Edgar, still in disguise, still not recognized by his blind father, now assuming yet another vocal disguise:

EDGAR   Yet he revives—
              What are you, sir?
GLOUCESTER   Away and let me die.
EDGAR   Hadst thou been aught but gossamer, feathers, air,
              So many fathom down precipitating,
              Thou'dst shivered like an egg; but thou dost breathe;
              Hast heavy substance; bleed'st not; speak'st; art sound.
              . . . .
              Thy life's a miracle. Speak yet again.
GLOUCESTER   But have I fallen, or no?
EDGAR   From the dread summit of this chalky bourn.
              Look up a-height; the shrill-gorged lark so far
              Cannot be seen or heard. Do but look up.
GLOUCESTER   Alack, I have no eyes.

                                                    4.6.47–60

Kott's existential view of the Dover Cliff scene is at the same time hyper-theatrical: "[T]he Shakespearean precipice at Dover exists and does not exist. It is the abyss, waiting all the time. The abyss, into which one can jump, is everywhere."[37] He understands, too, what "pure theatre" is—that is, theater that is emblematic, symbolic, iconic, and self-referential, not referring (merely) to the "outside," to historical events or human characteristics—"The white precipice at Dover performs a different function. Gloucester does not jump from the top of the cliff. . . . For once, in *King Lear,* Shakespeare shows the paradox of pure theatre."[38] And he sees, very clearly, that the connection be-tween blindness and insight is "read" by Beckett: "Edgar is leading the blind Gloucester to the precipice at Dover. This is just the theme of *Endgame;* Beck-ett was the first to see it in *King Lear;* he eliminated all action, everything external, and repeated it in its skeleton form."[39]

The scene in *Endgame* that comes closest to the Dover Cliff scene is the one of stasis rather than action. The blind man, Hamm, sits in a wheelchair and receives descriptions from his sighted servant (or son), Clov, who describes the room, the stage, the world outside the stage set's two windows, and finally the toy dog that is said to regard him as a master.

Hamm: Where is he?
        Is he gazing at me?

> As if he were asking me to take him for a walk?
> Or as if he were begging me for a bone.
> Leave him like that, standing there imploring me.[40]

The toy dog is black. "He's white, isn't he?" asks Hamm, and Clov replies, "Nearly."

> *Hamm:* What do you mean, nearly? Is he white, or isn't he?
> *Clov:* He isn't.[41]

The "endgame" is the last set of moves in a game of chess, when there are only a few pieces left. One of the most common is that of king and pawn. When Hamm says "Me— / —to play"[42] he is recognizing or acknowledging that fact.

Hamm, whose name has been associated with everything from Hamlet to ham actors, is "like King Lear . . . a 'ruined piece of nature.' "[43] His wheelchair is his throne. "Hamm who cannot get up, and Clov who cannot sit down."[44] Kott cites what he calls the "Endgame of *King Lear*."[45]

LEAR Read.
GLOUCESTER What, with the case of eyes?
. . . .
LEAR What, art mad? A man may see how this world goes with no eyes.
Look with thine ears.

4.6.140–47

But perhaps most Beckettian of all encounters in Shakespeare's play takes place when the mad Lear meets the blind Gloucester and Gloucester says, "O, let me kiss that hand!" To which Lear replies, "Let me wipe it first; it smells of mortality" (4.6.130–31).

KOTT PUT THE QUESTION of *King Lear* and the grotesque together with horrific developments in European politics. But the fact that the play had affinities with the grotesque had been noticed by critics as well, perhaps most importantly in G. Wilson Knight's essay "King Lear and the Comedy of the Grotesque," published in a collection called *The Wheel of Fire* (1930).[46] Wilson Knight's phrase "the wheel of fire" is taken from *Lear:* King Lear's anguished speech to Cordelia, when he awakens and thinks he has been dead—a death he longs for:

> You do me wrong to take me out o' th' grave.
> Thou art a soul in bliss; but I am bound

Upon a wheel of fire, that mine own tears
Do scald like molten lead.[47]

4.7.45–48

The "wheel of fire" is Ixion's wheel: his punishment in hell, to be bound to an ever-whirling wheel. It was not Ixion, however, but another classical icon of eternal punishment who was to become the model for mid-century philosophical speculations about the absurdity of modern life. *The Myth of Sisyphus*, published in 1940 ("amid the French and European disaster"[48]) by the French-Algerian writer Albert Camus, became the talismanic book of a generation. "There is but one truly serious philosophical problem," the book declared forthrightly, "and that is suicide."[49]

Sisyphus was doomed to roll a rock up a steep hill for all eternity. When the rock was almost at the top, it rolled down again, and Sisyphus had to begin his task all over again. Sisyphus is Camus's hero, a man for whom happiness and the absurd are inseparable. The absurd "makes of fate a human matter, which must be settled among men,"[50] Camus declared. "The struggle itself toward the heights is enough to fill a man's heart. One must imagine Sisyphus happy."[51] This is the famous last sentence of the book.

The idea of the absurd was, in the period, on many philosophers' minds. Camus's friend Sartre was intrigued by it, and so was Søren Kierkegaard. For Camus, the absurd, and existential philosophy more generally, were tied to the concept of "the leap," an image that calls to mind the grotesque stage "leap" of the blind Gloucester, a leap that, in the theater, requires him to jump—grotesquely, absurdly—from flat stage to flat stage. "There are many ways of leaping, the essential being to leap," is how Camus will describe "the leap" for existentialists.[52] But ultimately Camus himself will say, apropos of what he calls "plain suicide" (as distinct from "philosophical suicide"): "The leap does not represent an extreme danger as Kierkegaard would have it. The danger, on the contrary, lies in the subtle instant that precedes the leap. Being able to remain in that dizzying crest—that is integrity and the rest is subterfuge."[53]

We have already seen Jan Kott's view of "the leap" in *King Lear*: "The Shakespearean precipice at Dover exists and does not exist. It is the abyss, waiting all the time. The abyss, into which one can jump, is everywhere." The fact that Gloucester "does not jump from the top of the cliff" became, for him, an example of "the paradox of pure theatre."

Camus worked for much of his life in the theater, and *The Myth of Sisyphus*, a work of French philosophy, makes easy and regular reference to phrases from *Hamlet*[54] and turns at key moments to *King Lear*, and indeed, to Gloucester. "Take Shakespeare, for instance," he writes.

Never would King Lear keep the appointment set by madness without the brutal gesture that exiles Cordelia and condemns Edgar. It is just that the unfolding of that tragedy should thenceforth be dominated by madness. Souls are given over to the demons and their saraband. No fewer than four madmen: one by trade, another by intention, and the last two through suffering—four disordered bodies, four unutterable aspects of a single condition.

One by trade—the Fool. Another by intention—the disguised Edgar as Poor Tom. The last two through suffering—Lear and Gloucester.[55] And of Gloucester specifically, Camus writes, "In that short space of time [the actor] makes [him] come to life and die on fifty square yards of boards. Never has the absurd been so well illustrated or at such length."[56]

The actor, in fact, is one of Camus's types of the absurd man:

[H]is vocation becomes clear: to apply himself wholeheartedly to being nothing or to being several. The narrower the limits allotted him for creating his character, the more necessary his talent. He will die in three hours under the mask he has assumed today. Within three hours he must experience and express a whole exceptional life. That is called losing oneself to find oneself. In those three hours he travels the whole course of the dead-end path that the man in the audience takes a lifetime to cover.[57]

This passage brings us back to *Endgame.* Here there certainly is no "leap," since Hamm can't stand and Clov can't sit, and when Clov takes his ladder over to the window what he sees (even through the telescope) is "zero." The stage set, with its windows high on either side and the wheelchair/throne in the middle, might be imagined to look like the inside of a human head, the eyes on either side (seeing, like Hamm's eyes, nothing). The first line of the play is a last line, Clov's: "Finished, it's finished, nearly finished, it must be nearly finished." The last line of the play is Hamm's, as he has become finally, like Lear in the first act of *his* play, stripped of all possessions and relations: father, dog, whistle, Clov. Only the bloody handkerchief remains: "You . . . remain."[58]

When we look and listen closely to the play, the resonances are there. Hamm, as king, wants to make sure his chair is in the center, the very center. "Am I right in the center?" "I'm more or less in the center?" "I feel a little too far to the left." "Now I feel a little too far to the right." "I feel a little too far forward." "Now I feel a little too far back." All this time Clov is moving the chair.[59]

Beckett's favorite line in the play was said to be the exchange between Hamm and Clov about Nagg, Hamm's father, who is in one of the dustbins:

Hamm: What's he doing?
Clov: He's crying.
Hamm: Then he's living.[60]

It takes no stretch at all to recall here Lear's "When we are born we cry that we are come / To this great stage of fools" (4.6.176–77). There's something of Lear and Cordelia here, too, again eviscerated of content.

Hamm's question-and-answer game with Clov ends with Hamm's expression of (apparent) pleasure: "I love the old questions. Ah, the old questions, the old answers, there's nothing like them!"[61] But Clov doesn't have the right answers, any more than Cordelia did at the beginning of *King Lear*.

Hamm: Why do you stay with me?
Clov: Why do you keep me?
Hamm: There's no one else.
Clov: There's nowhere else.
Hamm: You're leaving me all the same.
Clov: I'm trying.
Hamm: You don't love me.
Clov: No.
Hamm: You loved me once.
Clov: Once![62]

Later in the play, Hamm demands of Clov "A few words . . . from your heart"—and gets a toneless rambling narrative that ends with the notion that "the words that remain . . . have nothing to say."[63] And Hamm repeats the word "Nothing" as Clov prepares to depart. The short and funny exchange about Nature ("Nature has forgotten us. / There's no more nature. / . . . But we breathe, we change! / . . . Then she hasn't forgotten us")[64] rivals, in its spareness, the eloquent invocations to an unresponsive Nature—and to truth—throughout Shakespeare's play.

THE WORD "ABSURD" comes from a root that means inharmonious or deaf, insufferable to the ear. Remember Edgar and Gloucester in the Dover Cliff scene:

EDGAR   Hark, do you hear the sea?
GLOUCESTER   No, truly.
EDGAR   Why, then, your other senses grow imperfect
     By your eyes' anguish.

                                        4.6.4–6

And the mad Lear to the blind Gloucester at the end of act 4: "A man may see how this world goes with no eyes. Look with thine ears" (4.6.46–47).

In *Endgame,* Beckett has a little joke about this, too, in the conversation between the two aged parents stuck in the ashbins:

> Our sight has failed.
> Yes.
> Can you hear me?
> Yes.
> . . . .
> Our hearing hasn't failed.
> Our what?
> Our hearing.[65]

Throughout the play we hear questions like Kent's "Is this the promised end?" and Edgar's "Or image of that horror?" (5.3.262–63)—but here without any context:

> What's happening?
> Something is taking its course.
> We're not beginning . . . to . . . to . . . mean something?[66]

But perhaps the most powerful refrain in the play is Hamm's constant call for his painkiller. Is it time yet? Not yet. Is it time yet? Not yet. Is it time yet? Not yet. And finally it is time—and there is no more painkiller.

LEAR'S PLAY STARTS with passion, and ends with compassion:

> KENT He hates him much
> That would upon the rack of this tough world
> Stretch him out longer.
>
> *5.3.312–14*

Hamm's play starts and ends with the notion that it is his move. "Me— / — to play" are his very first words, and we hear them again near the close:

> *Hamm:* Cover me with the sheet.
> No? Good.
> Me to play.[67]

And *Act Without Words* ends without words: "He does not move. . . . He looks at his hands."[68]

They, too, smell of mortality.

KING LEAR AND ENDGAME are both concerned with stripping, divestiture, and loss. Lear's discovery that mankind is a "bare, forked animal"—"the thing itself"—lies at the heart of this comparison.

These lines come in the storm scene, in act 3, scene 4, when Lear confronts Poor Tom (the disguised Edgar), and asks him not who he is, but who he has been. Edgar replies with a speech right out of the social satire of the time: "A servingman, proud in heart and mind, that curled my hair, wore gloves in my cap, served the lust of my mistress' heart, and did the act of darkness with her . . . Wine loved I deeply, dice dearly, and in woman, out-paramoured the Turk" (3.4.80–87). This is a social critique of the excesses of the court—Lear, the mad Lear, penetrates to the essential human animal behind the social, erotic, and cultural veneer: "Poor Tom" is, says Lear, better off as he is than as he was: "thou art the thing itself. Unaccommodated man is no more but such a poor, bare, forked animal as thou art" (3.4.98–100).

And Lear now tries to emulate this state of "unaccommodation," tearing off his own clothing: "Off, off, you lendings! come unbutton here" (3.4.100–1).

In Beckett's *Endgame,* not only are the characters pared down to the essentials of living—Hamm, Clov, Nagg, and Nell in their ashbins—but also the stage, and indeed the language of the play, is reduced, or expanded, to "the thing itself"—unadorned, bare, forked (mildly ridiculous), and, paradoxically, *therefore* ennobled.

Lear's recognition of Poor Tom as a version of himself—a poor, bare, forked animal—was anticipated by his encounter with his daughters Goneril and Regan at the end of act 2, in that terrible scene where they begin, mathematically, to strip him of his knights and entourage. Lear had wanted a "reservation" of one hundred knights—that is, to keep one hundred knights for his own private service even as he prepared to abdicate his throne.

In act 2, scene 2, Goneril tells Lear that he can indeed come to her household for a time, but only if he dismisses "half your train," keeping only fifty knights. The desperate Lear looks about him for comfort, and turns to the other daughter, Regan: "I can be patient, I can stay with Regan, / I and my hundred knights" (2.4.225).

"Not altogether so," says Regan. In fact, not so at all. Regan agrees with her sister. "What, fifty followers? / Is it not well? What should you need of more?" (2.4.232–33). She continues:

> If you will come to me—
> . . . I entreat you
> To bring but five-and-twenty. To no more
> Will I give place or notice.
>
> *2.4.241–44*

So Lear turns back to Goneril:

> I'll go with thee;
> Thy fifty yet doth double five-and-twenty,
> And thou art twice her love.
> GONERIL   Hear me, my lord.
> What need you five-and-twenty, ten, or five?
> To follow in a house where twice so many
> Have a command to tend you?
> REGAN   What need one?
>
> *2.4.253–58*

This methodical—and mathematical—stripping is what leads immediately, then, to Lear's great speech about necessity, and thus to the storm scene:

> O, reason not the need! Our basest beggars
> Are in the poorest things superfluous.
> Allow not nature more than nature needs,
> Man's life is cheap as beast's. Thou art a lady;
> If only to go warm were gorgeous,
> Why, nature needs not what thou gorgeous wear'st,
> Which scarcely keeps thee warm. But, for true need—
> You heavens, give me that patience, patience I need!
>
> *2.4.259–66*

In this magnificent speech, his invocation to the gods, his imprecations on his daughters, and his pledge not to weep are followed by the stage direction "*Storm and tempest*," as nature weeps for him, and he leaves the stage with the Fool—"O fool, I shall go mad."

WHILE MUCH ATTENTION at mid-century was devoted to the existential *Lear*, the *Lear* of conscious absurdity in an already grotesque world, another strand of political thinking was directed at the play's social and economic relevance to the present day. When the political scientist Marshall Berman came to write his book *All That Is Solid Melts into Air: The Experience of Modernity,*

he read the lines about "unaccommodated man" from *King Lear* in the context of a passage of Marx from the *Communist Manifesto* about stripping and nakedness:

> The bourgeoisie has stripped of its halo every occupation hitherto honored and looked up to with reverent awe. . . . The bourgeoisie has torn away from the family its sentimental veil, and turned the family relation into a pure money relation. . . . In place of exploitation veiled by religious and political illusions, it has put open, shameless, direct, naked exploitation.[69]

For Berman, this passage seemed directly to invoke *King Lear*. "The dialectic of nakedness that culminates in Marx," he wrote, "is defined at the very start of the modern age, in Shakespeare's *King Lear*. For Lear, the naked truth is what a man is forced to face when he has lost everything that other men can take away, except life itself. We see his voracious family, aided by his own blind vanity, tear away the sentimental veil."[70]

Existentialist critics had focused on Lear's madness and, especially, on the scene of Gloucester's "leap." Marxist and social critics pointed toward another key moment—Lear's realization, in the midst of the storm, that he was now suffering as others in his land had long suffered:

> Poor naked wretches, wheresoe'er you are,
> That bide the pelting of this pitiless storm,
> How shall your houseless heads and unfed sides,
> Your loop'd and windowed raggedness defend you
> From seasons such as these? O, I have ta'en
> Too little care of this! Take physic, pomp;
> Expose yourself to feel what wretches feel,
> That thou mayst shake the superflux to them,
> And show the heavens more just.[71]

3.4.28–36

To many in the sixties and seventies, these lines seemed to describe a disparity between rich and poor, privileged and underprivileged, that spoke of "now" rather than "then." Berman, writing in the wake of these concerns, made the link to theory and to Marx. "Shakespeare is telling us," Berman says, "that the dreadful naked reality of the 'unaccommodated man' is the point from which accommodation must be made, the only ground on which real community can grow."[72] This is Shakespeare applied, as if he were himself writing a manifesto. "Marx's hope is that once the unaccommodated men of the working class are 'forced to face . . . the real conditions of their lives and their relations with their fellow men,' they will come together to overcome the cold that cuts through them all." Thus "one of the Manifesto's primary aims is to point the way out of the cold, to nourish and focus the common yearning for communal warmth."

Berman is interested, but somewhat skeptical. "It isn't hard to imagine alternate endings to the dialectic of nakedness," he suggests, endings far less ideal or idealized. And he speculates, too, about the changes that modernism has brought:

> The nature of the newly naked modern man may turn out to be just as elusive and mysterious as that of the old, clothed one, maybe even more elusive, because there will no longer be any illusion of a real self underneath the masks. Thus, along with community and society, individuality itself may be melting into the modern air.[73]

The final phrase is again from Marx ("all that is solid melts into air") but it could, of course, come from Shakespeare, from *The Tempest:* "Our revels now are ended, / These our actors, / As I foretold you, are all spirits, / And are melted into air, into thin air."

———

SAMUEL BECKETT's *Endgame,* first performed in 1957, had become a modernist classic. Its hypertheatricality, its spareness, its ferocious humor, and its combination of philosophical abstraction and residual pathos made it an iconic work for its time. A decade and a half later, when the British playwright Edward Bond came to write his own *Lear,* the darkness remained, but the dramatic mode shifted into something much closer to Grand Guignol, or to the horror film—or to the news of the world.

Endgame was a kind of astringent philosophical redaction of the essence of *King Lear.* The characters in Beckett's play do not bear the same names as those in Shakespeare's. In fact the name of the central figure, Hamm, has led some critics to associate him with Hamlet rather than with Lear. Yet the visions, or blindnesses, of *King Lear* and *Endgame* brought them, at midcentury, into a compelling relation with each other. Beckett derealized the "bare, forked animal" that Lear noticed in the storm and recognized not only as Poor Tom, or the Fool, but also as himself. The language of Beckett's play is minimal, its resonances vast. Its mode, we might say, is allegorical, but it is an allegory of a state of mind, not of a narrative. It performs a *condition.* Something that, if the phrase had not been made banal by overuse, we might call "the human condition." It performs, that is to say, a condition very like the condition encountered in, and by, Lear. Or by, at least, the *King Lear* staged and performed (and then filmed) by Peter Brook—a *Lear* that had been, of course, inspired and motivated by Brook's own encounter with Jan Kott's *Shakespeare Our Contemporary* and its key chapter, *"King Lear or Endgame."* So that, in a nice reversal of literary history, critics could come to say things like this: "Brook's production reclaimed Shakespeare's text for a post-Holocaust age by highlighting (often grotesquely) its bleakest, most Beckettian aspects."[74] Shakespeare has thus become Beckettian.

EDWARD BOND had quite a different view. Bond's career as a playwright, director, screenwriter, and theorist flourished in Britain and, especially, in Germany and mainland Europe. His plays, like Brecht's, are concerned with the relation between history and the individual, and with class and the capacity for political action. "Human consciousness is class consciousness," he has said.[75] Bond's other plays—like his *Lear*—are concerned with a dialectical learning process, an experience of the social that calls for a kind of moral action, but never on the elevated plane of the abstract. Instead the plays gain power from what seems like the almost detached acceleration and particularity of violence. What Bond calls "aggro-effects"—a version of Brecht's alienation effects—are scenarios of extreme experience, often extreme violence, presented almost matter-of-factly on the stage.[76] For example, in Bond's *Lear,* the blinding scene, in which Lear (notice it is not Gloucester but Lear who is blinded) is confined to a chair, his head immobilized, and his eyes plucked out, methodically, in a procedure repeatedly called "scientific."[77] Lear has just said, ironically, that he "must open [his] eyes and see,"[78] and in the next scene he is put in a straitjacket ("now the buttons," says his genial torturer, the Fourth Prisoner, in an echo of Shakespeare's play), his head put in a frame ("your crown"), and the unspeakable operation begins. "You've turned me into a king again," says Lear, before he understands what is about to happen. And the Fourth Prisoner, with his infernal machine ("Understand, this isn't an instrument of torture, but a scientific device") sets about his business.[79] His motivation is preferment: "This is a chance to bring myself to notice."[80]

We might compare this bleeding and blinded Lear, tied to a chair, with the figure of Hamm in *Endgame.* The physical position and the suffering of the two figures are quite similar, in iconic ways—but the context of their experiences, and their stage presence, is profoundly different. Beckett's dramatic world is a world of quizzical isolation. Bond's dramatic world is "social," in an extreme sense—not the happy sociality of love and small talk, but the impassioned political social world, populated by soldiers, prisoners, farmers, and random rifle shots.

The *Lear* of Edward Bond, in a way, responds to and rejects, or overgoes, both the classic idea of Shakespeare's *King Lear* as a redemptive high culture parable of noble suffering, and the nihilistic view of Brook and Kott.[81] Brook's production of *King Lear,* with Paul Scofield in the lead role, was enjoying its enormous theatrical success at just the time when Bond was beginning as a struggling playwright in London, and for him, it seems, the nihilistic view of the "new" Lear was becoming as canonical, and as celebrated, as the old. What was needed was a shock to the system—the social system as well as the physical, and moral, system. Instead of being an icon of magnificent and pathetic human suffering—suffering raised to the place of high art—this *Lear* is a powerful incentive to see drama as continuous with social action.[82]

As Bond wrote in a program note to his play:

> Shakespeare's *Lear* is usually seen as an image of high, academic culture. The play is seen as a sublime action and the audience are expected to show the depth of their culture by the extent to which they penetrate its mysteries. . . . But the social moral of Shakespeare's *Lear* is this: endure till in time the world

will be made right. That's a dangerous moral for us. We have less time than Shakespeare. Time is running out.[83]

Bond's *Lear* begins with a wall, a dead man, and a pistol shot. Lear shoots a worker. The play ends with a wall, a pistol shot, and a dead man. The dead man is Lear. He is shot by a farmer's son, who has entered the army for instrumental, contingent, social reasons. His family has been displaced; they used to live by the side of the disused wall, and when the wall building began again, they were homeless, the son in need of a job.

The wall is Lear's project: "I started this wall when I was young. I stopped my enemies in the field, but there were always more of them. How could we ever be free? So I built the wall to keep our enemies out."[84] But like any Shakespearean king he soon finds, or rediscovers, that the enemies are already inside, that all wars are civil wars. His two daughters, Bodice and Fontanelle, announce that they are marrying the Dukes of North and Cornwall, whom they have "met" by mail, sending each other photographs. "Can't you see that they only want to get over the wall?" asks Lear. And Bodice pooh-poohs him: "Wall, wall, wall. This wall must be pulled down."

"Certainly," says Fontanelle. "My husband insists on that as part of the marriage contract." And Lear sees.[85] "I knew it would come to this! I knew you were malicious! I built my wall against *you* as well as my other enemies! You talk of marriage? You have murdered your family. There will be no more children. Your husbands are impotent." "I pity the men who share your beds," he continues. "I am ashamed of my tears! You have done this to me. The people will judge between you and me."[86]

Much of this is recognizable—the curse on Goneril ("into her womb convey sterility"), the weeping Lear ("No, I'll not weep") as he moves forward into the storm scene. But the tone and tenor are very different. Unlike Beckett's abstraction and reduction, this play spills, spills over, becomes multiply historical. The Berlin Wall is identifiable by any late twentieth-century audience, but it is also other walls, other kinds of walls. Just as the condition called "wall death"—your feet always wet, feeling like you are "living in a grave"—has echoes of World Wars I and II.

Lear has, in this version, two daughters, not three. (Cordelia will appear later, and in another form.) Their names are words that sound "feminine" but are, in different ways, comic or ridiculous: Bodice (the Goneril figure, the more dominant sister) and Fontanelle. A bodice is a body-restraining garment, but what is a Fontanelle? It is actually a word encountered in Beckett's *Endgame,* when Hamm muses to Clov that a vein had been dripping in his head "ever since the fontanelles."[87] *Fontanelle:* a membrane in the head of an infant, or an outlet for secretions; derived from the French word for fountain. An accident? A coincidence? Surely. But still . . . This seems to me a remarkable, uncanny verbal connection between two plays that seem on the surface to have little in common.

BOND'S *LEAR* IS IN THREE ACTS. In the first one Lear, having been supplanted by his daughters, finds himself in a country setting, with a young man called the Gravedigger's Boy and his wife. The pastoral paradise to which Lear thinks he has come is abruptly turned into nightmare, as soldiers arrive, kill the Gravedigger's Boy (who dies wrapped in a sheet on a clothesline, blood staining his winding sheet/shroud), and rape the boy's wife, who is pregnant. By the end of the first act domesticity has turned to horror, and the Carpenter who has brought a cradle as a gift for the expected baby now kills the rapist-soldier and seizes a rifle.

We will shortly learn that the nameless wife is called Cordelia, and in the course of the next two acts she will grow increasingly powerful, as the head of the rebel forces. The Carpenter becomes her new husband, and Lear is haunted by the Ghost of the Gravedigger's Boy, who becomes the Fool figure, recurring throughout the play. The Boy, grotesquely, dies twice, the second time gored by his own pigs—uttering that "impossible sentence" displaced from *Hamlet,* "O Lear, I am dead!"[88]—and Lear, having moved from madness to sanity, and from blindness to insight, enjoys for a brief moment the celebrity of a Trotsky-like prophet, admired and inspiring to the people, before he meets his own pointless death as he tries, again, to build the wall. Building the wall up, and tearing it down, only to build it again, becomes the common life of the people, and has a fateful effect, since the farmer's son who kills Lear is only a soldier because he needs the work. "Leave that," he says to his soldiers about the body of the dead Lear.[89] Someone else will pick it up.

THE PLAY VERY CLEVERLY, artfully, and effectively recycles props, scenes, and language from Shakespeare's *King Lear.* One recycled artifact is a mode of literalization—the literalization of figurative language, of metaphor. Again in the mode of matter-of-fact violence that will not allow for idealization, "Then let them anatomize Regan," Shakespeare's mad Lear says to Poor Tom in the storm, "see what breeds about her heart" (3.6.70–71). In Bond's version, the anatomization is literal—a bloody, explicit autopsy of the dead Fontanelle, performed by that same upwardly mobile Fourth Prisoner, who used to be the prison doctor. "I'm just making a few incisions to satisfy the authorities," he says as he reveals the lungs, the liver, the stomach—and the womb.[90]

And to Lear they are beautiful. The inner organs of his daughter are beautiful. "She sleeps inside like a lion and a lamb and a child. The things are so beautiful. . . . Did I make this—and destroy it?"[91]

If the first mode of recycling is *literalization* and *unmetaphoring,* a second mode is *dissemination*—in this case, the diminishment of the huge map unfurled at the beginning of Shakespeare's play into many smaller maps, all somehow out-of-date, or lacking the right detail or address.

Shakespeare's Lear's map is produced in the first act, when Lear says (without irony) that he will "express our darker purpose. / Give me the map there." And when the elder daughters speak their pretty speeches, he bestows land upon them, from the map:

> Of all these bounds, even from this line to this,
> With shadowy forests and with champaigns riched,
> With plenteous rivers and wide-skirted meads,
> We make thee lady.
>
> *1.1.61–64*

In Bond's version, the maps are small, dirty, and useless. In the very first scene of the play, as Lear and his daughters come to inspect the construction of the wall, the old councilor (who will appear in every act, the classic bureaucrat always seeking Lear's favor) is trying to read a map to tell him where he is: "Isn't it a swamp on this map?"[92] Their feet are wet—he hardly needs a map to tell him so. Cornwall and Bodice both read maps in their headquarters: "[T]he map's my straitjacket," she says—she has to move the men from one place to another, and thus can't pull the wall down.[93] "Useless bloody map!" says soldier J to soldier K, and his companion agrees: "We're lost." J, trying to consult it, gives up: "They must a issued this for the Crimea."[94] The deliberate trivialization of the big prop, and its grandiose language, into so many pointless small ones, tells its own tale—as does a third example: the restaging of the "reunion" scene between Lear and Cordelia.

But this Cordelia is no relation to Lear—in his exile as prophet he writes to her, thinking he can set her straight, but when they encounter each other, in act 3, scene 3, it is far from a sentimental scene. The stage direction tells us that she holds Lear's hand for a moment (another echo of the Shakespeare scene), but she is all business, arriving with her new husband, the Carpenter, as her former husband, the Ghost, looks on in anguish (she has no idea, of course, that he is there):

Lear: Don't build the wall.
Cordelia: We must.
Lear: Then nothing's changed! A revolution must at least reform.
Cordelia: Everything else is changed!
Lear: Not if you keep the wall! Pull it down.
Cordelia: We'd be attacked by our enemies!
Lear: The wall will destroy you. It's already doing it. How can I make you see?[95]

Bond's major characters—the Ghost of the Gravedigger's Boy, the Carpenter, and Cordelia—all become more cynical and more desperate as the play goes on. The Carpenter, lovesick builder of the cradle, becomes a guerrilla leader; and Cordelia, first a shy wife, then a rebel, is finally an idealistic tyrant. "You only understand self-pity," she says to Lear. "We must go back, the government's waiting. There are things you haven't been told. We have other opponents, more ruthless than you. . . . I knew you wouldn't cooperate, but I wanted to come and tell you this before we put you on trial: we'll make the society you only dream of."[96] And Lear says to her, calmly, "It's strange that you should have me killed, Cordelia, but it's obvious you would. How simple! Your law always does more harm than crime, and your morality is a form of violence."[97]

The final scene is a replay not of Lear but of Gloucester on "Dover Cliff," which we have seen through Kott, Camus, and others to be the emblematic "modern" moment of Shakespeare's play. The blind Lear, now without a stick, is led to the wall and left there. He climbs the wall, he reaches the top, he shovels, and he is shot.

SIGNIFICANTLY, Bond recovers Cordelia's lost history as a queen (of course he doesn't call her that). The historical Cordelia, according to Geoffrey of Monmouth and *Holinshed's Chronicles,* reigned for five years after the death of Lear, and waged war, and, when her nephews decided to try to unseat her because they thought a woman should not be the ruler of a kingdom, she committed suicide. This is not the after-story one could possibly have imagined from Shakespeare's Cordelia, even if she had, in the version of Nahum Tate, lived to the end of the play.

The avant-garde theater troupe Mabou Mines tried to address the gender question by reversing the genders in a 1990 production, with a powerful, autocratic, and transgressive female Lear right out of Tennessee Williams, and a male Goneril and Regan played as backwoods good ol' boys. But in many ways Edward Bond's play, described, aptly enough, by Frank Rich as a "gutsy post-Marx 'Lear,' " is a bolder way to unpack the question. (As Rich contended, Bond shows that "an icon like 'King Lear' may have to be dismantled entirely in order to make cogent new ideological points.")[98]

Bond's Cordelia, the unsentimental political leader, may be an uncomfortable stretch from the loving and supportive—and forgiving—daughter we can locate in Shakespeare's text ("no cause, no cause") and see on pages and stages wherever the play is to be found. But the steel frame of this queenly character is there in Shakespeare's play, in her principled resistance to the charade of the love test, her role, much occluded in the play, as queen of France, and her strong return in act 4. Although Cordelia is often linked with silence—"Her voice was ever soft, / Gentle, and low, an excellent thing in woman" (5.3.273–74)—it is important to remember how defiant she is, and indeed how brave, in refusing to say the scripted words, and thus meekly receive her "opulent" third of the kingdom.

Bond's *Lear*, like its Cordelia, refuses pity. It refuses, in fact, all classical tragic emotions, coming periodically to the edge of pathos, but always pulling back, toward the political and the social.

Why rewrite *King Lear*? What is at stake in doing so, in taking on a project of this kind at the very moment when the play—once deemed unactable—had become the cultural hallmark of sublimity? Sublime and grotesque, pathos and bathos, are not only the flip sides of each other, but also (in Shakespeare's play as well as in modern and modernist versions) constantly on the verge of turning into each other. Bond's play is suspicious of both kinds of emotions. It is resistant to pity and terror, the Aristotelian benchmarks of tragedy. It is resolutely material and materialist, resisting idealism at every turn. In that resistance lies its paradoxical idealism, its idealism despite itself.

IN THE TRANSFORMATION wrought on *King Lear* by Bond and by Beckett, each engaging with Shakespeare's play as a vehicle for interrogating what is left of the sublime in its relationship to comedy and terror, the play's famous thematic of "nothing" was, over and over again, brought to bear on the possibility of theater. But "nothing" also speaks another language, and it is in fact at the intersection between words and numbers, words and figures, that we encounter another way of reading Shakespeare together with modern culture. Here, as we will see, the preoccupations of mathematics (early modern and modern), and the allegories of first and last, all and nothing, one hundred and zero, come together to provide a second—or perhaps a first or primary—language for attending to *King Lear*.

SHAKESPEARE'S *KING LEAR* WAS written and performed at a moment of high volatility and change in the use of mathematics, pictorial perspective, and, indeed, in the use of paper money for financial transactions. All of these changes were related to the importation into Europe, and the gradual adoption, of the concept and sign for zero—and of zero's relationship to the equally problematic philosophical and religious question of "nothing." The argument is brilliantly made in *Signifying Nothing: The Semiotics of Zero,* a book by the mathematician and philosopher Brian Rotman, to which my understanding of this cultural history is greatly indebted.[99]

"Nothing will come of nothing," Lear's famous rebuke—or encouragement—to his daughter Cordelia, was in fact a familiar proverb, often expressed in its Latin form: *Ex nihilo nihil fit* (From nothing, nothing comes). In fact, it is as if he replies with an impatient cliché to her heartfelt "Nothing" in response to his question, "what can you say to draw / A third more opulent than your sisters? Speak" (1.1.84–85).

Does "nothing" come of nothing? What about the creation of the world? Or, said Renaissance scholars, what about the egg? The egg, which was the symbol of generation, was shaped like a zero. As a result, writers in the period often used it as an emblem of the paradox of everything and nothing.

This is the point, perhaps, or one of the points, of the Fool's joke about the egg:

FOOL . . . Give me an egg, nuncle, and I'll give thee two crowns.
LEAR What two crowns shall they be?
FOOL Why, after I have cut the egg i' the middle, and eat up the meat, the
    two crowns of the egg.

1.4.136–39

The image here is that of "nothing" (the yolk of the egg has been eaten by the practical Fool) inside two crowns that are now hollow and empty. And of course the devolution from royal crown to this homely image makes its own point. It's in the same scene, and just before this, that the Fool offers his own catechism to Lear: "Can you make no use of nothing, nuncle?" And he gets the same reply Lear made to Cordelia, "Why, no, boy; nothing can be made out of nothing."

It is also the Fool who makes the equation of zero with nothing: "now thou art an O without a figure. I am better than thou art now; I am a fool, thou art nothing" (1.4.168–69). This is an image from the new mathematics, the mathematics of Hindu or Arabic numbers. The number system that *has* a zero. The system that understands that zero is a sign, not the absence of a sign.

Zero is in a multiple, punning sense a *cipher* here: a symbol or character of no value by itself, which increases or decreases the value of other figures according to its position; a person or thing of no value; a numeral; a hieroglyph; and a cryptograph—a secret or disguised manner of writing. In other words, in a modern sense, a code.

Notice too that, in this very arithmetically minded play, all thirds are apparently not equal. Lear has already elaborately given thirds of his kingdom to Goneril and to Regan, in response to their glozing words (their "glib and oily art"). But he has clearly kept the best part for Cordelia. Until she takes the Fifth: "I love your majesty / According to my bond; nor more nor less" (1.1.91–92).

King Lear is set in ancient Britain, and is often performed, as we have noted, in some timeless "yore" of Druids or Picts or primeval England, in caves, with fur wraps and rough wooden utensils, even for the king. But the play was written and performed at a moment of transition in Europe and in England, from one kind of economy to another, and therefore, of necessity, from one kind of numerical system to another. With the rise of mercantile capitalism—trade, commerce, financial futures, all things at issue in Shakespeare's *The Merchant of Venice* as well—in addition to the new attention to perspective "vanishing points" in painting and in architecture, it became important to have a notation system that could handle these concepts and these transactions.[100]

By the time Shakespeare came to write *King Lear,* the old system of Roman numerals and calculation on the abacus was on the way out, and the new system of Hindu/Arabic numerals based on zero was on its way in. So the play's preoccupation with questions of counting, fractions, worth, and "nothing" (not to mention whether anything could actually come of nothing) was, we may say, "overdetermined." That is to say, it came from many motivations at once—from the old Lear story, from the new capitalism, from the old theology, and from the new science and philosophy.

King Lear, in this sense, is a play about nothing. Shakespeare scholars had long discussed "nothing" in *King Lear* from standpoints physical and metaphysical: in the Renaissance, the word was a slang term for female sexual organs; because an "O" was an unbroken circle it also, paradoxically, connoted "everything." Rotman, a mathematician, saw the relevance of zero in this connection, and made the link from cultural history to the play.

Cordelia's "Nothing, my lord," is a powerful affirmation, if only Lear could hear it as such. She claims that her love for him is right and natural—"according to my bond." What she resists is the love test, not the love. (And what Lear tests is the love test, not the love.) When the scene is replayed, in the fourth act, and Lear again asks her the same question, tell me how much you love me, it is striking—to me—that she answers it again in the negative.

The scene is perhaps the most moving episode in the whole play: Lear has awakened ("you do me wrong to take me out of the grave") and does not know whether he is alive or dead ("Would I were assured of my condition"). Cordelia, heartbroken, kneels before him:

> LEAR Pray, do not mock me.
> I am a very foolish fond old man,
> Fourscore and upward, not an hour more nor
>   less;
> And, to deal plainly,
> I fear I am not in my perfect mind.
> Methinks I should know you, and know this
>   man;
> Yet I am doubtful; for I am mainly ignorant
> What place this is; and all the skill I have
> Remembers not these garments; nor I know not
> Where I did lodge last night. Do not laugh at me;
> For, as I am a man, I think this lady
> To be my child Cordelia.
> CORDELIA   And so I am, I am.
> LEAR Be your tears wet? Yes, faith. I pray, weep not.
> If you have poison for me, I will drink it.
> I know you do not love me; for your sisters
> Have, as I do remember, done me wrong.
> You have some cause, they have not.
> CORDELIA   No cause, no cause.
> LEAR Am I in France?
> CORDELIA   In your own kingdom, sir.
>
>   *4.7.60–78*

"No cause, no cause."

AT THE END OF THE PLAY the death of Cordelia is met by Lear with the same emphasis by the negative:

> No, no, no life!
> Why should a dog, a horse, a rat have life,
> And thou no breath at all? Thou'lt come no more,
> Never, never, never, never, never!
>
> *5.3.304–7*

What has this "nothing" to do with zero?

Cordelia's "economics" of love are a matter of obligation. Her "nothing" makes Lear's script and props (the map, the procession) into a broken play, like the Mousetrap play in *Hamlet*, where "the king rises." Hers is not an economics of exchange but of natural "use." Notice her language to Lear. Brian Rotman nicely notes that "Shakespeare puts it all into the verbs":[101]

> You have begot me, bred me, loved me; I
> Return those duties back as are right fit.
> Obey you, love you, and most honor you.
>
> *1.1.95–97*

But Lear makes this domestic relation into a financial transaction, "forcefully inserting it into a system of mercantile exchange."[102] Seeking to commodify love, or praise, he destroys it.

THE ANTI-TYPE OF CORDELIA here is Edmund, who also mobilizes that word "nothing," in act 1, scene 2, right after Lear's love test. Edmund is often described by critics as the type of the "new man" and the capitalist entrepreneur. During the aftermath of World War II in England he was characterized as a rampant capitalist and even a figure conducive to fascism. Yet he has an undoubted charm. (No wonder the elder two Lear girls fall for him.) In the scene with his father, Gloucester, we first hear his voice in soliloquy—the Machiavel's device—confiding in the audience ("Thou, nature, art my goddess; to thy law / My services are bound"[1.2.1–2]), and we hear about the letter he has written to deceive his father. (Hamlet, of course, did the same to condemn Rosencrantz and Guildenstern to death.)

The scene is quite domestic, the opposite of the Lear court scene. And Edmund ostentatiously hides the letter:

GLOUCESTER What paper were you reading?
EDMUND Nothing, my lord.
GLOUCESTER No? What needed, then, that terrible dispatch of it into

your pocket? The quality of nothing hath not such need to hide itself. Let's see. Come, if it be nothing, I shall not need spectacles.

1.2.30–35

The last line is full of predictive irony, since Gloucester will have his eyes plucked out in the play's most terrible scene. (And here the effect of a play that becomes a "classic" is redoubled, for many in the audience will know what is coming, and will wince in anticipation. "Were all the letters suns, I could not see one," the blind Gloucester will tell the mad Lear later in act 4, scene 6, when Lear thrusts toward him a real or imaginary "challenge" he has "penned." Whether there is an echo of "sons" in "suns" will be up to the listener to determine.)

But in this first scene of reading the "letter," of course, is a forgery, purporting to come from Edgar, the loyal and legitimate son, and purporting, too, to invite Edmund into a conspiracy to kill their father and share his estate. Something will come of this "nothing"—Edgar flees, disguises himself; Edmund is for the moment preferred. And his motives are, he claims, financial. "Wherefore should I / Stand in the plague of custom, and permit / The curiosity of nations to deprive me" (1.2.2–3). That is, why should being a younger son—and a bastard—mean that he does not inherit?

To the list of the Fool, Cordelia, Edmund, Goneril, and Regan as figures for zero or nothing could easily be added the disguised Kent (who is a walking cipher, since he has lost his name) and Poor Tom, the disguised Edgar ("Edgar I nothing am"). In the various ways in which the *economic* sphere is mobilized and emblematized by these characters, we can see something of the play's visionary modernity, its modernity despite itself.

THE PLAY, AS BRIAN ROTMAN NOTED, IS POISED on the brink of a shift between the old and the new, the feudal family and the capitalist entrepreneur, the Roman numerals of computation and the Arabic numbers with which equations can be solved. A world without zero becomes a world—very like ours—in which many zeros are counted. Even the last line of the play, spoken to the audience on and off the stage, is cast in the negative: "Speak what we feel, not what we ought to say . . . we that are young / Shall never see so much, nor live so long."

But the redemptive view of the play's ending—Lear learns from his suffering; "we" who are left at the close have gained something from this powerful tragedy—was overtaken by the events of the mid- and late twentieth century.

Maynard Mack in his book *King Lear in Our Time* (1965) gave voice to the general sentiment of "we who are young" in his own time: "After two world wars and Auschwitz, our sensibility is significantly more in touch than our grandparents' was with the play's jagged violence, its sadism, madness, and processional of deaths, its wild blends of levity and horror, selfishness and self-lessness."[103] How many zeroes in six million?

And, as we have already noted, the horrors of the century had more to expose. The atom bomb was dropped on Hiroshima and Nagasaki. Where it fell was "ground zero"—the hypocenter—the part of the ground situated immediately under an exploding bomb, especially an atomic one. The term originated with the Manhattan Project, but as we know, it has had an afterlife (and a half-life).

The term emerged again in the wake of September 11, 2001. There are, I am sure, people alive today who know only the World Trade Center site as "ground zero"—for whom the earlier atomic usages were never known, or are now forgotten. But it is in this new context of *zero* that the play of *King Lear* has been produced, and read, and understood in *our* time. Although the dev-astations wrought by these two "ground zero" events may look similar, their efficient causes and their relationship to the technologized world are different. The Manhattan Project was Big Science; the World Trade Center, Pentagon, and Pennsylvania plane crashes were low tech, actions performed by recruited agents who may have seen their position as "the worst," in Edgar's terms. When zero enters the equation, what remains?

In this avalanche of "zero degree" catastrophes, we should also recall the story of the so-called Patient Zero, the supposed first case in the AIDS epi-demic. A "patient zero" is an index case in the transmission of a disease out-break—it's a technical term of art in epidemiological investigations. In the case of AIDS in the United States, however, the Patient Zero story turned out to be both a vilifying narrative and a typographical error. There is no clear evi-dence that any one person was the first to pass AIDS to the gay population in the 1980s; and in fact the numeral *zero* was an erroneous transcription from the letter O; "Patient O," for "Out of California," was how this individual was recorded in medical files. Thus yet again *zero* does not mark an origin (it is not referential) but an absence. A mistake, and a dissemination, not a cause.

An O without a figure.

IS THIS THE PROMISED end, or image of that horror? The feared nuclear holocaust of the mid-twentieth century, which haunted the *King Lear* of the cold war years, has not materialized. The Berlin Wall came down. But the nuclear threat remains, now joined with global terrorism, poverty, and the consciousness of impending ecological disaster. The play today seems to speak from a new ground zero—as, in a sense, it has always done:

> The weight of this sad time we must obey;
> Speak what we feel, not what we ought to say.
> The oldest hath borne most; we that are young
> Shall never see so much, nor live so long.

5.3.322–25

SHAKESPEARE'S TIME

I F EVERY PERFORMANCE is an interpretation, every interpretation, in a time of new media and unexampled cultural access, is also a performance. By "performance" we would include all of the kinds of rehearsal, homage, and citation that have provided material for this book, from new plays and fictions to advertisements, cartoons, case studies, and cultural clichés. Shakespeare's plays are living things; they grow and change over time.

At the outset, I suggested that Shakespeare has shaped many of the categories and themes through which we have come to understand human life, human nature, and human culture. Using a term that the philosopher Michel Foucault applied to innovators like Freud and Marx, I noted that Shakespeare was an initiator of discursive practices—which is to say, a writer and thinker who changed the fundamental ways in which people write, read, and think. But—as I also noted—Shakespeare's double place in the cultural pantheon as both an initiator and a great author means that we meet him coming and going. In his language, characters, and plots we "recognize" cultural scenarios that may be traced to the effect of his works—just as, to take one example, contemporary ideas about femininity, female empowerment, and womanliness often find reference points in characters like Juliet, Rosalind, Lady Macbeth, and Cleopatra, even though all those parts were originally written for male performers.

Each of the plays discussed here has intersected in significant—and different—ways with the events of recent times, as well as with modern writers and thinkers. *The Merchant of Venice* is not the same play that it was before the Holocaust, even though the text may remain exactly as it was. The experience of reading Shakespeare is as timely and time-inflected as it is timeless and universal.

It may therefore be useful here to say a word about the question of Shakespeare's vaunted "timelessness," a laudatory concept often paired with "universality"; two traits that have been used to distinguish Shakespeare's greatness from the more local or time-bound fame of lesser writers. "Timeless and universal," as a phrase, seems unassailable, the highest compliment possible to a creative artist, the mark, indeed, of artistic genius.

In this case, as so often, Shakespeare himself may be said to have created—

or at least promoted—the taste by which he is enjoyed. His sonnets offer what is perhaps the most eloquent, and most sustained, testimony to the triumph of timelessness over time.

> Not marble nor the gilded monuments
> Of princes shall outlive this powerful rhyme,
> But you shall shine more bright in these contents
> Than unswept stone, besmeared with sluttish time.
>
> *Sonnet 55, 1–4*

Sonnet after sonnet offers similar testimony, both to the power of love and to the power of poetry.

> But thy eternal summer shall not fade,
> Nor lose possession of that fair thou ow'st,
> Nor shall death brag thou wander'st in his shade
> When in eternal lines to time thou grow'st.
>   So long as men can breathe or eyes can see,
>   So long lives this, and this gives life to thee.
>
> *Sonnet 18, 9–14*

But the history of reception of the sonnets is also a testimony to the opposite sentiment—not that they have ever, to my knowledge, been seen as supporting artistic oblivion, but rather that they have themselves been taken, by poets like Wordsworth and Wilde, and by many twentieth-century critics, as an autobiographical testimony to Shakespeare's own love life, his passion for the "dark lady," his bisexuality or homosexuality, his gay sensibility, his queer identity. Whether it was out of concern about the sonnets' male addressee, or a sales technique, or mere carelessness (all three hypotheses have been advanced), John Benson's 1640 edition of Shakespeare's sonnets, *Poems: Written by Wil. Shakespeare, Gent.,* rearranged the order of the poems, combined some, gave them titles, and changed some pronouns, converting poems to a man into poems to a woman. This unauthorized and jumbled text became the basis of many eighteenth-century editions, even though more responsible scholarly editions of the sonnets continued to be published.[1]

Nineteenth-century poets and writers found the personal aspect of the sonnets of special fascination. "With this key / Shakespeare unlock'd his heart," declared Wordsworth in his sonnet on the sonnet, to which Robert Browning retorted, "If so, the less Shakespeare he!"[2] Wilde created a playful fantasy about one "Willie Hughes," the fictional boy player to whom the sonnets, dedicated to "Mr. W.H.," might have been written.[3] W. H. Auden (who did not, so far as I know, comment on his own initials in this context) wrote that "what is astonishing about the sonnets, especially when one remembers the age in which they were written, is the impression they make of naked autobiographical confession."[4] Many critical studies of the sonnets followed in this direction, seeking clues to the life and inner feelings of the poet through a close look at evidence in the poems.[5] By the mid- to late twentieth century Shakespeare was being cited, together with other "timeless" writers like Plato and Proust, as a forerunner of queer theory.[6] The ideology of "timelessness" voiced in so many of the sonnets was not in competition with, but rather in consort with, the twentieth-century "timeliness" of the sonnets written to a man—made more poignant, and thus even more powerful, by comments like Auden's about the sociopolitical prescience of the sonnets "when one remembers the age in which they were written." And in this case, as in so many others, Shakespeare's "greatness" and Shakespearean exceptionalism are yoked to—rather than in tension with—a certain topicality. This itinerary might well be taken as a prime case of the effect of Shakespeare in, and on, modern culture.

We might also note that this theme, that of the tension between timelessness and time, monumentality and history, so essential to the poetry of the sonnets, is revisited in a vivid onstage moment toward the end of Shakespeare's career. The moment I have in mind is the awakening of the "statue" of Hermione in *The Winter's Tale*, a scene that critics have often, and rightly, taken as a metaphor for the power of theater and of art. But in this case, as so often, Shakespeare again anticipates the question:

> LEONTES Chide me, dear stone, that I may say indeed
> Thou art Hermione; or rather, thou art she
> In thy not chiding; for she was as tender
> As infancy and grace. But yet, Paulina,
> Hermione was not so much wrinkled, nothing
> So aged as this seems.
> . . . .
> PAULINA So much the more our carver's excellence,
> Which lets go by some sixteen years, and makes her
> As she lived now.
>
> *5.3.24–32*

The word "now" is again a shifter, indicating the present moment. The work of art, the supposed statue that is—and reveals itself to be—a living woman, has itself changed over time. In Paulina's trenchant commentary the excellence of the artist is in imagining and anticipating the future, not (merely) in memorializing the past.

WHEN I SUGGEST THAT TIMELESSNESS is a cultural effect, and indeed an aspect of what I'd claim as the overall Shakespeare effect within modernity, I do not want to be misunderstood as seeming to say that such a quality is either delusory or negligible, nor yet that it is simply a naïve response to the plays or to Shakespeare's reputation. To the contrary, I think the idea of timelessness, especially when sutured to Shakespeare, may represent a wish: the same kind of wish represented by the "eternizing" rhetoric of the sonnets, and, collaterally, the English Renaissance preoccupation with mutability, *vanitas,* death, and the progress of the soul. The wish that *something* should endure, something made by man, something to show that we have been here and touched the world.

Timelessness and timeliness go hand in hand. The sense of, and reputation for, timelessness is produced by multiple timely moments, in which the event, or the play, or the character, or the quoted phrase or speech, coincides with the current moment and its concerns. The timelessness of Shakespeare is achieved by his recurrent timeliness, the way his plays seem to reflect upon, and to speak to, what Cassius, with blind confidence in the verdict of the future, called "states unborn and accents unknown."

NOTES

INTRODUCTION

1. Bruce Eric Kaplan, "I don't mind if something's Shakespearean, just as long as it's not Shakespeare." (A man talks to his wife while walking.) *The New Yorker* (January 29, 2001).
2. Diane Francis, "Black Failed to Grasp the U.S. Way: A Downfall of Shakespearean Proportions," *Financial Post* (July 14, 2007).
3. E.g., "In a fall from grace of Shakespearean proportions, [Conrad] Black will trade his tailored suits and over-the-top extravagance for an orange prison jumpsuit." Stephanie Balogh, "Conrad Black Jailed for Fraud," *Daily Telegraph* (December 11, 2007).
4. Ross Todd, "Small-Firm Stars Set to Defend Conrad Black," *American Lawyer* (March 15, 2007).
5. Michael Scheuer, *Marching Toward Hell: America and Islam After Iraq* (New York: Free Press, 2008). Passage cited by Michiko Kakutani in "Fighting the Wrong Foe With the Wrong Weapons." *New York Times* (March 14, 2008), Section E, 31.
6. Riad Saloojee, "Muslim Anger Over Danish Cartoon Displays Global Disconnect," *Edmonton Journal* (February 5, 2006).
7. Victor Dwyer, Elizabeth Renzetti, and Johanna Schneller, "Out With a Bang," *Toronto Globe and Mail* (June 9, 2007).
8. "It started out as a full-court media press to clear Roger Clemens of the taint of the George Mitchell steroid investigation, but now the plot has thickened to Shakespearean proportions. With apologies to the Queen in Act 3 (Scene 2) of Hamlet, methinks Roger might have protested too much." Peter Schmuck, "No Closer to Truth: Pitcher's Denials on '60 Minutes' Leave Us Hanging," *Baltimore Sun* (January 7, 2008), 2Z.
9. Randall Balmer, professor of religion, in a lecture, "God in the White House: Faith and the Presidency from John F. Kennedy to George W. Bush," quoted in Aimee Lin, "Dartmouth Professor Looks at Religion, Presidents," *The Dartmouth* (February 7, 2008). Eric Hamburg, ed., *Nixon: An Oliver Stone Film* (New York: Hyperion, 1995); Ben Procter, *William Randolph Hearst: The Later Years, 1911–1951* (New York: Oxford University Press, 1998).
10. Selim Algar and Leonard Greene, "'DWI' Drag Death: 'Woman Kills Beau,'" *New York Post* (July 23, 2007).
11. Jane Austen, *Mansfield Park* (1814; New York: Penguin Books, 1985), 335.
12. Jane Martineau, *Shakespeare in Art* (London and New York: Merrell, 2003), 210.
13. Ralph Waldo Emerson, "Shakespeare; Or, The Poet," in *Representative Men: Nature Addresses, and Lectures* (Boston: Houghton Mifflin, 1883), 194–95.
14. Ibid., 201.
15. Ernest Jones, *Hamlet and Oedipus* (1949; New York: Norton, 1976), 151.
16. *Reader's Digest Asia* (November 2005); TimesOnLine UK, November 24, 2007; *Chip*

Scale Review (November–December 2006); Wilson D. St.Pierre, "Out, Damned Spot!" *Foreign Affairs* (January/February 2006); www.hardcandy.com.

17. *Star Trek VI: The Undiscovered Country* (1991); "The Undiscovered Country," Hammer Museum, October 3, 2004–January 16, 2005; Undiscovered Country Tours, Palo Alto, CA.

18. Carol Rador, "Alas, Poor Yorick De-Parts," *FDA Consumer Magazine* (November–December 2003).

19. Greg Mankiw's blog, October 13, 2007, http://gregmankiw.blogspot.com/2007/10/strange-bedfellows.html.

20. Marjorie Garber, "Roman Numerals," in *Symptoms of Culture* (New York: Routledge, 1998), 179–98; reprinted in Garber, *Profiling Shakespeare* (New York: Routledge, 2008), 151–66. For more on this question, see below, in the chapter on *King Lear.*

21. E.g., Movers and Shakespeares, based in Washington, D.C., and run by Ken and Carole Adelman. "Will Power," *People* (March 11, 2003); "Chairman of the Board," *Fortune* (April 1, 2002); Bruce Weber, "Friends, Generals, and Captains of Industry, Lend Me Your Ears," *New York Times* (January 31, 2005), etc.

22. Harriet Rubin, "Lessons in Shakespeare, From Stage to Boardroom," *New York Times* (November 10, 2007), B4.

23. A version of this disquieting sentiment appears in play after play, not always in the voice of a schemer or a Machiavel. It is the mise en abyme, the black hole, Freud's navel of the dream—the lost point of origin, which is at the core of acting, and of literariness—and of Shakespeare.

24. Evan Thomas notes in his biography of Robert Kennedy that RFK had a special fondness for quoting Shakespeare's English history plays. On a family camping trip, when the group encountered dauntingly hot weather and rough terrain, he recited some lines from the St. Crispin's Day speech in *Henry V* ("We few, we happy few, we band of brothers"). When the poet Robert Lowell, on another occasion, teased Kennedy for comparing himself to Henry V, RFK responded by "pulling down a volume of Shakespeare's Histories and reading from Henry IV's deathbed scene. ('For what in me was purchased, / Falls upon thee in a more fairer sort. . . .') 'Henry the Fourth,' said Kennedy, without apparent irony, 'that's my father.'" Thomas, *Robert Kennedy: His Life* (New York: Simon & Schuster, 2000), 18, 22.

25. Marjorie Garber, "Bartlett's Familiar Shakespeare," in *Profiling Shakespeare* (New York: Routledge, 2008), 278–301.

26. Michel Foucault, "What Is an Author?," in *Language, Counter-Memory, and Practice,* ed. Donald F. Bouchard, trans. Bouchard and Sherry Simon (Ithaca: Cornell University Press, 1977), 132.

27. Ibid., 131.

28. Karl Marx, *Capital,* trans. Samuel Moore and Edward Aveling (New York: International Publishers, 1967), 1: 87.

29. Karl Marx, "Speech at the Anniversary of the *People's Paper,*" published in the *People's Paper* (April 19, 1856), reprinted in *Marx/Engels Selected Works,* trans. Samuel Moore (Moscow: Progress Publishers, 1968), 1: 500.

30. Karl Marx, "Debates on the Freedom of the Press," in Karl Marx and Friedrich Engels, *Collected Works,* vol. 1, *Marx: 1835–1843,* trans. Richard Dixon et al. (New York: International Publishers, 1975), 139.

31. Walter Benjamin, "One-Way Street," in *Reflections,* ed. and trans. Peter Demetz (New York: Schocken Books, 1986), 91.

32. A one-way street as a mode of traffic control was itself a "modern" development; the first one-way streets in Paris were designated in 1909.

33. Hannah Arendt, Introduction to *Illuminations,* by Walter Benjamin, ed. and trans. Hannah Arendt (New York: Schocken Books, 1968), 18.

34. Benjamin, "Karl Kraus," in *Reflections,* 263.
35. Ibid., 264. Benjamin's friend Theodor Adorno used the same theme of "blood" in his own comparison of Kraus with a Shakespearean character: "Kraus is a Shylock who pours forth his own heart's blood, where Shakespeare's Shylock wanted to cut the guarantor's heart out." Theodor W. Adorno, "Morals and Criminality," in *Notes to Literature,* ed. Rolf Tiedemann, trans. Shierry Weber Nicholsen (New York: Columbia University Press, 1974), 2: 43–44.
36. Benjamin, "The Work of Art in the Age of Mechanical Reproduction," in *Illuminations,* 221–22.
37. Benjamin, "Theses on the Philosophy of History," in *Illuminations,* 257–58.
38. Friedrich Nietzsche, "On the Uses and Disadvantages of History for Life," in *Untimely Meditations,* trans. R. J. Hollingdale (1894; Cambridge: Cambridge University Press, 1983), 81.
39. Bertolt Brecht, "Shouldn't We Abolish Aesthetics?," in *Brecht on Theatre: The Development of an Aesthetic,* ed. and trans. John Willett (New York: Hill and Wang, 1964), 20.
40. Bertolt Brecht, "Does Use of the Model Restrict the Artist's Freedom?" interview with E. A. Winds, 1949. In Willett, ed., *Brecht on Theatre,* 225.
41. Ludwig Wittgenstein, *Culture and Value,* ed. G. H. von Wright in collaboration with Heikki Nyman, trans. Peter Winch (Oxford: Basil Blackwell, 1980).
42. The girls today in society
    Go for classical poetry.
    So to win their hearts one must quote with ease
    Aeschylus and Euripides.

    . . . .

    But the poet of them all
    Who will start 'em simply ravin'
    Is the poet people call
    The bard of Stratford-on-Avon.

    Brush up your Shakespeare.
    Start quoting him now.
    Brush up your Shakespeare
    And the women you will wow.
    Just declaim a few lines from "Othella"
    And they'll think you're a helluva fella.
    If your blonde won't respond when you flatter 'er,
    Tell her what Tony told Cleopaterer.
    If she fights when her clothes you are mussing,
    What are clothes? "Much Ado About Nussing!"
    Brush up your Shakespeare
    And they'll all kowtow.

    . . . .

    Brush up your Shakespeare.
    Start quoting him now.
    Brush up your Shakespeare
    And the women you will wow.
    If your goil is a Washington Heights dream
    Treat the kid to "A Midsummer Night's Dream."
    If she then wants an all-by-herself night
    Let her rest ev'ry 'leventh or "Twelfth Night."
    If because of your heat she gets huffy
    Simply play on and "Lay on, Macduffy!"

Brush up your Shakespeare
And they'll all kowtow.
Cole Porter, "Brush Up Your Shakespeare," in *The Complete Lyrics of Cole Porter,* ed.
Robert Kimball (New York: Da Capo Press, 1992), 395–96.

43. Victor Turner, *The Ritual Process* (Ithaca: Cornell University Press, 1969), 134–36; Martin Buber, *I and Thou,* trans. R. G. Smith (Edinburgh: Clark, 1958).

44. Niklas Luhmann, "Paradox of Observing Systems," in *Theories of Distinction: Redescribing the Descriptions of Modernity,* ed. William Rasch (Stanford: Stanford University Press, 2002), 81 (original text in English). Luhmann was a major—and controversial—theorist of modernity, a concept he described as related to the distinction between the problem of truth and the problem of reference—and, further, to "the distinction between the distinction true / untrue and the distinction self-reference / external reference." Niklas Luhmann, "The Modernity of Science," trans. Kerstin Behnke, in *Theories of Distinction,* 65.

45. E. O. Wilson, *Sociobiology* (Cambridge: Belknap Press of Harvard University Press, 1980), 58.

46. Laura Bohannan, "Shakespeare in the Bush," *Natural History* 75 (1966): 28–33, reprinted in David Scott Kastan, *Critical Essays on Shakespeare's Hamlet* (New York: G. K. Hall, 1995), 9–18. When Bohannan's narrative was retold in Pierre Bayard's *How to Talk About Books You Haven't Read,* Jay McInerney singled it out as "the funniest section in the book." See Pierre Bayard, *How to Talk About Books You Haven't Read,* trans. Jeffrey Mehlmann (New York: Bloomsbury, 2007), and Jay McInerney, "Faking It," *New York Times* (November 11, 2007).

47. Claude Lévi-Strauss, *The Raw and the Cooked: Introduction to a Science of Mythology: I,* trans. John and Doreen Weightman (New York: Harper & Row, 1964), 12, 13.

48. Jacques Lacan, "The Four Fundamental Concepts of Psychoanalysis," in *The Seminar, Book 11, 1964;* trans. Alan Sheridan (London: Hogarth Press and Institute of Psycho-Analysis, 1977), 232.

49. Sigmund Freud, *The Interpretation of Dreams,* in *The Standard Edition of the Complete Psychological Works of Sigmund Freud,* 24 vols., ed. and trans. James Strachey (London: Hogarth Press and the Institute of Psycho-Analysis, 1961), 4: 264.

50. A. C. Bradley, "The Substance of Tragedy," in *Shakespearean Tragedy* (London: Macmillan, 1904), 12.

51. Inaugural Address, Kennedy Draft, 01/17/1961; Papers of John F. Kennedy: President's Office Files, 01/20/1961–11/22/1963; John F. Kennedy Library, National Archives and Records Administration.

ONE

THE TEMPEST: *The Conundrum of Man*

1. *Shakespeare Behind Bars,* directed by Hank Rogerson (Philomath Films, 2005).

2. Jean-François Lyotard, Introduction to *The Postmodern Condition: A Report on Knowledge,* trans. Geoff Bennington and Brian Massumi, *Theory and History of Literature,* vol. 10 (Minneapolis: University of Minnesota Press, 1984), xxiv.

3. Daniel Wilson, *Caliban: The Missing Link* (London: Macmillan, 1873).

4. Quoted in Virginia Mason Vaughan and Alden T. Vaughan, Introduction to *The Tempest,* Arden Shakespeare (London: Thomas Nelson and Sons, 1999), 96.

5. Jacques Derrida, *Of Grammatology,* trans. Gayatri Chakravorty Spivak (Baltimore: Johns Hopkins University Press, 1976), 23. It might be helpful here to use the deconstructive technique of putting a word "under erasure," that is, of both crossing it out and letting

the world and its definition stand, thus indicating that the word marks out a key concept, but is problematic. This is a technique Derrida borrowed from Heidegger, who famously put the word "being" under erasure: "he lets the word 'being' be read only if it is crossed out. . . . Is effaced while still remaining legible, is destroyed while making visible the very idea of the sign."

6. H.D. (Hilda Doolittle), *By Avon River*. See Susan Stanford Friedman, "Remembering Shakespeare Differently: H.D.'s *By Avon River*," *Women's Re-Visions of Shakespeare*, ed. Marianne Novy (Urbana: University of Illinois Press, 1990), 142–64.

7. Christopher Marlowe, *Doctor Faustus, English Renaissance Drama*, eds. Lars Engle, Katharine Eisaman Maus, and Eric Rasmussen (New York and London: W. W. Norton & Company, 2002), 1.1.51–64.

8. See Benjamin Woolley, *The Queen's Conjurer: The Science and Magic of Dr. John Dee, Adviser to Queen Elizabeth I* (New York: Henry Holt, 2001).

9. The panopticon, "a circular prison with cells around a central well, from which inmates can be observed at all times" (*Oxford English Dictionary*) was first proposed by Jeremy Bentham in 1787, and has become a key image for modern discussions of visibility and surveillance as a result of its use in the works of Michel Foucault. See Foucault, *Discipline and Punish: The Birth of the Prison*, trans. Alan Sheridan (New York: Vintage, 1979), 195–228.

10. For a more extended discussion of this projection onto the inner life of Shakespeare, see my "Bartlett's Familiar Shakespeare," published in *Profiling Shakespeare* (New York: Routledge, 2008), from which this analysis of the "revels" speech is excerpted.

11. Peter Greenaway, *Prospero's Books: A Film of Shakespeare's* The Tempest (London: Chatto & Windus, 1991), 164.

12. Ibid., 17.

13. Ibid., 25.

14. William Hazlitt, *Characters of Shakespeare's Plays* (New York: Wiley and Putnam, 1845), 89–90.

15. Jeremy Maas, Pamela White Trimpe, Charlotte Gere, et al., *Victorian Fairy Painting*, ed. Jane Martineau (London: Royal Academy of Arts, 1997), 114–18.

16. John William Cole, *The Life and Theatrical Times of Charles Kean, F.S.A.* (London: Richard Bentley, 1859), 2: 217.

17. Quoted in Alicia Finkel, *Romantic Stages: Set and Costume Design in Victorian England* (Jefferson, NC, and London: McFarland & Company, 1996), 51.

18. Vaughan and Vaughan, eds., *The Tempest*, 28.

19. José Enrique Rodó, *Ariel*, trans. Margaret Sayers Peden (Austin: University of Texas Press, 1988), quoted in Vaughan and Vaughan, eds., *The Tempest*, 326.

20. Ibid.

21. Ibid., 327.

22. Ibid., 328.

23. Ibid., 330.

24. Quoted in Vaughan and Vaughan, eds., *The Tempest*, 98–99.

25. Octave Mannoni, *Prospero and Caliban: The Psychology of Colonization* (New York: Praeger, 1956), quoted in Vaughan and Vaughan, eds., *The Tempest*, "Appendix 2: Appropriations," 331–42.

26. Ibid., 332.

27. Ibid., 333.

28. Ibid., 334.

29. Ibid., 336.

30. Ibid.

31. Ibid., 337.

32. Ibid.
33. Ibid., 339–40.
34. Ibid., 342.
35. Frantz Fanon, "The So-Called Dependency Complex of Colonized Peoples," *Black Skin White Masks* (London: Pluto Press, 1986), 107.
36. Ibid., 108.
37. Aimé Césaire, *A Tempest,* trans. Philip Crispin, quoted in Peter Hulme and William H. Sherman, eds., *The Tempest and Its Travels* (Philadelphia: University of Pennsylvania Press, 2000), 153–54.
38. Ibid.
39. Ibid., 156.
40. Roberto Fernández Retamer, "Caliban: Notes Toward a Discussion of Culture in America," *Caliban and Other Essays,* trans. Edward Baker (Minneapolis: University of Minnesota Press, 1989), 14.
41. T. S. Eliot, *The Waste Land,* in *The Waste Land and Other Poems* (New York: Penguin Putnam, 2003), 53–70.
42. Robert Browning, "Caliban Upon Setebos; or, Natural Theology in the Island," quoted in Vaughn and Vaughn, eds., *The Tempest,* 320, 322, 323.
43. Ibid., 324.
44. Ibid., 325.
45. Oscar Wilde, *The Picture of Dorian Gray,* ed. Joseph Bristow (New York: Oxford University Press, 2006), 3.
46. Ibid., 3–4.
47. James Joyce, *Ulysses,* ed. Jeri Johnson (New York: Oxford University Press, 1993), 6.
48. W. H. Auden, *The Sea and the Mirror: A Commentary on Shakespeare's The Tempest,* ed. Arthur Kirsch (Princeton and Oxford: Princeton University Press, 2003).
49. Ibid., 27.
50. Ibid., 35.
51. Ibid., 42.
52. Thus Marianne Moore would define poetry as "imaginary gardens with real toads in them," while Wallace Stevens writes that "the dump is full of images." Marianne Moore, "Poetry," in *Perspectives on Poetry,* eds. James L. Calderwood and Harold E. Toliver (Oxford: Oxford University Press, 1968), 93. Wallace Stevens, "The Man on the Dump," in ibid., 243.
53. Quoted in Auden, *The Sea and the Mirror,* xxx.

TWO

ROMEO AND JULIET: *The Untimeliness of Youth*

1. Marc Norman and Tom Stoppard, *Shakespeare in Love: A Screenplay* (New York: Hyperion, 1998).
2. Marjorie Garber, "Shakespeare's Dogs," reprinted in *Profiling Shakespeare* (New York: Routledge, 2008), 182–94; *Beethoven's 2nd,* directed by Rod Daniel (Northern Lights Entertainment, 1993).
3. Luigi da Porto, *Istoria novellamente ritrovata di due Nobili Amanti* (c. 1530); Bandello, *Le Novelle del Bandello* (1540); Adrien Sevin, *Halquadrich and Burglipha* (French, 1542); Arthur Brooke, *The Tragicall Historye of Romeus and Juliet* (1562). Geoffrey Bullough, ed., *Narrative and Dramatic Sources of Shakespeare* (New York: Columbia University Press, 1966), 1: 27–275.
4. *Oxford English Dictionary,* "Romeo," sense 1.

5. Lothario is the name of the libertine seducer in Nicholas Rowe's play *The Fair Penitent* (1703). A more accurate, but currently a far less frequently heard, label for a man who pursues women, sometimes called (why, I wonder?) a "lady-killer."

6. Besides Brooke's poem, a version was published in William Painter's *Palace of Pleasure* (1567).

7. Bullough, *Narrative and Dramatic Sources,* 275.

8. E.g., Bernard McElroy, *Shakespeare's Mature Tragedies* (Princeton: Princeton University Press, 1973); Piotr Sadowski, *Dynamism of Character in Shakespeare's Mature Tragedies* (Wilmington: University of Delaware Press, 2003).

9. A. C. Bradley, *Shakespearean Tragedy* (London: Macmillan, 1932), 3, 80.

10. August Wilhelm Schlegel, *A Course of Lectures on Dramatic Art and Literature,* trans. John Black (London: Bell & Daldy, 1871), 401.

11. John Dryden, *Defence of the Epilogue, or An Essay on the Dramatic Poetry of the Last Age,* in *Collected Essays,* 2 vols., ed. W. Ker (London, 1925), 1: 174. This is Samuel Johnson's citation from memory, in his notes on *Romeo and Juliet.* Samuel Johnson, *Johnson on Shakespeare,* ed. Arthur Sherbo (New Haven: Yale University Press, 1968), 8: 57.

12. Johnson, *Johnson on Shakespeare,* 8: 958.

13. Ibid., 8: 946, 954, 953.

14. Samuel Pepys, cited in Gamini Salgado, *Eyewitnesses of Shakespeare* (London: Sussex University Press, 1975), 50.

15. Thomas Campbell, *Life of Mrs. Siddons* (London, 1839; New York: Benjamin Blom, 1972), 250–51.

16. James Boaden, quoted in William Winter, *Shakespeare on the Stage* (New York: Moffat, Yard and Company, 1911), 125.

17. Ibid.

18. Joseph Leach, *Bright Particular Star: The Life and Times of Charlotte Cushman* (New Haven: Yale University Press, 1970), 175.

19. Winter, *Shakespeare on the Stage,* 201.

20. William Hazlitt, *Characters of Shakespeare's Plays* (1817; London: Oxford University Press, 1975), 105.

21. Camille Cole Howard, *The Staging of Shakespeare's* Romeo and Juliet *as a Ballet* (San Francisco: Mellen Research University Press, 1992), xi; Leslie Hotson, *The Commonwealth and Restoration Stage* (New York: Russell and Russell, 1962), 42.

22. Howard, *The Staging of Shakespeare's* Romeo and Juliet *as a Ballet,* 14–15.

23. Tobi Tobias, "A Portrait of the Artist as a Young Man," *Voice of Dance* (August 27, 2007).

24. Press Release, Mark Morris Dance Group, January 25, 2007.

25. M.M.D.G., "Bard's Fisher Center and the Mark Morris Dance Group Announce Historic World Premiere of the Original Version of Prokofiev's Ballet *Romeo and Juliet.*" Mark Morris Dance Group, http://markmorrisdancegroup.org/press_releases/55 (accessed January 25, 2007).

26. Quoted by Richard Finkelstein, *Artslynx International Arts Resources, Dance,* "Romeo & Juliet: A Ballet Timeline," 1998.

27. "Bernstein's Studio—West Side Story—Bernstein's inspiration from Romeo and Juliet," http://www.leonardbernstein.com/studio/element2.asp?FeatID=8&AssetID=9.

28. Leonard Bernstein, interview with Al Kasha and Joel Hirschhorn, in *Notes on Broadway: Conversations with the Great Songwriters* (Chicago: Contemporary Books, 1985), 14.

29. Dramatists' Guild, *West Side Story* panel, April 18, 1985.

30. Martha Gellhorn, letter to Leonard Bernstein (undated in source). *Bernstein's Studio, West Side Story,* online archive.

31. Leonard Bernstein, interview with Jonathan Cott. *Rolling Stone,* no. 592 (November 29, 1990), 70–130.

32. Leonard Bernstein, Diary, July 8, 1957, quoted in Keith Garebian, *The Making of West Side Story* (Toronto: ECW Press, 1995), 115.

33. Irene Sharaff, cited in ibid., 55.

34. Bob Dylan, "The Times They Are a-Changin'," copyright 1963, renewed 1991, Special Rider Music.

35. Peter S. Donaldson, *Shakespearean Films/Shakespearean Directors* (Boston: Unwin Hyman, 1990), 158.

36. Jack J. Jorgens, *Shakespeare on Film* (Bloomington: Indiana University Press, 1977), 83–84.

37. Ibid., 89. Jaly L. Halio, *Romeo and Juliet: A Guide to the Play* (Westport, CT: Greenwood Press, 1998), 110.

38. Ali MacGraw, introduction to AMC showing of Zeffirelli's 1968 *Romeo and Juliet*, http://students.ed.uiuc.edu/bach/rnj24/rj1968.html.

39. For example, www.bookrags.com/studyguide-love-story. There are many other citations online.

40. Hiller B. Zobel, "The Play's the Thing," *The Harvard Crimson* (August 14, 1957). Barbara Tettlebach played Juliet. The reporter—who later went on to become a Superior Court judge in Massachusetts—preferred Tettlebach's performance to Segal's: "He delivered his lines effectively, but too often he exchanged light-of-love look for a wide-eyed stare."

41. Dick Hebdige, *Subculture: The Meaning of Style* (London: Methuen, 1979), 75.

42. Albert Cohen, *Delinquent Boys: The Culture of the Gang* (New York: Free Press, 1955); Walter Miller, "Lower-Class Culture as a Generating Milieu of Gang Delinquency," *Journal of Social Issues* 14 (1958): 15.

43. Arthur Laurents, "The Growth of an Idea," *New York Herald Tribune* (August 4, 1957).

44. Ibid.

45. Bob Hamilton and Fred Gorman, "(Just Like) Romeo and Juliet." Produced by Rob Reeco on Golden World Records.

46. Robert F. Kennedy, "Tribute to John F. Kennedy at the Democratic National Convention," Atlantic City, New Jersey, August 27, 1964. John F. Kennedy Presidential Library and Museum Archives, Boston, Massachusetts.

47. In commenting on the dance production *Nevermind,* based in part on the *Nirvana* album and premiering at Seattle's Moore Theatre in March 2007, choreographer Donald Byrd was quoted in the *Seattle Times:* "It's like sometimes when you're watching *Romeo and Juliet,* you think, if they had just waited. You want to say, hold on, everything changes. Even if it seems unbearable, it's going to change."

48. Richard Driscoll, Keith E. Davis, and Milton E. Lipetz, "Parental Interference and Romantic Love: The Romeo and Juliet Effect," *Journal of Personality and Social Psychology* 24 (1972): 9.

49. Susan Sprecher and Diane Felmlee, "The Influence of Parents and Friends on the Quality and Stability of Romantic Relationships: A Three-Wave Longitudinal Investigation," *Journal of Marriage and the Family* 54 (November 1992): 888, 897.

50. See also Robert Hinde, *Relationships: A Dialectical Perspective* (East Sussex: Psychology Press, 1997), 441–42.

51. Linda Lowen, "Romeo and Juliet Laws—What They Mean for Teens," About.com: Women's Issues, http://womensissues.about.com/od/datingandsex/a/Romeo_and_Juliet .htm. The Kansas Supreme Court ruled in 2005 in *State of Kansas v. Limon* that the "Romeo and Juliet law" must be amended to treat same-sex conduct on an equal basis with heterosexual conduct.

52. Nextel advertisement, TBWA/Chiat/Day New York, 2003. Copywriter Richard Overall, art director Simon McQuoid, producer Ozzie Spenningsby, director Joe Pytka.

THREE

CORIOLANUS: *The Estrangement of Self*

1. Cole Porter, "Brush Up Your Shakespeare," *Kiss Me, Kate,* 1948.

2. The pun on "anus" was revisited half a century later by queer theorist Jonathan Goldberg in the title of his essay, "The Anus in Coriolanus." *Historicism, Psychoanalysis and Early Modern Culture,* ed. Carla Mazzio and Douglas Trevor (New York: Routledge, 2000), 260–71. As Goldberg points out, Kenneth Burke, in his essay on the play, had commented on the same question: "In the light of Freudian theories concerning the fecal nature of invective, the last two syllables of the hero's name are so 'right,' people now often seek to dodge the issues by altering the traditional pronunciation (making the *a* broad instead of long)." Kenneth Burke, "*Coriolanus*—and the Delights of Faction," in *Language as Symbolic Action* (Berkeley: University of California Press, 1966), 96. This "delicacy" in phrasing is doubtless one of the targets of Cole Porter's witty lyric.

3. Samuel Taylor Coleridge, *Essays and Lectures on Shakespeare and Some Other Old Poets and Dramatists* (London and Toronto: J. M. Dent, 1907), 92.

4. Bernhard Krytzler, *Shakespeare Jahrbuch* 57 (1921): 163; Martin Brunkhorst, *Shakespeare's "Coriolanus,"* in *Deutscher Bearbeitung* (Berlin and New York: De Gruyter, 1973), 157. Both quoted in Philip Brockbank, ed., *Coriolanus,* Arden Shakespeare (London: Methuen, 1976), 86.

5. An index of the importance of this term is its inclusion in the *Oxford English Dictionary* (*Verfrumdungseffekt,* an alienation effect) with citations going back as far as 1945. Arguments for one translation over another have tried to separate out the sense of political or economic alienation (Marx's *Entfremdung,* alienation of labor from production under capitalism) from the resistance to sensation, emotion, or identification in favor of education, learning, pedagogy.

6. Walter Benjamin, "What Is Epic Theater?," trans. Harry Zohn, in *Illuminations,* ed. Hannah Arendt (New York: Schocken Books, 1968), 150; originally published in *Mass und Wert,* 1939.

7. Bertolt Brecht, "Short Description of a New Technique of Acting which Produces an Alienation Effect," in *Brecht on Theatre: The Development of an Aesthetic,* ed. and trans. John Willett (New York: Hill and Wang, 1964), 141.

8. Ibid., 137.

9. Ibid., 143.

10. Ibid., 140.

11. Bertolt Brecht, "Alienation Effects in Chinese Acting," in Willett, ed., *Brecht on Theatre,* 91. See also Willett's discussion in the notes on page 99 for Brecht's encounter with Mei Lan-Fang's company and its relationship to his theory and terminology.

12. Bertolt Brecht, *Coriolanus,* trans. Ralph Manheim, in *Collected Plays,* 9, eds. Ralph Manheim and John Willett (New York: Pantheon, 1972), 141.

13. Bertolt Brecht, "The Literarization of the Theatre," in Willett, ed., *Brecht on Theatre,* 45.

14. Ibid., note, 46.

15. Laurence Kitchin, *Mid-Century Drama* (London: Faber and Faber, 1960); quoted in Anthony Holden, *Laurence Olivier* (New York: Atheneum, 1988), 339.

16. Cynthia Marshall, "Coriolanus," in Richard Dutton, ed., *A Companion to Shakespeare's Works* (Oxford: Blackwell, 2003), 1: 468.

17. Erving Goffman, *The Presentation of Self in Everyday Life* (New York: Doubleday Anchor, 1959), 15.

18. E.g., Michel de Certeau, *The Practice of Everyday Life,* trans. Steven Rendall (Berkeley: University of California Press, 1984).

19. "self, *n.*" *The Oxford English Dictionary,* 2nd ed. (Oxford University Press, 1989), *OED Online,* http://cgi/entry/50218807 (accessed August 22, 2008).

20. Goffman, *The Presentation of Self in Everyday Life,* 254–55.

21. Freud, "The Uncanny," *The Standard Edition of the Complete Psychological Works of Sigmund Freud* (London: Hogarth Press and the Institute of Psycho-Analysis, 1955) 17: 250.

22. J. L. Austin, *How to Do Things with Words* (Cambridge: Harvard University Press, 1962), 22.

23. Daniel J. Boorstin, *The Image: A Guide to Pseudo-Events in America* (New York: Harper & Row, 1964).

24. The first reference for both sense one and sense two is the *Ancrene Riwle* (c. 1230). *OED Online,* http://dictionary.oed.com/cgi/entry/50218807. The more commonly used modern meaning of "person" is listed second, after this one: "A human being, and related senses." So even in the *OED* the role comes before the reality, although the two meanings, in this historical dictionary, seem to begin at the same early date.

25. Kenneth Burke, "Antony in Behalf of the Play," originally published in the *Southern Review* 1 (1935); reprinted in *Kenneth Burke on Shakespeare,* ed. Scott L. Newstok (West Lafayette, IN: Parlor Press, 2007), 38–48. In this rewriting of Antony's speech, Antony alludes at the close to "our Great Demagogue," the playwright.

26. Bertolt Brecht, *The Resistible Rise of Arturo Ui* (New York: Samuel French, 1972), scene 7, 62–63.

27. This is the title given to the speech in William Holmes McGuffey's *McGuffey's New Sixth Eclectic Reader* (Cincinnati: Van Antwerp, Bragg, and Co., 1857). The name of the play from which the speech is excerpted is not given; the speech, not the play, is the thing.

28. Stanley Fish, "How to Do Things with Austin and Searle," in *Is There a Text in This Class? The Authority of Interpretive Communities* (Cambridge: Harvard University Press, 1980), 197–245.

29. Günter Grass, "The Prehistory and Posthistory of the Tragedy of *Coriolanus* from Livy and Plutarch via Shakespeare down to Brecht and Myself," in Grass, *The Plebeians Rehearse the Uprising: A German Tragedy,* trans. Ralph Manheim (New York: Harcourt, Brace & World, 1966), vii–xxxvi.

30. Ibid., xxvii.

31. Ibid., xxviii.

32. Ibid., xxix.

33. Ibid., xxx–xxxi.

34. Ibid., xxxii.

35. Grass, *The Plebeians Rehearse the Uprising,* 102.

36. Ibid., 107. The history of Brecht's written statement is told in Uta Gerhardt, "The Uprising of June 17, 1953," in Grass, *The Plebeians Rehearse the Uprising,* 121–22. Grass's Volumnia explains the duplicity, and describes what did in fact take place: the East German newspaper *Neues Deutschland* printed only the third paragraph, and the whole text was not reprinted until 1965.

     Volumnia: Why read this pussyfooting document aloud? Three succinct paragraphs. The first two are critical; you say the measures taken by the government, in other words the Party, were premature. In the third and last something makes you proclaim your solidarity with the same people you attacked in the first two. . . . [T]hey'll cross out your critical paragraphs and trumpet the solidarity until you die of shame.

37. Grass, *The Plebeians Rehearse the Uprising,* 111.

38. Brecht, "Short Description of a New Technique of Acting which Produces an Alienation Effect," in Willett, ed., *Brecht on Theatre,* 136. A typical passage occurs in his description of the "alienation effect" and its relationship to a new technique of acting: "It is of course

necessary to drop the assumption that there is a fourth wall cutting the audience off from the stage and the consequent illusion that the stage action is taking place in reality and without an audience. That being so, it is possible for the actor in principle to address the audience direct."

39. Grass, *The Plebeians Rehearse the Uprising*, 31–32.
40. Ibid., 107.
41. E.g., Christopher Hitchens, "Snake in the Grass," Slate.com (August 22, 2006).
42. Henrik Ibsen, *Peer Gynt*, trans. Michael Meyer (Garden City, NY: Anchor Books), 133–34.
43. H.W., "Enough to Make You Cry," *Guernica* (June 16, 2007).
44. "The Betrayal of Memory." *New York Times* (August 18, 2006).

FOUR

MACBETH: *The Necessity of Interpretation*

1. King James VI and I, "Daemonologie," *Selected Writings,* eds. Neil Rhodes, Jennifer Richards, and Joseph Marshall (Aldershot, Hampshire: Ashgate Publishing, 2003), 176.
2. W. Davenport Adams, *A Dictionary of the Drama: A Guide to the Plays, Playwrights, Players, and Playhouses of the United Kingdom and America, from the Earliest Times to the Present* (Philadelphia: J.B. Lippincott Company, 1904), 539.
3. Lawrence Levine, "William Shakespeare and the American People," *American Historical Review* 89 (February 1984): 61.
4. Ibid., 62.
5. Quoted in Michael Knox Beran, "Lincoln, *Macbeth,* and the Moral Imagination," *Humanitas* 2, 2 (1998): 5.
6. Ibid., 13–14.
7. These rituals include turning three times, spitting over your left shoulder, swearing, or reciting a line from either *The Merchant of Venice* ("Fair thoughts and happy hours attend on you" [3.4.41]) or *Hamlet* ("Angels and ministers of grace defend us" [1.4.20]).
8. For more on this phenomenon, see, for example, Richard Huggett, *Supernatural on Stage* (New York: Taplinger, 1975).
9. Susan McCloskey, "Shakespeare, Orson Welles, and the 'Voodoo' *Macbeth,*" *Shakespeare Quarterly* 36 (Winter 1985): 406.
10. Courtney Lehmann, "Out Damned Scot: Dislocating *Macbeth* in Transnational Film and Media Culture," *Shakespeare the Movie II: Popularizing the Plays on Film, TV, Video, and DVD,* eds. Richard Burt and Lynda E. Boose (New York: Routledge, 2003), 234.
11. Sigmund Freud, "Some Character-Types Met with in Psycho-Analytic Work," *The Standard Edition of the Complete Psychological Works of Sigmund Freud,* 24 vols., ed. and trans. James Strachey (London: Hogarth Press, 1957), 14: 318.
12. Ibid., 319.
13. Ibid., 324.
14. Ibid., 323.
15. Sigmund Freud, "The Uncanny," *Standard Edition,* 17: 250.
16. Sigmund Freud, "Fetishism," *Standard Edition,* 21:149–57.
17. Daniel Wattenberg, "The Lady Macbeth of Little Rock," *American Spectator* 25 (August 1992): 25–32.
18. Brenda Maddox, "The True Believer: Margaret Thatcher," *New York Times* (November 24, 1996).
19. Michael Carmichael, "Condi's Bogus Journey," *Planetary Movement* [Weblog] (December 6, 2005).

20. Ben Shapiro, "Shock Story: Nancy Pelosi Is a Woman," *Human Events* (January 10, 2007).
21. Barbara Garson, *Macbird* (Berkeley, CA: Grassy Knoll Press, 1966).
22. Ibid., 27.
23. Ibid., 28.
24. Quoted in Tom Blackburn, "*MacBird!* and *Macbeth:* Topicality and Imitation in Barbara Garson's Satirical Pastiche," *Shakespeare Survey 57: Macbeth and Its Afterlife,* ed. Peter Holland (Cambridge: Cambridge University Press, 2004), 138.
25. Garson, *MacBird,* 1.
26. Ibid., i.
27. Ibid., 5.
28. Ibid., 2.
29. Ibid., 4.
30. Ibid., 14.
31. Ibid., 15.
32. Ibid., 21.
33. Ibid., 18.
34. Ibid., 30.
35. Ibid.
36. Ibid., 41.
37. Ibid., 43.
38. Ibid., 56.
39. Katherine Q. Seelye, "Clinton Remark on Kennedy's Killing Stirs Uproar," *New York Times* (May 24, 2008).
40. Michael Goodwin, "Hillary Clinton's Colossal Blunder Simply the Last Straw," *New York Daily News* (May 24, 2008).
41. Ronald Wilcox, posted response at Documentary Films.NET, January 25, 2007, http://www.documentaryfilms.net/index.php/dick-morris-trying-to-fund-a-hillary-clinton-documentary/.
42. Ibid.
43. Ibid.

FIVE

RICHARD III: *The Problem of Fact*

1. Senior army officers knew the truth within days after the event, but nonetheless approved Tillman for the award of a Silver Star, a Purple Heart, and a posthumous promotion. It was months before his family learned the actual facts about his death. Tillman's younger brother, Kevin, noted that the only problem with the army's account was that "it was utter fiction." Quoted in Bob Herbert, "Working the Truth Beat," *New York Times* (April 30, 2007).
2. Quoted in ibid.
3. Ross Terrill, "China Is Not Just Rising, but Also Changing," *New York Times* (September 9, 2006).
4. "A Million Little Lies: James Frey's Fiction Addiction," www.thesmokinggun.com (January 8, 2006).
5. Deborah Caulfield Rybak, "Taking Liberties: Memoir Writer Walks a Wavy Line Between Reality and Invention," *Minneapolis Star Tribune* (July 27, 2003).
6. Herbert, "Working the Truth Beat."
7. Marjorie Garber, "*Richard III,*" in *Shakespeare After All* (New York: Anchor Books, 2004), 132.

8. James R. Siemon, "Between the Lines: Bodies/Languages/Times," *Shakespeare Studies* 29 (2001): 38, 40.
9. *Looking for Richard,* directed by Al Pacino (Fox Searchlight Pictures, 1996).
10. Bruce Weber, "The Eternal Now of a Shakespeare Play," *New York Times* (November 23, 2003).
11. Molly Ivins, "Nixon's Ghost Haunts White House," *Buffalo News* (December 29, 2005).
12. Mary Jacoby, "McCain Stays a Pesky Thorn in Bush's Side," *St. Petersburg Times* (February 18, 2001).
13. E. M. Forster, *Aspects of the Novel* (1927; New York: Harcourt Brace, 1954), 86.
14. The third reference in *OED,* dated forty years later, is to Shakespeare's play.
15. The technique of shot reverse shot (or shot/countershot) reinforces the sense of continuous, linear, and logical action, and emphasizes the sense of narrative and discursive realism. See David Bordwell and Kristin Thompson, *Film Art: An Introduction* (New York: McGraw-Hill, 2006).
16. *Oxford English Dictionary,* "now," 6.
17. Sigmund Freud, "Some Character-Types Met with in Psycho-Analytic Work," *The Standard Edition of the Complete Psychological Works of Sigmund Freud,* 24 vols., ed. and trans. James Strachey (London: Hogarth Press, 1957), 14: 314.
18. Richard H. Rovere, *Senator Joe McCarthy* (Berkeley, Los Angeles, and London: University of California Press, 1996) 244.
19. Josephine Tey, *The Daughter of Time* (New York: Scribner, 1995), 40.
20. Such as *The Franchise Affair, Miss Pym Disposes,* and *Brat Farrar.*
21. Francis Bacon, *Novum Organum: Collected Works of Francis Bacon* (London: Routledge/Thoemmes, 1996), 4: 82. "And with regard to authority, it shows a feeble mind to grant so much to authors and yet deny time his rights, who is the author of authors, nay, rather of all authority. For rightly is truth called the daughter of time, not of authority."
22. Tey, *The Daughter of Time,* 42.
23. Ibid., 131.
24. Ibid., 36.
25. Ibid., 38.
26. Ibid., 201.
27. Ibid., 188–89.
28. Ibid., 47.
29. Ibid., 111.
30. Ibid., 182.
31. Ibid., 195.
32. Clements Markham, *Richard III: His Life and Character Reviewed in Light of Recent Research* (Bath, UK: Chivers, 1906).
33. James Joyce, *A Portrait of the Artist as a Young Man* (1916; New York: Viking Press, 1968), 15.

SIX

THE MERCHANT OF VENICE: *The Question of Intention*

1. John Dover Wilson, *The Essential Shakespeare: A Biographical Adventure* (Cambridge, UK: 1932), 7–8, quoted in S. Schoenbaum, *Shakespeare's Lives* (Oxford: Clarendon Press; New York: Oxford University Press, 1970), 662.
2. George Steevens, quoted in Schoenbaum, *Shakespeare's Lives,* 282.
3. J. Hain Friswell, *Life Portraits of William Shakespeare* (London, 1864), 31.
4. J. Parker Norris, *The Portraits of Shakespeare* (Philadelphia: Robert M. Lindsay, 1885).

5. Abraham Wivell, *An Inquiry into the History, Authenticity, and Characteristics of the Shakespeare Portraits* (London, 1827), 140.

6. William Dunlap, *The Life of George Friedrich Cooke* (London: H. Colburn, 1815), 26; David Erskine Baker, *Biographia Dramatica, or, A Companion to the Playhouse* (London: Rivington, 1782), vol. 1, part 2, 469.

7. Representative Dana Rohrabacher (R-CA), *Congressional Record,* February 7, 2007, Section 75.

8. "Demanding Our Pounds of Flesh," *Herald Sun* (Australia), February 2, 2007; "Kinross Won't Raise Takeover Bid for Berma Despite Opposition," (Canadian Press) *Resource Investor* (January 21, 2007).

9. Michael Ordoña, "*Saw III,*" *Los Angeles Times* (October 30, 2006).

10. Carrie Johnson and Brooke A. Masters, "Cook the Books, Get Life in Prison: Is Justice Served?" *Washington Post* (September 25, 2006).

11. Charles Isherwood, "O Villain, Villain, Loosed in Elizabethan Minds," *New York Times* (February 5, 2007), http://theater2.nytimes.com./2007/02/05/theater/reviews/osmerc .html

12. Patricia Cohen, "Essay Linking Liberal Jews and Anti-Semitism Sparks a Furor," *New York Times* (January 31, 2007), http://www.nytimes.com/2007/01/31/arts/31Jews.html

13. Moe Lane, "Shoot at a Senator . . . And You Had Better Not Miss," http://archive.redstate .com/stories/featured_stories/shoot_at_a_senator (online: Eagle Publishing, Inc., 2006).

14. William Hazlitt, "On Shakespeare and Milton," *Lectures on the English Comic Writers* (New York: William and Putnam, 1845), 55–56.

15. Samuel Taylor Coleridge, *Biographia Literaria: Or, Biographical Sketches of My Literary Life and Opinions* (New York: American Book Exchange, 1881), 1: 460.

16. T. S. Eliot, "Christopher Marlowe" [1918], in *Selected Essays 1917–1932* (New York: Harcourt, Brace and Company, 1932), 104–5.

17. John Gross, *Shylock: A Legend and Its Legacy* (New York: Touchstone, 1992), 35.

18. Ibid., 54–55.

19. James Shapiro, *Shakespeare and the Jews* (New York: Columbia University Press, 1996), 73.

20. Charles Macklin's account appeared in the *European Magazine,* April 1800; Gamini Salgado, ed., *Eyewitnesses of Shakespeare: First Hand Accounts of Performances, 1590–1890* (New York: Barnes and Noble, 1975), 127.

21. Georg Christoph Lichtenberg, *Visits to England: As Described in His Letters and Diaries,* eds. and trans. Margaret L. Mare and W. H. Quarrell, in Salgado, ed., *Eyewitnesses of Shakespeare,* 128.

22. Sander Gilman, "The Jewish Voice," in *The Jew's Body* (New York: Routledge, 1991), 14–15.

23. Shapiro, *Shakespeare and the Jews,* 196–224.

24. Samuel Taylor Coleridge and Henry Nelson Coleridge, *Specimens of the Table Talk of Samuel Taylor Coleridge* (London: John Murray, 1836), 13.

25. William Hazlitt, *A View of the English Stage,* in Salgado, ed., *Eyewitnesses of Shakespeare,* 131.

26. William Hazlitt, *Characters of Shakespeare's Plays* (1817; London: Oxford University Press, 1975), 212.

27. Bryant, quoted in Gross, *Shylock,* 143–44.

28. *Between Actor and Critic: Selected Letters of Edwin Booth and William Winter,* ed. Daniel J. Watermeier (Princeton: Princeton University Press, 1971), 256.

29. Garber, *Vested Interests,* 230.

30. Cited from the *Literary Digest* (October 26, 1929), in Toby Lelyveld, *Shylock on the Stage* (Cleveland: Western Reserve University, 1960), 126.

31. *The Times* (London), November 3, 1879, in Salgado, ed., *Eyewitnesses of Shakespeare,* 137–38.

32. George du Maurier, *Trilby: A Novel* (New York: Harper and Brothers, 1894), 370.

33. Nahma Sandrow, *Vagabond Stars: A World History of Yiddish Theater* (New York: Harper & Row, 1977), 158; *The Jewish King Lear* was written by Jacob Gordin.

34. Gross, *Shylock,* 278.

35. Quoted in *Jacob Adler: A Life on the Stage, A Memoir,* trans. and with a commentary by Lulla Rosenfeld (New York: Applause, 2001), 348.

36. Ibid.

37. Gross, *Shylock,* 241.

38. "Jacob Adler—the Bowery Garrick," *Theatre* (November 1902): 18, quoted in Rosenfeld, *Jacob Adler,* 345.

39. Henriette von Schirach, *The Price of Glory,* trans. Willi Frischauer (London: Frederick Muller, 1960), 173, quoted in Andrew G. Bonnell, *Shylock in Germany* (London: Tauris, 2008), 49.

40. Gross, *Shylock* 239–41.

41. Ibid., 241–42.

42. Ibid., 321–23. Gross quotes here from Werner Krauss's autobiography, *Das Schauspiel meines Lebens* (Stuttgart: Goverts, 1958), 199–209. For more extended quotations from reviews of the time, see Bonnell, *Shylock in Germany,* 162.

43. Quoted in Bonnell, *Shylock in Germany,* 162.

44. Ibid., 161–62.

45. Henry Ford, *The International Jew: The World's Foremost Problem* (Dearborn, MI: Dearborn Publishing, 1920).

46. Ibid., 105.

47. Ibid., 104.

48. Richard Hofstadter, *The Paranoid Style in American Politics and Other Essays* (Cambridge: Harvard University Press, 1965), 301.

49. James Harvey Rogers, *America Weighs Her Gold* (New Haven: Yale University Press, 1931); Aijaz Ahmad, "Colonialism, Fascism and 'Uncle Shylock,'" *Frontline,* India's National Magazine 17, no. 17 (September 1, 2000); William F. Buckley, "Uncle Shylock?" *National Review Online,* January 3, 2005.

50. Theodor Adorno, *Prisms* (Cambridge: MIT Press, 1955); Adorno, "Is Art Lighthearted?" *Notes to Literature,* vol. 2, trans. Shierry Weber Nicholsen (New York: Columbia University Press, 1992), 251, 253.

51. Karl Marx, "The Working-Day," in *Capital, A Critique of Political Economy,* trans. Samuel Moore and Edward Averling (New York: The Modern Library, 1906), 315.

52. Karl Marx and Friedrich Engels, footnote to *The Communist Manifesto* (London, 1848), 5.

53. Sigmund Freud, "The Theme of the Three Caskets," *The Freud Reader,* ed. Peter Gay (New York: W. W. Norton & Company, 1995), 514.

54. Ibid.

55. Marjorie Garber, "Freud's Choice: The Theme of the Three Caskets," in *Shakespeare's Ghost Writers: Literature as Uncanny Causality* (New York and London: Routledge, 1987), 86.

56. "Hath not a Jew eyes? Hath not a Jew hands, organs, dimensions, senses, affections, passions; fed with the same food, hurt with the same weapons, subject to the same diseases, healed by the same means, warmed and cooled by the same winter and summer as a Christian is? If you prick us do we not bleed? If you tickle us do we not laugh? If you poison us do we not die? And if you wrong us shall we not revenge? If we are like you in the rest, we will resemble you in that." (3.1.49–57)

57. Jean-Paul Sartre, *Anti-Semite and Jew* [1948], trans. George J. Becker (New York: Schocken Books, 1995), 19.

58. Ibid., 20.

59. Ibid., 22.

60. Ibid., 28.

61. Michael Walzer, Preface to Jean-Paul Sartre, *Anti-Semite and Jew,* trans. George J. Becker (New York: Schocken Books, 1995), vii.

62. Ibid., xi.

63. Ibid., xviii.

SEVEN

OTHELLO: *The Persistence of Difference*

1. Mac E. Barrick, "The Newspaper Riddle Joke," *Journal of American Folklore* 87, 345 (July–September 1974): 253–57.

2. Sigmund Freud, *Jokes and Their Relation to the Unconscious* (1905), *The Standard Edition of the Complete Psychological Works of Sigmund Freud,* 24 vols., ed. and trans. James Strachey (London: Hogarth Press and the Institute of Psycho-Analysis, 1960) 7: 234.

3. Theodore Sorensen, "A Time to Weep," 2004 Commencement Address at the New School University, May 21, 2004.

4. Sandra Block, "Don't Fall Prey to Identity Thieves," *USA Today* (September 12, 2000), 3B; James J. Kilpatrick, "Curbing the Power of Credit Bureaus," *St. Petersburg Times* (July 10, 1991), 13A.

5. Jay M. Shafritz, *Shakespeare on Management: Wise Business Counsel from the Bard* (New York: HarperPerennial, 1999), 2.

6. Ibid., 107–8.

7. Ibid., 108.

8. O. J. Simpson, letter discovered June 17, 1994.

9. Lawyer and novelist Scott Turow gave voice to the general pop-cultural sentiment when he told *USA Today,* "There is a Shakespearean dimension to the tragedy of what has gone on. O. J. Simpson is the Othello of the 20th century." Scott Turow, quoted in Joe Urschel, "Case That Captivated U.S.," *USA Today* (September 19, 1995), 1A. The analogy with *Othello* was, perhaps, too glaring to be ignored (though columnist Frank Rich, for one, insisted that "Mr. Simpson is no Othello—he commanded a playing field, not a battlefield," before going on to analyze the overwhelming power of celebrity in American culture. Frank Rich, "Addicted to O.J.," *New York Times* (June 23, 1994), A23.

10. Mary McGrory, "Clinton, Nixon, and Common Sense," *Washington Post* (February 1, 1998).

11. Maureen Dowd, "All Tripped Up," *New York Times* (June 28, 1998), Section 4, 17.

12. "The Trial of the President; White House Counsel: 'There Was No Basis for the House to Impeach,'" *New York Times* (January 20, 1999), A26ff.

13. *Today* show, March 4, 1999; Andrew Morton, *Monica's Story* (New York: St. Martins Press, 1999).

14. Liz Langley, "Great Balls of Ire," *Orlando Weekly* (October 7, 1999).

15. Karen DeCrow, "Stain Resistance," *Syracuse New Times* (August 19–26, 1998), 5.

16. Bruce Fein, News Conference, August 11, 1998.

17. "Shakespearean Tragedy and the Bush Administration: Cheney as Iago," *Media Jihad* (June 9, 2004); "The guru delivers his message" ("Rove is the political guru of this Republican administration, Iago to George . . ."), *Toronto Star* (September 2, 2004); "Iago in a silk suit," *Barista* (February 24, 2004); "Where Is Iraq War Instigator, Richard Perle?," message board by American Patriot Friends Network, August 21, 2003, http://codshit.blogspot.com/2003/07/where-is-iraq-war-instigator-richard.html.

18. G. K. Hunter, "Othello and Colour Prejudice," in *Dramatic Identities and Cultural Tradi-*

tion: Studies in Shakespeare and His Contemporaries (Liverpool: Liverpool University Press, 1978), 45, first published in *Proceedings of the British Academy,* 53 (1967).

19. E. A. J. Honigman, ed., *Othello,* Arden 3rd edition (Surrey: Thomas Nelson and Sons, 1997), 22–23.

20. Ibrahim Amin, "Killing with One's Mind: Iago and the War on Terror," Free Muslims Coalition, Anti-Terrorism Resources, 2006.

21. Jeffrey Rothfeder, "Terror Games," *Popular Science* 264, no. 3 (March 2004): 82–115.

22. John Hiles, personal communication (e-mail), August 30, 2006.

23. Bernard Spivak, *Shakespeare and the Allegory of Evil: The History of a Metaphor in Relation to His Major Villains* (New York: Columbia University Press, 1958).

24. Christine M. Flowers, "An American Tragedy," post to http://www.philly.com. In *Othello,* Cassio says, "Reputation, reputation, reputation—O, I ha' lost my reputation, I ha' lost my reputation, I ha' lost the immortal part of myself, and what remains is bestial!" (2.3.246–48).

25. Richard H. Brodhead, quoted in Peter J. Boyer, "Big Men on Campus," *The New Yorker* (September 4, 2006), 61, 53.

26. Stephen Jay Gould, "How the Zebra Gets Its Stripes," in *Hen's Teeth and Horse's Toes* (New York: W. W. Norton, 1983), 366.

27. J. B. L. Bard, "A Model for Generating Aspects of Zebra and Other Mammalian Coat Patterns," *Journal of Theoretical Biology* 19: 363–85, quoted in ibid., 375.

28. Gould, "How the Zebra Got Its Stripes," 375.

29. E. H. Gombrich, *Art and Illusion: A Study in the Psychology of Pictorial Representation* (Princeton: Princeton University Press, 1960), 5.

30. T. S. Eliot, "Shakespeare and the Stoicism of Seneca" [1927], in *Selected Essays* (New York: Harcourt Brace, 1932), 111.

31. Sigmund Freud, "Some Neurotic Mechanisms in Jealousy, Paranoia, and Homosexuality" [1922], in *Standard Edition* 18: 221–32.

32. C. L. R. James, "*Othello* and *The Merchant of Venice*" [1963], *Spheres of Influence: Selected Writings* (London: Allison & Busby, 1980), 141.

33. Honigman, ed., *Othello,* 3.

34. "1601. Negroes and Blackamoors.—Whereas the Queen's Majesty is discontented at the great number of 'negars and blackamoores' which are crept into the realm since the troubles between her Highness and the King of Spain, and are fostered here to the annoyance of her own people. . . . In order to discharge them out of this country, her Majesty hath appointed Caspar Van Zeuden, merchant of Lubeck, for their transportation. . . . This is to require you to assist him to collect such negroes and blackamoore for this purpose." Historical Manuscripts Commission, Hatfield House, Part XI (1601), (1906), 569, cited in Honigman, ed., *Othello,* 29.

35. Thomas Rymer, *A Short View of Tragedy* (1693), in Edward Pechter, ed., *Othello: A Norton Critical Edition* (New York: W. W. Norton, 2004), 202–3.

36. T. S. Eliot, "Hamlet and His Problems" [1919], in *Selected Essays 1917–1932* (New York: Harcourt, Brace, 1932), 121n.

37. Samuel Taylor Coleridge, *The Complete Works of Samuel Taylor Coleridge* (New York: Harper and Brothers, 1858), 4: 179.

38. Abigail Adams, cited in David McCullough, *John Adams* (New York: Simon and Schuster, 2001), 345–46. See also *Adams Family Correspondence,* ed. L. H. Butterfield (New York: Atheneum, 1965) 6: 366.

39. John Quincy Adams, "The Character of Desdemona," *Atlantic Monthly* (March 1836), 210.

40. James Henry Hackett, *Notes and Comments Upon Certain Plays and Actors of Shakespeare, with Criticism and Correspondence* (New York: Carleton, 1863), 224.

41. W. T. Lhamon Jr., *Jump Jim Crow: Lost Plays, Lyrics, and Street Prose of the First Atlantic Popular Culture* (Cambridge: Harvard University Press, 2003), 24; Tilden G. Edelstein, "*Othello* in America: The Drama of Racial Intermarriage," in *Region, Race, and Reconstruction: Essays in Honor of C. Vann Woodward,* eds. J. Morgan Kousser and James M. McPherson (New York: Oxford University Press, 1982), 179–97.

42. The playbill for a performance in Cincinnati in 1846 lists the availability of seating as follows: "Private Boxes $1.00, Dress Circle and Second Tier, 75. Pit, 35, Boxes for Persons of Color, 50, and Gallery, 25." Playbill for Cincinnati National Theatre, May 9, 1846, Harvard Theatre Collection, Houghton Library. Reproduced in Lhamon, *Jump Jim Crow,* 82.

43. Mary Preston, *Studies in Shakespeare* (Philadelphia: Clexton, Remson and Haffelfinger, 1869), cited in Horace Howard Furness, *A New Variorum Edition of Shakespeare, Othello* (reprint, New York: American Scholar Publications, 1965), 395.

44. A. C. Bradley, *Shakespearean Tragedy: Lectures on* Hamlet, Othello, King Lear, Macbeth (London: Macmillan, 1904; rpt. 1932), 200.

45. Ibid., 201.

46. Ibid., 202.

47. Ibid., 202n.

48. *Daily Sketch,* May 21, 1930, quoted in Martin Duberman, *Paul Robeson* (New York: New Press, 2005), 135.

49. *Variety,* August 12, 1942, quoted in ibid., 265.

50. Maureen Dowd, "Jeremy Irons Is Looking for Passion in His Roles," *New York Times* (September 23, 1984). This tradition is alive and well today: in a recent production at Shakespeare and Company in the Berkshires, Jonathan Epstein and Tony Molina alternated in the parts.

51. See Gordon Heath, *Deep Are the Roots: Memoirs of a Black Expatriate* (Amherst: University of Massachusetts Press, 1992), 146, quoted in Scott Newstock, "*Touch* of Shakespeare: Welles Unmoors *Othello,*" *Shakespeare Bulletin* 23, 1 (2005): 29–86.

52. Margo Hendricks, "Surveying 'Race' in Shakespeare," in Catherine M. S. Alexander and Stanley Wells, *Shakespeare and Race* (Cambridge: Cambridge University Press, 2000), 19.

53. W. E. B. Du Bois, *The Souls of Black Folk* [1903], in *W. E. B. Du Bois: Writings* (New York: Library of America, 1986), 364–65.

54. Ralph Ellison, "*An American Dilemma:* A Review" [1944], in John Callahan, ed., *The Collected Essays of Ralph Ellison* (New York: Modern Library, 1995). Emphasis added.

55. Quoted in Ruth Bader Ginsburg, "*Brown v. Board of Education* in International Context," Centre for Human Rights, University of Pretoria, South Africa, February 7, 2006. Emphasis added.

56. For this suggestion, and for a generous reading of this lecture in draft, I am indebted to William Germano.

57. And again, in the kind of locution that the HUAC hearing made famous, "I put it to you as a fact, and ask you to affirm or deny the fact, that your Communist Party name was 'John Thomas.'" This was an accusation the FBI had made for ten years without adducing any proof. Duberman, *Paul Robeson,* 440.

58. Testimony of Paul Robeson before the House Committee on Un-American Activities, June 12, 1956.

59. *Sex and the City,* Episode 52, "What's Sex Got to Do With It?"

60. James R. Andreas, "Othello's African American Progeny," *South Atlantic Review* 57 (November 1992): 45.

61. The chair of HUAC, Francis Walter, was the cosponsor of the McCarran-Walter Act (1952), which placed entry quotas on immigrants and barred supposed "subversives" from the country. And he was also a director of the Pioneer Fund, a controversial nonprofit foundation that has funded research on supposed genetic variations of IQ among races,

research that later surfaced in the publication of Richard J. Herrnstein and Charles Murray's *The Bell Curve* (New York: Free Press, 1994).

62. Testimony of Paul Robeson before the House Un-American Activities Committee, June 12, 1956.

63. "This accident is not unlike my dream," says Brabantio, when he hears Iago's nighttime description of Othello and Desdemona making the beast with two backs. It's not the fact (they are married, they are in love) but the fantasy, the sexual and animal fantasy, that is "like his dream." Just as the curious little narrative called "Cassio's dream" is actually Iago's made-up story about sharing a bed with Cassio and being kissed by him, by mistake, in his "dream," for Desdemona. Whose dream? Whose mistake? Whose kiss?

64. Freud, *Jokes and Their Relation to the Unconscious, Standard Edition,* 7: 90n.

65. Sigmund Freud, *The Joke and Its Relation to the Unconscious,* trans. Joyce Crick (London: Penguin, 2002), 87.

66. Samuel Taylor Coleridge, "Notes on *Othello,*" *Coleridge's Essays and Lectures on Shakespeare and Some Other Old Poets and Dramatists* (London: J. M. Dent, 1907), 172.

67. Freud, *Jokes and Their Relation to the Unconscious, Standard Edition,* 7: 90.

EIGHT

HENRY V: *The Quest for Exemplarity*

1. James Agee, *Time Magazine,* April 8, 1946, reprinted in *Agee on Film: Criticism and Comment on the Movies* (New York: McDowell-Obolensky, 1958).

2. Ibid.

3. François Rigolot, letter to the editor, *New York Times* (February 18, 1990).

4. Chris Fitter, "A Tale of Two Branaghs: Henry V, Ideology, and the Mekong Agincourt," in *Shakespeare Left and Right,* eds. Ivo Kamps et al. (New York: Routledge, 1991), 274–75.

5. Kenneth Branagh, quoted in Sally Ogle Davis, "Under the Lion's Skin: Young Kenneth Branagh Continues to Defy Critics of His Remarkable Career," *Weekend Australian* (December 23–24, 1989).

6. Kenneth Branagh, quoted in Alan Roberts, "*Henry V:* Once More Unto the Screen," *Literature/Film Quarterly* 20 (1992), no. 4.

7. *Oxford English Dictionary,* "theatre, theater," 5.c.

8. David Ira Goldstein, Arizona Theatre Company, quoted in Kyle Lawson, "Bard's Complex 'Henry V' Rises in Times of War," *Arizona Republic* (April 3, 2005).

9. Arianna Huffington, "Shakespeare Turns a Spotlight on Bush and Iraq," Salon.com (June 4, 2004), http://dir.salon.com/story/opinion/huffington/2004/06/04/bush_and_shakespeare/index.html.

10. Charles Austin Beard, "Giddy Minds and Foreign Quarrels: An Estimate of American Foreign Policy," *Harper's* (September 1939). For an excellent summary of the range of political commentary, see Scott Newstrok, "Step Aside, I'll Show Thee a President: George W. as Henry V?," http://www.poppolitics.com (May 2003).

11. Paul Corrigan, "Henry V: 'All Things Are Ready, If Our Minds Be So,' " *Shakespeare on Management: Leadership Lessons for Today's Managers* (London: Kogan Page, 1999), 137.

12. Ibid., 139.

13. Ibid., 147.

14. Ibid., 172.

15. Ibid., 177.

16. Ibid., 178.

17. Ibid.

18. Corrigan, "From Shakespeare to Tom Peters," *Shakespeare on Management,* 11.

19. Movers & Shakespeares, "Leadership Training . . . The Bard boom hits the conference room," http://www.moversandshakespeares.com/leadership.html.

20. Ibid., "About Us," http://www.moversandshakespeares.com/about.html.

21. Norman Augustine and Kenneth Adelman, *Shakespeare in Charge: The Bard's Guide to Leading and Succeeding on the Business Stage* (New York: Hyperion-Talk-Miramax, 2001).

22. Ibid., 1, 3–4.

23. Ibid., 6.

24. Ibid., 13.

25. Ibid., 14.

26. Ibid., 18–20.

27. Ibid., 24; Augustine and Adelman's book is divided into chapters as follows: "On Leadership" (*Henry V*); "Confronting Change" (*Taming of the Shrew*); "Making Your Play in Business" (*Julius Caesar*); "Risk Management" (*The Merchant of Venice*); and "Crisis Management" (*Hamlet*). Tag lines from other Shakespeare plays ornament and augment these how-to chapters, which are basically a kind of "case study" approach using Shakespeare as the raw material for decision making.

28. Jay M. Shafritz, *Shakespeare on Management: Wise Business Counsel from the Bard* (New York: Harper Business, 1999), 62.

29. Thomas Leech, *Say It Like Shakespeare: How to Give a Speech like Hamlet, Persuade Like Henry V, and Other Secrets from the World's Greatest Communicator* (New York: McGraw-Hill, 2001), 153–54.

30. Ibid., 241.

31. Ibid., 292.

32. Kyle Lawson, "Bard's Complex 'Henry V' Rises in Times of War," *Arizona Republic* (April 3, 2005).

33. This is an issue that has had a great effect upon literary studies in the works of theorists like Jacques Derrida, Paul de Man, and Judith Butler, as well as in those readers and critics who would like to appropriate literary characters and events for "real life" issues, whether in ethics, in law, or in business. See, for instance, Jacques Derrida, *Glas,* trans. John P. Leavey Jr. and Richard Rand (Lincoln: University of Nebraska Press, 1986), 28–30; Derrida, *The Truth in Painting,* trans. Geoff Bennington and Ian McLeod (Chicago: University of Chicago Press, 1987), 63, 105; Derrida, "The Law of Genre," *Glyph: Textual Studies* 7 (1988): 206; Derrida, "Passions: 'An Oblique Offering,'" in *Derrida: A Critical Reader* (Oxford: Blackwell, 1992), 33–35n14; Paul de Man, "Aesthetic Formalization: Kleist's Über das Marionettentheater," *The Rhetoric of Romanticism* (New York: Columbia University Press, 1984), 276; Judith Butler, *Bodies That Matter: On the Discursive Limits of "Sex"* (New York and London: Routledge, 1993), 200; Butler, "Conscience Doth Make Subjects of Us All," *The Psychic Life of Power: Theories in Subjection* (Stanford: Stanford University Press, 1997), 110–14; Butler, "Competing Universalities," *Contingency, Hegemony, Universality: Contemporary Dialogues on the Left* (London and New York: Verso, 2000), 157.

34. Ralph Waldo Emerson, *Representative Men: Nature, Addresses, Lectures* (Boston: Houghton Mifflin and Co., 1883), 5.

35. Jonathan Culler, *The Literary in Theory* (Stanford: Stanford University Press, 2007), 35.

36. Jacques Derrida, "Limited Inc a b c," *Limited Inc* (Evanston, IL: Northwestern University Press, 1988), 61.

NINE
HAMLET: *The Matter of Character*

1. There is an excellent essay on this question by the critic Alan Sinfield, called "When Is a Character Not a Character? Desdemona, Olivia, Lady Macbeth, and Subjectivity," in *Faultlines: Cultural Materialism and the Politics of Dissident Reading* (Berkeley: University of California Press, 1992), 52–79.

2. Samuel Taylor Coleridge and Henry Nelson Coleridge, *Specimens of the Table Talk of Samuel Taylor Coleridge* (London: John Murray, 1836), 37.

3. Johann Wolfgang von Goethe, *Wilhelm Meister's Apprenticeship,* trans. Thomas Carlyle (London: Olver & Boyd, 1824), 2: 75.

4. Samuel Taylor Coleridge, *Notes and Lectures upon Shakespeare and the Old Dramatists* (New York, 1868), 4: 144.

5. Edward P. Vining, *The Mystery of Hamlet: An Attempt to Solve an Old Problem* (Philadelphia: Lippincott & Co., 1881), 11–12.

6. Ibid., 7–8.

7. Ibid., 9.

8. Ibid., 9–10.

9. Ibid., 61.

10. Ibid., 59.

11. Ibid.

12. See Ann Thompson, "Asta Nielsen and the Mystery of Hamlet," in *Shakespeare the Movie: Popularizing the Plays on Film, TV, and Video,* eds. Lynda E. Goose and Richard Burt (New York: Routledge, 1997), 215–24. Also, see Garber, *Vested Interests,* 38.

13. Quoted in Garber, *Vested Interests,* 38.

14. Sigmund Freud, *The Complete Letters of Sigmund Freud to Wilhelm Fliess,* ed. J. M. Masson (Cambridge: Harvard University Press, 1985), 272.

15. Ibid., 277.

16. Sigmund Freud, *The Interpretation of Dreams* (1900; New York: Avon, 1980), 298.

17. Ibid., 299.

18. Sigmund Freud, "A Special Type of Object-Choice Made by Men" [1910], *The Standard Edition of the Complete Psychological Works of Sigmund Freud,* 24 vols., ed. and trans. James Strachey (London: Hogarth Press, 1953–74), 11: 171.

19. Virginia Woolf, "Character in Fiction" (1924), *The Essays of Virginia Woolf, Vol. 3, 1919–1924,* ed. Andrew McNeillie (London: Hogarth Press, 1988), 421. *The Complete Works of Freud* would later be published by Virginia and Leonard Woolf's Hogarth Press and translated by Lytton Strachey's brother James. In 1924 the Hogarth Press took over the publication of the papers of the International Psycho-Analytical Institute, for which Jones was the general editor. We are talking here about a founding moment of modernity, in which the literary (and economic) interests of Bloomsbury crossed over into psychoanalysis, and made it available for the first time in English.

20. Ernest Jones, *Hamlet and Oedipus* (New York: Norton, 1976).

21. Ibid., 19.

22. A. C. Bradley, *Shakespearean Tragedy: Lectures on* Hamlet, Othello, King Lear, Macbeth, 4th ed. (Hampshire, UK, and New York: Palgrave Macmillan, 2007), 83.

23. Ibid.

24. Ibid., 85.

25. Jones, *Hamlet and Oedipus,* 68.

26. Ibid., 69.

27. T. S. Eliot, "Hamlet and His Problems," in *The Sacred Wood* (1920; Mineola, NY: Dover Publications), 55.

28. The title character of Goethe's novella *The Sorrows of Young Werther* (1774).

29. Ibid.

30. Eliot, "Hamlet and His Problems," 57.

31. Jones notes of his mentor, in an admiring footnote, "It is but fitting that Freud should have solved the riddle of this Sphinx, as he has that of the Theban one." Jones, *Hamlet and Oedipus*, 22.

32. Eliot, "Hamlet and His Problems," 57.

33. Ibid., 58.

34. Ibid., 59.

35. George Bernard Shaw, *Shaw on Shakespeare: An Anthology of Bernard Shaw's Writings on the Plays and Productions of Shakespeare*, ed. Edwin Wilson (New York: Dutton, 1961), 82.

36. D. H. Lawrence, "Twilight in Italy," *D. H. Lawrence and Italy*, introduced by Anthony Burgess (New York: Viking Press, 1972), 68.

37. D. H. Lawrence, "When I Read Shakespeare," *Complete Poems*, eds. Vivian de Sola Pinto and F. Warren Roberts (New York: Penguin, 1993), 494.

38. Albert Sonnenfeld, "Mallarmé: The Poet as Actor as Reader," *Yale French Studies* 54 (1977): 167–92.

39. For further discussion of *Ulysses* and *Hamlet*, see, for instance, Hugh Kenner, "Joyce's *Ulysses*: Homer and Hamlet," *Essays in Criticism* 2 (1952): 100–4; William M. Schutte, *Joyce and Shakespeare: A Study of the Meaning of* Ulysses (New Haven: Yale University Press, 1957), esp. Appendix B, "The Sources of Stephen's Shakespeare Theory," 153–77; Richard Ellman, *The Consciousness of Joyce* (London: Faber, 1977), ch. 2, "Shakespeare," 45–72; and Richard Kearney, "Hamlet's Ghosts: From Shakespeare to Joyce," *Strangers, Gods and Monsters: Interpreting Otherness* (London and New York: Routledge, 2003), 141–62.

40. See, for instance, Nicholas Rowe, Shakespeare's earliest biographer, in "Some Account of the Life, &c., of Mr. William Shakespeare," in *The Works of Mr. William Shakespeare, in Six Volumes* (London: Jacob Tonson, 1709), 1: vi.

41. James Joyce, *Ulysses*, ed. Hans Walter Gabler (New York: Vintage Books, 1986), 151–79.

42. Ibid., 158.

43. Ibid., 151.

44. Quoted in John Jowett, ed., *The Tragedy of King Richard III*, Oxford World's Classics (New York: Oxford University Press, 2000), 74.

45. Joyce, *Ulysses*, 172.

46. Ibid., 163.

47. Ibid., 15.

48. Ibid., 154.

49. Ibid., 155.

50. Ibid.

51. Ibid.

52. Emerson concedes, "We have to thank the researches of antiquaries, and the Shakespeare Society . . . they have left no bookstall unsearched, no chest in a garret unopened, no file of old yellow accounts to decompose in damp and worms." He adds, "The Shakespeare Society have inquired in all directions, advertised the missing facts, offered money for any information that will lead to proof,—and with what result? . . . I admit the importance of this information. It was well worth the pains that have been taken to procure it. But whatever scraps of information concerning his condition these researches may have rescued, they can shed no light upon that infinite invention which is the concealed magnet of his attraction for us." Finally: "Shakespeare is the only biographer of Shakespeare; and even he can tell nothing, except to the Shakespeare in us." Ralph Waldo Emerson, "Shakespeare, or, The Poet," *Representative Men* (Boston: Houghton Mifflin, 1883), 192, 195–96, 198.

53. Joyce, *Ulysses,* 155.

54. Ibid., 159.

55. Ibid., 166.

56. Ibid., 170.

57. Ibid., 174.

58. Ibid., 171.

59. Ibid., 170.

60. See also Roland Barthes on authorial paternity in *The Pleasure of the Text,* trans. Richard Miller (New York: Hill and Wang, 1975), 27, and Michel Foucault, "What Is an Author?," *Language, Counter-Memory, and Practice,* ed. Donald F. Bouchard, trans. Bouchard and Sherry Simon (Ithaca: Cornell University Press, 1977).

61. Joyce, *Ulysses,* 168.

62. Both are cited as accepting as a genuine Shakespeare play *Pericles,* which has a plot very like *Ulysses,* with a wandering hero in quest of a lost wife and a lost child. But both are also, in fact, the sources of much of what Stephen Dedalus has to say, both about Hamlet and about Shylock; ibid., 160.

63. Ibid., 554.

64. Joyce, *Ulysses,* 155.

65. Walter Benjamin, "The Work of Art in the Age of Mechanical Reproduction," *Illuminations: Essays and Reflections,* ed. Hannah Arendt (New York: Schocken Books, 1969), 220.

66. Ibid.

67. W. G. Sebald, *Campo Santo,* trans. Anthea Bell (New York: Random House, 2005), 24.

68. Susan Sontag, *On Photography* (New York: Picador USA, 2001), 154.

69. Jacques Derrida, *Spectres of Marx,* trans. Peggy Kamuf (New York and London: Routledge, 1995).

70. Ibid., 5.

71. Ibid., 7.

72. Ibid., 10–11.

73. Tom Stoppard, *Rosencrantz and Guildenstern Are Dead* (New York: Grove Press, 1991), 123.

74. For a discussion of the device of the "unscene," and of its various manifestations in a number of Shakespeare's plays, see Marjorie Garber, *Shakespeare After All* (New York: Pantheon, 2004).

75. Ihab Hassan, *The Dismemberment of Orpheus: Toward a Postmodern Literature* (Madison: University of Wisconsin Press, 1982), 267–68.

76. Tom Stoppard, interview with Ronald Hayman, *Tom Stoppard* (London: Contemporary Playwrights Series, 1977), 8.

77. Stoppard, *Rosencrantz and Guildenstern Are Dead,* 42.

78. Maynard Mack, "The World of Hamlet," in Leonard F. Dean, ed., *Shakespeare: Modern Essays in Criticism* (New York: Oxford University Press, 1961), 239. Originally published in *The Yale Review* 41 (1952): 502–23.

79. Stoppard, *Rosencrantz and Guildenstern are Dead,* 56–57.

80. Ibid., 49–50.

81. Ibid., 116–17.

82. Stoppard, *Rosencrantz and Guildenstern Are Dead,* 125.

83. Ibid., 126.

84. Stoppard, *Rosencrantz and Guildenstern Are Dead,* 11.

85. Ibid.

86. Ibid., 70.

87. Ibid., 63.

88. Ibid., 83.

89. Ibid., 122.

90. Ibid., 123.
91. Ibid.
92. Ibid., 124.
93. Roland Barthes, "Textual Analysis of a Tale by Edgar Allan Poe," in Roland Barthes, *The Semiotic Challenge*, trans. Richard Howard (Berkeley and Los Angeles: University of California Press, 1994), 287.
94. Stoppard, *Rosencrantz and Guildenstern Are Dead*, 125.
95. Ibid., 126.
96. Ibid.

TEN

KING LEAR: *The Dream of Sublimity*

1. R. A. Foakes, *Hamlet versus Lear: Cultural Politics and Shakespeare's Art* (Cambridge: Cambridge University Press, 1993).
2. Ibid., 3–4.
3. Ibid., 1–3.
4. "We have a saying in the movement that we don't trust anybody over 30," Jack Weinberg, a leader of the Free Speech movement, told a *San Francisco Chronicle* reporter. Revisiting his comment a few years later, Weinberg said that he did not hold literally to the statement, but had said it "as a kind of taunt," in response to questions about whether older adults were manipulating the campus organization. *Washington Post* (March 23, 1970), A1.
5. Foakes, *Hamlet versus Lear*, 224.
6. Ralph Waldo Emerson, "The American Scholar," an oration delivered before the Phi Beta Kappa Society at Cambridge [Massachusetts], August 31, 1837, in Ralph Waldo Emerson, *Essays and Lectures* (New York: Library of America, 1983), 68.
7. George Brandes, *William Shakespeare: A Critical Study*, trans. William Archer, Mary Marison, and Diana White (London: W. Heinemann, 1898), 2: 39, quoted in Foakes, *Hamlet versus Lear*, 16.
8. Foakes, *Hamlet versus Lear*, 18.
9. Paul Claudel, "The Catastrophe of *Igitur*," *Nouvelle revue française* (November 1, 1926), quoted in Stéphane Mallarmé, *Selected Poetry and Prose*, trans. Mary Ann Caws (New York: New Directions Books, 1982), 101.
10. *Oxford English Dictionary*, "Hamlet." See also Foakes, *Hamlet versus Lear*, 19ff.
11. Eugene O'Neill, *A Moon for the Misbegotten* (New Haven: Yale University Press, 2006), 142.
12. "Shultz Says U.S. Should Use Force Against Terrorism," *New York Times* (October 26, 1984).
13. William Hazlitt, *Characters of Shakespeare's Plays* (1817; London: Oxford University Press, 1975), 119, 137.
14. A. C. Bradley, *Shakespearean Tragedy: Lectures on* Hamlet, Othello, King Lear, Macbeth (1904; London: Macmillan, 1932), 244.
15. Ibid., 243.
16. Ibid., 91, 174.
17. Ibid., 244.
18. M. H. Abrams et al., *The Norton Anthology of English Literature* (New York: W. W. Norton, 1962).
19. Maynard Mack, *King Lear in Our Time* (Berkeley: University of California Press, 1965); Jan Kott, *Shakespeare Our Contemporary* (New York: Doubleday, 1964).
20. Samuel Johnson, "General Observations on the Plays of Shakespeare," in *The Works of Samuel Johnson*, ed. Arthur Murphy (New York: Alexander V. Blake, 1843), 2: 491.

21. See Gary Taylor and Michael Warren, eds., *The Division of the Kingdoms: Shakespeare's Two Versions of "King Lear"* (Oxford: Oxford University Press, 1983).

22. Charles Lamb, "On the Tragedies of Shakespeare," in *The Works of Charles Lamb* (London: Edward Moxon, 1852), 523.

23. William Hazlitt, quoted in *The Tragedian: An Essay on the Histrionic Genius of Junius Brutus Booth* (Cambridge: Riverside Press, 1868), 146.

24. Sigmund Freud, "The Theme of the Three Caskets," in *The Standard Edition of the Complete Psychological Works of Sigmund Freud: The Case of Schreber, Papers on Technique and Other Works* (1911–13), 24 vols., ed. and trans. James Strachey (London: Hogarth Press, 1958), 12: 289–302; see also Marjorie Garber, "Freud's Choice: The Theme of the Three Caskets," in *Shakespeare's Ghost Writers: Literature as Uncanny Causality* (New York: Routledge, 1987), 74–86.

25. Sigmund Freud to Martha Bernays, June 12, 1883. In *Letters of Sigmund Freud*, selected and edited by Ernst L. Freud, trans. Tania and James Stern (New York: Basic Books, 1960), 41. See also Garber, "Freud's Choice: The Theme of the Three Caskets."

26. For more on various treatments of the Fool—and the notion of the Fool as Cordelia's "alter ego"—see Foakes, *Hamlet versus Lear,* 99–105.

27. W. B. Yeats, "Lapis Lazuli," *New Poems* [1938], in *Yeats's Poetry, Drama, and Prose: Authoritative Texts, Contexts, Criticism* (New York: W. W. Norton, 2000), 115–16.

28. "[S]uch, however, was the drop-scene of his Excellency's memorable Campaign—the finale of his administration," wrote Edward Napier in *Excursions in Southern Africa* (London: William Shoberl, 1849), 412.

29. W. B. Yeats, "Emotion of Multitude," in *Ideas of Good and Evil* (London: Kessinger, 2006), 340.

30. Foakes quotes the preface to the English edition of Jan Kott's book *Shakespeare Our Contemporary,* where Brook, who was to be powerfully influenced by Kott's resituation of the Shakespeare plays in light of what was happening in Eastern European politics, says: "[Jan] Kott is undoubtedly the only writer on Elizabethan matters who assumes without question that every one of his readers will at some point or another have been woken by the police in the middle of the night." Peter Brook, Preface, in Jan Kott, *Shakespeare Our Contemporary,* trans. Boleslaw Taborski (London: Methuen, 1965), vii.

31. Martin Esslin, Introduction, in ibid., xxi.

32. Ibid.

33. Ibid., 165.

34. Ibid., 149.

35. Ibid., 132.

36. Ibid.

37. Ibid., 145–46.

38. Ibid., 146.

39. Ibid., 157.

40. Samuel Beckett, *Endgame: A Play in One Act* (New York: Grove Press, 1958), 41.

41. Ibid., 40.

42. Beckett, *Endgame,* 2.

43. Kott, *Shakespeare Our Contemporary,* 155.

44. Ibid., 160.

45. Ibid.

46. G. Wilson Knight, "King Lear and the Comedy of the Grotesque," in *The Wheel of Fire* (London and New York: Routledge, 2001).

47. Quoted in ibid., v.

48. Albert Camus, *The Myth of Sisyphus: And Other Essays,* trans. Justin O'Brien (New York: Vintage, 1991), v.

49. Ibid., 3.

50. Ibid., 122.
51. Ibid., 123.
52. Ibid., 42.
53. Ibid., 50.
54. Ibid., 25, 35, 77, 79, 80, 82: "the time is out of joint"; "the play's the thing, wherein I'll catch the conscience of the king."
55. Ibid., 80, 81.
56. Ibid., 78.
57. Ibid., 79–80.
58. Beckett, *Endgame,* 1, 84.
59. Ibid., 26–27.
60. Ibid., 62.
61. Ibid., 38.
62. Ibid., 6.
63. Ibid., 80, 81.
64. Ibid., 11.
65. Ibid., 15–16.
66. Ibid., 32.
67. Ibid., 82.
68. Ibid., 91.
69. Karl Marx, *The Communist Manifesto,* quoted in Marshall Berman, *All That Is Solid Melts into Air: The Experience of Modernity* (London: Verso, 1983), 106.
70. Ibid., 107.
71. Quoted in ibid., 107–108.
72. Ibid., 108.
73. Ibid., 109.
74. Jenny S. Spenser, *Dramatic Strategies in the Plays of Edward Bond* (Cambridge: Cambridge University Press, 1992), 80.
75. "Letter to Tony Coult," in Malcom Hay and Philip Roberts, *Edward Bond: A Companion to the Plays* (London: T. Q. Publications, 1978), 74.
76. Spenser, *Dramatic Strategies,* 8.
77. Edward Bond, *Lear,* in *Plays* (London: Methuen, 1977), 77.
78. Ibid., 74.
79. Ibid., 77.
80. Ibid., 76.
81. Edward Bond's *Lear,* written and first performed in 1971, was produced by the Royal Shakespeare Company in 1982, the same season in which they staged a production of Shakespeare's *King Lear.* Clearly the plays "read" each other, just as Bond's adaptation or rewriting (more than "revived with alterations") offered a new context for the Shakespearean source, while also introducing some elements of jarring contemporary relevance. The play is both old and new, never timeless, always urgent.
82. See Spenser, *Dramatic Strategies,* 80–81.
83. Hay and Roberts, *Edward Bond,* 53.
84. Bond, *Lear,* 17.
85. Ibid., 20.
86. Ibid., 21.
87. Beckett, *Endgame,* 50.
88. Ibid., 100.
89. Ibid., 70.
90. Ibid., 73.
91. Ibid.

92. Ibid., 16.
93. Ibid., 62.
94. Ibid., 63–64.
95. Ibid., 98.
96. Ibid., 99.
97. Ibid.
98. Frank Rich, "Mabou Mines Creates a 'King Lear' All Its Own," *New York Times* (January 26, 1990).
99. Brian Rotman, *Signifying Nothing: The Semiotics of Zero* (Stanford: Stanford University Press, 1987).
100. Ibid., 1, 5, 17–21.
101. Ibid., 80.
102. Ibid.
103. Mack, *King Lear in Our Time,* 25.

AFTERWORD: SHAKESPEARE'S TIME

1. Stephen Booth, *Shakespeare's Sonnets* (1977; reprint, New Haven: Yale University Press, 2000), 543.
2. William Wordsworth, "The Sonnet," *Poems by William Wordsworth*, ed. Stopford A. Brooke (New York: McClure Phillips & Co., 1907), 259; Robert Browning, "House," *The Complete Poetic and Dramatic Works of Robert Browning* (New York: Houghton Mifflin, 1895), 809.
3. Oscar Wilde, *The Portrait of Mr. W.H.* (Whitefish, MT: Kessinger, 2004).
4. W. H. Auden, "Shakespeare's Sonnets," in W. H. Auden and Edward Mendelson, *Forewords and Afterwords* (New York: Random House, 1973), 104.
5. For example, Joseph Pequigney, *Such Is My Love: A Study of Shakespeare's Sonnets* (Chicago: University of Chicago Press, 1985).
6. Eve Kosofsky Sedgwick, *Between Men: English Literature and Male Homosocial Desire* (New York: Columbia University Press, 1985), 28–48.

ACKNOWLEDGMENTS

THIS BOOK COULD NOT HAVE HAPPENED were it not for the loving labors of many friends and colleagues. Moira Gallagher Weigel assisted at the initial stages, finding images and commenting helpfully on the text. Brett Gamboa, Melissa Pino, David Saunder, Larry Switzky, Rikita Tyson, and Steve Gilbert listened carefully to early versions of these arguments and responded to them. Eliza Hornig, Daniel Wenger, Chris Barrett, Max Freeman, and Suparna Roychoudhury chased down references and brought their attentive sensibilities to the project. Sol Kim Bentley read through the text more than once, and painstakingly hunted down art permissions, often engaging international interlocutors in order to do so. Laura Starrett, the copy editor, made many judicious suggestions, and responded with care and understanding to the text. Lily Evans at Pantheon coordinated matters with skill and care. To Sara Bartel, my assistant, my debt is especially great. Sara participated in all of these activities, from line editing to finding references to proofreading and the scouting of permissions, and she also managed the entire project, keeping track of people, deadlines, text, and images, undertaking all these tasks with wisdom, patience, and admirable literary sense. I am enormously grateful to her, and to all of those who listened to, and talked through, versions of these chapters. The book is dedicated to Erroll McDonald, my editor, and to Beth Vesel, my literary agent. Both have understood from the beginning that this was for me an intensely personal project as well as a scholarly labor of love, and each offered wise counsel at many crucial stages. I am immensely fortunate to have them as friends, advisers, and readers.

INDEX

Page numbers beginning with 275 refer to notes. Numbers in *italics* refer to illustrations.

PERMISSIONS ACKNOWLEDGMENTS

GRATEFUL ACKNOWLEDGMENT IS MADE to the following for permission to reprint previously published material:

Alfred Publishing Co., Inc.: Excerpt from "Brush Up Your Shakespeare" from *Kiss Me Kate,* words and music by Cole Porter, copyright © 1949 (Renewed) by Chappell & Co. All rights reserved. Reprinted by permission of Alfred Publishing Co., Inc.

Faber and Faber Ltd.: Excerpt from "The Love Song of J. Alfred Prufrock" from *Prufrock and Other Observations* by T. S. Eliot. Reprinted by permission of Faber and Faber Ltd.

Grove/Atlantic, Inc., and Faber and Faber, Ltd.: Excerpt from *Endgame* by Samuel Beckett, copyright © 1958 by Grove Press, Inc. Reprinted by permission of Grove/Atlantic, Inc., and Faber and Faber, Ltd.

Hal Leonard Corporation: Excerpt from "(Just Like) Romeo and Juliet," words and music by Freddie Gorman and Bob Hamilton, copyright © 1964 (Renewed 1992) by Jobete Music Co., Inc. All rights controlled and administered by EMI April Music Inc. and EMI Blackwood Music Inc. on behalf of Jobete Music Co., Inc. and Stone Agate Music (a division of Jobete Music Co., Inc.). All rights reserved. International copyright secured. Reprinted by permission of Hal Leonard Corporation.

Hill and Wang and Methuen Drama: Excerpts from "Study of the First Scene of Shakespeare's *Coriolanus*" from *Brecht on Theatre*, edited and translated by John Willett, translation copyright © 1964, renewed 1992 by John Willett. Reprinted by permission of Hill and Wang, a division of Farrar, Straus and Giroux, LLC and Methuen Drama, an imprint of A&C Black Publishers.

Houghton Mifflin Harcourt Publishing Company and Steidl Verlag: Excerpt from *The Plebeians Rehearse the Uprising: A German Tragedy* by Günter Grass, translated by Richard Manheim, copyright © 1966 by Hermann Luchterhand Verlag GmbH, Neuwied und Berlin. Copyright © 1997 by Steidl Verlag, Göttingen, Germany. English translation copyright © 1966 and renewed 1994 by Martin Secker and Warburg Limited and Houghton Mifflin Harcourt Publishing Company. Reprinted by permission of Houghton Mifflin Harcourt Publishing Company and Steidl Verlag.

International Creative Management, Inc.: Excerpts from *MacBird* by Barbara Garson, copyright © 1966 by Barbara Garson. Reprinted by permission of International Creative Management, Inc.

Oberon Books Ltd.: Excerpt from *The Tempest* by Aimé Césaire, translated by Philip Crispin. Reprinted by permission of Oberon Books Ltd.

Rondor Music International: Excerpt from "Romeo and Juliet" by Mark Knopfler, copyright © 1980 by Straitjacket Songs Ltd. All rights administered by Almo Music Corp. (ASCAP). All rights reserved. Reprinted by permission of Rondor Music International.

Scribner and AP Watt Ltd.: Excerpt from "Lapis Lazuli" from *The Complete Works of W. B. Yeats, Volume I: The Poems,* edited by Richard J. Finneran, copyright © 1940 by Georgie Yeats. Copyright renewed 1968 by Bertha Georgie Yeats, Michael Butler Yeats, and Anne Yeats. All rights reserved. Reprinted by permission of Scribner, a division of Simon & Schuster Adult Publishing Group and AP Watt Ltd. on behalf of Gráinne Yeats.

ILLUSTRATION CREDITS

ALSO BY MARJORIE GARBER

SEX AND REAL ESTATE
Why We Love Houses

"When you stop to think about it, buying and selling a house is a lot like dating," says Marjorie Garber, "the same quickening of the pulse, the lingering around the phone, willing it to ring." In this witty and incisive study of how we relate to ideas of house and home, Garber makes a host of ingenious parallels between house love and human love: the house as mother (it loves you as you are); the Cinderella house (a fixer-upper to be transformed with love); the house as beloved (the dream date and the dream mate). And at a time when we've never been so obsessed with real estate, Garber pronounces it a new form of yuppie pornography. Brilliantly drawing on cultural references such as Chaucer, Waugh, and Woolf, as well as movies and shelter magazines, *Sex and Real Estate* is as provocative as it is pleasurable, multiply enriching our understanding of our homes and the houses we covet.

Cultural Studies/978-0-385-72039-7

SHAKESPEARE AFTER ALL

A brilliant and companionable tour through all thirty-eight plays, *Shakespeare After All* is the perfect introduction to the bard by one of the country's foremost authorities on his life and work. Drawing on her hugely popular lecture courses at Yale and Harvard over the past thirty years, Marjorie Garber offers passionate and revealing readings of the plays in chronological sequence, from *The Two Gentlemen of Verona* to *The Two Noble Kinsmen*. Supremely readable and engaging, and complete with a comprehensive introduction to Shakespeare's life and times and an extensive bibliography, this magisterial work is an ever-replenishing fount of insight on the most celebrated writer of all time.

Literary Criticism/978-0-385-72214-8

ANCHOR BOOKS
Available at your local bookstore, or visit
www.randomhouse.com